Leadership Handbook of Outreach and Care

Other Leadership Handbooks

Leadership Handbook of Preaching and Worship
Leadership Handbook of Management and Administration

Leadership Handbook of Outreach and Care

GENERAL EDITOR
James D. Berkley

A Division of Baker Book House Co.
Grand Rapids, Michigan 49516

To my son,
Peter James Berkley,
who deeply cares about people.

First paperback edition copublished in 1997 by Christianity Today, Inc., and Baker Book House Company.

Previously copublished in 1994 by Christianity Today, Inc., and Baker Book House Company as *Leadership Handbooks of Practical Theology*, vol. 2: *Outreach & Care*.

Copublished by Christianity Today, Inc., and Baker Book House Company. Distributed by Baker Book House Company.

Printed in the United States of America

ISBN 0-8010-9042-3

For information about academic books, resources for Christian leaders, and all new releases from Baker Book House, visit our web site:
http://www.bakerbooks.com

Contents

PART III: Social Involvement

PART IV: Pastoral Care

PART VII: Chaplaincies

Introduction

Years of study and experience rest in your hands in this second volume of the *Leadership Handbooks of Practical Theology*. The editors of LEADERSHIP, a practical journal for church leaders (published by Christianity Today, Inc.), want Christian leaders to have the down-to-earth, comprehensive counsel they need for every aspect of pastoral ministry. *Outreach & Care,* this second volume of a three-book series, continues toward that goal.

The first volume—*Word & Worship*—provided practical wisdom on preaching, worship, music, the sacraments, weddings, and funerals. Here in *Outreach & Care,* you will find a practitioner's storehouse of help for evangelism, missions, ministries of social involvement, pastoral care, pastoral counseling, Christian education, and chaplaincies. The final volume, *Leadership & Administration* will cover church business management, the pastor as a person, and other issues of leading a church.

How to Use This Book

The *Leadership Handbooks of Practical Theology* can be read cover to cover for a thorough exploration of pastoral practice. But they also lend themselves to quick reference for items of particular interest or need. Articles are arranged topically, both by volume and by section within each volume. Thus, the following features will help you find what you seek:

- *Table of contents.* Look here first for a complete listing of the topics covered in each volume. Articles are titled for clarity rather than artistry, to give you a clear understanding of the subject matter. Authors' names accompany article titles.

- *Main section headings.* This volume is divided into seven main subject areas, denoted by Parts I through VII. Here you find sets of articles on Evangelism, Missions, Pastoral Care, Pastoral Counseling, Social Involvement, Christian Education, and Chaplaincies. In each of these main parts, you should find the counsel you need in chapters organized by subject matter.
- *Chapter essays.* Each of the 32 chapters is anchored by a main essay that covers the central issues of the topic. Look for the title to indicate the chapter's specific subject matter.
- *Brief sidebar articles.* Most chapters contain a number of concise articles that cover a specific aspect of the subject at hand. If a chapter essay doesn't appear to address your needs, a sidebar probably will fit the bill. The sidebars also provide background and insights in addition to those found in the chapter essays.

Give It a Try

With this search apparatus in place, you can take a trial run at finding a subject of interest. Suppose you want to know more about why Christians are involved with helping the oppressed. In the table of contents, you find a major section on "Social Involvement." That's a good start. The initial chapter essay on "The Purpose of Social Compassion and Social Action" appears a good candidate to meet your needs, and the sidebar on "Social Action or Social Service?" might help you better understand the terms.

Or if you face a counseling situation with parents of a cult member, you would discover "Part V: Pastoral Counseling" in the table of contents. Scanning the chapters in that section, you don't find one about your particular need, but Chapter 21 on "Distinctively Christian Counseling" has a number of sidebars about specific counseling cases. There you strike gold with the sidebar "Counseling Cult Members."

If you don't find such obvious matches, scan the table of contents again, looking for subject headings similar to your needs. The logic of the table of contents is somewhat similar to a filing system.

More Than Information

The author's name can be found at the end of each article (as well as in the table of contents), and information about the authors fills the "Contributors" section. At the end of most of the chapter essays, you will find "Resources," a combination of footnotes and bibliography for further study.

Here in *Outreach & Care*—and indeed in the other *Leadership Handbooks of Practical Theology*—you find hundreds of pages of information about *doing* pastoral ministry. The authors provide it out of their wealth of practical experience and scholarly inquiry.

But even more important than the encyclopedic ideas and techniques presented here is the mission of this series: That Christian pastors, better prepared to serve as shepherds, will bring people to a saving knowledge of the Lord Jesus Christ and to maturity in their walk with him. May wise practices empowered by spiritual strength lead to pastoral effectiveness that produces healthy citizens of the kingdom of God.

Contributors

General Editor
James D. Berkley

Executive Editor
Marshall B. Shelley

Editorial Administrator
Bonnie Rice

Editorial Assistant
Cynthia Thomas

Consulting Editor
Paul E. Engle

Senior Copy Editor
Gary Wilde

Associate Copy Editors
Richard Doebler
David Goetz
Craig Brian Larson
Kevin D. Miller

Writers

Gordon Aeschliman. Editor, *Prism*, Colfax, Washington.

Michael J. Anthony, Ph.D., Claremont Graduate School. Associate Professor of Christian Education, Talbot School of Theology, La Mirada, California.

Charles Arn, Ed.D., University of Southern California. President, Church Growth, Inc., Monrovia, California.

Win Arn, D.R.E., Eastern Baptist Seminary. President, L.I.F.E., Monrovia, California.

John Ashmen, B.S., Philadelphia College of Bible. Director of Member Services, Christian Camping International/USA, Colorado Springs, Colorado.

Myron Augsburger, Th.D., Union Theological Seminary (Richmond). President, Christian College Coalition, Washington, D.C.

Nancy D. Becker, M.Div., Union Theological Seminary (New York). Pastor, Ogden Dunes (Indiana) Presbyterian Church.

James D. Berkley, D.Min., Fuller Theological Seminary. Editor, YOUR CHURCH, Carol Stream, Illinois

Warren Bird, M.Div., Alliance Theological Seminary. Writer and editor, Suffern, New York.

Paul Borthwick, M.Div., Gordon-Conwell Theological Seminary. Minister of Missions, Grace Chapel, Lexington, Massachusetts.

Douglas J. Brouwer, D.Min., Princeton Theological Seminary. Senior Pastor, First Presbyterian Church of Wheaton, Illinois.

John A. Burgess, Ed.D., Harvard University. Professor of Education, Emeritus, Gordon College, Wenham, Massachusetts.

Andre Bustanoby, Th.M., Dallas Theological Seminary. Marriage and family therapist, Bowie, Maryland.

Kenneth W. Campbell, M.Div., Trinity Evangelical Divinity School. Director of Ministries, ACMC, Inc., Wheaton, Illinois.

Scott Campbell, Th.M., Boston University School of Theology. Senior Pastor, International Protestant Church, Brussels, Belgium.

Douglas M. Cecil, D.Min., Dallas Theological Seminary. Assistant Professor of Pastoral Ministries, Dallas Theological Seminary, Dallas, Texas.

Linwood H. Chamberlain, Jr., M.Div., Hamma School of Theology, Wittenberg University. Co-pastor, First Evangelical Lutheran Church, Lorain, Ohio.

Randy Christian, D.Min., Fuller Theological Seminary. Associate Minister, Adult Education and Family Ministry, Beaverton (Oregon) Christian Church.

John Cionca, Ph.D., Arizona State University. Associate Dean, Bethel Theological Seminary, St. Paul, Minnesota.

Lyman Coleman, S.T.B., Biblical Seminary in New York. Founder, Serendipity Foundation, Littleton, Colorado.

Gary R. Collins, Ph.D., Purdue University. Executive Director, American Association of Christian Counselors, Kildeer, Illinois.

Harvie M. Conn, Litt.D., Geneva College. Professor of Missions, Westminster Theological Seminary, Philadelphia, Pennsylvania.

Eleanor A. Daniel, Ph.D., University of Illinois. Professor of Christian Education, Cincinnati Bible College and Seminary, Cincinnati, Ohio.

Edward G. Dobson, Ed.D., University of Virginia. Senior Pastor, Calvary Church, Grand Rapids, Michigan.

Dave Dolan, M.P.H., University of the City of Los Angeles. Executive Director, Center for Ministry Resources, San Anselmo, California.

William Donahue, M.A., Dallas Theological Seminary. Director of Couples Ministry, Willow Creek Community Church, South Barrington, Illinois.

Brett Eastman, M.Div., Talbot School of Theology. Area Director of Small Groups, Willow Creek Community Church, South Barrington, Illinois.

James Andrew Edgren, D.Min., Wesley Theological Seminary. Director, Chaplain's Commission, National Association of Evangelicals, Washington, D.C.

Chris Ellerman, M.S.W., George Williams College. Executive Director, Outreach Community Ministries, Inc., Wheaton, Illinois.

Roger Razzari Elrod, M.A., California State University, Chico. Golden Gate Area Director, InterVarsity Christian Fellowship, San Jose, California.

Douglas Fagerstrom, M.C.E., Bethel Theological Seminary. Minister of Adults, Calvary Church, Grand Rapids, Michigan.

Mark Galli, M.Div., Fuller Theological Seminary. Managing Editor, CHRISTIAN HISTORY, Carol Stream, Illinois.

Carl F. George. Adjunct Professor, Fuller Theological Seminary, School of World Mission, Pasadena, California.

Eddy Gibbs, D.Min., Fuller Theological Seminary. Associate Rector for Discipleship, All Saints Church, Beverly Hills, California.

Peggy M. Gilbert, M.S., University of Bridgeport. Director of Migration Services, World Relief, NAE, Congers, New York.

Wayne L. Gordon, M.A., Northern Baptist Theological School. Pastor, Lawndale Community Church, Chicago, Illinois.

Michael P. Green, Ph.D., University of North Texas. Associate Professor, Moody Graduate School, Chicago, Illinois.

Gary Gulbranson, Ph.D., Loyola University. Senior Minister, Westminster Chapel, Bellevue, Washington.

Ronald T. Habermas, Ph.D., Michigan State University. McGee Professor of Biblical Studies, John Brown University, Siloam Springs, Arkansas.

David C. Hacker, M.Div., Church Divinity School of the Pacific. Executive Director, Emergency Food Bank, Stockton, California.

John D. Hambrick, M.Div., Fuller Theological Seminary. Assistant Pastor, American Church in London (England).

Richard R. Hammar, L.L.M., Harvard Law School. Attorney at Law, CPA, Springfield, Missouri.

Quentin L. Hand, Ph.D., Boston University. Pastoral Psychotherapist, The Key Pastoral Counseling Center, Huntsville, Alabama.

Tim Hansel, M.A., Stanford University. Founder, Summit Adventure, Bass Lake, California.

Archibald D. Hart, Ph.D., Fuller Theological Seminary. Professor of Pschology, Dean, Graduate School of Psychology, Fuller Theological Seminary, Pasadena, California.

Paul H. Heidebrecht, Ph.D., University of Illinois. Administrator, Immanuel Presbyterian Church, Warrenville, Illinois.

Roberta Hestenes, D.Min., Fuller Theological Seminary. President, Eastern College, St. Davids, Pennsylvania.

Dennis P. Hollinger, Ph.D., Drew University. Pastor, Washington Community Fellowship, Washington, D.C.

Michael Jinkins, Ph.D., University of Aberdeen, Scotland. Pastor, Brenham (Texas) Presbyterian Church.

Darrell W. Johnson, M.Div., Fuller Theological Seminary. Senior Pastor, Glendale (California) Presbyterian Church.

H. Deen Kaplan, M.Div., Gordon-Conwell Theological Seminary. Vice-President, Public Policy & International Networks, National Coalition Against Pornography, Washington, D.C.

D. James Kennedy, Ph.D., New York University, New York City. Senior Minister, Coral Ridge Presbyterian Church, Fort Lauderdale, Florida.

Jerry R. Kirk, D.L., Grove City College. President, National Coalition Against Pornography, Cincinnati, Ohio.

Ronald S. Kraybill, M.Div., Harvard Divinity School. Director of Training, Center for Intergroup Studies, Cape Town, South Africa.

Bruce Larson, D.D., Seattle Pacific University. Co-pastor, The Crystal Cathedral, Garden Grove, California.

Ann A. Letson, M.Div., Louisville Presbyterian Theological Seminary. Associate Director, Department of Pastoral Care, Spartansburg Regional Medical Center, Spartansburg, South Carolina.

Steve Levicoff, Ph.D., Union Institute. Lecturer, Institute on Religion and Law, Ambler, Pennsylvania.

Roy W. Lowrie, Jr., Ed.D., Temple University. Professor of Christian School Administration, Columbia Bible College and Seminary, Columbia, South Carolina.

Aubrey Malphurs, Th.D., Dallas Theological Seminary. Professor and Department Chairman of Field Education, Dallas Theological Seminary, Dallas, Texas.

Conrad Mandsager, B.A., Wartburg College. Director of Field Ministries, JAF Ministries, Agoura Hills, California.

James E. Martin, Ph.D., Trinity Theological Seminary. Senior Pastor, Mt. Olivet Baptist Church, Portland, Oregon.

Gary L. McIntosh, D.Min., Fuller Theological Seminary. Associate Professor of Practical Theology, Talbot School of Theology of Biola University, La Mirada, California.

Brent Mitchell, M.Div., Fuller Theological Seminary. Pastor, Harvest Presbyterian Church, Ceres, California.

Terry C. Muck, Ph.D., Northwestern University. Professor of Comparative Religions, Austin Theological Seminary, Austin, Texas.

Arthur Nazigian, L.L.D., Indiana Christian University. Headmaster, Mid-Vermont Christian School, White River Junction, Vermont.

Sheri Noah, M.Div., McCormick Theological Seminary. Coordinator of Volunteers, Emergency Food Bank, Stockton, California.

Ronald B. Oertli, M.B.A., University of Washington. Consultant, Church Discipleship Ministry, The Navigators, Colorado Springs, Colorado.

Steven L. Ogne, M.A., Talbot Theological Seminary. Church Consultant, Church Resource Ministries, Fullerton, California.

Luis Palau, D.D., Wheaton College (Illinois). President, Luis Palau Evangelistic Association, Portland, Oregon.

Earl Palmer, B.D., Princeton Theological Seminary. Minister, University Presbyterian Church, Seattle, Washington.

Leslie Parrott, M.A., Fuller Theological Seminary. Co-direcator, Center for Relationship Development, Seattle Pacific University, Seattle, Washington.

Les Parrott III, Ph.D., Fuller Theological Seminary Graduate School of Psychology. Associate Professor of Psychology and Director of Center for Relationship Development, Seattle Pacific University, Seattle, Washington.

John M. Perkins, D.L., Wheaton College (Illinois). Publisher, *Urban Family,* Pasadena, California.

David Philips, D.Min., Fuller Theological Seminary. Senior Pastor, Desert Hills Presbyterian Church, Carefree, Arizona.

Michael E. Phillips, B.Th., Canadian Bible College. Senior Pastor, Riverside Alliance Church, Kalispell, Montana.

Rebecca Manley Pippert, M.A., University of Illinois. Author and speaker, Rockville, Maryland.

Michael Pocock, D.Miss., Trinity Evangelical Divinity School. Chairman, Department of World Missions, Dallas Theological Seminary, Dallas, Texas.

Calvin C. Ratz, M.A., Syracuse University. Senior Pastor, Brightmoor Tabernacle, Southfield, Michigan.

James W. Reapsome, Th.M., Dallas Theological Seminary. Editor, *Evangelical Missions Quarterly,* Wheaton, Illinois.

Robert Redman, Dr.Theol., University of Erlangen, Germany. Director, Doctor of Ministry Program and Associate Professor of Theology of Ministry, Fuller Theological Seminary, Pasadena, California.

Donald P. Regier, Th.M., Dallas Theological Seminary. Associate Professor of Christian Education, Dallas Theological Seminary, Dallas, Texas.

Gerald T. Richards, Th.M., Duke Divinity School. Consultant in Chaplaincy and Military Ministry, Southern Baptist State Convention of North Carolina, Cary, North Carolina.

Richard A. Roberts. Chief Executive Officer, Chicago Christian Industrial League, Chicago, Illinois.

Edward Rommen, D.Th., University of Munich, Germany. Associate Professor of Mission, Trinity Evangelical Divinity School, Deerfield, Illinois.

Bruce Rowlison, D.Min., Jesuit Theological Seminary. Senior Pastor, Gilroy Presbyterian Church, Gilroy, California.

Kevin E. Ruffcorn, M.Div., Luther Northwestern Theological Seminary. Minister, Grace Lutheran Church, Oconto Falls, Wisconsin.

Denny Rydberg, B.A., Seattle Pacific University. President, Young Life International, Colorado Springs, Colorado.

Sonny Salsbury, B.A., Pasadena College. Executive Director, Camp Ghormley, Rimrock, Washington.

John S. Savage, D.Min., Colgate Rochester Divinity School. President, L.E.A.D. Consultants, Inc., Reynoldsburgh, Ohio.

Hal B. Schell, M.Lib.Sc., University of Syracuse. Chairman, Equipping Ministries, International, Cincinnati, Ohio.

Terry Schlossberg, M.A., George Washington University. Executive Director, Presbyterians Pro-Life, Research, Education & Care, Inc., Burke, Virginia.

Robert L. Schneider, M.Div., Trinity Evangelical Divinity School. Associate Pastor for Missions, The Chapel, Akron, Ohio.

Doug Self, D.Min., Denver Seminary. Pastor, Church at Carbondale (Colorado).

Mark H. Senter III, Ph.D., Loyola University. Dean of Extension and Continuing Education, Trinity Evangelical Divinity School, Deerfield, Illinois.

Bruce L. Shelley, Ph.D., University of Iowa. Senior Professor of Church History, Denver Seminary, Denver, Colorado.

Ernest D. Sillers, M.A., University of New Hampshire. Headmaster, St. John's Church and School, Rancho Santa Margarita, California.

Don Smarto. B.A., Lewis University. Director, Institute for Prison Ministry, Wheaton College, Wheaton, Illinois.

James H. Smith, B.A., University of Charleston. Former Executive Director, Family Life Center, Highland Park Presbyterian Church, Dallas, Texas. Deceased.

George Soltau, B.D., Faith Theological Seminary. Director, Faith Prison Ministries, Greenville, Mississippi.

Gary Sweeten, Ed.D., University of Cincinnati. President/CEO, LifeWay and Equipping Ministries, International, Cincinnati, Ohio.

John R. Throop, M.Div., School of Theology, University of the South. Vicar, St. Francis Episcopal Church, Chillicothe, Illinois.

James Townsend, Ph.D., Fuller Theological Seminary. Bible Editor, David C. Cook Publishing Company, Elgin, Illinois.

David Veerman, M.Div., Trinity Evangelical Divinity School. Executive Vice-President, The Livingstone Corporation, Naperville, Illinois.

Charles A. Ver Straten, D.Min., Denver Seminary. Senior Pastor, Bethel Baptist Church, Greeley, Colorado.

Jeffrey A. Watson, D.Min., Dallas Theological Seminary. Senior Pastor, Grace Bible Church, Seabrook, Maryland.

C. Peter Wagner, Ph.D., University of Southern California. Professor of Church Growth, Fuller Theological Seminary, Pasadena, California.

Gordon Weekley, M.Div., Southern Baptist Theological Seminary. Executive Director, Rebound Christian Rehabilitation Center, Inc., Charlotte, North Carolina.

Edward T. Welch, Ph.D., University of Utah. Director of Counseling, The Christian Counseling and Educational Foundation, Laverock, Pennsylvania.

David A. Wilkinson, M.Div., Fuller Theological Seminary. Pastor, Moorpark Presbyterian Church, Moorpark, California.

Dennis E. Williams, Ed.D., Southwestern Baptist Theological Seminary. Professor of Christian Education, Denver Seminary, Denver, Colorado.

Wayne Willis, D.Min., Louisville Presbyterian Theological Seminary. Director of Pastoral Care, Alliant Health System, Louisville, Kentucky.

Ralph Winter, Ph.D., Cornell University. General Director, U.S. Center for World Mission, and President, William Carey University, Pasadena, California.

Frank Milstead Woggon, M.Div., Southern Baptish Theological Seminary. Pediatric Oncology Chaplain, Alliant Health Systems, Louisville, Kentucky.

Penny J. Zettler, D.Min., Bethel Seminary. Pastor of Christian Education and Families, Friendship Church, Prior Lake, Wisconsin.

Part I:

Evangelism

At some point in each of our lives, someone—or perhaps a string of someones—related to us the good news of Jesus Christ. As we heard and responded, we became a link in a long and precious chain that stretches unbroken from Jesus directly to each of us. How many lives are linked in that chain? How many conversations did it take to carry the message of salvation from Jesus through the centuries to our ears?

That chain's path could not have been easy. The message had to be carried against ignorance and adversity. The carriers must have battled against hardship and self-interest. Before their death—perhaps for bearing the message itself—they had to pass on the vital gospel story. Yet somehow that relay of hope continued unbroken across barriers of language and people, through the rigors of war and famine, in the face of persecution and rage, over generations and centuries to our hearing, to our believing, to our regeneration. What a highly improbable yet joyfully real set of circumstances! What a powerful God who made it all possible!

Our job, since the chain has stretched thus far intact, is to forge the links to the next recipients. Many of us don't find that particularly easy. Evangelism is a joy to *have done* but is for many a terror to actually *do*. We want to be faithful and effective, but we need counsel and encouragement.

Good news is for sharing, and we have, in the gospel, the best news that ever entered an ear. Here, then, is help for designing and setting into place the next links in the chain of salvation for all those yet to hear the message that *is* life.

1

The Purpose of Evangelism

Before his Ascension, Christ left his followers with an immense task—the Great Commission command to make disciples of all nations. Evangelism is the first step in obeying this command.

God has done something about the evil that surrounds us and dwells within us. He has done something about restoring us to himself in a holy, personal and intimate, safe and eternal relationship. This deliverance from evil and restoration to relationship with God is great news for all human beings. But someone must spread this news, and blessed are those who do!

Let's look a little closer at the subject of evangelism by asking four questions that will help us define its purpose with more precision: What, exactly, is the basic content of the evangelistic message? What are some of the key characteristics of the proclamation task? What troublesome challenges face the outreach efforts of the contemporary church? What will empower those who take the gospel message into the world?

The Gospel Message in a Nutshell

If the gospel is a message, what is that message? In the contemporary, worldwide church, perhaps the most widely accepted definition of what the gospel message is (and is not) comes from the Lausanne Covenant (see article 4, The Nature of Evangelism):

> To evangelize is to spread the Good News that Jesus Christ died for our sins and was raised from the dead according to the Scriptures, and that as the reigning Lord he now offers the forgiveness of sins and the liberating gift of the Spirit to all who repent and believe. Our Christian presence in the world is indispensable to evangelism, and so is the kind of dialogue whose purpose is to listen sensitively in order to understand. But evangelism itself is proclamation: telling about the historical, biblical Christ as Savior and Lord, with a view to persuading people to come to him personally and so be reconciled to God. In issuing the gospel invitation we have no liberty to conceal the cost of discipleship. Jesus still calls all who would follow him to deny themselves, take up their cross, and identify themselves with his new community. The results of evangelism include ongoing obedience to Christ, incorporation into his church, and responsible service in the world.

Evangelism is the proclamation of the gospel. It deals with how to *become* a Christian.

The Great Commission also requires that we teach people to *be* Christians in lifestyle, to disciple them so that they begin observing daily all that Christ has commanded (Matt. 28:18–20). As such, believers must become involved in a continuing process of growth, called follow-up, discipleship, or edification. Much of the criticism of evangelistic efforts that do not result in new church members is really a reflection of the failure to establish new believers in the faith and to equip them to continue following Christ in discipleship. As the Lausanne Covenant states, although discipling is not a part of evangelism's strict definition, it is not an optional task for the church.

Key Characteristics of the Evangelistic Task

What a unique message was proclaimed by the first Christians! New Testament scholar Joachim Jeremias comments: "The message that God wants to have dealings with sinners and only with sinners and that his love extends to them is without parallel at the time. It is unique. The literature of Qumran has confirmed this uniqueness. They confirm that nothing comparable is to be found in contemporary Judaism" (Jeremias 1971, 121). What should we know about the call to spread this unique message?

• *We are commanded to do the work.* Evangelism is not an optional ministry that churches can decide to do or not to do. The call to evangelize is recorded by all four gospel writers (Matt. 28:16–20; Mark 16:14–18; Luke 22:44–49 and Acts 1:8; John 20:19–23). To fulfill this command, believers were given the Holy Spirit and appointed to go into all the world as Christ's ambassadors entrusted with the message of reconciliation (Acts 1:8; 2 Cor. 5:18–20).

Notice, too, that the appointment and the message were given not just to those who "had the gift" or were "good communicators" but to people described by the gospel writers as depressed (mourning and weeping), afraid of those outside their little group (the Jews), and struggling with unbelief. Most modern believers can relate to such feelings. Nevertheless, like the first believers, we are commanded to tell the world the message of salvation.

• *God alone is responsible for the results.* Though our clear responsibility is to proclaim the message, it is God's responsibility to produce the results; we follow, and God works through us to bring in the catch (Matt. 4:19). In our society, with its emphasis on measurable outcomes, it is easy to think of evangelistic efforts as successful only if they produce significant numbers of contacts, converts, and church members. While some measurements may help us evaluate an effort in terms of our stewardship of resources, God defines success in terms of our obedience and faithfulness. Bill Bright has expressed it well: "Success in evangelism is simply taking the initiative to share the gospel in the power of the Holy Spirit and leaving the results to God" (Bright 1987, 67). The entire process of salvation, from the first awareness of God to our ultimate glorification, is the work of God alone.

• *The task is greater than the methods used.* Just as we must not define the gospel in terms of the response to its proclamation, so we must avoid defining it in terms of a particular method of communication. When evangelism means only a particular method to us, we limit our availability to be used by the Spirit, since we may look for him to work only through our preferred methods. A method-based definition of evangelism can confuse the method of communication (form) with the message itself (substance). Thus arises the danger of preserving a gospel form without the gospel content, or of using a method inappropriate to a unique audience.

• *External response mechanisms still require inner faith.* A method-based understanding of the gospel sometimes tempts churches to think of evangelism as a supernatural technology. The gospel becomes a standard procedure or religious ritual, which, when used properly (saying the prayer, walking the aisle, signing the card, being immersed or sprinkled), always yields the desired result: salvation. This, of course, is faulty thinking and faulty theology, since actions or words apart from faith do not produce salvation.

Generally, it is wise to give the seeker a concrete way to express his or her faith, and many of the above actions can potentially do this. Yet we must remain aware that standard "sinner's prayers" and other response mechanisms have no inherent value for salvation. To think otherwise is to believe in a form of spiritual magic.

Contemporary Challenges to Outreach

Several factors complicate the evangelistic task for the contemporary church, making it especially challenging. Consider these three:

- *The widespread secularization of society*. Great numbers of people in our society now have absolutely no exposure to the Bible and Christianity, either at a cultural or personal level. These people will find little immediate meaning or relevance in our words about God, religion, morality, sin, evil, salvation, holiness, faith, heaven, hell, judgment, and other concepts essential to understanding the gospel message.

Those reaching out to a secularized, post-Christian society must learn to expand the traditional fifteen-minute gospel presentation if their audience is to find it meaningful. They'll need to redefine, de-

The Great Commission

The Great Commission (see Mark 16:8, 14–18; Luke 24:46–49; John 17:18; 20:21–23; and Matt. 28:18–20) has become the Great Omission in the life of many churches, especially in the Western world. Yet, for the early Christian community, those Great Commission statements were not used to motivate the reluctant to get involved in mission. Rather, the Great Commission provided the foundation for everything the early disciples were doing.

A Command in Context

One of the problems in studying the so-called Great Commission is that it is often examined in isolation, rather than as a great outcome following the climax of the gospel story. When cut from the preceding contexts, the comprehensive and radical nature of this text—the challenge to make disciples—is severely diminished. Matthew's version provides the clearest illustration.

Matthew's gospel was clearly written for a community of Jewish followers of Jesus. Most New Testament scholars believe the community was located in a predominantly Gentile environment, possibly in Syria. Matthew's distinctive emphasis is on what it means to be a disciple of Jesus amid the growing tension between one's Jewish identity and being part of a Christian community becoming increasingly Gentile.

Matthew helps these people live through the transition time between Jesus' earthly ministry (directed to the lost sheep of the house of Israel [Matt. 15:24]) and the disciples' later calling to go into all the world and make disciples. So Jesus is presented as the New Moses, who proclaims the "laws" of kingdom living. Until Matthew's hearers know how to live in this new reality, they cannot have an effective ministry in the wider world.

velop, and explain old concepts with new words and anecdotes. They'll need to focus on general revelation until hearers have a context for understanding the authority and function of the Bible. The idea that God has communicated in Scripture is no longer assumed; it must often be defended with the best apologetics we can winsomely bring to the conversation. Whether considered part of the evangelistic task or as pre-evangelism, this communication of a gospel context will become essential to evangelizing the ultrasecularized.

For example, for many people "God" now means "a life-force that is both in the universe and in me." "Love" is a term that many children growing up in a single-parent home equate with lust, as the media have portrayed it. The biblical concept of love as *chesed* (loyal love) and *agape* (unconditional love) has no parallel in the experience

Matthew's emphasis is equally important to the contemporary church. His gospel challenges today's believers to make sure the gospel message is never reduced to a culturally monitored, private commitment. In other words, only people enrolled in the school of discipleship, grappling with the faith-stretching reality of living in God's kingdom, can go out and make other disciples in the kingdom of this world.

Baptismal initiation is followed by teaching the new converts everything the Lord has commanded as guidelines for kingdom living. Consequently, whenever the Great Commission is studied in isolation from the rest of this gospel, the question becomes: What, exactly, are we commanded to make? To the extent the contemporary church down plays the importance of discipleship living and fails to provide support for it within the context of community, so the Great Commission becomes an empty slogan. In other words, if we want to stay in business, we need to know precisely what we are in business to do in the church and harness our energies to that end.

A Call to Commitment

For Matthew, the Great Commission does not so much signify going to all nations in order to rescue people out of the world, but rather calling people to Christ in order to live out their commitment to him in the world. The Great Commission should never be isolated from the Great Commandment "to love our neighbors as ourselves." Jesus' words do not begin with the command to go, but with the Sovereign's declaration that "all authority in heaven and on earth has been given to me." Therefore, with confidence the church can venture forth from its cultural cocoon into the world.

As the church responds to the disciple-making challenge, it will discover that the Lord's presence is not only cosmic and global but also intimate. In a special sense, it will prove his promise holds true: "Surely, I am with you always, to the very end of the age."

—*Eddie Gibbs*

of many people—and thus no meaning. A contemporary concept of heaven, if people believe it even exists, will likely resemble a hedonist's paradise (having a good time forever). Few people understand heaven to be a place of intimate and personal relationship with God (John 17:3).

As we carry out the evangelistic mandate in our secularized society, we must recognize that God has communicated about himself in many ways in the world. These forms of witness include divine mercy (through circumstances and "coincidences"), general revelation (through Creation and conscience), the redeemed lives of Christians, the Word of God, and the Holy Spirit. While only the Scriptures communicate a saving knowledge of God (Rom. 10:17; John 16:8–11), we can start with these other forms of revelation to enhance our witness to those who have opened their hearts to God on at least some level.

- *The cultural values of relativism and pluralism.* As these twin values increasingly affect the general world-view, people will indig-

The Gift of Evangelism and the Role of Witness

Would that God's people more freely and joyfully accept the great privilege and responsibility of representing Jesus Christ to the world! Tragically, so many miss out because of the fear—and consequent guilt—born of confusing the words *evangelist* and *witness.* Put simply, while Jesus Christ calls *all* believers to the role of witness, only a few are called to serve as evangelists.

Evangelists

An evangelist is a person uniquely empowered by the Holy Spirit to bring people to a saving encounter with Jesus Christ (see Eph. 4:11 and Acts 8:26–40). The gift can be exercised in large gatherings or in personal conversations. Persons with this spiritual gift sense when people are open, and know where and how to lead seekers to receive Christ as Savior. Evangelists need to be set free from institutional responsibilities in order to exercise their unique gift.

Witnesses

A witness is not necessarily an evangelist. In the only place the term is used in the New Testament, Jesus says, "You will receive power when the Holy Spirit comes upon you; and you shall be my witnesses" (Acts 1:8). Carefully consider four key words used here.

- *Witness.* This is a legal term. Why does Jesus apply the language of the courtroom? Because he himself is on trial. The claims he has made about himself, especially that the long-awaited kingdom of God is breaking in upon the world (Mark 1:15), put him on trial before everyone. Is he right? Can he substantiate the claims? "When the Holy Spirit comes upon you, you shall be

nantly challenge the "narrow-minded notion" that Christ is unique and the gospel message exclusive. Culture has historically shaped gospel preaching in America, often to a large degree. Couple the cultural values of relativism and pluralism with the American passion for pragmatism, and the potential for heretical preaching grows large. Evangelicals must guard the uniqueness of Christ and the gospel message in the face of growing cultural objections.

• *The controversy over strategies.* Do we use traditional proclamation methods or the newer friendship methods? Acts 1:8 provides a solution that avoids the polarizing of these two strategies. Jesus promised that believers would "receive power when the Holy Spirit comes on you; and you will be my witnesses in Jerusalem, and in all Judea and Samaria, and to the ends of the earth" (Acts 1:8). According to the Book of Acts, the believers, empowered by the Holy Spirit, employed various methods of witnessing. For example, they proclaimed the Good News through witness as presence, through deeds of integ-

my witness." To paraphrase, "You will be the evidence that I am who I say I am and am doing what I say I can do."

You have likely heard the question, "If you were on trial for being a Christian, would there be enough evidence to convict you?" It's a good question but off target. Instead, the key question is, "If Jesus Christ were on trial (which he is) for being the Sovereign Lord of Life, would there be enough evidence to convict him?"

Jesus is saying, "Yes! And you, my people, are the evidence."

• *Be.* "You shall *be* my witnesses." Not *do*. We serve as evidence by being who we are in Christ. Something about who we are, what we do, and what we say witnesses to him and his work in the world. Something about our character, deeds, and speech witnesses to the new reality he is bringing about. The role of witness involves the totality of our being.

• *Shall be.* Jesus does not command us to be his evidence. Rather, Jesus promises to do something to us and in us that makes us his evidence. He promises to send his Spirit upon us. It is the presence and power of his Spirit that makes us witnesses.

Because of Christ's promise, we need not exhort each other to "get out there." God's people are already "out there," in homes, in schools, in factories, in board rooms. The exhortation should rather be: "Open up out there," or "Surrender out there," to the Holy Spirit who makes us into winsome, contagious, irrefutable evidence that Jesus is who he says he is and can do what he claims to be able to do.

Let's continue to pray that God raises up and frees those gifted to be evangelists. May we pray, too, that God so fills us with the Spirit that Jesus Christ will "be convicted"—on clear evidence—of the charge of being the world's Redeemer.

—Darrell Johnson

rity and mercy, through acts of Christian love and compassion, through brief statements of values and beliefs, through testimony about the works of God (in conversion and otherwise), through gospel presentations (personal and public), and through evangelistic Bible studies.

These Spirit-empowered forms of witness fall into two main categories: witness by walk and witness by words. They are never presented in Acts in the form of a sequential progression. We find relationships and conversations developing within each of these forms of witness. In Acts these forms of witness do not fall into any kind of hierarchy, as though any of the forms might be better than others.

Acts does reveal to us that God gave his Spirit to Christians to enable all of life (our walk and our words) to be a witness for Jesus Christ. Thus, the debate between initiative/proclamation versus friendship/life-style methods becomes unnecessary; the Spirit uses both. A strategy based on recognizing that Acts 1:8 calls the believer to be a witness, rather than just an evangelist, enables the believer to see all of life as an opportunity for Spirit-empowered witness and gives guidance for a continued witness to an unbeliever who has rejected the gospel proclamation. This understanding of Acts 1:8 also preserves the theological content of the gospel message, which is propositional and doctrinal, while mandating and affirming the need for all of our life to be a witness.

Ministries that do their work in short-term relational environments, such as many campus and military ministries and programs in areas with transient populations, generally have emphasized "witness with words" strategies. When these groups move into long-term relational environments such as the local church, they also begin to emphasize relational strategies. As the youth culture has become more relationally intense, effective youth ministries have switched from proclamation strategies to relational strategies, just as this understanding of effective witnessing predicts.

The Power of God for Success

In his classic work, *Evangelism in the Early Church,* Michael Green (no relation to this article writer) states of the early Christians and the task of evangelism: "It is almost impossible to exaggerate the obstacles that lay in their way" (Green 1970, 13). He summarizes:

> Those who have never lived in a society which has been won over from paganism by Christianity find it hard to imagine how extensive are the obstacles presented to the Christian faith by religion, vice, custom and sheer laissez-faire. Wherever they went, Christians were opposed as anti-social, atheistic and depraved. Their message proclaimed a crucified criminal, and nothing

> could have been less calculated than that to win them converts. To the Greeks such a story showed how ridiculous the new faith was; to the Romans how weak and ineffective it was; while the Jews could not bring themselves to stomach it at all. To Jew and Gentile alike Christians were offensive, on account both of the doctrines and the behavior credited to them. All this they had to live down if they were going to win anybody at all for Jesus Christ. (Green 1970, 29)

Yet, in spite of the external challenge from a culture that opposed them and equally significant internal problems (such as small numbers, lack of trained leadership, weak organization, numerous leaders bound by custom and tradition, and so forth), the first Christians changed the world. How? Through immersing themselves in the Word, through constantly bathing their plans in prayer, and through relying on the Holy Spirit to empower them to be witnesses. They were few and weak, but in a dark room it doesn't take much light to make people squint!

Although uncompromising in their message, the early Christians were creative when it came to communicating that message. They used any method available to proclaim the Good News: open-air preaching, home meetings, one-on-one encounters. They created a new literary form, the Gospels, to get the word out. They launched an effective literature ministry using the papyri codex, a cheap, easy-to-produce form of literature. When famine or plagues struck, the hated Christians responded with acts of nearly superhuman mercy, courage, and selflessness toward all who were suffering, friend or foe.

These bold evangelizers transformed martyrdom and other forms of persecution and suffering into opportunities for witness that even their most hardened opponents could not ignore. Eusebius' *Ecclesiastical History* tells of an overwhelming series of martyrs whose moral purity and faithful love for God emerged as more powerful than torture or execution. The lesson for the contemporary church is that there will be far more success in the basic proclamation of our faith when it is Spirit-empowered than in all of the media and high-tech strategies we could devise and attempt apart from the Spirit's direction.

There was, however, one great failure in the evangelistic efforts of the early church. After the Christians fled Jerusalem during the Jewish rebellion in A.D. 70, the attitude toward the Jews expressed by Paul in Romans 9:3–5 no longer characterized Christians in general. Jewish-Christian relations soured, and efforts to evangelize the Jews failed. Green comments, "If ever any evangelistic enterprise taught the lesson that the gospel cannot be preached without love, this was it" (Green 1970, 108).

After the collapse of the Roman Empire, Christianity tried to replace and control the state, with results that eventually would lead to the Protestant Reformation. Yet in a time of moral and social decay, there emerged groups of men and women who voluntarily banded together in religious communities to develop in their faith, to serve their fellow human beings, and to preach the gospel.

The Irish monks, for instance, who preserved Christianity in the darkest of times in Europe and then carried it throughout a pantheistic Europe, present a possible model for contemporary believers wondering how to be holy and active in a fallen world. The disciplined monasticism of Benedict and his followers shone like a light upon a hill in a dark land. The love, humility, and servanthood of St. Francis of Assisi stand in utter contrast to the linking of Christianity with the European expansionism that resulted in the Crusades.

The gospel is the power of God for salvation, no matter what the challenges or setbacks. Even though opposed, it cannot be overcome (see 1 Thess. 2:2; 2 Tim. 2:9). Our task is to proclaim this message of ultimate liberation, of ultimate freedom, of eternal salvation with boldness to all people.

—Michael P. Green

Resources

Bright, B. 1987. Witnessing without fear. San Bernardino, Cal.: Here's Life.
Coleman, R. 1963. The master plan of evangelism. Old Tappan, N.J.: Revell.
Green, M. 1970. Evangelism in the early church. Grand Rapids: Eerdmans.
Jeremias, J. 1971. New Testament theology. New York: Scribner's.
McCloskey, M. 1985. Tell it often, tell it well. San Bernardino, Cal.: Here's Life.
Petersen, J. 1989. Living proof. Colorado Springs: NavPress.

The Pastor's Role in Evangelism

Paul told Timothy, "Do the work of an evangelist," and ever since, evangelism has belonged in a pastor's job portfolio. But how, exactly, do we go about evangelism as pastors?

Intentional Modeling

People want to be led, inspired, challenged. Pastors who lead their churches into evangelism do it primarily by example, by intentionally modeling what they want to see developing in others. Even though we sometimes are poor models, we can aim to model well and joyfully. To do that, we may tell stories about the joy of seeing a life transformed by Christ, the gratitude of people who thank us for sharing Christ, and the satisfaction of leading someone to Christ for eternity.

In addition, if we are to model

our joyful commitment to evangelism, we can do at least three basic things as pastors:

• *Make evangelism a personal, passionate priority.* If we don't live it, we can't preach it with conviction. Passion has to exist — somewhere — for evangelism to work. Paul said, "For Christ's love compels us, because we are convinced that one died for all" (2 Cor. 5:14a). It is hard to pastor effectively without a passionate care for the lost, because if evangelism doesn't bubble to the surface in a pastor's life, how will others catch the vision to evangelize? Every pastor needs to be appropriately driven to share the gospel.

• *Get out of the office.* Some pastors prefer to manage church affairs, study, and prepare sermons, activities that keep them in an office with the door closed. But spending an inordinate amount of time away from people is not modeling evangelism.

Tom Peters, in *A Passion for Excellence,* encourages "management by walking around." He says a manager should be out of his or her office a third of the time. So why not learn to minister by walking around? "Peoplework" keeps us fresh and makes us visible. When we're among people, they can *see* our priority for evangelism at work. And getting out puts us in contact with non-Christians.

• *Use methods of integrity.* If we go to the Bible for what we believe, we shouldn't look only to the world for methodology. Our evangelistic methods should lead people to repentance and faith, and a decision to follow Jesus Christ, not just to attend church programs. The church has to be built on biblical principles, and so does the evangelism we model.

We could attract a crowd with a Christian cowboy riding an Appaloosa pony across the platform, but that is hardly a biblical model of evangelism. We don't want to sacrifice the integrity of the gospel for the sake of pulling a crowd, or compromise the message in order to make the gospel more palatable.

Purposeful Praying

Along with modeling, we'll need to pray for an increase of harvesters. We don't have to pray for the harvest; it's there. But the harvesters are few, so they need our prayers. We can pray that evangelism will happen through the people of the church. We also do well to pray for more passion for the lost, for opportunities, and for courage and faith to grab the opportunities as they come.

A friend was distributing food in Ethiopia, and while there, he talked to some Catholic sisters who did similar work. "How do you handle the devastation and the hurt and agony you see day after day?" he asked them.

"Prayer," replied one. "If we do not have God in our hearts, nothing else works." Likewise, only if we have God in our hearts will evangelism "work" in the local church.

—*Calvin C. Ratz*

2

Planning Evangelism

There's no three-step, money-back-guaranteed approach to positioning a church for evangelism. Rather, it's an ongoing process of personal growth and evaluation, coupled with sensitivity to the history and needs of a congregation. It goes far beyond implementing a program or hiring additional staff. Ultimately, it takes a corporate change of heart.

Pastors can engender that attitude, but only the Holy Spirit can bring about an intense passion for spiritual harvesting. Here are important considerations for those wanting to create an environment in which evangelism flourishes.

Establish the Church's Vision

A church, if it expects to rouse from lethargy, must know why it exists and what God expects it to accomplish. This means going beyond knowing that it is God's intention for all churches to evangelize. A church must discover God's plan for *its* particular contribution to the kingdom. Some congregations are called to be spiritual hospitals, some social activists, some teaching centers. Still others are front-line attack forces.

So we must ask two questions at the outset: First, what direction should *this* church take? Second, how best can we reach our community with the gospel?

After considerable discussion and prayer, a church board often will come to consensus. For example, a church committed to growth may decide to construct a larger sanctuary. In addition, the congregation may outline basic principles to follow in reaching its evangelism goals, such as prayer, an emphasis on Scripture, an appeal to the unchurched, and strong pastoral leadership.

Such principles must become more than vague notions; they must be specifically described. For example, a congregation may decide that evangelistically strong churches usually have one dominant preacher, rather than a rotating team. Consequently, the senior pastor is asked to do the bulk of the preaching.

Excite the Congregation with the Vision

When a pastor blows the trumpet for evangelism, it can scare the congregation as much as excite it. The call to evangelism is first of all a call for change, and change can be threatening. So care is needed to woo the congregation toward evangelism. For example, in one church I pastored, our initial pastor-board discussions about evangelism brought unanimity, faith, and excitement. But we held the information to ourselves, proceeding slowly, because we knew the importance of building confidence and trust within the congregation.

A new vision for a church can be both thrilling and traumatic for the congregation. For those who buy the vision, it's exhilarating; for those who are threatened, it can mean fear and confusion. Sometimes leaders get so far ahead of their people that they are perceived as the enemy. The people have to feel a personal conviction for evangelism. They have to want to touch their community and grow.

Church leaders can use a variety of means to encourage people to fulfill the vision God has given them:

• *The pulpit.* The pulpit can elevate the vision from the secular to the spiritual. We can challenge our people with the needs of the community, keeping the focus on not how many people we can get to join our church but on how many in our community are lost without Jesus Christ. Of course, we will try to avoid creating guilt, a poor motivator with only short-term benefits. Its long-term effect is usually cynicism and fear. But we can affirm the pioneers of a church by acknowledging that the strength of the church today is a result of their vision and faithful service.

• *Conversations.* Tom Peters, in his book *Thriving on Chaos,* suggests a leader should become the vision's foremost itinerant preacher: "Do not let a single day pass without taking at least two or three opportunities to deliver a three-minute stump speech on the vision." Pastors must develop ways to introduce their vision into many conversations, to summarize their dreams repeatedly.

A couple of questions can help turn conversations toward a church's vision for evangelism: "What's God been telling you about our church lately?" and "Are you aware of some of the things God is doing in our church?" In the discussion that follows, a pastor can summarize what he or she believes God is saying to the church and how the collective leadership is responding.

- *Encouraging ownership of the vision.* Deacons or elders may sometimes tip us off to a nascent problem: "Pastor, some people think this is just your project. We've got to correct that impression." Some people may think we just want a larger church to feed our egos.

For example, one person called plans my church had for a new sanctuary "the pastor's pet project." Because of this mistaken notion, we devised a program to share the vision while taking the spotlight off me by working through the committees, particularly our leadership council. At several meetings, we dealt with the question: What will enable us to evangelize our community? We allowed time for free expression of ideas, fears, and concerns. Lay leaders chaired many of these sessions.

- *Opinion leaders.* It works well to reach out through those perceived to be congregational opinion leaders. These opinion leaders aren't necessarily the elected officials; they are simply the people who command attention when they speak. Their influence may be felt in a business meeting, but more likely it's felt over coffee after church or in parking lot conversations.

- *Testimonials.* In a church I pastored, once a month we had someone share what the church meant to him and how he was praying for the church to reach out to our community. God spoke to the congregation through these testimonials. People began to realize that concern for growth was widespread.

One particularly helpful testimonial came from a man who had been in the church about three years and was working in the Sunday school. People heard the passionate concern of someone who wasn't part of the church establishment or even closely associated with me. He described how the Sunday school was growing, how we had several classes meeting in hallways, and how the youth department was meeting in a nearby school. His words weren't the most polished, but the congregation was moved.

- *An abundance of information and means.* There are dangers in relying solely on verbally announcing key information. The spoken word can be misunderstood and forgotten. In addition, at least 30 percent of most congregations are absent on a given Sunday, so the only sure way to inform all the people is through the mail. Though it's expensive, it will pay good dividends in terms of regular communication.

One church board circulated a "Facing the Future, Fulfilling Our Mission" document to the congregation. It detailed growth goals and methods, outlined the church's ten-year plan, showed the projected growth for the community, and explained the idea of planting another congregation.

• *Themes and emphases.* A well-stated theme can mobilize people to a vision. When the theme is visible continually—posters, bulletins, signs, bookmarks—it constantly reminds people of the church's passion for evangelism.

Each year the church can set a theme tied to its vision of evangelistic and spiritual growth. Phrases such as "Growing Together" and "Building for the Future" communicate the church's expectations. One church called a year simply "The Year of Evangelism" and taught personal evangelism and programmed several special events during that year. Gradually the vision spreads.

Reshape the Ministries

As a vision for evangelism begins to grow, new challenges emerge. First, it may become obvious that *many church programs are intro-*

Evangelism Training

Most Christians intuitively know that evangelism belongs not in the sales department but in the public relations department. Common sense tells us we must both proclaim the Word and live it out among the people with whom our lives naturally intersect. Whenever evangelism majors in technique and strategy, and minors in love and respect for individuals, there is trouble.

Loving Communication

When I ask people to tell me where they struggle in witnessing, their answers fall into three categories: 2 percent say they struggle with intellectual questions they can't answer, 1 percent say they struggle with mechanics ("How do I lead a person to Christ?"), and 97 percent say they need help with their communication skills ("How do I move from secular to spiritual conversation in a natural way?" "How do I disagree or withdraw from an activity without seeming 'holier than thou'?" "How can I be myself when I feel the world puts me in a Christian box?").

People seem to be saying they need more help with communication skills. While we certainly need to know *what* to say, we acutely need to know *how* to say it.

The communication process is so complex and multifaceted that it is easy to feel overwhelmed. Yet the simple key to good evangelistic communication is the ability to love as Christ loved. Christians who break nearly every rule of communication can yet be effective evangelists if they genuinely love the person with whom they are talking.

Relational Skills Training

After establishing Christ's love as the foundation for communication, we can analyze our own rela-

verted. A lot of a typical church's programs are geared to meet the needs of its people rather than touch those in the community. In a church I pastored, research indicated that 95 percent of our ministries had little or no evangelistic focus!

While the need to provide support and encouragement to existing Christians is legitimate, that's not spiritual harvesting. Growing churches find ways to build an evangelistic component into their programs; they also establish programs with evangelism as a primary purpose.

Second, there is *a need to realign the personnel in the church's programs.* Those with both a heart and an aptitude for evangelism can be shifted into positions where their gifts reap the maximum benefits. For example, a secretary for the music department might be gifted in sharing her faith. But by being buried in a church office, she's cut off from the people to whom she could witness. If she were redeployed,

tional weaknesses: Are we shy and timid? Is it difficult for us to start a conversation, much less get it around to God? Do we miss detecting people's needs? Do we listen well?

It is helpful to devise exercises for the specific relational skills we are trying to teach: listening skills, affirming skills, dealing with hostility, disagreeing without being disagreeable, and so on. For instance, information theorists tell us that to communicate effectively, we must recognize the way we stereotype people, especially those to whom we are speaking. So I developed this exercise: "Turn to the person next to you. Assume this is a Christian friend. I want one of you to say, 'Hi. How was your weekend?' Then the other person needs to reply with where he or she has been this weekend and tell about one thing he or she has learned recently."

After a few minutes, I say, "Now, reverse the roles. This time the other person says 'How was your weekend?' and you answer. But this time you know the person asking the question is *not* a Christian."

In step one, everyone chatters, and the atmosphere is relaxed. After I explain step two, there is initial silence and then groans, nervous laughter, and uneasiness. Afterward I ask participants to tell me how they felt in going from one conversation to the next. The answer is always the same: "I felt relaxed in the first but very uncomfortable in the second. I felt the non-Christian wouldn't be interested. I knew she would think I was strange. I felt defensive and uneasy."

Then we examine why, having been told only that the questioner wasn't a believer, the speakers assumed the worst. Was that fair? If this is our basic reaction toward nonbelievers, is it any wonder we feel uncomfortable witnessing? In learning about ourselves and how we relate to others, we can learn to better relate the gospel.

—Rebecca Manley Pippert

perhaps she could be leading neighborhood Bible studies and helping in counseling ministries.

Not all department leaders will live comfortably with the implications of a new emphasis on evangelism. Some will find it threatening. Some solid workers who enjoy working among Christians will be intimidated by the thought of working with non-Christians. We can try to help them find less threatening but equally important ministries.

Third, as a vision for evangelism takes hold, it becomes clear that *a church has to rethink its target audience.* It has to look outside its four walls to identify the groups it is most capable of reaching.

No community is likely to become fully evangelized, and most churches fall short of the capacity to reach everyone. So, without playing God, it's best to identify those groups most apt to respond positively to the gospel in a particular setting. This enables a church to target local needs and maximize the use of its workers.

One church identified four groups they are most likely to reach:

Evangelistic Calling by Lay People

Over the years, one of the most prevalent misconceptions about the evangelistic work of the church has been the idea that only professional ministers are called to share the gospel. Today there is a growing trend in the opposite direction, as lay people are realizing and accepting their responsibility to witness. Pastors are working to encourage this movement and build a calling program that recruits and trains church members to do the job of evangelism.

Recruiting the Workers

When Christ called his apostles, he first prayed all night. Then he called them by name. An apostle is one sent forth with a commission. In its broader sense, the term refers to every Christian who has been sent forth by Christ with a commission to witness for him. After much prayer, therefore, pastors should select people to take with them to learn how to evangelize.

One method is to select two people for morning calling and two others for evening calling. For example, at our church we have set aside Wednesday mornings from 9:00 to 12:00 and Thursday evenings from 7:15 to 10:30 as our calling times. On Wednesday noon we enjoy a bag lunch together, and on Thursday we have a light snack. In each case we have a report-back meeting to hear about the results of our efforts. These reporting sessions help reduce dropouts due to discouragement, because people have an opportunity to hear how God has worked through each witnessing team that day.

• *The hurting.* Naaman came to God at a time of crisis. Jesus attracted the diseased, the deluded, and the depressed. He appealed to the ostracized and the social misfits. It's the same today; people in need are prime candidates for responding to the gospel.

The gospel has always appealed to those in the lower half of society. The trouble is, people in many churches have been saved for several years. God has blessed them in the interval, and they become socially and economically removed from the most responsive segment of society. Yuppies and dinks (double income, no kids) don't relate well with people on welfare.

A church can take this into consideration in planning for evangelism. Perhaps the youth can run a coffee house for the mentally and physically handicapped, for example. Or new converts can be redeployed among their unsaved friends.

• *Young adults.* Several consultants have indicated that churches usually grow in the 18–35 age bracket, in which people are making

Training the Workers

It is essential to teach and model this progression: how to find out where the hearer is spiritually, how to present the gospel message itself, and how to bring the person to a commitment to Christ at the conclusion of the presentation. With the goal of developing these skills, a calling program normally consists of three main types of training:

• *Class instruction.* Classes can be held at least once a week on the day people come to the church for visitation. People normally meet for about a half hour and then go out on calls. Participants receive a brief lecture on the topic of the week and are given study assignments for the following week. In our program, we also have class members pair up to role play what they learned the previous week.

• *Homework assignments.* Since many Christians do not know how to make an intelligible, interesting presentation of the gospel, part of the homework should involve learning and practicing a scripted gospel presentation. Most people need a model to use as a basic pattern, which they can adapt to their individual experiences and personalities.

Leaders can prepare a notebook that contains instructions on how to present the gospel logically and interestingly. Portions of the notebooks are then given as assignments each week. One good way to check the assignments is through weekly recitation during the classroom instruction.

• *On-the-job training.* This, typically, is the missing link of modern evangelistic training. The average person can no more learn to evangelize in a classroom than he or she can learn to fly an airplane in the living room. In effective programs, trainees go out with experienced partners and listen as these trained people endeavor to lead others to Christ. Evangelism is more caught than taught.

—D. James Kennedy

major choices and establishing family lifestyles. The church set up age-grouped programs with these people to reach out, integrate them into the church, and provide teaching and pastoral care. Singles are made to feel welcome not by segregating them (though the church has a singles class) but by integrating them into the life of the church. One way is by including at least one single adult on the committee for each adult fellowship group.

• *The over-55 crowd.* Seniors are responsive to the gospel. Programming to meet their needs includes a monthly luncheon and a midweek recreational program. In addition, a seniors choir, handbell choir, orchestra, or small ensemble provides ways for seniors to devote their time and talent to the church.

• *Children.* Children are still the segment of society most responsive to the gospel. The church divided this potential harvest into two groups: children of church families and those from non-Christian homes.

The church, after investigating its success rate at keeping its own children, determined that "biological evangelism" doesn't happen automatically. So, to meet the need, the church holds children's crusades and emphasizes Sunday school and several midweek activities.

A pastor established an informal group for parents of older teens and young adults who aren't living for God. He meets with these parents, helps them deal with their sense of failure, and assists them in finding ways to reach their grown children.

Upgrade the Worship Experience

What happens in worship is critical for evangelism, because it touches newcomers and influences people on the fringe. Consequently, churches may need to upgrade the effectiveness of their Sunday worship. We don't want to be so concerned about keeping the Christians happy that we make outsiders feel uncomfortable.

Twenty-five years ago, 88 percent of Canadian university students said it was important to have a philosophy of life. A recent survey indicated that number has dropped to 39 percent. People obviously have changed. The truth is, if we are presenting the gospel the same way we did ten years ago, we are probably missing the mark today.

To hit the mark, a church may need to implement worship goals, such as:

• *We will make church a positive experience for outsiders.* Ours is an experience-oriented generation, not a thinking generation, and our churches have felt the shift. Those entering a church sanctuary today are more interested in feeling good spiritually than in gaining biblical knowledge. Inspiration has replaced information as the hot button in today's church market.

This presents a dilemma, because religious experience without biblical knowledge fosters fanaticism and confusion. Fortunately, authentic, biblical Christianity does provide an experience. In the New Testament, both the gathering of believers and the public proclamation of the gospel to outsiders were intense, heart-moving encounters. People experienced relationship and emotion. There was joy, anger, conviction, sorrow, and tension. Everyone who touched New Testament Christians experienced something.

People do need to have a legitimate experience that brings them closer to both God and their friends. We may offer this experience through warm interaction in the foyer, the tasteful use of humor, soaring music, or a well-developed illustration that touches the emotions. All our services can lead to an encounter with Almighty God—the most heart-stopping, life-changing experience possible.

• *We will provide a warm, relaxed atmosphere.* Obviously the atmosphere of the service ought to usher people into the presence of God. But how does that happen? Today, more than ever, people respond to a relaxed atmosphere. People don't want to come to church to be lectured, and they certainly won't bring a guest to a setting that feels strained, heavy, or eccentric.

We can work at closing the emotional distance between pulpit and pew. We can take time to chat with the people (though keeping it separate from the sermon). A friend calls this "pastoring from the pulpit." We can be transparent, to let people see that those at the front are essentially no different from those in the pew.

• *We will waste no time.* It's amazing how easily worship time is wasted. Radio and television preachers know the danger of dead spots. The fact is, dead time hurts any service by inviting thoughts to wander. Here are some ways to honor the time of member and visitor:

—Eliminate 95 percent of verbal announcements. They're in the bulletin, and that's enough.

—Eliminate introductions of musical groups. The information is listed in the bulletin. If musicians are trained to be in place at the appropriate moment, time isn't lost while they're walking to the platform.

—Increase the number of offering plates and ushers. This can cut minutes from the time it takes to collect the offering.

—Rearrange the logistics of serving Communion elements, saving significant time in that portion of the service.

• *Preaching will relate to life.* Preaching has been called "the fine art of talking in someone else's sleep." Regrettably, we must all plead guilty to putting more than one person to sleep on Sunday morning, and when we have, it's usually because we haven't been touching people where they live. Every Sunday, we have to earn our credentials, our right to speak.

If a church is to be evangelistic, the people in the pew have to feel the preacher understands them and knows what is going on in today's world. Illustrations have to be current. Facts must be accurate, statements substantiated. We're not called to be pop psychologists, but we *are* called to lift up Jesus Christ in such a way that people recognize him as the solution to their frustrations, hurts, and despair.

In positioning a church for evangelism, pastors may need to rework both the style and content of their preaching. Considering the following four rules for evangelistic sermons can help us stay on track. First, plan the invitation prior to writing the final draft. Every sermon should be designed to get a response. Second, try to write the sermon concept in seventeen words or less. If you can't, the sermon may not have focus. Third, write a description of one person you're trying to reach and ask yourself, *Will this person relate to what I'm trying to say?* Fourth, ask yourself, *Will a non-Christian understand the language I'm using?*

• *We will provide special events and services especially for outsiders.* People don't want to bring a neighbor to church on the morning their pastor speaks on stewardship. They want to know when it's a good time to invite friends. Thus, special events and services aimed at evangelism are important, and we should tell the people that these services are designed with outsiders in mind.

For example, I dealt with age groupings in one set of Sunday evening services: for seniors, "When I'm Old and Gray"; for young adults, "The Generic Generation"; and for those in between, "Handling the Middle Ages." Other evenings hit contemporary issues, family life, and practical ways of coping with life. Drama has also proved an effective way to explain the gospel to non-Christians.

In many and various ways the church needs to be structured so that the word gets out: We have a message of Good News that we can hardly wait to share with you.

—*Calvin C. Ratz*

Crusade Evangelism

Crusade evangelism not only wins individuals to the Savior; it also contributes tremendously to the health and vitality of the local church.

The Local Church Benefits

Even critics of crusade evangelism agree it has helped build the church in America. The goal is not to eclipse the witness of local churches but to enlarge it. The evangelist is simply a servant of the churches, as well as of Jesus Christ. Interestingly, up to 42 percent of those who trust Christ at a crusade report leading someone else to the Lord within six months.

Any united, cross-denominational, citywide crusade is really the task of hundreds of local churches in a given city, not just the evangelist. Such a crusade, under the guidance and power of the Holy Spirit, provides many opportunities that can lead to local-church renewal and growth. Here are just five of the ways churches benefit:

• *The increase in praying.* Prayer is foundational to any crusade, and Christians get involved interceding privately, in small groups, and in large-scale concerts of prayer. Many church members learn to pray specifically and effectively for the first time. Part of the purpose of the training is to get Christians into the mindset to invite friends, family, neighbors, and work associates to specific crusade events. Through prayerful interaction with others, they develop this inclination.

• *The effects of training.* Church members learn how to do friendship evangelism, how to serve as a counselor, and how to follow up decision makers after the crusade. Such training emphasizes the importance of building relationships with nonbelievers. Crusades provide excellent opportunities to put this training into practice, something that benefits local churches long after the crusade is over.

• *The prospect of revival.* On occasion full-blown revivals of Christianity both precede and flow out of crusade evangelism. The backslidden come back to Christ, new believers become established in local churches, and older Christians renew their faith and zeal.

During a large crusade, a God-consciousness often sweeps a city. This in turn helps Christians become bolder in their personal witness. Many lead someone to Christ for the first time, while others become all the more effective at personal evangelism. As thousands commit their lives to Jesus Christ and join local churches, God is glorified.

• *The renewal of pastors.* Involvement with the wider body of Christ is a key benefit to pastors, personally, because of its encouraging effects ("There are a lot of Christians in this city, after all!"). So it is wise for pastors to lead by example and take the training. They can experience the joy of renewing the vows they made in the early days of their call to ministry.

• *The growth in membership.* Recent research suggests that pastors who actively participate in a crusade see seven times more growth in their churches afterward than pastors who limit their involvement because they've heard, "Your church won't benefit that much from the crusade." Such thinking inevitably becomes a self-fulfilling prophecy.

Carefully planned and executed follow-up discipleship produces membership growth. Not all the sown seed will bear fruit, but independent studies have verified that systematic follow-up can bring tremendous results, incorporating from 54 to 78 percent of all adult decision makers into local churches.

—Luis Palau

Friendship Evangelism

What happens when people want to obey Jesus' command in Matthew 28 to make disciples but don't know how? What happens when people view some popular evangelistic methods as coercive, manipulative, or otherwise unhealthy? What happens when people realize that they do not have the rhetorical skills of a great evangelist?

What happens is a whole new form of outreach: friendship evangelism.

Golden-Rule Evangelism

Actually, the term "friendship evangelism" covers a rather large and growing number of new approaches to evangelism. What they have in common, though, is a recognition that not all believers are great orators who will preach to packed soccer stadiums around the world. These approaches also share a strong desire to move away from heavy-handed strategies of the past. To put it another way, guilt-producing questions and ambush tactics are out; the Golden Rule is in.

Some of the new forms of friendship evangelism offer sophisticated lessons in listening skills, so that, as one writer puts it, "needs are discovered *before* solutions are shared." Still other forms embrace cultural sensitivity as an important feature. What all forms of friendship evangelism seem to agree on is this: The unbeliever is a person to be taken seriously, not to be targeted simply as an object for conversion but as a subject for a caring relationship. The approach begins with *presence,* the loving presence of the evangelist with the unbeliever.

Theologically, friendship evangelism rests heavily on the teaching of the Incarnation. Jesus, for example, didn't just talk about love; he loved. He didn't just preach forgiveness; he forgave. He didn't just proclaim the Good News; he was the Good News—in the flesh. Jesus also saw to the immediate, physical needs of the people he encountered *before* he spoke to them of sin and forgiveness. Similarly, those who practice friendship evangelism do more than talk, preach, and proclaim; they attempt to incarnate the very truths they wish to communicate.

A Caring Alternative

Friendship evangelism is an attractive alternative for many church people because it fits with what they see themselves to be — not gifted preachers, not bold faith sharers, but caring people. Furthermore, the product of friendship evangelism is not simply new converts to the faith, but, in many cases, a revitalized fellowship. This form of outreach nearly always strengthens the fellowship ties within the church. After all, what church would not benefit from members who earnestly attempt to incarnate the very attributes of Christ they wish to tell others about?

Friendship evangelism also has the advantage of being able to involve every person in a church. Creating a climate of hospitality in worship, where the stranger feels welcomed, is quite conceivably a task for every church member. With friendship evangelism, not every church member must be willing to make door-to-door calls. In practice, there are many different ways that church members can participate, depending on their particular gifts.

As with most church efforts, this relationship-building approach to evangelism requires strong pastoral leadership and benefits from professional assistance. If a church wants to become more friendly, for example, a consultant from outside the church may visit the services and provide arresting insights about the way newcomers actually feel. Long-time members of a church are often unaware of the strong, unwelcoming signals they inadvertently send.

In many ways, friendship evangelism may be the most difficult form of evangelism to practice. What sounds on first hearing like the easiest and most natural form of evangelism may actually require the hardest work of those who would adopt it.

—Doug Brouwer

Records and Statistics

Some church leaders hate keeping records. According to them, churches should not be in the numbers game; keeping records leads to pride and an unholy trust in statistics. Numbers, though, are not necessarily evil. The writer of Acts carefully communicated the growth of the early church using records and statistics. From 120 persons (Acts 1:15) the early church grew to 3,000 (Acts 2:41) and added another 5,000 men (Acts 4:4). Then, when the numbers expanded, the growth was recorded as simply "more and more men and women" (Acts 5:14). Reporting statistics was an acceptable and useful means to evaluate the results of evangelistic outreach.

When we go to a doctor's office, a nurse carefully records our temperature, blood pressure, weight, height, and pulse rate. Using these statistics, the doctor formulates a judgment about our health. In no way, of course, do such measurements heal us. However, they do give the doctor an objective way to gauge our health and prescribe treatment.

Measuring Ministry

Keeping accurate ministry records gives us an objective read-out of the health of our church. While statistics certainly do not lead anyone to Christ, they do help us know where, when, and how our outreach ministry may be most influential.

For example, if we want to increase the effectiveness of our evangelism ministries, we will find it helpful to know:

• *What attracts people to our churches.* Few churches know exactly why they attract visitors. Asking newcomers how they heard about the church and carefully recording their answers will present a picture of what attracts people and will help us focus more efforts in that direction.

• *What keeps people in our*

churches. Visitors tend to stay in a church if they build friendships, become involved in a small group or class, and find a way to serve. Tracking all new members to see if they are becoming involved in these three ways helps assimilate the folks who have begun attending as a result of our outreach efforts.

• *How people become members of our churches.* People become members through one of the three modes of church growth—conversion, transfer, and biological (members' children joining the church). Tracing the conversion, transfer, and biological growth rates during the last three years allows us to see where our church's outreach is strongest and where it needs strengthening.

• *How people find Christ in our churches.* The majority of a church's new converts enter the church through only one or two of its ministries. Interviewing new converts to find out how they made commitments to Christ, and recording the responses, will highlight our most effective ministries.

• *How often people attend our churches.* The key statistic every church needs to track is composite membership — the average of Sunday-morning worship attendance, Sunday-school attendance, and formal church membership. Charting yearly composite membership on a graph will establish a trend line that helps us spot changes in congregational growth patterns. We then can adjust ministry strategy.

Tracking Trends

How is data gathered? The most common methods include interviews (in person or by phone), completion of attendance cards during services, and the regular recording of membership changes. Attendance records are most accurate when kept on a weekly basis, but if that seems a bit much, we can keep records during the months of October and May and project findings into the total year.

Keeping good records helps a church fulfill its part in the Great Commission. The first steps? Think: *What records do we already keep? What kinds of records do we need to begin keeping?*

—*Gary L. McIntosh*

Parking and Buildings

Pastors recognize that numerous theological, relational, sociological, and administrative factors influence whether or not a church will grow. However, many church leaders overlook two other crucial factors that also have significant effect on church attendance: the parking situation and the state of the church facilities.

What's the Parking Message?

Parking is a major concern for many churches because limited spaces can limit membership growth. Churches struggling with a lack of parking space should first look for nearby parking lots not being used on Sundays and put them to use as shuttle parking areas. For example, our church uses some college lots near our church and buses people from those lots to the church.

Next, church leaders can encourage regular attenders to park in these shuttle lots, freeing prime parking space for visitors. When staff members regularly park in the shuttle lots, it encourages other members to do the same.

Finally, the best parking spaces can be reserved for first-time visitors. Once these people are assimilated into church membership, they can be asked if they would be willing to put up with more distant parking as a form of sacrificial service.

A visitor's first—and last—impression of a church occurs in the parking lot. Thus it is wise to evaluate the parking situation regularly. For example, a number of years ago, our church hired nonmembers to direct traffic in the parking lot. While these folks were efficient, they were not interested in making people feel welcomed by our congregation. Consequently, we decided to set up a completely volunteer crew to work the parking lot as a ministry. We still park with efficiency, but we also do it with a servant attitude.

Are the Buildings Inviting?

A second environmental factor that impacts church ministry is the state of the church buildings themselves. At a bare minimum, growth-conscious leaders will want to evaluate these four items regularly:

• *Appearance.* People will judge the quality of church services, at least in part, by the appearance of the facilities. This does not mean the buildings need to be expensive. It does mean that they should be clean and neat.

• *Size.* The size of the facilities will limit church growth to some degree. People may tolerate crowded rooms for a while if there is some hope of relief; however, they will not tolerate uncomfortable overcrowding forever. If adjustments are not made, they will soon go elsewhere for worship.

• *Flexibility.* All spaces should be capable of multipurpose use. Educational space that is reserved for only one kind of use or one kind of ministry will become wasted space. This fact needs consideration when designing new space, since greater efficiency is gained when all church space can be used many times over.

For example, a church that is out of space for worship or for Sunday school can try offering double services and classes. Those already doing that can consider offering on Saturday nights what they do on Sunday mornings. This approach demonstrates wiser stewardship than plans to build more space that would only be used once a week.

• *Expansion possibilities.* As much as is possible, facility designs should incorporate the possibility of expansion. One sanctuary was built a number of years ago to seat 2,100 people. This seemed rather optimistic, since the church was running about 1,200 in Sunday worship attendance, so it was built without the possibility of expansion. Seven years after moving into the new sanctuary, the church had three morning services that ministered to over 4,000 people. With building, as with parking, we should always plan room for more.

—Edward G. Dobson

3

The Church Growth Movement

In the 1950s and 60s, few people had heard the term "church growth." Evangelistic pessimism dominated many missions agencies and churches in North America, as denominations and congregations suffered significant numerical decline. Today, however, dozens of denominations have embraced church growth thinking. Local churches and denominations have added specialists in church growth to their staffs, and seminaries now teach academic courses in church growth, both at the master's and doctoral levels.

Church growth has come into its own. But what, exactly, is it? The term was coined by Donald A. McGavran. Put simply, church growth describes "all that is involved in bringing men and women who do not have a personal relationship to Jesus Christ into fellowship with Him and into responsible church membership" (Wagner 1984, 14).

Technically, church growth is a contemporary missions movement stressing a scientific approach to planting, multiplying, nurturing, and renewing churches. It is based on a pragmatic analysis of existing churches, and it emphasizes numerical growth as an indication of church health. The movement strongly advocates commitment to the lordship of Jesus Christ and obedience to his Great Commission to "make disciples of all the nations."

The History of the Movement

In the United States, the Church Growth Movement has been primarily associated with Donald McGavran, C. Peter Wagner, Win Arn, and the School of World Mission at Fuller Theological Seminary in Pasadena, California. The "Father of Church Growth," Donald McGavran (1897–1990), was a third-generation missionary in India, serving there for thirty years. As a young man at a youth conference in Lake Geneva, Wisconsin, in 1919, he heard the claims of the gospel and made a lifelong commitment to Jesus Christ. At a Student Volunteer convention in Des Moines in December 1919, he sensed God's call to the mission field. After graduating from Yale Divinity School, McGavran went to India in 1923. He learned to speak Hindi and won recognition as an educator in the United Christian Missionary Society.

In 1932, after receiving his Ph.D. at Columbia University, McGavran was elected executive secretary-treasurer of his mission in India. His responsibilities included administrating an extensive mission of eighty missionaries, schools, a leprosy home, hospitals, and evangelistic-outreach programs. After reading *Christian Mass Movements in India* (Pickett 1933), McGavran began to study his own mission's success in the mid-India area. Frustrated to find only ten growing churches out of 145 missions stations, McGavran asked the Mid-India Christian Council to recruit J. Waskom Pickett to conduct a survey. He assisted Pickett in conducting the research, and eventually their work was published in 1936 under the title, *The Mass Movement Survey of Mid-India,* revised in 1958 to *Church Growth and Group Conversion.*

After becoming convinced that all the missions in his area needed to become more effective in evangelism, McGavran left his executive position to devote the next 18 years to evangelistic work, from 1936 to 1954. While testing his ideas in the real world of missionary endeavor, he saw about 1,000 individuals won to Christ and 15 churches established.

In 1951 McGavran began writing his ideas, resulting in publication of *Bridges of God* (McGavran 1955, rev. 1981). (The Church Growth Movement traces its official beginning to the publication of this book, which is considered the Magna Carta of the movement.) Returning to the United States in 1954, McGavran was asked by his mission board to complete a series of church growth case studies on its other nine mission fields, such as Mexico, Latin America, the Philippines, Thailand, Congo, Jamaica, and Puerto Rico. In each field, he studied the work being carried on by Baptists, Episcopalians, Methodists, Presbyterians, Pentecostals and others. He published his findings in *How Churches Grow* (1959).

A number of key events then began to bring the Church Growth Movement into prominence. The first was the establishment of the Institute of Church Growth at Northwest Christian College in Eugene, Oregon, in 1961. While only a small handful of students had studied church growth there by 1965, the institute had developed courses, reading lists, research projects, and a faculty that would be important when the school moved to Pasadena.

At this time, the Evangelical Foreign Missions Association began sponsoring annual church growth seminars for missionaries home on furlough. Seminars were held each September at Winona Lake, Indiana; on the campus of the Alliance School of Missions in Nyack, New York; and on the campus of Biola College in La Mirada, California. Along with seminars came the publication of the *Church Growth Bulletin* (first circulated in 1964), a 16-page bimonthly periodical published by Overseas Crusades, Inc. Today the *Church Growth Bulletin* remains in print as *Global Church Growth* and is one of the chief publications of the Church Growth Movement.

The next key event was the establishment of the School of World Mission at Fuller Theological Seminary in 1965. As the founding dean, McGavran assembled a team of professors who would communicate church growth principles around the globe, notably: Alan R. Tippett, J. Edwin Orr, Ralph D. Winter, Charles H. Kraft, Arthur F. Glasser, and C. Peter Wagner. Along with these leaders, a significant vehicle for communicating church growth thinking in the early years was the William Carey Library, a publishing house devoted to producing books about Great Commission missions.

The publication of McGavran's magnum opus, *Understanding Church Growth* (McGavran 1970, rev. 1980), played a major role in preparing the United States for church growth. In the fall of 1972, Peter Wagner and Donald McGavran taught a pilot course in church growth, designed specifically for American church leaders. One student, Winfield C. Arn, due to the influence of the course, decided to leave his executive position with the Evangelical Covenant Church and establish the Institute for American Church Growth, with McGavran as chairman of the board. This agency promoted church growth through seminars, workshops, pastors conferences, films, and the first magazine devoted to American church growth, *Church Growth, America* (later the *Win Arn Growth Report*).

John Wimber pioneered the new field of church growth consulting when in 1975 he became the founding director of the Charles E. Fuller Institute of Evangelism and Church Growth. His successor, Carl F. George, has become widely recognized as the "dean of church growth consultants." From this beginning in 1975, church growth consulting groups have grown to number over 100 today. While church consultants have existed for many years, church growth consultants focus on pragmatic research and a trained understanding of how all parts of church ministry work together to further the growth of local congregations.

The early church growth pioneers were primarily generalists. They asked questions, made observations, suggested hypotheses, discovered principles, and articulated church growth philosophy. Their major strength was their communication skill, both through writing and speaking. George G. Hunter III, Elmer L. Towns, Alan R. Tippet, Ar-

The Homogeneous Unit Principle

The classic statement of the homogeneous unit principle comes from missiologist and church growth pioneer Donald McGavran: "People like to become Christians without crossing racial, linguistic, or class barriers." An underlying assumption of the principle has always been that once people become Christians and are growing in their application of biblical ethical principles to their daily lives, they will lose their inclinations toward racism and prejudice. Christians, therefore, become free to group themselves in churches in whatever way they want along homogeneous or heterogeneous lines.

But to what extent should Christians encourage conscious group identity, or ethnicity, in congregational life? Can Christians advocate the establishment of culturally homogeneous congregations?

The Church Is Broad

Christianity prides itself on being a religion of all people. Jesus' Great Commission to his followers was to "go therefore and make disciples of all nations" (Matt. 28:19). Multicolored international gatherings of Christians give tangible evidence that people of many ethnic, racial, national, and linguistic identities call themselves Christians and identify not only with Jesus as Lord, but also in some tangible way with each other as brothers and sisters.

Clearly some individual Christian congregations — though few — are heterogeneous and do mix different kinds of people to significant degrees. However, is the heterogeneous church growing? My impression is that if any truly heterogeneous churches in America are growing, they are exceptions to the rule.

Homogeneity and Growth

My studies of a large number of churches showing membership growth consistently indicate that they are growing within fairly homogeneous units.

Most Christian congregations, whether they ought to be or not, are culturally homogeneous. Even in pluralistic societies where different groups of people live closely together and speak mutually intelligible languages, churches seem to develop in homogeneous units.

An increasing body of missiological research worldwide and sociological research within America indicates that most Christian people meet together for worship and fellowship within the basic sociological groupings into which they are born. Where Christianity is tak-

thur F. Glasser, Medford H. Jones, and Paul Benjamin are some of the most well-known early church growth leaders in North America.

Not to discount the contributions of these early pioneers, but few would debate the fact that C. Peter Wagner and Win Arn did the most

ing root in different nations and cultures of the world, it seems to develop most vigorously when it is allowed or even encouraged to grow in specific homogeneous units rather than forced to include different groups.

Donald Hohensee reported from Burundi, for example, that Christian churches developed very well among the Hutu, fairly well among the Tutsi, but hardly at all among the Twa. In his opinion, one of the reasons for this lack of success among the Twa, a locally despised race of pygmies, was that they had been required to join Hutu or Tutsi churches upon becoming Christians rather than being encouraged to develop new churches within their own Twa homogeneous unit.

Can We Grow Together?

Because Christian churches do tend to be culturally homogeneous and because they do seem to maintain more growth and vitality when they remain as such does not, of course, lead to the conclusion that they should necessarily be homogeneous. A description of what *is* cannot be taken as what *ought to be;* more substantive ethical considerations must be brought to bear on the issue.

The debate continues and probably will for some time to come. If the option of crossing homogeneous unit lines and mixing two or more different groups in the congregation is chosen, the positive effect is that Christians will feel good about their success in breaking through racial or class barriers. They also will be enriched by the interaction with and exposure to people of other cultures.

The evangelistic potential of the church, however, will likely be seriously curtailed. Most of the few truly interracial or otherwise heterogeneous churches that have flourished have grown largely through transfer of membership rather than individual conversions. Few non-Christians from outside the congregation are likely to be attracted to such a different community.

If the option of allowing a homogeneous congregation is chosen, the direct benefit of close intercultural relationships will be sacrificed, unless the church works to bring about other means of structured contact between churches that otherwise are homogeneous. But in all probability, the evangelistic potential of a homogeneous congregation will be higher. Other things being equal, a higher rate of conversion growth can be predicted for the homogeneous unit church.

The issue that needs urgent attention is how to do both. Congregations must discover ways and means to evidence Christian unity to the greatest possible extent, while at the same time maintaining a high evangelistic potential.

—*Peter Wagner*

to spread church growth thinking in North America. Two of their books—*How to Grow a Church* (McGavran and Arn 1973) and *Your Church Can Grow* (Wagner 1976, rev. 1984)—remain the top-selling church growth books in North America.

Arn's influential Institute for American Church Growth, with its prime purpose of interpreting and applying church growth principles to congregations in North America, was the primary vehicle for communicating church growth insights to pastors and church leaders for the first 20 years of the movement in the United States.

Today's second generation of church growth leaders tends to be specialists. Practitioners, innovators, and adaptors of church growth, they typically specialize in areas such as church planting, consulting, megachurch research, and other narrowly defined fields. Some of those in this second generation of church growth leadership today are

Removing Barriers to Church Growth

Many churches encounter numerous obstacles as they work toward growth, particularly when they fail to think through the real implications of growth. Most growth problems stem from some form of attitudinal, structural, or functional barrier.

Attitudinal Barriers

Since the single most important requirement for church growth is the *desire* to grow, one of the most serious barriers to growth is a congregation, governing board, or pastor who, perhaps subconsciously, does not want to grow. In congregations where the key people see growth as threatening, growth potential suffers, even when the church is otherwise well-positioned to grow. No matter how attractive the meeting space, no matter how close the church is to a major artery or expressway, no matter how many other fine attributes a church has, the secret desire to keep things small and familiar—"the way they used to be"—will fatally inhibit growth.

Structural Barriers

In comparison, most of the other barriers to growth are much easier to overcome; they are essentially structural in nature, easy to identify, and fairly painless to fix. For example, a church board can attack structural barriers to growth by candidly exploring and responding to questions such as these:

- *Is the church physically accessible?* Is there adequate (off-street) parking? Is the church wheelchair accessible? Is there a place for a parent to go with a crying infant? Are there signs (indoor or outdoor) to point people in the right direction — to the sanctuary, nursery, Sunday school rooms?
- *Is worship user friendly?* In other words, can a newcomer com-

Robert E. Logan, Kent R. Hunter, W. Charles Arn, Eddie Gibbs, R. Daniel Reeves, Carl F. George, Gary L. McIntosh, Bill M. Sullivan, George Barna, and John N. Vaughan. The Church Growth Movement continues to grow, serving two main groups of church leaders—those involved in cross-cultural missions and those in monocultural ministry (such as most pastors in North America).

The Theory Behind the Movement

Over 150 distinct principles of church growth have been identified by a score of authors during the first 30 years of the movement. However, church growth theory may be summarized in seven broad, foundational concepts.

• *People movements.* "People like to become Christians without

fortably follow the order of service? Are there large-print worship bulletins or hymn books? Are there hearing devices for people with hearing impairment? Does the worship bulletin provide information about how to participate in the Lord's Prayer, the Apostles' Creed, or other parts of worship that may be unfamiliar to the unchurched? Are the words of choruses and musical responses printed for those who don't have them memorized?

• *Does the church have "entry points" other than worship?* Since worship is often not the first contact a person has with the church, where else can people enter into the church's inner life? Are there midweek Bible studies, small support groups, choir programs, youth groups, a weekday nursery school, a men's breakfast, or a local mission project? How could any one of these entry points more effectively lead people into membership?

• *Is there a well-planned visitor follow-up process?* Who is responsible for doing the follow-up? How soon will a visitor be contacted? What are the strategies for assimilating new members? How does the church track the attendance of its members in order to know when someone is heading toward the "back door"?

Functional Barriers

In order to grow, a church must be staffed to grow, ready to function at a higher level of ministry. Some churches, simply by the way they are staffed, will decline or remain on a membership plateau. When a church invites people to be a part of its life, it must be able to "keep its promise." Not having a singles ministry would be a barrier to inviting singles; not having an educational ministry would be a barrier to inviting parents with young children; not having an older adult ministry would be a barrier to inviting older adults. In other words, if a church does not have the ministries or programs to back up its invitation, it will not grow.

—Douglas J. Brouwer

crossing racial, linguistic, or class barriers" (Wagner 1986, 17). No concept of church growth has received as much attention as its cornerstone principle. Known popularly as the homogeneous unit principle, it has been misunderstood to be a principle of exclusion, when in fact it is a principle of inclusion: how to bring more people to Christ.

• *Pragmatic research.* A distinctive of church growth theory is that it is based on pragmatic research. Practitioners use questionnaires, interviews, field observations, and historical analyses in their research projects. "Church Growth takes a fiercely pragmatic approach in evaluating results, employing data to determine faithfulness and effectiveness in the Church's missions" (McGavran 1980, 335).

• *Scientific research.* Viewing all truth as God's truth, church growth researchers take advantage of all scientific disciplines that will help them fulfill Christ's commission. Church leaders study the social sciences, such as anthropology and sociology, in order to learn about cultural dynamics and trends. Such information is put to use in any way that might aid the growth of local congregations.

• *Social networks.* Church growth studies have found that Christianity spreads most rapidly along the natural networks of people and in their social units, rather than across networks. Popular approaches to outreach, such as lifestyle evangelism, friendship evangelism, and household evangelism, trace their roots to this insight.

• *Receptivity.* An early discovery of church growth research found that people are more responsive to the gospel message when they can come to faith without having to cross linguistic or cultural barriers. Outreach strategies then, should focus on specific groups of people, with resources targeted toward those who seem to be the most responsive.

• *Priority.* Christians are to be involved in "discipling" and "perfecting." These terms are basically synonymous with "evangelizing" and "nurturing," and both are to be important aspects of church ministry. However, there is a tendency for Christians to focus on perfecting their own lives, while virtually ignoring those who have yet to hear the gospel. The priority of the church must be on discipling, however. "Perfecting the saints is impossible without discipling. People who do not win converts do not prosper spiritually. Whenever I have seen Christians concentrating on perfecting their own lives and neglecting their mission, there I have seen people going backward spiritually" (McGavran 1959, 8).

• *Purpose.* The central purpose of the church is to reach lost men and women and bring them into responsible membership in Christian churches. It is not enough simply to persuade people to make decisions for Christ. Proclamation and persuasion must lead to assimilation of converts into local congregations—pragmatic, purposeful discipleship.

As it developed its theoretical underpinnings, the Church Growth Movement also made significant practical contributions to church ministry in the early years of its existence. Consider these areas:

• The identification of hidden peoples. Over 16,000 unreached people groups have been identified and targeted for future evangelistic emphasis.

• The concern for church planting. The recent emphasis on church planting in the United States is rooted firmly in the Church Growth Movement.

• The emphasis on the Great Commission. The continuing focus on world evangelism through analysis and research arose from the church growth focus on pragmatic research.

• The establishment of a new academic field. Most seminaries now offer an educational emphasis in church growth studies, particularly in Doctor of Ministry programs.

• The revitalization of churches. Dozens of denominations and thousands of churches have been alerted to their decline and have been given specific help to renew their growth.

• The understanding of churches. Church leaders now have a better understanding of the life cycles, growth patterns, barriers, and needs of various sizes of churches.

The Future of Church Growth

The Church Growth Movement in the United States has gone through three phases of development. Phase one took place in the United States from about 1970 to 1980. It was during these years that most of the principles for church growth in North America were discovered, categorized, and communicated. This was a time of researching and disseminating church growth information to the Christian community.

Phase two occurred primarily in the 1980s. During these years the principles of church growth were actually put into practice in large scale. This phase saw the development of church growth consulting, strategic planning, intentional church planting, hidden-peoples targeting, and citywide outreach planning.

Today the Church Growth Movement is entering phase three, which will take it into the twenty-first century. While church growth leaders have always assumed the presence and direction of the Holy Spirit in their efforts, only recently has this important aspect of the movement received much attention in its published literature. This third phase will no doubt see a new emphasis on the spiritual aspects of church growth. Research will be conducted on issues such as power encounters, prayer, intercession, spiritual warfare, signs and wonders, world view, and supernatural power. As the Church Growth

Movement matures, there will be a balancing of pragmatic research and practice with the spiritual dynamics of the growth mix. Specifically, church growth will stress:

- *Accurate research.* Formerly research has sometimes been built on subjective analysis and anecdotal evidence. Such research is not necessarily inaccurate, but in the future church growth studies will focus on developing a rigorous and sophisticated accuracy.
- *Entire-city evangelism.* As the population of the world continues to grow, more and more people will be living in what are called the "world-class cities." Any strategic plan to win people to Christ and assimilate them into responsible church membership will need to focus on such cities.
- *Information networks.* With information doubling every four to five years, the movement will need to systematize, classify, store, and share information with others in the larger Christian community if the world is to be won for Christ.
- *Quality assessment.* The Church Growth Movement will continue to balance its stress on numerical growth as a measurement of quality with the development of research methods that will help evaluate a church's overall spiritual health.
- *Multicultural studies.* The monocultural experience of North American church leaders is being challenged as God brings the world to our doorstep. Cross-cultural ministry is a reality throughout the United States, especially in larger cities such as New York and Los Angeles. Effective church growth will require church leaders to tune in to multicultural ministry in the coming years.

Some people continue to see church growth as a passing fad. However, careful observation reveals that wherever people seriously seek to find God's lost sheep and fold them into his church, church growth principles are—and will be—a major force.

Church growth is here to stay because it is now a widely recognized, worldwide movement. For the first 15 years of its history, church growth was promoted exclusively in the Third World. However, it has expanded into the Western world and has strong advocates in nearly every country of the world.

Today, before planting new churches, leaders seek information from church growth studies; they hire consultants and listen closely to them before proceeding. Bible schools and seminaries have introduced courses in church growth into their curriculums, especially at the master's and graduate levels; it is a recognized arena for publication. Church growth books, articles, and newsletters continue to thrive, such as *Net Results, Church Growth Network, Church Growth Today,* and *Growing Churches.*

In the early years, only two church growth agencies provided the bulk of training and materials for the movement in North America.

Win Arn's Institute for American Church Growth offered seminars, books, films, and resources, and the Charles E. Fuller Institute for Evangelism and Church Growth responded to the need for growth consultation. More recently, new organizations promote church growth, such as the North American Society for Church Growth, a professional society for professors, pastors, consultants, and denominational executives specializing in church growth. "The Church Growth Movement is alive and well," writes Peter Wagner, "and I believe it will make an increasingly significant contribution to spreading the good news of the kingdom here in North America and around the world" (Wagner 1985, 27).

—Gary L. McIntosh

Resources

George, C. 1993. How to break growth barriers. Grand Rapids: Baker.

Logan, R. 1989. Beyond church growth. Old Tappan, N.J.: Revell.

McGavran, D. 1959. How churches grow. New York: Friendship.

McGavran, D. 1980. Understanding church growth. Grand Rapids: Eerdmans.

McGavran, D., and W. Arn. 1973. How to grow a church. Ventura: Regal.

Wagner, C. 1986. Church growth: State of the art. Wheaton: Tyndale.

Wagner, C. 1985. The state of the art in church growth today. Unpublished manuscript presented at the North American Society for Church Growth, November 21, 1985, in Pasadena, Cal.

Wagner, C. 1984. Your church can grow. Ventura: Regal.

Objections to Church Growth

Many voices have been raised in opposition to Church Growth. Some seem embarrassed by talk of lost souls, and others decry the technical terminology and emphasis on results. Others generally favor the thrust of Church Growth but take exception with specific points. A full understanding of Church Growth involves wrestling with objections.

Points of Contention

Following are three of the major hot spots in the conflict:

• *Numbering and statistics.* The reliance on head counts, charts, trends, and statistics bothers some, who point out David's punishment for numbering Israel (1 Chron. 21). While attendance is measurable, they point out, much in the Christian life isn't, and people can make a fetish out of numbers.

Church Growth contends, however, that quantitative growth is measurable and should be measured. Churches keep their budgets accurate to the last cent, so why shouldn't people be watched as closely? The *heads* in head counts are precious to God—new creations, changed lives. What should be decried is the success syndrome's obsession with numbers, not the shepherd's careful count of the sheep so he knows one is missing.

• *Pragmatism and methodology.* "Where is the transcendent dimension?" asks one critic. Is Church Growth trying to computerize the kingdom rather than depend on God's providence? Just because a method works, *should* it be used?

Certainly immoral or deceitful methods ought to be eschewed, and Church Growth's pragmatism is more about effectiveness than expedience. If a moral and effective plan can be used in place of a moral but ineffective one, they'll choose the effective version.

Peter Wagner says, "Rather than compete with the Holy Spirit, strategy is to be used by the Holy Spirit." So Church Growth people baptize compatible ideas from sociology, psychology, anthropology, demographics, and a number of other disciplines. For traditionalists, it may not *look* like theology, but it is.

• *Homogeneous unit principle.* Stated simply that people are more likely to become Christians if they don't have to cross cultural barriers, this principle has caused a storm of controversy. It is accused of being racist, unethical, and contrary to the inclusive church Christ commanded. The assumption is that differences among people are bad; those sociological factors that give a homogeneous unit identity also separate it from others, so they must be eliminated. While sociological distinctives may cause people to voluntarily group themselves in society, critics argue they ought not affect church life.

Church Growth practitioners affirm that believers are one in Jesus Christ, but that shouldn't mean shedding cultural distinctives to become blandly alike, especially if that means being forced to abandon one's culture to *become* a Christian. The "scandal of the Cross" is barrier enough, so Church Growth thinkers don't want to force people to cross social or language barriers. If people can become Christians among people like themselves, they are much more likely to make that decision; if people's natural groupings can help the task of evangelism, all the better! Some people prefer Bach to rock, and God can use that to cause affinity with a group of believers, which can lead to conversion.

Unity, not uniformity, is God's desire for his people. That unity can be worked out *among* distinct and basically homogeneous churches; it doesn't have to come from each church containing diverse elements forced into an uncharacteristic uniformity under one roof. The church universal would be impoverished if it were to require conformity to one set of traditions, one language, one way of doing things, one culture. Instead, God's church can be a mosaic with each unique and distinct element adding its brilliance to the overall work.

—James D. Berkley

4

Innovations in Evangelism

People who have descended from home-grown American denominations tend to picture evangelism in terms of yesteryear's firebrand preaching. They may think of pulpits as moving, over time, from the stump on the street corner to the inside of church buildings. As a result, many evangelicals feel public preaching is still the primary means by which the gospel is propagated—from Bible conferences, to revival meetings, to the Sunday-morning worship service.

Today, as with long ago, the good news frequently travels within preexisting social settings, such as a church, a geographic neighborhood, or a college campus. So what does it mean to be *innovative* in evangelism? What are some of the breakthrough ways churches are going about the task of evangelism?

Is High-Tech Innovative?

Some would point to the use of radio, television, and computers as being on the cutting edge of innovation in evangelism.

• *Radio and television.* Though both are powerful mediums, they have had limited evangelistic effect. The greatest fruit of most religious programming on radio and television may be more an increase in ecumenicity than actual evangelism. While numerous conversions may be reported, most people who support broadcasts do so because they hear a consonance of values in that programming: the message that Christ is Savior and that the grace of God is available for day-today concerns, the proclamation of miracles, the publicizing of large rallies, and the opportunity for preevangelism. Only the last of these emphases directly speaks to non-Christians.

Christian broadcasts tap into the hunger people have for a practical exposition of the Word as it relates to their daily lives and relationships, and especially as it relates to their family values. They illustrate a wide hearing for a conservative approach to biblical exegesis and for the reinforcement of traditional family values, neither of which is primarily evangelistic in thrust. Broadcast mediums, therefore, do not primarily represent innovative evangelism.

• *Computers.* What innovations in evangelism have computers generated? When computers came to churches, they were harnessed to automatically mail tithing envelopes, send receipts for tax-deductible donations, and encourage people's financial faithfulness by showing them their developing record of donations against faith promises.

Computers can help a church reach more people than ever before and in a more economical fashion than was previously possible. Yet even with all the quantum leaps forward in computer and broadcast technology, few of the advances have made churches more capable, qualitatively speaking, of drawing in new people or holding existing members.

Indeed the most important breakthroughs in evangelism during this era are based on the realization that we cannot build caring church groups if the evangelistic message (*kerygma*) is not preceded by genuine friendship (*koinonia*). Perhaps the most consistently cited reason for why someone drops out of church stems from the care factor: "I didn't feel cared about."

Even in churches that want to be evangelistic, then, the challenge is not a logistical problem that a computer or a citywide broadcast can untangle. Rather, in most cases, the biggest evangelistic blockades involve the unwillingness of Christians to allow others into their lives, accepting those who do come and making room for them in their day-to-day wealth of activities.

The Essence of Evangelistic Innovation

The most important evangelistic innovations of our time are a consequence of a shift from specific programming efforts to a more systemic view of the process by which evangelizing and congregationalizing takes place. In other words, the innovation of recent decades is the view that if a new convert fails to become involved in the social fabric of a local church, the evangelism was somehow incomplete.

Consider just four fairly recent attempts at innovation that work according to this principle:

• *Sequence evangelism and support-group evangelism.* In 1984, Russ Potter, a lay person who runs a Christian publishing house in Siloam Springs, Arkansas, coined the term *sequence evangelism.* "It expresses a sense of evangelistic flow," he says. "It reminds Christians that their neighbors must be moved gradually from their felt needs into Christian nurture."

Sequence evangelism has gained popularity in a number of pockets around the continent. Potter, himself, has developed an entire curriculum around the idea. The idea's appeal, however, is far greater than a particular publishing effort. It seems to underlie what Dale Galloway, founding pastor of New Hope Community Church, in Portland, Oregon, means when he teaches his flock about need-based evangelism, telling them: "Start with someone's felt need. Be the good news to them and then share the good news."

It's what Matt Hanna, pastor of a Vancouver, Washington, church (that rocketed from 300 to 850 members in less than two years, predominantly through new believers) means when he describes his church's community evangelism as doing process evangelism: "You have to anticipate that there will be multiple elements in the process."

In many ways the sequence-evangelism concept also describes evangelism that occurs through the recovery movement. Perhaps the hottest side-door entry to the church today is taking place through support-group and 12-step-group ministries. Participants in these groups bond together in community. As they become whole as persons, they share their spiritual stories as well and grow together in Christ.

A study released in 1993, based on a three-year project run by the Princeton Center for the Study of Religion, documents that 40 percent of the American adult public is involved in some kind of support group (whether religious or not). Truly this is a movement in society today that churches are tapping into, and they are experiencing breakthrough results in evangelism. The key to this evangelistic tool is more the concept of socially binding relationships than the specific topics addressed by these self-help groups.

• *Servant evangelism.* This method uses creative points of contact to meet people's needs right where they are. For example, one Friday evening traffic in Cincinnati was at its worst of the summer. Cars were backed up for a mile from the intersection where Vineyard Christian Fellowship's building is located. The 90-degree temperature made everyone's temper short on this Labor Day weekend.

Church people quickly went into action. They iced down 400 soft drinks and posted signs along the road: FREE DRINKS AHEAD. As the cars came to the stop sign, members of the Vineyard team asked, "Would you prefer diet or regular?"

"Diet or regular what?" came the skeptical reply.

"We're giving away free drinks to show people God's love in a simple and practical way."

"Why?"

"Because God loves you."

Some motorists smiled, and some shook their heads in disbelief, and a few mouths dropped open. A UPS driver couldn't understand. "But I don't even know you guys," he protested. "Why would you do this for me?"

But lots of people took the soda and thought hard about the church. In less than an hour, the church team had spoken with about 600 people, given away every soda, and received positive coverage on a

Evangelism Materials and Resources

Scottish theologian James Denney commented that if evangelists were theologians and theologians were evangelists, the church would be in a much healthier condition. Taking his point to heart, let us begin this listing with some key textbooks on the theology of evangelism.

• *Theology of evangelism.* From a Reformed theological perspective, J. I. Packer's *Evangelism and the Sovereignty of God* (IVP 1961) is a classic text. William J. Abraham, a Methodist theologian, in his *Logic of Evangelism* (Eerdmans 1989) provides a much-needed kingdom perspective, and Robert Kolb, from a Lutheran point of view, has made a significant contribution in *Speaking the Gospel Today* (Concordia 1984). A recent contribution from Lewis Drummond is *Word of the Cross* (Broadman 1992). And William Pannell gives a spirited response to the evangelistic challenge presented by urban America in *Evangelism from the Bottom Up* (Zondervan 1992).

• *Evangelistic preaching.* For help in the preparation and delivery of evangelistic sermons, try the self-study kit put out by the Billy Graham Institute of Evangelism Training Center, published by World Wide Publications in Minneapolis. The kit has six audio cassettes and a workbook. One of the most difficult aspects of evangelistic preaching is knowing how to call for a decision for Christ with theological and psychological integrity. This is skillfully handled by R. T. Kendal in *Stand Up and Be Counted* (Zondervan 1985).

Evangelism Programs

• *Cross-denominational programs.* The most popular program continues to be *Evangelism Explosion,* by D. James Kennedy. Less well-know is the *Magnetic Evangelism* kit put out by Archie Parrish of Serve International (120 Interstate North Parkway East, Suite 404, Atlanta, GA 30339). It is less confrontational

local radio station's traffic report that day.

The philosophy behind this often-retold story is what Steve Sjogren, founding pastor of this church, calls "servant evangelism." "If we can somehow lighten some of the pain people are going through, maybe we would get their attention," he explains. "By serving our way into their hearts, maybe we could gain their ears."

As the idea of servant evangelism crystallized, church people organized an absolutely free car wash. They stationed a couple of former cheerleaders on the corner with signs that directed dirty cars to the rest of the crew. As the cars arrived, motorists had their windows washed and floors vacuumed, while a couple of "designated evangelists" shared why the church would do this.

---

than many programs, being based on "the ancient Chinese secret of how to live forever."

• *One-on-one evangelism.* For personal evangelism, there are the well-tried *Four Spiritual Laws* and *Getting to Know God Personally* from Campus Crusade for Christ, and *Steps to Peace with God* from the Billy Graham Evangelistic Association (P.O. Box 779, Minneapolis, MN 55440-0779). Among tracts, some of the most attractive and wide-ranging come from Dick Innes of ACTS (P.O. Box 157, Claremont, CA 91711).

• *Small-group outreach.* Most of North America's 100 million unchurched will best be reached on their own turf in small groups. Richard Peace, in *Small Group Evangelism* (IVP 1983), and Bob and Betty Jacks with Ron Wormser, Sr., in *Your Home a Lighthouse* (NavPress 1989), tell how to go about it. Other information can be found by writing for catalogs from Neighborhood Bible Studies (Tyndale House Publishers, Box 80, Wheaton, IL 60187), Serendipity (Box 1012, Littleton, CO 80160; 800/525-9563), InterVarsity Press (5206 Main Street, Downers Grove, IL 60515), and NavPress (P.O. Box 35001, Colorado Springs, CO 80935).

Another program for small-group evangelism has been introduced to the U.S. from Australia by Scripture Union (7000 Ludlow Street, Upper Darby, PA 19082; 800/621-LAMP). It is developed by Michael L. B. Bennett, who also conducts seminars.

• *Evangelism training.* Church leaders looking for help in developing evangelistic strategies can consult Michael Green's *Evangelism Through the Local Church* (Oliver Nelson 1992), as well as *Mastering Outreach and Evangelism* (Multnomah 1990) by Calvin Ratz, Frank Tillapaugh, and Myron Augsburger.

In preparing training programs, the following make excellent resources: Rebecca Manley Pippert's *Out of the Saltshaker* (IVP 1979), Joseph C. Aldrich's *Gentle Persuasion* (Multnomah 1988), Paul Little's *How to Give Away Your Faith* (IVP revised 1988), and Donald C. Posterski's *Reinventing Our Evangelism* (IVP 1989).

—*Eddie Gibbs*

"Our first car was a station wagon driven by a single mom accompanied by six squirming kids," reports Sjogren. "She cried as we shared with her and prayed for her." The owner of the second car turned out to be a well-known Cincinnati businessman. As the service team finished its work, he asked, "To whom shall I make out my check?"

"No, sir," someone replied. "We aren't receiving money. We did this just because God loves you." It was one thing to see the mother cry, but quite another to see this powerful businessman wipe away his tears.

The Vineyard Cincinnati typically launches about 40 creative outreaches each year. They've even scrubbed the bathrooms in local gas

Community Image and Visibility

Many churchgoers view their worship services and facilities through honeymooners' eyes. They forget their own first-visit confusions about where to park or which door was the "proper" one to use. Perhaps they no longer notice the rotting pile of grass clippings along the sidewalk, the nursery wallpaper that hasn't been changed since 1950, or the absence of signs pointing to the rest rooms. They may be unaware that guests can feel uncomfortable, exposed, afraid of doing something wrong, and vulnerable to embarrassment.

In spite of this common attitude among members, most churches no doubt harbor far more community-impact potential than they presently utilize. It is possible to reposition a church in the surrounding community, strengthening the church image in such a way that its evangelistic efforts will be fortified, too. Here are two beginner's tools to use for just that purpose.

A Photographic Second Look

One tool that creates the greatest ownership in addressing these issues is a task force to examine the entire church through a visitor's eyes. Several key people of influence, such as a trustee, a longtime leader in the women's ministry, and an energetic newcomer, should conduct this self-study.

So should a camera. Numerous congregations discover blind spots only with the help of a slide presentation (or a display of photographs) that documents everything from the first, distant glimpse of the church's location to the patterns of socializing occurring after the Sunday worship service.

It makes no difference whether a visitor's perception of a church is accurate. The fact remains: If visitors are adversely impressed, they probably will not return and may never benefit from the church's ministry. If they are favorably im-

stations. They calculate that they touch more than 60,000 people each year. Is it any wonder that their fellowship has grown from 35 people to 2,500 in eight years, with five weekend services? Plus it has planted six other fellowships in the Cincinnati area.

The church's philosophy of ministry defines evangelism with this formula: Deeds of God's love, plus words of God's love, plus time. "As we go for the hearts of people, we bypass their defenses," explains Sjogren. When Christians genuinely reach out, build bridges of affection and love to other people, and offer a social context in which newcomers can be accepted and assimilated, a church can't help but be evangelistically effective.

These creative points of contact are but one part of an equation,

---

pressed, they may return to receive Christ or find spiritual renewal. Therefore, careful, intentional self-study is a crucial image-strengthening tool.

A Communications Strategy

A second tool for improving a church's community image is a renewed public communications plan. The most obvious way to begin is to examine how the phone is answered and how community needs are handled day by day. A more long-range issue, however, involves the media coverage a church receives and the image it projects.

Most communities have a newspaper that will include stories about churches if the editors feel the stories warrant communitywide interest. Sometimes a church will mail the local paper a photo of an event that happened a month previously, featuring the pastor shaking hands with an out-of-town denominational official. Then the church moans that the media is biased against religion when the story goes unpublished.

Why not, instead, recruit a church member who is a photography buff and get a close-up photo of the three toothless first-graders grinning as they receive a Scripture memory award? Pay for overnight developing and have the church secretary drive the photos to the newspaper's news desk, with accompanying background information crisply typed on church letterhead. Or why not skip a month of the church newsletter and instead ask the writers to develop three or four human-interest stories—"My Most Memorable Easter," "Church Cares for Family Whose Home Burned Down," or "Church Sends Three Couples on Short-Term Mission to Russia"? If the material is specific, factual, and of broad human interest, chances are the local paper will be delighted to use it.

Many churches miss these and other opportunities to affect their communities, not because no one thinks about them but because volunteer energy and leadership are missing. Perhaps some energy needs to be redeployed to be invested in transmitting the fact that God is doing some exciting things through the church.

—*Carl F. George with Warren Bird*

however. Pastor Sjogren invests an equal amount of energy in creating an affinity-based network of small groups so that these new contacts will feel at home in the church and will grow in Christ as a result. In this way, the Cincinnati Vineyard is one of the best North American models of the technology used in most of the world's largest churches.

• *Cell-based evangelism.* When David Yonggi Cho, founding pastor of the largest church in the history of Christendom was asked, "What do you see as the future of evangelism?" he replied, "You know, we don't do evangelism in Korea the way you do it in the West. Our church involves 700,000 people, and we're asking God for a million. We'll probably have 100,000 new members and converts this year. How will God accomplish this? We have 50,000 cell groups, and each group will love 2 people to Christ. They select someone who's not a Christian whom they can pray for, love, and serve. They bring meals, help sweep out the person's store—whatever it takes to show we really care. When the person asks, 'Why are you treating me so well?' our people answer, 'Jesus told us we're supposed to do good to all men, and we want you to know that we love you and so does Jesus.' After two or three months of that, the hardest soul softens up and surrenders to Christ."

Dr. Cho is not talking about two "decision cards" per group. Rather, the groups have won a person to the Lord and to the church, and then to the specific tenets of the faith. New people, without realizing what is happening, are caught within the pastoral-care network of these groups. That linking becomes the binding social context in which the Holy Spirit is greatly freed to do a convicting work and then to knit the hearts of people into the social fabric of the church as a whole.

That's why they're effective! The making of disciples includes the congregationalizing of converts. Many of the strategies and methods used today may differ in their specific practice from previous generations. But their real distinction is in their ability to articulate a larger plan and to see its connections—the relationship of preevangelism to evangelism, the responsibility the proclaimer has for follow-up, the preengineering of a plan of proclamation so that it will also include a plan of congregationalization. The use of technology—whether the telephone, the mailing list, or the airwaves—becomes almost incidental to the larger sweep of these processes.

• *Law-of-large numbers evangelism.* The law of large numbers teaches that whether the telephone is hand dialed or machine dialed, whether you distribute flyers at the county fair or at the rapid transit depot, if you talk with 100 people, you're likely to find one or two who are susceptible to an invitation to a meeting. There have been numerous applications of this principle:

1. Direct mail. The Christian & Missionary Alliance started 100 new churches on Easter Sunday 1987 using a direct-mail approach. A pastor moved to a new community, researched its demographics and areas of felt need, and then cooperated with previously existing C&MA churches to hand address an invitation to every household listed in the phone book.

2. Telemarketing. The Presbyterian Church of America used "The Phone's for You!" to start dozens of new churches. At one time, this phone program was the PCA's predominant method of church planting. The program has been used by some 100 denominations to place more than 30 million phone calls.

3. Telecare. Churches of many denominations, following a model pioneered by Harold Grindal of the Evangelical Lutheran Church, are instituting a monthly phone call to their entire constituency. They are creating, in effect, a care net to undergird their existing groups and programs.

Teams of lay volunteers, supervised by a staff member or trained lay person, initiate these calls. The calls avoid scolding ("Why weren't you there?") and recruitment ("By the way, we have a need . . ."). Instead, they increase the churchwide level of "touch."

A recent survey of telecare implementers indicates that the most frequently identified content of a telecare call is a prayer concern. In response, prayer may be offered during that very phone call. Sometimes the need is transferred to a printed prayer list, and sometimes the need is relayed to the pastoral staff.

4. Niche marketing. The Charles E. Fuller Institute for years conducted a seminar across North America on the topic of "Baby Boomers," and, as boomers matured, on "Baby Busters." Numerous churches and denominations used the seminar to create a plan for targeting new ministries to these particular market niches. Win and Charles Arn's 1993 book, *Catch the Age Wave,* does the same with the other end of the age spectrum: How to reach senior adults for Christ. Many growing churches even personalize the kind of niche they are trying to target, such as "Saddleback Sam" (Rick Warren's church in southern Los Angeles) or "Unchurched Harry" (Bill Hybels's church, currently the largest in North America, near Chicago).

Not all law-of-large numbers ministries require sophisticated, fancy-named, technically loaded programming, however. The same principles can be put to work when a large percentage of any church gets back to the old business of wiping noses, bandaging bruises, and sharing cups of tea in Jesus' name.

The lesson from Third World churches, and especially from David Yonggi Cho's church, is that if you have a group of six or eight praying Christians and they earnestly ask the Holy Spirit for guidance about whom to target for service, that person is almost compelled to the gospel. Similarly, if any church group in North America prayerfully searches among all the people it knows, it likely will find the four or five people who are ready to do business with God. The law of large numbers will be applied in a most personal way, without even the aid of a computer or mailing list.

Service and Fellowship Before Preaching

A church can experiment with every marketing gadget available and still not improve on the idea of serving one's neighbor. Put enough individual Christians in a service mode, and if anyone around them is susceptible to the gospel message, they'll find them. Targeting is no good if it doesn't produce the results of one changed life at a time.

The ever-present danger is a plethora of "gospel blimps," as Joe Bayly forewarned so prophetically in his 1960 book by that title. Mass evangelism, TV evangelism, automatic telephone dialers, direct-mail evangelism—any of this technology for evangelism, though exciting, can be a colossal waste of Christian resources. It will be effective only to the degree that it builds community, ideally in a *koinonia*-before-*kerygma* sequence.

Any time we redefine evangelism in terms of truth apart from community, we have not produced a New Testament form of discipleship. Any time the ideas can be announced apart from an invitation to be part of the church, we have lost our biblical moorings.

Numerical growth is not always a sign of spiritual vitality, nor does it necessarily indicate that evangelism is present. The tendency in North America, verified by research across dozens of denominations, is that the bigger a church grows, the smaller its percentage of newcomers who are new converts. In a church with average worship attendance of 400 or more, between 60 and 95 percent of its growth comes from transfers, in most cases.

Here, then, are the methodologies for innovative evangelism today: On the one hand are the caring groups (or cells) that are open and experiencing new conversions regularly. The other methodologies get a church involved in building bridges to its neighborhood, causing itself to be perceived in the eyes of the surrounding community as people who do good—people in common cause with those who are not already Christians—so that acquaintance networks can be extended.

Of these, the single most important evangelistic innovation of our time is the open cell in which unbelieving, unchurched people are loved into fellowship. The open cell achieves a socially binding context through connection, interaction, and service to others. Through the gifts and ministry of the Holy Spirit, Jesus is present in these groups.

With each passing year, evangelistic innovations will continue to take on new forms. However, the need for evangelism to include congregationalizing will remain constant.

—Carl F. George with Warren Bird

Resources

Barna, G. 1992. A step-by-step guide to church marketing: Breaking ground for the harvest. Ventura: Regal.

George, C. 1990. What visitors see. Pasadena: The Charles E. Fuller Institute.

Gerber, M. 1986. The e-myth: Why most small businesses don't work and what to do about it. New York: HarperBusiness.

Shawchuck, N., et. al. 1992. Marketing for congregations: Choosing to serve people more effectively. Nashville: Abingdon.

Towns, E. 1993. Ten Sunday schools that dared to change. Ventura: Regal.

5

Evangelizing Target Groups

Just a couple decades ago, churches typically evangelized by going from door to door visiting people. We hardly considered other possibilities. In those days, people were suspicious of other methods. Door-to-door was the accepted way to reach out with the gospel, and if we strayed from the norm, local residents might call our orthodoxy into question.

Today, things are different. Some believe door-to-door evangelism is out of date; families are just too busy to entertain drop-in visitors. With multiple-career couples and fast-paced elementary and high school schedules, families are not home much, and when they are, they may prefer privacy over some stranger ringing the doorbell.

So what are we to do? One approach that has worked for many churches is target-group evangelism. This involves identifying a specific target group—single moms, people who have lost jobs, teenagers, and so on—building a relationship with them, and sharing the gospel in a relevant way.

The Biblical Basis

Target-group evangelism is nothing new. The apostle Paul pioneered this strategy. He outlined a few of his techniques in a letter to friends in Corinth: "To the Jews I became like a Jew, to win the Jews. To those under the law I became like one under the law. . . . To those not having the law I became like one not having the law. . . . To the weak I became weak, to win the weak" (1 Cor. 9:20–22). To sum up this evangelism strategy, he wrote, "I have become all things to all men so that by all possible means I might save some" (1 Cor. 9:22). That's target group evangelism at its best.

In Paul's case the target groups were Jews, Gentiles (without the law), and the weak. To each of these groups, Paul adapts himself and his evangelistic message. For example, in reaching the Jews, he based his approach on the Old Testament Scriptures. He reviewed the Scriptures, explained them, and applied them (see Acts 13:13–41). In dealing with the Gentiles, he used a different method: Greek philosophy and secular poetry (see Acts 17:16–34). He did *not* use Scripture or even refer to it. In fact, he even used the Greek name for God, not the Hebrew one.

From Paul's strategy, we can identify three key principles for our target-group evangelism:

- *Adjust to each target group.* As we have seen, Paul's strategy for evangelism was to target the particular needs and interests of a specific group.
- *Build relationships with different people groups.* Paul recognized cultural diversity and adapted his style to each unique cultural situation.
- *Realize that methods will often seem in conflict.* When Paul was with the Jews, his behavior was kosher. When he was with the Gentiles, it was not. One day he was strong; the next day he was weak. Paul could have been accused of being inconsistent, but his behavior was not based on selfish or capricious choices. Rather, he acted in prayerful wisdom according to what he believed was necessary to share the gospel effectively with each group he sought to reach.

Identifying Target Groups

Paul's target groups were Jews, Gentiles, and the weak. What are ours today, and how do we identify them? Here are a few suggestions:

- *The target group at our fingertips.* Every believer has a target group close at hand. Such groups include neighbors, work associates, friends, and extended family. All we have to do is open our spiritual eyes.
- *Need-related groups.* We can identify the felt needs of people and build target groups around them. The list of needs is endless. For example, we might develop groups around people who are having to cope with stress, such as in a marriage, in raising teenagers, in work-related politics, or in trying to survive in today's economy. Other groups can form around people who are facing any number of crises, including death, divorce, single parenthood, AIDS, dysfunctional families, and physical, sexual, or emotional abuse. Others might suffer addictions to alcohol, drugs, food, pornography. The list goes on.

• *Age-related groups.* We might want to explore the specific needs of various age groups and build a set of target groups accordingly. These might include children, teenagers, college students, singles of all ages, young marrieds, young families, empty nesters, senior adults and many subcategories in each of these groupings.

Working with Different Target Groups

Once we have identified target groups, what do we do next? We build bridges. That is, based on the unique needs of each group, we develop target-group programs that will encourage relationship, open sharing, and intimacy in such a way that sharing Jesus Christ will follow naturally.

Note the progression here: need, relationship, Christ. Our intention is to recognize and help people with their struggles, but also to move them beyond their struggle to a personal relationship with Jesus Christ. We do not substitute spiritual growth for self-help principles. For that reason, it is critical that those who lead these groups recognize the priority of bringing people to Christ and encouraging them on their spiritual journey.

Following are a few illustrations for working with target groups, beginning with the group closest to us.

• *The group at our fingertips.* We can begin our strategy of target-group evangelism by praying for this "fingertip group," especially for those who do not know the Lord. Second, we can cultivate deeper relationships with these people until, third, the time is ripe to share the gospel.

Many churches build such a bridge by taking advantage of special holidays. Why not hold a special Christmas coffee, a neighborly gathering that features refreshments, spontaneous sharing of holiday traditions, and perhaps a nonthreatening inspirational message. The format is an effective bridge to the community and gives an opportunity to present the gospel to neighbors in a relaxed home setting.

God will lead in a sensitive way toward other methods of sharing the gospel as well. We might do this one on one or through small-group programs at church. As those in the fingertip group come to faith in Christ, we can offer compassion and discipleship, possibly through our own congregation but not necessarily so. We need to depend on the Spirit to give us wisdom for each situation, because each situation is different, even within the same target group.

• *Need-related support groups.* Those of us who live in the trenches of ministry are increasingly aware of the pain people carry. That pain (emotional and physical) is one of God's strategies to gain people's attention. For this reason we can offer a number of support groups for people who struggle in different ways. Following are a few examples of what churches might offer the community:

Divorce-recovery workshops. Divorce is a reality that must not be ignored by the church. If we believe the gospel offers forgiveness and a new beginning, then those who have endured the nightmare of divorce need to hear this good news. Workshops may meet once a week for several weeks and include lectures and small-group discussion.

Activities for children of divorce. In our church, for example, Club Rainbow groups meet at the same time as divorce-recovery workshops. They are targeted toward the children of the divorced parents who are enrolled in the divorce workshop.

Support groups. These groups gather people with a number of needs: men struggling with sexual desires, women who have survived sexual abuse, people who have lost a loved one through death, women

Windows of Opportunity

Our Lord encourages us to "Walk in wisdom toward those who are outside, redeeming the time" (Col. 4:5, NKJV). "Time" is a limited season when people are open to the good news of the gospel. Our job is to take advantage of these "windows of opportunity" to win people to Christ. The time is changing, and windows that are now open may soon be closed.

Research has found that people go through times of receptivity and resistance to the gospel message. At certain times people will be more open to the gospel, while at other times they will be resistant.

For example, pastors often have observed that young couples seem to be most open to church attendance immediately after the birth of a baby. Likewise, church planters realize it is much easier to start a church in a new neighborhood than an older one.

Open Windows

People tend to be most receptive to the gospel when they face change in their lives. Here are a few windows — times of significant change — that we might find open around our churches right now.

• *Following the birth of a child.* New parents wake up quickly to the physical and spiritual needs that arise with the brand new challenge of raising children. Young parents go back to church propelled by a desire to give their children spiritual guidance.

• *Following a move.* In a mobile society like the United States, relational networks constantly break up and form again in different locations. People who have recently moved into a new community are searching for friends, doctors, dentists, places to shop—and churches.

• *Following a divorce.* With over 50 percent of marriages ending in

who live with or love someone who has abused alcohol, single adults and others who are without jobs or in transition, adult children of alcoholics or dysfunctional families, single mothers, children of single parents, and those suffering from the effects of serious mental illness in the family.

• *Age-related groups.* Churches can also develop support groups based on age. For example, our church has Campus Safari, an annual outreach of our youth department. They rent a gym on a Sunday morning, and for weeks ahead of time, students from our church invite school friends, teachers, and administrators to come for a morning of competition among area schools.

Another program, Backyard Bible Clubs, reaches a younger age group. After many years of traditional daily vacation Bible school, we

divorce, a number of people in every community seek healing from broken relationships. Many churches find divorce-recovery workshops effective in reaching out to these people.

• *During a crisis event.* Death, injury, a job layoff, and other kinds of crises cause people to consider the big questions of life: What is the purpose of my life? Why do bad things happen to me? What do I do when I can't fix things on my own? Is there a God who cares about me? Where can I find others who will support me during this crisis?

• *During a time of hurt.* Today's younger generation is a hurting generation. Divorce, drugs, and various forms of abuse have taken an emotional toll. The growth of the support-group movement is a direct response to this open window of opportunity.

• *During a period of physical renewal.* The physical fitness revolution has created fitness centers and spas around the country. Many people are renewing their commitments to walking, jogging, or participating regularly in sports programs such as softball, volleyball, or basketball. Churches can reach out to these unchurched folks through various sports-oriented programs.

• *During the transition to single parenting.* More people are single today than at any other time in the history of the United States. However, while singles are open to the gospel, singles ministry is more complex than simply offering a college and career Bible study as we did in the past. One of the windows open the widest today is that of ministry to new parents who are single. Such ministry may well offer spiritual-growth opportunities along with practical support and help for real-life problems.

• *During the child-care years.* The continuing need for two-income families produces the corresponding need for child care. Here is a window wide open to the unchurched.

Churches that respond to these and other open windows of opportunity will find their evangelism efforts blessed as "God gives the increase."

—*Gary L. McIntosh*

made a major change in our focus by taking our program out into the community. In August, we run about forty Backyard Bible Clubs the same week, multiplying the opportunities to reach unchurched children and their families because we are out where the needs are.

Whenever we can shift evangelism out of the walls of the church and into the community, we can be more effective in attracting special target groups among the unchurched.

Getting Started

No church can reach every potential target group. It's important, therefore, to develop a careful strategy that will accomplish the goal of evangelism with carefully selected target groups. Consider these crucial steps:

Urban Evangelism

In cities such as New York and Los Angeles, as many as a hundred different people groups live within two miles of one another. But the obstacles to reaching these nearby peoples are uniquely difficult. Many of the urban lost are crushed spirits with little hope for a better future for themselves or their children. Years of separation and neglect from the mainstream have raised high walls of distrust, anger, and blame.

The Mission Field Next Door

Reaching this difficult mission field for Christ must begin with a proper understanding of the gospel, which is the visible demonstration of God's love (see Luke 7:18–23). How do we strategically put the gospel into loving action among urban people? After thirty years of ministry among the poor, I believe we must recognize four key characteristics of effective urban evangelism as we address the unique challenges of outreach within the mission field next door.

• *Effective urban evangelism is incarnational.* "The Word became flesh and dwelt among us" (John 1:14). Jesus did not commune in the morning, pass out tracts, and head back to heaven at night. Because Jesus identified with our sufferings, because he faced the same temptations we do, his teachings are trustworthy. Urban people are open to the gospel to the extent they trust the messenger, so people who have made the urban community their home do the most effective outreach.

The first step, then, to the most effective urban evangelism is *relocation.* While not all of us are called to go, churches must seek to build supply lines to those in the trenches of the urban community.

• *Effective urban evangelists are reconcilers.* If we were to go to China to reach the lost, we would learn the language, eat the food, learn all

• *Establish a core group.* A core group consists of up to twelve people with a passion for evangelism. They need to accomplish two primary objectives: identify the potential target groups and evaluate which target groups could be reached most effectively through the church's resources.

• *Seek board approval.* The core group presents its findings to the board and seeks their approval.

• *Present the plan to the congregation.* The core group, with board endorsement, then informs the congregation of the prospective target groups and establishes a time to meet with people interested in being involved.

• *Train the leadership.* It is wise to choose leaders who have personal experience that directly relates to the target group. After training, the group can begin its outreach.

we could about the history and the culture, and seek to build trusting relationships with the people there. If we arrive unable to distinguish between our culture and our Christ, if we arrive as do-gooders unwilling to receive and learn as well as give and teach, then our efforts will be severely handicapped.

Urban minorities tend to be more relationship oriented than program oriented. If they don't trust us, they won't trust our ideas. Effective urban evangelists are cross-culturally skilled reconcilers.

• *Effective urban evangelism is holistic.* In the urban context, wishing for our neighbor what we wish for our own family means such things as working alongside our neighbors for a community free of crime, creating educational opportunities that make youth job-ready, or making home ownership broadly available. As we love our urban neighbors by focusing on their needs, we create opportunities to share the gospel.

We can intentionally build evangelism into housing programs through seminars that share the gospel as well as home-ownership skills; into health care through doctors who probe beneath physical illness to spiritual disease; into tutoring through materials that use the Bible for reading.

One of the most effective ways to win urban adults to Christ is to love their children. As we love the children through meeting their needs for recreation, affirmation, self-esteem, and education, we'll win the respect and trust of their parents.

• *Effective urban evangelism results in the development of indigenous Christian leaders.* Indigenous leaders are the most effective, trustworthy evangelists in the urban community. The absence of such visible, dedicated, faithful, skilled leaders is a major contributor to the erosion of urban America's moral and spiritual foundation. As we win young people to Christ, we must seek to develop them into Christian leaders who no longer want to escape from their communities but want to heal them.

—John Perkins

• *Evaluate progress.* After several months, the core group that began the process should evaluate the progress. Important questions include: What kind of people are attending? What problems have arisen? Have people made a commitment to Christ? Do people continue to attend after a first visit? What changes need to be made?

Danger Signals

While it is exciting to see people come to Christ through target-group evangelism, there are also dangers to avoid. For example:

• *Meeting the felt need but not the gospel need.* Some groups do extremely well in addressing the particular needs of the target group but fail to present the gospel. The key is to make sure evangelism is ongoing without pushing the gospel in an obnoxious way.

• *Promoting the gospel but not meeting the felt need.* If a church ignores a target group's needs and attempts to evangelize only with words, it will alienate people from the gospel.

• *Pushing the gospel as the only solution to felt needs.* Accepting Christ is the most important decision a person can make, but it may not restore a relationship or annul the consequences of bad choices. People need help with some practical matters as well as the profound.

• *Using ill-prepared leaders.* Those who lead must be extremely sensitive to the people they seek to befriend for Christ. Insensitivity will further alienate target groups outside the fold of the faithful.

Great Opportunities

In today's world, we face tremendous problems: increasing secularization of the broader culture, the breakdown of the traditional family, the increased complexity of modern living, violent nationalism that goes hand in hand with international terrorism, the lack of purpose beyond materialism.

But let's not despair. By the grace of God, it is precisely because of these problems that the church has tremendous opportunities to share the gospel.

This is no time to be out of touch with the needs of people in the trenches of life, no time to invite needy people to church only if they buy into the church's definition of what is acceptable. To evangelize effectively, we must meet people where they are, not where we are or where we think they ought to be.

One way to do this is through target-group evangelism. The possibilities for effective outreach are as limitless as the problems people face in a broken world.

—Edward G. Dobson

Resources

Aldrich, J. 1981. Life-style evangelism. Portland, Ore.: Multnomah.

Eims, L. 1980. The lost art of disciple making. Grand Rapids: Zondervan.

Hess, M., and B. Hess. 1977. The power of a loving church. Glendale, Cal.: Regal Books.

Jacks, B., and B. Jacks. 1987. Your home a lighthouse. Colorado Springs: Navpress.

Tillapaugh, F. 1982. Unleashing the church. Ventura, Cal.: Regal.

6

Church Planting

Church planting is the exciting venture of beginning and growing new local churches in obedience to Christ's Great Commission. Hebrews 11:6 states that "without faith it is impossible to please God." Those who launch new churches must be men and women of strong faith and energetic spirit. It's hard, exhausting work! Church planters can expect to put in long days networking with people over the phone or counseling over a cup of coffee. Because they are birthing culturally contemporary churches, these pioneers must be prepared for large doses of criticism, which can be emotionally exhausting.

Since the work involves both beginning and growing a new congregation, church planters must be familiar not only with spiritual birthing principles but also with biblical church growth principles, or they will see their new churches plateau and begin to decline. The planting of the church itself is a process analogous to birthing a child. It will move through certain stages such as conception, development, birth, and so on. However, once the church is started, it should reproduce itself by spawning other churches in the area and abroad.

Church planting rests squarely on Jesus' promise in Matthew 16:18: "I will build my church, and the gates of Hades will not overcome it." While deep, dark clouds hover over American Christianity at the end of the twentieth century, this promise of Jesus serves as a ray of hope breaking through those clouds, reminding us that Jesus Christ himself is the Planter and Master Builder of every church.

While church planting is exhausting, it is also most exciting. It appeals to the pioneer spirit resident within so many Americans. There is a sense of anticipation; God is about to do something—and we're going to be a part of it!

Why to Plant a Church

The question may be asked, "With so many churches in America, do we really need more?" Some Christians would have us focus all our efforts on missions overseas. Others feel we must revitalize our existing churches first. However, there are several critical reasons for birthing new churches.

The first is to obey the Great Commission. Christ gave the commission in Matthew 28:19–20, calling us to pursue and win lost people, and then to disciple them. A careful reading of the Book of Acts reveals that the early church understood and responded to Christ's mandate by planting churches. A study of the missionary journeys recorded in Acts demonstrates that those trips were, in fact, church-planting forays into a predominantly pagan culture.

A second reason for birthing churches is to display our faith in the Savior's promise of success. While the future of American Christianity may look grim to some, Jesus' promise in Matthew 16:18 to build his church, no matter what the opposition, gives us great hope for the future of the church. Though the history of the church shows periods of both numerical growth and decline, the point of the promise is that the church will continue to exist, regardless of its size. Some church leaders predict revival early in the twenty-first century, due to the planting of a great number of high-impact, cutting-edge churches that will reach vast numbers of lost people.

The third reason for planting new churches is perhaps the most practical and obvious: to confront the fact that the majority of American churches are plateaued, in decline, or dying. In *The Pastor's Manual for Effective Ministry,* Win Arn writes that 80 to 85 percent of the churches in America are plateaued or declining (Arn 1988, 43). This figure includes both mainline and evangelical churches, though hardest hit are the more liberal mainline churches. According to *The Yearbook of American and Canadian Churches,* in 1965 the United Methodist Church reported approximately 11 million members; in 1988 they reported 9 million. In 1965, the Presbyterian Church (U.S.A.) reported 4 million members, but in 1988 reported a drop to 3 million people. The Disciples of Christ reported 2 million members in 1965; this figure dropped to 1 million in 1988. Finally, the Episcopal Church reported around 3.4 million members in 1965 and 2.5 million in 1988 (Jacquet 1989, 261).

Many churches of evangelical persuasion are struggling as well. The Southern Baptists, Missouri Synod Lutherans, and others are reporting plateaus and declines. While evangelical churches are growing more in comparison to mainline churches, much of that growth comes from transfers and biological growth in membership, not from conversion. Martin Marty describes this growth as "a kind of circulation process, by which evangelicals move from one conservative church to another" (Carroll, Johnson, and Marty 1979, 16). Not only are churches struggling, but a large number are actually closing. According to Arn, 3,500 to 4,000 churches die every year (Arn 1988, 16). Lyle Schaller writes that "an estimated 30,000 congregations ceased to exist sometime during the 1980s" (Schaller 1991, 17). There is a great need for a new crop of healthy, growing churches.

Healthy Characteristics

Before planting any crop, farmers must first decide what kinds of crops to plant. To fling out just any seed randomly across any kind of soil could spell disaster. So it is with church planting. Someone has said that it takes all kinds of churches to reach all kinds of people. Nevertheless, church planters must determine what kinds of churches they're going to plant in which areas. Though each new church will have a particular, specialized focus, any new church should have at least seven biblical characteristics.

• *A Great Commission vision.* The new church must have a single, clear vision. It must know where it's going. Without a vision, the church will quickly plateau, turn inward, and simply begin to maintain itself. Mere maintenance leads to a downward spiral that hastens the church's ultimate, untimely demise. Unfortunately, many churches have little or no vision, while some churches try to juggle several visions that conflict and lead to splits among the people. Some churches may have a single, clear vision, but it's the *wrong* vision!

Church planters constantly must ask themselves the basic question, "What is Christ's church supposed to be doing—in this place, at this time?" Asking this question forces them to stay with the basics.

The Great Commission mandate consists of three basic components that unfold chronologically. The first is the intentional *pursuit* of lost people, reflected in the word *go* found at the beginning of the commission. The second component is the *evangelization* of those we pursue. A Great Commission church makes telling the gospel message a high priority. The final component is the *edification* of those who accept the message. Once the church reaches lost people, it must not drop them, but rather enfold and disciple them, moving these new believers toward Christlikeness (see Eph. 4:11–16).

• *A strong servant-leadership focus.* A Great Commission vision is vital to any planted church, but it takes leadership excellence to implement this vision in a given situation.

What is a strong servant-leader? We might define Christian leaders as godly people (character) who know where they are going (vision) and have followers (influence). Godly character is the essential element that qualifies Christians to lead others. It earns people's respect and produces trust, the most critical factor in all relationships. A leader must be trusted to be followed. This type of character is portrayed in 1 Timothy 3:1–7 and Titus 1:6–9. The leaders' vision helps people see where they are going and supplies the motivation to get there. Finally, leaders exert influence in the world because other people are following them. Godly leaders who cast a clear, significant vision for their ministries attract followers.

Not only must church planters be leaders, they must be *strong* leaders. A group of people, such as a part-time voluntary committee, cannot lead a church with the power and effectiveness of a single,

Church-Planting Pastors

"If you were to select an organizing pastor for a new church, what would you look for?" This question, posed to effective church planters from a range of denominations, brought surprising agreement. In general, effective church planters want to help create the future and can see the future in small beginnings. Their egos are not tied to immediate results. They are prayerful, with the spiritual insight to recognize and handle the focused spiritual opposition every new church faces.

Clues from Personality

Research conducted by the Presbyterian National Office of New Church Development suggests some interesting relationships between effective church planters and the personality types in the Meyers-Briggs Type Indicator. Most crucial was the finding that the church planter needs to be able to at least function as an "E"—or extrovert—because relational abilities are vital to the strength of the ministry, especially at the beginning. In a new church, there are few if any strong bonds among people in the congregation that will help tie people to the church, so the relationship to the pastor must be perceived as warm. This fact puts a tremendous strain on the pastor to be always "on."

However, this does not mean the church planter has to be a strong extrovert. In fact, research suggests that it may be better if he or she is balanced between "I" (introvert) and "E," or is even a slight introvert. This is because new churches, except those begun by large teams, tend to be lonely. An extreme extrovert, who receives energy by involvement with other people, may find this source of vital energy to be in short supply. An introvert, on the other hand, derives energy from time alone in recreation,

strong leader. It's not that the groups aren't capable of leading an organization, but they have neither the time nor the training to meet the unique leadership demands of a newly planted church. This particular challenge calls for a pastor who functions as the "point person" at a time in the church's life cycle when it needs clear, unambiguous marching orders.

Such pastors must have the authority to exercise that power in leading the new church (see 1 Thes. 5:12–13; Heb. 13:7, 17). They should be serving full-time, just as the elders in the early church served. Because the churches were large, the elders took much time to minister as shepherds, and they were paid (1 Tim. 5:17–18 and 1 Pet. 5:2). Strong leaders must still remain accountable servants, however. The great example is the Savior, who led with a servant's heart (Mark 10:45; Matt. 20:28; and John 13).

• *A mobilized lay army.* God's plan is that all Christians be involved

---

reflection, and study. He or she is then equipped to go out and function as an extrovert in the ministry.

Characteristics for Success

In a recent interview, Lyle Schaller said, "Fifteen years ago, the key to a strong new church was 'location, location, location.' Today the key is 'the pastor, the pastor, the pastor.'" This makes finding the right pastor crucial. Consider these key characteristics of those who successfully plant new churches:

• *Target-group similarity.* The church planter typically will be similar in age and ethnicity to the target group in the community.

• *A self-starter.* He or she should be a strong preacher and teacher, skilled in personal evangelism and able to train others to do it.

• *A high level of productivity.* The successful planter can "make the sale," bringing things to closure. He or she operates with energy and enthusiasm on a daily basis to get things done.

• *A history of church growth.* There is no reason to think that a person who has not been effective in growing an established church will be effective in starting a new one..

• *A flexible approach.* This includes the ability to hunt for the "buttons" in the community, push them all, and go forward with those that work. Church planters who arrive with a specific program to plug in and make work often fail.

• *An enthusiasm for the new.* He or she wants to try new things, despite old models or denominational styles. This also means the ability to adapt quickly to each new phase in the life of the growing church.

• *A willingness to lead.* Successful church planters are usually strong, directive leaders. As church-development expert Lyle Schaller writes in *44 Questions for Church Planters* (Abingdon), "relatively few self-identified 'enablers' or 'facilitators' have been effective church planters."

—Dave Wilkinson

in some form of ministry, since all have the indwelling Holy Spirit (Eph. 3:16, 20), spiritual gifts (Eph. 4:7–11), and believer-priest identities (1 Pet. 2:5–9). The great tragedy is that far too many Christians aren't involved in any form of service for Christ. A survey by Gallup indicates that only 10 percent of church members do 90 percent of church ministry.

The solution to this problem is to set up a good lay-mobilization program that not only seeks to place people in established ministries but also designs ministries around its people. Program startup occurs in three phases. The first is the education phase, in which people discover their ministry gifts through classes and assessment tools. Then comes the consultation phase, in which people meet with a leader who helps confirm the accuracy of the assessments and seeks to place each individual in a gift-matching ministry. Finally, the mobilization phase gets each person involved in the ministry and then evaluates to determine if the first two phases produced a good fit.

Financing New Churches

In any practical discussion of church planting, the issue of funding demands immediate attention. Unfortunately, this is the issue that sometimes clouds our vision for the harvest and causes outreach plans to wither on the vine. But coupling our vision for winning souls with a sensible approach to funding new churches paves the way for success.

Finding Sources of Support

The most common source of support for a new church is its denomination. Some denominations will provide grants or monthly support to pay the church planter's salary and start-up costs for a designated time. The difficulty with such funding is when a church plant is subsidized too long. This can result in a congregation that becomes rather lethargic in its stewardship while depending on denominational support. Subsidies from a denomination sometimes stifle the independence and creativity that a new congregation needs to grow.

Some church planters provide for their own salaries, supplementing church finances with employment outside the church. The best jobs for church planters have flexible hours and are not highly stressful. A pastor should decline any bivocational position in which business practices could negatively influence relationships. Bivocational church planting is most effective when the pastor views his or her job as a means of modeling evangelism and connecting with individuals in the community.

Family, friends, associates, and other churches are other sources of support for many church-planting pastors. Such funds give pastors freedom to focus exclusively on their church-planting tasks, and

• *A culturally relevant ministry.* Since our world is changing, the church must change as it attempts to communicate the message of Jesus Christ. The cultural leap from the typical unchurched mentality to that of most American churches is too vast. Consequently, our new churches must be culturally relevant if they are to reach this and future unchurched generations for the Savior. They must follow the example of the men of Issachar in 1 Chronicles 12:32 "who understood the times and knew what Israel should do." This means exegeting the culture as well as the Bible.

• *A holistic, authentic worship.* Authentic worship is an active response to God in which we acknowledge his great worth, recognizing that of all we value in life, we value him the most. Holistic worship affects the entire person. It not only touches the intellect but also affects the emotions, as reflected by the worship found in the Psalms. The result of involving both the mind and the emotions in worship is a changed life (see Rom. 12:1).

they also help generate valuable prayer support. Such support generally lasts for a longer term than that received from other sources. Consequently, it is an effective means of support for church planting among the urban poor and among some ethnic groups.

Foundations and private funding agencies can also become sources of financial support. The key is to find organizations or individuals interested in new-church development or community impact. Raising money from foundations requires patience, persistence, and possibly the help of a professional fund raiser.

Finally, some new churches receive funding directly from a wealthy person. This can be a great blessing, but it can become a burden, as well. There are two potential problems: the amount of intentional — or often unintentional — control the individual maintains in the church, and the irresponsible attitude the young church may develop about its need to grow into financial independence.

Moving Toward Independence

New churches may be funded by one or more of the methods mentioned above. To be successful, each church planter should determine his or her needs before beginning, selecting the methods or resources that are available in the particular situation. Yet it's important to remember that each new congregation should become financially independent as soon as possible.

Generally speaking, a church should begin to cover its own operating expenses within the first year. During the second year, the church should pay the pastor's entire salary. The third year is a good time to help sponsor another church plant. In later years, church leaders can begin seeking a permanent facility for the congregation.

—*Steven L. Ogne*

• *A biblical, relevant outreach.* Effective evangelism needs to be characterized by cultural relevance. Little evangelism takes place in and through churches that don't know how to relate to the real-life concerns of the unchurched. While the methodology of evangelism must change and adjust to the culture, the biblical principles remain the same. As Jesus did, churches must value lost people, spend time with them, and understand their needs. Ultimately, evangelism is best accomplished through a well-designed strategy that pursues lost people right where they are.

• *A robust small-group network.* At the end of the twentieth century, the pattern among churches has been a move away from smaller churches toward larger churches. People are leaving the smaller churches for larger churches that have large ministry "menus" to offer. Consequently, the small church is dying, and the large church is growing.

If this trend continues, how will larger churches minister effectively to people's friendship and fellowship needs? The answer: The larger they get, the smaller they must become! They must place more and more emphasis on the ministry of small groups, just as the large churches in the first century did (Acts 2:46; 5:42; 20:20).

The Process of Planting

Eventually, farmers reach a point when it's time to start the planting process. This involves the sowing of seed, watering, fertilizing, and protecting the crop. Church planting requires similar work, involving six stages analogous to the human birth and growth process.

• *Conception.* The conception stage consists of three steps. The first is the birthing of a clear, succinct ministry vision. Vision provides direction, promotes unity, produces motivation, encourages giving, and forms the basis for future evaluation. The church's vision will be a clear, challenging picture of the future of the ministry as the planters believe it can and must be.

In birthing a vision, we must ask two important questions. The first is, "*Who* will develop the vision?" Initially, the answer is the team's leader of leaders. Just as a group or board can't lead a new church effectively, neither can it develop a powerful vision. It's far more expedient for visionary pastors to bring to their boards a vision they've already developed and then let the board gain ownership by interacting with it.

The second question is "*How* will I develop the vision?" A vision normally results from recognizing an untapped ministry opportunity or a general dissatisfaction with the status quo. Then the visionary "sees" some exciting solutions that ultimately lead to the final vision statement.

The second step of the conception phase is to recruit a dynamic, gifted church-planting leadership team that will both own and play a major role in realizing the dream. Several qualifications must characterize this team, but along with godly character and vision, the key qualification is desire—an overwhelming God-given desire to plant a church.

The third step is to develop a specific strategy. A talented ministry team cannot accomplish the vision without a strategy. Rather than attempting to duplicate another successful church, the team must develop its own unique strategy. It must identify its target group, determine where that group is located in the community, and design creative methods to reach it.

- *Development.* There is no church without people. Consequently, the development stage begins with the gathering of an initial core group of people. Once gathered, they must be cultivated through personal-ministry assessment, leadership training, and inclusion in a smaller fellowship cell. Finally, the core group grows as people begin reaching out to personal contacts and recruiting other interested people.
- *Birth.* Here is where the church goes public in a big way. Once the core group has grown to fifty or more people, the church is ready to target and reach out to its community in a strategic, corporate effort. For example, the group might use a well-designed mailer, a telemarketing approach, or word of mouth to invite people in the community to a public service. This initial service is important to the credibility of the church in the target community and must be planned and executed with great care.
- *Growth.* The growth stage determines the church's ultimate size in numbers. It will likely either plateau at around two hundred people or push through this barrier. During this stage, church planters need to direct their efforts toward such critical areas as leadership training, vision casting, staffing, mobilization, and assimilation.
- *Maturity.* As the church enters the maturity stage, it continues to grow spiritually and numerically because its members haven't forgotten the Great Commission. If a daughter church, it is ready to wean itself from the mother church and survive on its own. Most likely the new church has been in existence from twelve to twenty months or more. Its ministries are expanding, and it is developing additional ministries to implement growth strategies. The leadership has given some thought to a building but doesn't want to build too soon and thus limit the ultimate growth and outreach of the young church's ministry.
- *Reproduction.* This final stage isn't meant to be a separate, distinct stage from the growth and maturity stages but could begin during either one. During this stage the new church itself becomes a

mother church, planting its own strategic, high-impact churches throughout America and in other countries as well.

—*Aubrey Malphurs*

Resources

Arn, W. 1988. The pastor's manual for effective ministry. Monrovia, Cal.: Church Growth, Inc.

Carroll, J., D. Johnson, and M. Marty. 1979. Religion in America: 1950 to the present. San Francisco: Harper & Row.

Jacquet, C. 1989. Yearbook of American and Canadian churches, 1988. Nashville: Abingdon.

Malphurs, A. 1992. Planting growing churches for the 21st century. Grand Rapids: Baker.

Malphurs, A. 1992. Developing a vision for ministry in the 21st Century. Grand Rapids: Baker.

Schaller, L. 1991. 44 questions for church planters. Nashville: Abingdon.

Building a First Facility

Challenge and demand await those who build. A building project should not be rushed into without plenty of forethought, since a premature building program hinders growth rather than encourages it. For example, raising funds for the facility can take several months, even years. Taking time to study all the issues up front will be critical to the success of the program. Then a church will be ready to launch into the four foundational steps in the process.

Four Steps to Building

• *Step 1: Choose a facilities team.* Along with strong lay leaders, place key staff members on the team; they have a broad understanding of the church's needs. If possible, include the architect as a team member. The architect can help with the whole project, including designing the master plan, selecting the site, obtaining permits, and selecting contractors and subcontractors.

Including the building contractor as well on the facilities team gives him or her positive ownership of the project. Suggestions from both the architect and contractor will help avert expensive modifications after construction begins.

• *Step 2: Develop a master plan.* Develop your master plan by thoroughly reviewing the church's mission and ministry philosophy, and the programs that result from them. The whole team will benefit from an in-depth understanding of the church's history and its goals for future growth. The church's programs should be the greatest single factor influencing future facility needs.

The master plan should incorporate: short-, medium-, and long-term facility needs; site needs, including location and the acreage required; specific plans for site development and first-phase facilities; and plans for subsequent building phases.

• *Step 3: Select the site.* Consider the church's primary market when selecting a site. Is the location in close proximity to the majority of people who will be attending services? Does the property have good visibility and easy access?

Size is also an important factor. A church with a goal of reaching 500 in regular attendance needs three to five acres to provide space for worship, parking, education programs, fellowship events, and recreational activities. The minimum space for even a small, neighborhood church is 2.5 acres. Larger, regional churches require as much as 10 to 50 acres.

Since zoning regulations vary from one community to the next, the construction professionals on your team will prove invaluable at this time. Their prior knowledge of the area and their existing relationships with key people in local agencies will be an advantage.

• *Step 4: Plan the facility.* Consider carefully the style and size of the future facility. Team members should base their plans on both realistic expectations and limitations.

Ask these questions: Should the facility be contemporary or traditional, simple or ornate? Is the emphasis on form or function? Design a building that will accommodate the existing congregation plus the projected attendance growth for the next two years. After that, the church can add multiple services to accommodate growth.

Plan large, flexible spaces to facilitate long-term growth. Strike a balance between parking, worship, and programming space, based on the age of the congregation, the projected number of children and youth, and the types of programming offered. Overcrowding in any one area will stifle growth.

Estimating the costs of building is difficult. Try to get firm numbers — specific to the site and plan — before proceeding. It's important not to get carried away by all the options; emotions lead to excessive spending. A 10 percent overage margin for both the budget and the calendar helps offset delays and increased costs, since even the best-planned facilities experience such difficulties.

—Steven L. Ogne

7

Revitalizing Churches

Like a giant tidal wave, megachange is sweeping across America in the decade of the nineties. It has flowed into every area of society, accomplishing both good and bad, and has deeply impacted the American church. Various writers of different backgrounds have put some figures on accelerating change in America. From the business perspective, Michael Gerber writes, "Today's world is a difficult place. Mankind has experienced more change in the past twenty years than in the 2,000 that preceded them" (Gerber 1986, 156). Today, some estimate that human knowledge doubles every five to eight years.

The Church and Megachange

While American society is living for change, the American church is dying for change. Church growth specialist Kirk Hadaway writes, "The typical church in almost any American denomination is either plateaued or declining in membership and participation. Rapid growth is atypical, and among older congregations the pattern is even more pronounced—plateau and decline are the rule; growth is the rare exception" (Hadaway 1991, 110). Win Arn estimates that 80 to 85 percent of the churches in America are plateaued or in decline and that 3,500 to 4,000 churches die every year (Arn 1988, 16, 41).

While the American church is struggling, the unchurched population is growing. In 1978, George Gallup surveyed American adults 18 or older and discovered that 41 percent were unchurched. In 1988, he conducted the same poll a second time, and the figure had climbed to 44 percent (Gallup 1988, 2). Some pastors in America believe that Gallup's figure is conservative, setting the percentage at around 70 to 80 percent.

A critical question is, "Can these unchurched people be reached?" Indications are that they certainly could be reached. The fact that they are unchurched doesn't mean they're not interested in spiritual matters. In fact, Gallup's studies indicate they are actually more religious than a decade ago (Gallup 1988, 3).

The problem isn't a lack of interest in spiritual matters; it is a lack of interest in the established, traditional church. About 85 percent of American churches are functioning much as they did in the 1940s and 1950s. Consequently, the baby-boom and baby-bust generations view them as culturally irrelevant and show little interest in them.

The Best Leadership for Change

The leadership of skilled, influential change agents will be the key to catalyzing change in our churches and revitalizing them. But who are these leaders? How can we identify those who have the abilities to lead churches through this needed change process?

Robert Thomas used the *Biblical Personal Profile* to discover specific personality characteristics of effective revitalization pastors. According to this profile, I-type persons like to be around people and are articulate and motivational. They generate lots of enthusiasm, enjoy participating in a group, and genuinely desire to help people. They are risk takers who don't like the status quo and are "up-front" and "out on the point" kinds of people.

D-type persons want immediate results, love a challenge, and are catalytic. They tend to be quick decision makers who take charge of situations and are good at managing conflict and solving problems.

Thomas's research discovered that effective revitalization pastors in Baptist General Conference churches fall within the Persuader Pattern on the profile. The Persuader Pattern results from combining the High I temperament with a secondary D. The High I predominates, but the D also affects the temperament.

Leaders who desire to revitalize churches, then, would be wise to examine their natural characteristics and abilities to help determine their own potential for effectiveness in this task. For a good biblical role model, we might look to Nehemiah. An effective change agent, he displayed many excellent characteristics as he lead the Jews through the difficult task of rebuilding the walls of Jerusalem. While biblical change agents will not have all of Nehemiah's characteristics, they should identify with some of the following: being a visionary, a catalyst, an outsider, a problem solver, a motivator, a persuader, a risk taker, an empathizer, a planner, an organizer, and a delegator.

Not only should today's church leaders be aware of the impact of societal change and consider whether or not they really are change agents, they also need to understand the process of change itself. In analyzing that process, they'll need to look at why people don't change and then try to understand the people who *do* change, the best *times* for change, the typical *process* of change, and the overall *principles* of change.

The People Who Don't Change

In order to lead a church successfully through the revitalization process, the astute change agent must be aware of the more common reasons people don't change. Consider some typical reasons:

- *Felt needs.* While every man, woman, and child passes through this life with certain basic needs, it's their felt needs that demand attention. In most typical churches, people resist change because they don't feel a need to change. Many aren't aware of the awesome changes taking place in society and don't understand how seriously the church has failed to make the gospel appealing to modern seekers.
- *Status quo.* Some people refuse to change because they prefer the way things are over the way they could be. To move out of one's comfort zone is to leave a place of perceived safety and take up a position of vulnerability.
- *Values.* A congregation's culture consists of the traditions and values the church has acquired over its years of existence. It's "the way we've always done things around here." Many people can't distinguish their own narrow culture from the broad "market" the gospel message targets—all people, everywhere. While church people may not die for their congregational culture, they will protect and even fight for it.
- *Vested interests.* Over a period of time, certain benefits accrue to the church's long-term faithful, such as position, power, and prestige. Change threatens all of this. It often means a loss of power and prestige, and poses a threat to those who have grown used to "having the say about what goes on around here."
- *Distrust.* People may consciously or unconsciously harbor distrust of the leadership. Some dislike change because they feel leaders are trying merely to build their own kingdoms rather than God's.
- *Stress.* Subjecting people to change in a brief span of time often produces shattering stress and disorientation. Consequently, people resist change because they've been taught to look to the church as a place of safety and protection from the stresses of daily living.
- *Sacred cows.* People often assign a sacred quality to things that aren't intrinsically sacred, such as the church's style of music, a par-

ticular version of the Bible, or the Wednesday night prayer meeting. For those who can't discern the difference, to tamper with these practices is tantamount to ripping a page out of Holy Writ.

• *Self-centeredness.* People rarely will admit selfishness as a reason for resisting change, but the reality is that many people are looking out for Number One. Unfortunately, the "meet my needs" mentality of the contemporary world has invaded the church.

The People Who Do Change

Who votes for change, and who votes against? When we introduce change, we should be aware of the categories of change response and

Retaining Converts

How sad when apparently genuine converts fail to proceed naturally into church involvement and continued growth! Closing the evangelistic back door is possible, however. Two keys produce significant increases in lasting disciples and growing churches. The first is *process;* the second concerns *ratios.*

The Evangelistic Process

The process by which people arrive at a point of Christian decision often determines whether they become responsible members or drop out. Consider four dropout-creating approaches:

• *A manipulative process.* In one study, 70 percent of those who are now active members came to Christ and joined their church as the result of a member who engaged them in nonmanipulative dialogue. Such dialogue views evangelism as a two-way process of honest interaction. The assumption is that not all people see things the same way, and one canned approach will not be appropriate in every situation. The relationship between Christian and non-Christian in this case is friend to friend, the goal being to share an honest concern for the other.

• *An evangelistic goal of "decision" rather than "disciple."* When the goal is "a soul saved," God's plan for making disciples may get short-circuited. The fact is that not all deciders become disciples; the two are not synonymous. The biblical goal is not simply an oral confession but rather a life transformed and a participating member of Christ's body.

Nowhere in Scripture is the word *decision* found, yet, the word *disciple* appears again and again. A decision is only one element of many in the goal of seeing people become disciples and responsible church members.

• *A one-time presentation.* Effective evangelistic strategy seeks to expose potential disciples to many

what categories our local opinion makers fall into. There are basically four categories of change response. The first category is the *early adopters*, who, when they hear a new idea or proposal for change, jump on board almost immediately. Second are the *never adopters*. They're the laggards or strongest resistors to change; chances are excellent that they'll never change. The *middle adopters* come next, located between the two extremes. They are the majority of the church members, who will ultimately determine whether or not the church will actually change. In the final category we find the *late adopters*, who eventually will accept the change but are the last to do so.

In most churches, change occurs when the early adopters persuade the middle adopters to embrace change, and eventually the late

---

and varied presentations of the gospel. We all know stories of people who heard the Good News once, were gloriously changed, and went on to become great men or women of faith. When these miraculous events happen — and they do — we can rejoice. It should be understood, however, that this is not the norm. More often, when someone comes to faith, that person has heard the message again and again and again—and then makes a Christian commitment.

• *An approach unrelated to a church body.* The closer evangelism is to the local church, the greater the fruit that remains. The new Christian must build friendships with members in the church. When the events leading up to a non-Christian's profession of faith occur outside any relationship with the people of the local church, no ties are established, and the perceived need for involvement in the church is low.

The Crucial Ratios

Here are seven ratios that have significant effect in closing the evangelistic back door:

• Friendship ratio—1:7. Each new person should be able to identify at least seven friends in the church within the first six months.

• Role/task ratio—60:100. At least 60 roles and tasks should be available for every 100 members in a church.

• Group ratio — 7:100. At least seven relational groups — places where friendships are built — should be available in a church for every 100 members.

• New-group ratio —1:5. Of every five relational groups in a church, one should have been started in the past two years.

• Committee member ratio — 1:5. One of every five committee members should have joined the church within the last two years.

• Staff ratio—1:150. A church should have one full-time staff member for every 150 persons in worship.

• Visitor ratio—3:10. Of the first-time visitors who live in the church's ministry area, three of every ten should be actively involved within a year.

—Win Arn and Charles Arn

adopters agree. However, change doesn't occur when the middle adopters are persuaded by the never adopters and late adopters. The problem is that most never adopters are very vocal, and most middle adopters want to appear fair, so they give in to the squeaky wheels to try to make them happy.

In his book *Dying for Change,* Leith Anderson points out that most organizations have levels of opinion makers who either formally or informally exert influence that can be used to accomplish change. In the church are four levels: (1) the people on the church board who represent the formal leadership, (2) the staff and other committee members, (3) the Sunday school teachers and subgroup leaders, and (4) the rest of the church (Anderson 1990, 178).

The wise change agent will examine each level of opinion makers and determine where the people are in light of the four categories of

Recovering Church Dropouts

Suppose you discover a family is having troubles at home, seems to be avoiding you, is feeling disappointed about the way other church members have treated them, and thinks they are overworked and unrewarded. You can probably predict the next stage: they cry for help.

The Cry for Help

The cry for help usually springs from anxiety in at least one of four major areas. The most common is *intrafamily conflict.* Husband and wife square off on some issue; parents and kids squabble. This kind of conflict is the most consistent characteristic of people who have left the church.

Conflict with pastors is the second most common problem, and the main cause is avoidance. When pastors avoid dealing with people's anxiety, the people simply avoid the pastors and their churches.

Family against family, *interfamily conflict,* is the third arena. It's the Hatfields against the McCoys; the people just don't get along with one another.

Overwork, or at least the perception of it, presents a fourth problem area. With volunteer church service, too much too soon or too long, with no reward, will drive people from the church.

So how does a cry for help sound? It comes in all forms, sizes, and intensities. If we miss the verbal cries for help, we at least have a whole string of nonverbal cries to alert us to the problem. The cries for help become behavioral as the person either leaves or begins the process of leaving.

The first behavior change is the leaving of worship. Second, people leave major committees and boards. They either don't show up or begin to show up sporadically.

change response. If any level is inundated with never adopters, especially the levels toward the top, the chances of implementing change are slight. Next, leaders will proceed to identify and persuade the primary informal leaders at each level, who, in turn, are in positions to convince everyone else.

The Best Times for Change

Every church has a life cycle of birth, growth, plateau, and eventual death. However, there are certain times in the history of the typical church when its cycle can be interrupted. These interventions disrupt the status quo and present windows of opportunity for the implementation of change. The skillful pastor must be alert to the various open windows and be ready to use them to accomplish revi-

Third, people begin to leave Sunday school. Most adults have their closest friends in their Sunday school classes, so backing away from friends is a major change. Fourth, the kids are pulled out of Sunday school. The parents decide they don't even want to bring them, let alone come themselves. Fifth comes the letter of resignation, and finally, interestingly enough, the financial pledge is dropped. That's the final gasp for help.

Responding to Cries for Help

So what do we do for these people? Some pastors start shooting with the gospel gun: "Hey, friend, what's the matter with you? You losing your faith or something?" That's confusing the symptoms with the disease, the behavior with the cause. Instead, we need to teach ourselves and our lay people to *hear the pain* of inactive people. Consider these basic suggestions:

• *Report on the hurting.* How about taking fifteen minutes at the end of every board meeting for the board members to report on who, in their estimation, is crying for help? Collect those names and give them to a team of trained callers.

• *Actively listening for the pain.* One pastor extends his secretary's hours so she can stand near him at the door on Sunday mornings to listen for cries for help. She is good at picking them up, and the pastor inconspicuously indicates others for her to note while he manages the flurry of smiles and handshakes and small talk. By the afternoon, she alerts the calling teams, who reach out to these people *before* their cries turn to the silence of absence.

• *Always take the initiative.* Remember, we will not get inactive members back by avoiding pain. We have to take the initiative, go to them, uncover the anxiety-provoking situations, and pave the road for a return. If the people come back as a result of our ministering to their pain, that is good. But if they don't, we still have reached out to them in the name of Jesus Christ.

—John S. Savage

talization before the opportunity is lost. There are no fewer than seven such windows.

• *A widely perceived crisis.* A crisis event has the greatest potential to initiate biblical change in the typical church. The power of a crisis is its pain. Crises interrupt the status quo in an emotionally painful way that gains everyone's attention. People are willing to accept change as a means of pain relief.

• *A change of pastors.* A new pastor can bring to the church a new vision. Since churches grant new pastors some leverage at the beginning of their ministries, the chances are good they can implement their visions and initiate renewal.

• *A renewal of the pastor.* As the pastor of the church goes, so goes the church. Or better—as the pastor of the church grows and changes, so the church grows and changes. In *Your Church Can Grow,* Peter Wagner writes, "In America, the primary catalytic factor for growth in a local church is the pastor" (Wagner 1984, 61).

• *The planting of a church.* Church birthing is a good option for established churches that are clinging to the status quo while experiencing a generational clash. As the baby-boom folks move into positions of leadership in traditional churches, they will demand radical change that some members will find intolerable. While those churches will need to experience some change to survive, planting a spin-off congregation may avoid a potential church split.

• *A renewal of the lay leadership.* Not only pastors experience renewal; lay leaders do, too. Pastors should take every opportunity to educate their boards in biblical principles of change. For example, a pastor could take his or her core group members to church growth conferences and seminars where they could see what God is doing in committed-to-growth churches.

• *The expertise of a church consultant.* Sometimes churches don't value or have confidence in their pastor's leadership for church revitalization. In these situations, a qualified, skilled church consultant can bring the kind of objectivity that instills confidence. Outside consultants can spot problems and suggest biblical and practical solutions that translate into change.

The Typical Process of Change

Change agents are involved in causing things to change, in being catalysts of the process. But, like farmers, before they sow the seeds of change, they must prepare the soil. Preparation precedes process. The preparation for change involves three steps: ample prayer, the proper leadership for change, and evaluation.

The last step gets change agents involved in determining whether their ministries are plateaued or declining. The rule is this: If a church is plateaued, a pastor should move the church through revitalization more slowly. If a church is declining, a pastor should move quickly—or *later* may become *never.*

As with the preparation for change, the process of change itself also consists of three steps. In 1943, Kurt Lewin developed this three-step formula that has stood the test of time: (1) unfreeze the present situation, (2) move to a new level, (3) refreeze at the new level. Leaders of change can initiate the transition by unfreezing their churches' present situations. In other words, churches must become discontent with "what is." This involves intentionally creating dissonance with the status quo.

God may accomplish this through such events as sickness, natural disasters, and various trials and tribulations within the congregation. Biblical examples of this phenomenon include Hezekiah's illness; various invasions from Babylon, Syria, and Egypt; and Paul's thorn in the flesh. Change agents may call attention to the church's desperate situation or point to the church's poor image in the community or remind people of the church's "better days."

Once the present situation is sufficiently thawed, the next step is to move the congregation to a new level. This consists of three phases. The first is the casting of a clear, significant vision so that people crave *what could be* over *what is.* Disrupting the congregational status quo isn't enough by itself to implement change. People need to see what could be—the exciting possibilities of the future. Therefore, it's imperative that leaders know how to cultivate, communicate, and clarify a powerful vision.

The second phase calls for developing an initial plan to implement the new vision in the church. Most struggling congregations expect the pastor to come up with a plan and a program. The pastor shouldn't disappoint them. The plan needs to focus primarily on people, programs, and the physical plant.

The final phase demands recruiting a vocal, articulate, visionary team to follow through on the implementation of the vision. New Testament ministry is team ministry. In most smaller churches, the team will consist of part-time, voluntary lay people, who, as key opinion makers, will champion the new vision among the congregation. Larger churches must also involve the professional staff.

Once the new changes are implemented, the ever-present temptation to slip back to the "good old days" of the status quo will dog the leaders' footsteps. As Israel wandered in the wilderness, her constant complaint to Moses was, "Wouldn't it be better for us to go back to Egypt?" So the final step is to refreeze change at the new level.

The question is how, and the answer is found in Numbers 14. First, Moses and Aaron remained resistant; they hung tough. Second, two early adopters, Caleb and Joshua, exhorted and encouraged people by pointing to all the advantages of the new vision and what had been accomplished. Finally, they identified the real issues — rebellion against God and fear.

The Overall Principles of Change

Change catalysts need a toolbox filled with various tools for accomplishing revitalization. As they lead churches through the change process described above, they'll constantly fall back on these basic statements of principle to keep the process running smoothly:

• *Vital prayer leads to vital change.* Not enough can be said about the importance of prayer to the change process. The battle over change in American churches is primarily a spiritual battle being fought in the heavenlies (see Eph. 6:10–20). Even a casual glance through the Bible reveals that most major events were prefaced with prayer.

• *Tough faith upholds change.* In addition to prayer, another spiritual revitalization tool is a tough faith. According to Hebrews 11:6, without faith it's impossible to please God. But this cannot be an easy faith, as illustrated by change agents such as Noah (who built an ark in spite of the fact he'd never seen rain) and Abraham (who traveled without knowing where he was going).

• *Change is the response to wise questions.* Insightful leaders encourage change more by asking the right questions than by laying down ultimatums. People who resist biblical change aren't thinking clearly. Asking good questions facilitates change, because such questions gently uncover needed improvements in the organization, challenge people to think for themselves, and help point them in the proper direction.

• *Change agents pay attention to the power of words.* Because we use words to express new and innovative ideas about change, leaders of change must pay strict attention to the terms they use to express their ideas. For example, using the term *change,* itself, may alienate certain people. Pastors who lead those with a negative view toward change would be wise to use other words and synonyms for change, such as "transition," "transformation," and "variation."

Churches that want to reach the unchurched can be encouraged by the fact that today's pervasive secularism doesn't satisfy the cravings of the human soul. The baby-boom and baby-bust generations are searching for spiritual truth. It's time to get every church involved in offering that truth in ways that meet the needs of twenty-first–century seekers.

—Aubrey Malphurs

Resources

Anderson, L. 1990. Dying for change. Minneapolis: Bethany.

Arn, W. 1988. The pastor's manual for effective ministry. Monrovia, Cal.: Church Growth, Inc.

Gallup, G. 1988. The unchurched American—ten years later. Princeton, N.J.: The Princeton Religion Center.

Gerber, M. 1986. The e-myth. New York: Harper Business.

Hadaway, K. 1991. Church growth principles. Nashville: Broadman.

Malphurs, A. 1993. Pouring new wine into old wineskins. Grand Rapids: Baker.

Malphurs, A. 1992. Developing a vision for ministry in the 21st. century. Grand Rapids: Baker.

Schaller, L. 1972. The change agent. Nashville: Abingdon.

Wagner, P. 1984. Your church can grow. Ventura, Cal.: Regal.

Part II:

Missions

It was commanded by Jesus himself, yet finally begun as the result of a dire persecution. It was limited ethnically at first, before the doors were finally flung open wide to all peoples. It flourished under adversity and waned in prosperity. It was nearly abandoned for a time, later to be pursued vigorously—and then discouraged in some quarters.

It has taken the Good News to every continent, most peoples and tongues, and hundreds of millions of individual souls. It has brought nearly a third of the world's population—1.734 billion people, according to Operation World—to the point of calling Jesus Christ Lord and Savior.

It, of course, is missions.

Since the church as a whole has marching orders to "Go into all the world and make disciples," and since each local congregation has a part to play in obeying that order, the success of missions at all levels is of utmost importance. So how can missions best be accomplished? This is what concerns the writers of this section, just as it concerns conscientious church leaders and people called into missions, and just as it ultimately concerns the Lord of the Harvest. Here, then, are the suggestions these experienced leaders offer.

8

The Purpose of Missions

Christians traditionally have understood missions to include at least four broad purposes: the conversion of the lost, the establishment of the church, the restoration of the Creation, and the glorifying of God's grace throughout the universe forever. Yet some Christians today might question whether God has such a worldwide concern and whether he wants the church at large to develop the same cosmic perspective.

If so, we'll need to find ways to convince our church members that the living God is—and has been, since the advent of sin—a missionary God. He does yearn for all his creatures to offer him praise. By surveying key themes in the history of God's people, we will see that God constantly has called his people to labor for that great purpose with him.

God's Worldwide Concern

At first glance, the themes of the Old Testament may appear more parochial than universal in scope. Very quickly these Scriptures zero in on Abraham and the Semitic history of his descendants. God's grace seems to narrow down to Isaac and not Ishmael, to Jacob and not Esau. Yet, woven through the history of Genesis 1–11 are vivid reminders of a divine mercy whose interests are global.

• *The Genesis history and the unity of all humankind.* The story of Creation begins with a sweep that is worldwide in concern. This history, unlike the religious myths of the Ancient Near East, points to a cosmic sovereign, not a local deity. God's territorial dwelling place is not limited to a city-state like the Baals; the heavens and the earth are his domain (Ps. 24:1–2). Unlike the Babylonian creation account, this history gives us no hint of ethnic superiority for Israel based on a special creation relationship to an ethnic god. Likewise, the great assumption of the narrative is the unity of all humankind in the royal responsibilities of covenant imagehood before God (Gen. 1:26–27). This imagehood does not omit the startling inclusion of women, either from the act of Creation or from the creature's rebellion against the Creator.

The subsequent history of humanity chronicles the effects of this act of rebellion on a similarly universal scale. Alienation from God becomes incorrigible perverseness that can be halted only by the divine intervention of a universal flood. But after this flood judgment—and through it—God still remains faithful to his creation blessing to Adam (Gen. 1:28). He desires to fill the earth with a multitude of peoples (Gen. 9:1).

The Table of Nations in Genesis 10 reinforces this promise. Its link to the earlier history reminds us of God's postflood promise. And linking with the history subsequent to Babel, the Table looks forward to the return of these peoples to the redemptive fold through the blessing of the Semites in Abraham.

• *Abraham's call and the promise of worldwide blessing.* With the call to Abraham (Gen. 12:2–3), the same God who promises "I will make you into a great nation" promises "All peoples on earth will be blessed through you." The blessing of Abraham will one day "come to the Gentiles through Jesus Christ" (Gal. 3:14). All of this is the *beginning* of the restoration of the lost unity of humanity, not the *ending.* "Abraham is chosen, not just for his own glory, the good fortune of his descendants, or the misery of his enemies; rather, with him Yahweh begins a new chapter in the history of man. Abraham is the instrument for the salvation of the world" (Martin-Achard 1962, 35).

• *Israel's election and her testimony to the nations.* This same nonparochial perspective shapes the history of Israel as a witness to God's sovereignty among all nations. Israel's mission was to sanctify God's name before the peoples (Deut. 28:10). The preface to the constituting words of the theocracy speak of God's right of possession over all nations: "The whole earth is mine" (Exod. 19:5). In this light Israel is elected by God as "a kingdom of priests and a holy nation" (Exod. 19:6; 1 Pet. 2:9). She is to "fulfill a priestly role as a people in the midst of the nations. She is to represent God in the world of nations. What priests are for a people, Israel as a people is for the world" (Blauw 1962, 24). What kind of witness is Israel to be?

First, before the nations she testifies to God's covenant purposes. Her identity is shaped not by ties of blood or genealogy but by the electing grace of God (Deut. 26:18–19). The surrounding nations see themselves as incarnations of deity, their victories over other peoples being victories over others' gods. Israel's identity, however, comes only through obedience to the covenant God.

Second, before the nations Israel testifies to God's sovereign power. At Sinai the all-powerful God had promised victory over all those who would threaten his vassal, Israel (Exod. 23:22–23). In covenant power Yahweh keeps that word as the Israelites possess the land. Pagan treaties of that day called on the gods to bear witness to the secular ruler's faithfulness; in God's covenant the nations are to bear witness to the power of God (Lev. 26:45; Josh. 2:10; Ezek. 5:8, 14).

Third, before the nations Israel testifies also to God's mercy. Formed out of a "mixed multitude" (Exod. 12:38, KJ), she finds room for a Rahab and a Moabite Ruth in her community. A widow in Sidon and a Syrian leper named Naaman become harbingers of God's healing for the nations (Luke 4:25–28). Israel's laws extend equally to Israelite and to resident alien, the stranger in her midst (Lev. 19:10, 34; Num. 9:14; Deut. 24:19).

Fourth, before the nations Israel testifies to God's justice. The nations around her constantly exhibited oppression and injustice; righteousness was defined as "doing your own thing," or "having your own way." Israel was to model God's new charter of reality, righteousness as the companion of justice (Jer. 9:24; Amos 5:24). Quite uniquely, the poor were to be protected, not exploited in this display of justice (Deut. 10:17–18). A wise Solomon "administers justice" (1 Kings 3:28), and even the pagan queen of Sheba marvels (1 Kings 10:4, 6–7).

• *Israel's apostasy and the gathering of all peoples.* Against this background, Israel's failure to maintain her distinctiveness before God becomes a failure to enact her role as witness before the nations. In idolatry she "plays the harlot" with the very peoples before whom she was to model covenant holiness. A notable sign of this syncretism is the oppression of the righteous poor (Amos 2:6–7; 5:12).

In the face of Israel's acceptance of the lifestyle of the nations, the prophets call on those same nations to execute the other responsibility of the covenant witness (Deut. 17:7). Assyria and Babylon now serve as the Lord's instruments to administer the curses of the covenant (Hos. 10:10; Amos 6:14). Dispersion and exile for the twelve tribes become the judgment for disobedience.

Alongside the message of God's wrath against Israel, there is also a renewed promise of God's grace, to be shared this time by the nations. "The last days" are approaching, when God will come to be King over all the earth (Zech. 14:9). Israel will taste again the mercies of God, and the nations will spontaneously come to the Lord (Zech. 8:23). Jerusalem will be the gathering place of a new Israel, its citizens drawn from its former enemies (Ps. 87:4–6; Isa. 56:3–8). It will be a great harvest day unparalleled in history (Isa. 27:12–13; Amos 9:13–15). Ushering it in will be the Messenger of the new covenant (Mal. 3:1), the Servant who, by his suffering, will "justify many" (Isa. 53:11). Around his ensign Israel and the nations will be gathered (Isa. 5:26; 11:10, 12) and then scattered again in a second exodus among the nations (Isa. 11:15–16; 52:10–12).

Christ's Harvesting Ministry

The great emphasis of the gospels is that this Jubilee day of liberation (Isa. 61:1–2) has come in Jesus.

• *The Son and the coming of the kingdom.* God's kingdom rule of peace and restoration has begun in the words and deeds of the saving King Jesus (Matt. 4:17; Luke 4:18–21; 11:20). John the Baptist announces the great harvest day of the prophets as he points to Jesus the

World Christians

Let us see ourselves as World Christians! What more appropriate term for us, especially now, when television news brings the whole globe into our living rooms every day? After all, we belong to him who says, "Go, make disciples of all the nations" (Matt. 28:18).

Worldwide Discipleship

The term "World Christian" can help remind us of key requirements for true discipleship. First, Christ's disciples are to enter into his deepest concerns. He is Lord of all the world and has made all the world his passion.

Someone has said, "The closer we get to the heart of Jesus, the closer we get to what is on his heart." What is on his heart is the whole world, in all its pain and need. Those who know his heart must share his passion.

Second, disciples of Jesus Christ are to recognize the interconnectedness of his *whole* body, the universal church. What happens in one part of the worldwide body of Christ affects all other parts. We are involved in kingdom work together. What the Holy Spirit is doing among Chinese believers will affect the Swedish believers, and vice versa. Disciples do not go it alone.

Third, Christian disciples must enter into others' perspectives to know Jesus Christ fully. The way each of us perceives Jesus is colored by our culture's world view. Our world view enables us to see something in him the other is *not* able to see, yet it blinds us to something in him the others *are* able to see.

For instance, my understanding of Jesus was wonderfully expanded while serving in the Philippines. In a course on Christology, I taught students from nine Southeast Asian

harvester (Matt. 3:12). And Jesus re-echoes that theme as he describes the harvesting ministry of his disciples (Luke 10:1–2).

The universal gathering of the nations is to begin. "Many will come from the east and the west, and will take their places at the feast with Abraham, Isaac and Jacob in the kingdom of heaven" (Matt. 8:11). The new Exodus will be launched with Jesus' departure death in Jerusalem (Luke 9:31; John 12:32). There are gospel hints that this ingathering has begun in part. As the Shepherd/Son of David (Ezek. 34:23), Jesus gathers his remnant flock given him by the Father (Luke 12:32). To the remnant poor he promises the kingdom's blessing (Matt. 5:3–10). Around the "lost" leftovers of Israel, he defines his messianic calling (Luke 15:3–7; 19:9).

He looks with compassion on the multitudes who come to him as scattered sheep (Matt. 9:36) and proclaims that the Father has "other sheep" also (John 10:16). He heals the daughter of a Greek woman

---

countries and the Middle East. These students helped me see aspects of Christ I never would have seen had I remained enmeshed in the American culture. World Christians have a bigger and richer Savior and Lord.

Expanding Perspectives

How can we learn to live as World Christians, especially if we do not have the opportunity to live in another country? Consider these four starting points:

• Ask the Spirit of God to place on your heart one country or people group for whom you can regularly pray. Ask, "Lord, for what part of the world can I share your passion?" We may never know the impact our intercession may make (see Dan. 10:12–11:1 for encouragement), but what will happen is an ever greater expression of our vision of him who with his blood "purchased men and women for God from every tribe and language and people and nation" (Rev. 5:9).

• Find out everything you can about your chosen country or people group by contacting denominational mission boards and other mission agencies. Write to missionaries in the field. Or better yet, write to the nationals themselves: government leaders, social workers, and teachers, for instance. Find out what the ministry needs are, and find out what Christ is already doing there.

• Listen to what believers and nonbelievers are saying about Jesus Christ in that part of the world. Search out articles being written in newspapers or journals. If possible, obtain copies of sermons being preached by nationals and immerse yourself in their experience of Christ.

• Finally, reach out to persons from that country or people group who might be living in your own area. Invite them to your home; visit them in their neighborhoods. With appropriate sensitivity, begin crossing the cultural line as a World Christian.

—*Darrell Johnson*

---

born in Syrian Phoenicia (Mark 7:25–26) and marvels at the pleading faith of a Roman centurion (Matt. 8:10).

• *The Gospel riddle and the Great Commission.* Nevertheless, Jesus' attitude toward the Gentiles seems still limited and narrow in its nature. He prohibits his disciples from going to non-Jews (Matt. 10:5–6) and confines his own ministry to the "lost sheep of Israel" (Matt. 15:24). The resolution of the tension lies in seeing the ministry of Jesus as initiating the fulfillment of the redemptive plan of God. The time had not yet come for a full proclamation to the Gentiles. Israel must first be invited to the wedding feast of salvation. Only after those who are invited refuse may the banquet doors be opened to outsiders (Matt. 22:8–10).

Unreached Peoples

Looking down from an airplane when landing, we first see whole square blocks. Eventually individual buildings come into focus.

Something similar happened when Protestants began to send missionaries out across a strange and mysterious world. The biblical command was simple: disciple the nations. As missionaries "landed," they discovered blocks of people. But when they tried to focus on individuals, they found winning them unexpectedly difficult.

People as a Concept

Highly individualistic Americans today are probably the most likely to be confused by the phenomenon of social and family constraints to evangelism in non-Western societies. Individuals live within the tight grip of a people, a social structure, a culture, an extended family. Our missionaries found it difficult to pry out individuals to be saved one-by-one.

Eventually they learned that the highest quality church movements were those that did not try to tear up or replace the social fabric of the people to which they were sent. Thus arose the concept of "peoples"—natural groupings among which people live.

More than anyone else, Donald A. McGavran, a third-generation missionary in India, championed the idea that missionaries ought not to consider their job done nor assume they have given any individual a real chance to accept Christ unless that person can become part of what he called a "people movement."

This radical idea required missionaries to do more than evangelism. They had to plant churches. McGavran would not let missionaries count raised hands. They could consider saved only those who had been securely "folded" into a vital, ongoing fellowship.

A further logical conclusion was that unless a people movement to Christ was set in motion, the basic

The kingdom offer to the Gentiles can be issued only after the death of the Passover Lamb. At his Resurrection, his atoning work will be vindicated. Then, in the full assurance of "all authority in heaven and on earth given" to him by the Father, his disciples can "go and make disciples of all nations" (Matt. 28:18–20). "On the basis of the earthly ministry, the death, and the Resurrection of Jesus, the 'road' of missions to the Gentiles is open" (Bosch 1991, 83).

• *Universal proclamation and the church.* Before this second exodus/dispersion begins, however, the fullness of the Holy Spirit must be poured out on the church (Acts 1:8). The Great Commission is to be the primary task of those working in the new kingdom, but the Spirit must come to empower them first. He comes on the day of harvest

---

missionary task had not yet been accomplished. Success couldn't be substantiated by a few converts, some missionaries, or even a Bible translation if there was not yet a substantial, indigenous social movement within which new believers could fellowship and grow.

This approach now precisely defines what is or isn't an unreached people. Unreached peoples are those where there is no viable, indigenous, evangelizing church movement.

Measuring the Progress

The people-movement approach to missions brings into focus precisely how to measure progress (Are we reaching new groups?) and what is yet to be accomplished (How many peoples are yet unreached?). Also, the question arises in any mission situation: How large is this group? If we can penetrate this group with a fully indigenous people movement, how many people can be brought to an unconfused opportunity to accept Christ and become part of his church?

This is a more difficult question than it sounds. For example, even the truly professional Wycliffe Bible Translators do not always know in advance how large a group — or how many people groups — will be able to read a printed translation they have developed. From their estimates of the "reading basins" of the translations they now have, their best guess is that they have about three thousand translations yet to produce. When the Bible is put on cassette or on the radio, however, the distinctions in intelligibility or acceptability are even finer, and the number of groups still to read could be three or four times as great as Wycliffe's estimate.

Thus, an estimate of the number of remaining unreached peoples is a subtle question; the number could be up around 11,000, even though all those groups can be listed under 6,000 or so commonly accepted names for groups.

Big as these number are, the global church movement is enormous by comparison. There are well over six hundred existing congregations for *each* remaining unreached people group.

—*Ralph Winter*

celebration, Pentecost (Acts 2:1–4). He is both a fulfillment of the harvest promise and the promise of a greater fulfillment yet to come (Rom. 8:23; Eph. 1:13–14).

The universal proclamation of the gospel promised as a sign of the end (Matt. 24:14) now begins. From Jerusalem, the Spirit widens the horizon of a reluctant church to include the half-Jew, half-Gentile Samaritans (Acts 8:14–17). With the falling of the same Pentecost Spirit on Cornelius, a Roman proselyte, the ancient problem of Jew and Gentile is solved for a slow-learning Peter and the church (Acts 10:34–35; 11:15–18). The Gentile mission, propelled again by the Spirit, becomes fact (Acts 13:2–4), and official sanctioning of Gentile inclusion takes place in the church's Jerusalem assembly (Acts 15:12–18). Paul's missionary work becomes the great symbol of this change. The Book of Acts follows his proclamation of Jesus as Lord through the Greek world and eventually to Rome, "the ends of the earth." Paul's journey becomes a trail of repeated rejection by the Jews and growing response from the Gentiles.

As the commentator on this mission history, Paul links the witnessing role of Israel to its fulfillment in the church. At the same time, he enlarges the Old Testament themes. Old Covenant signs of particularism are given a new slant. Jerusalem, receding into the background in Acts, is replaced by Jesus as the central point around which the nations will gather (John 4:21–23; Gal. 4:25–26). The church becomes the temple (2 Cor. 6:16; cf. 1 Pet. 2:4–5). And yet there still remain special promises for the Jews; the conversion of the Gentiles will prompt the Jews to believe (Rom. 11:11–12, 25–26). The mission from Israel to the Gentiles now becomes the mission from the new Israel (Jews and Gentiles) to the old Israel.

In this new Israel, the theocratic calling of old Israel before the nations is repeated. God's sovereign power in Christ breaks down social, political, and ethnic boundaries (1 Cor. 1:23–28; Gal. 3:28). Justice and compassion, now incarnate in Christ, still demand neighbor love in the Spirit (Gal. 5:13–23). Wealthy and poor, male and female fashion a new community in the Spirit. In all this we are called to be conscious of those "outside" (Col. 4:5; 1 Tim. 3:7). Whether in worship (1 Cor. 14:23) or at work (1 Thess. 4:11–12), the church lives before the witnessing eye of the world.

• *Mission and God's design for the world.* Important as the church is, however, it is not the ultimate aim for missions. As the beginning of the "new creation," the church is to model God's original Genesis design for the world. Calvary's saving victory over sin and death also makes Jesus Lord of the cosmos, the head of all things (Eph. 1:21), that he might "fill the whole universe" (Eph. 4:10).

In anticipation of that final reality, we participate in the transformation of the world. We challenge the world to what Christ intends all things one day to be: the total submission of all people and all earthly and cosmic powers to God's kingship and glorious rule (Phil. 2:9–11). When may we expect this complete renewal of all things? When the Son of Man sits on his glorious throne, with "a great multitude that no one could count from every nation, tribe, people, and language" (Rev. 7:9) gathered before him. Then, and only then, will God's mission be fulfilled, unmarred by failed efforts and human frailty. Then will the people of God sing the final mission doxology (Rev. 7:12).

Outreach in the Great Awakening and Beyond

In the years that have followed this biblical model of understanding missions, history has both chipped away at that vision and also underlined its riches. Paradigms formed by traditions have risen and fallen, some still surviving alongside others.

Not until the end of the eighteenth century, however, did the larger Protestant community widely view the church's mission in terms of being a co-laborer with God in the consummation of the work of redemption. The church at that time optimistically expected to convert the Jews and the Gentile nations and to usher in an era of glory when the gospel would triumph around the world.

To achieve those goals, the revived community turned to the pietist model of voluntary mission societies. Designed as temporary arrangements until the non-missionary-minded churches came on board, the societies quickly became permanent fixtures. Church-related missions followed the pattern, and the "faith mission movement" of later years repeated it.

The middle of the twentieth century marked a new beginning for missions. Colonialism would be dismantled, and Christianity would be well on the way to numbering a third of the world in its community. What had been a European-centered religion would at last be a truly global fellowship, as churches looked for new patterns of cooperation with one another and with western mission societies. The formation of the World Council of Churches in 1948 provided one instrument for that reexamination.

Initial malaise slowly began to give way to new energy. Fueled by the reform efforts of Vatican II (1962–1965), the Roman Catholic Church reexamined the missionary dimensions of the church as the body of Christ. It underlined the relationship between the church and the world and urged dialogue with other Christian churches and other world religions.

Protestant responses were more mixed. Mainline churches appeared more sensitive to the need for partnership with their "daughter" churches, and they also were more influenced by theological pluralism. They reduced their missionary force, concentrating missionaries in specialist roles.

The more evangelical missions, particularly in the United States, expanded their efforts, spurred on by the stimulation of the emerging Church Growth Movement. Questioning the theological pluralism represented by the World Council of Churches, evangelicals worldwide found an ecumenical base of expression and encouragement in the Lausanne Committee for World Evangelization, formed in 1974. Adding their strength to this new revival of missions is the emerging wave of Third World missionaries, estimated to reach 54 percent of the total force by the end of the century.

Where will missions go in the future? A growing agenda of issues makes some suspect that a new paradigm is now forming (Bosch 1991, 349–367). In any case, the questions multiply: What is the connection between missions and evangelism, or between evangelism and social transformation? What should be done about those still unreached by the gospel? How can missions become the calling of the whole people of God?

These are all tough questions, but Jesus still leads us by his Spirit into unique and creative solutions. We must continue to follow him—to the ends of the earth, until the end of time.

—*Harvie M. Conn*

Resources

Anderson, G. 1988. American Protestants in pursuit of mission: 1886–1986 *International Bulletin of Missionary Research* 12:98–118.

Blauw, J. 1962. The missionary nature of the church. London: Lutterworth.

Boer, H. 1961. Pentecost and missions. Grand Rapids: Eerdmans.

Bosch, D. 1980. Witness to the world. Atlanta: John Knox.

Bosch, D. 1991. Transforming mission: Paradigm shifts in theology of mission. Maryknoll: Orbis.

DeJong, J. 1970. As the waters cover the sea: Millennial expectations in the rise of Anglo-American missions, 1640–1810. Kampen: J. H. Kok.

Martin-Achard, R. 1962. A light to the nations. London: Oliver and Boyd.

Neill, S. 1966. Colonialism and Christian mission. London: Lutterworth.

Stamoolis, J. 1986. Eastern Orthodox mission theology today. Maryknoll: Orbis.

Evangelism or Service?

Where should the resources go, into evangelism or into social service? To what should we be giving our time, to evangelism or to social service?

Asking the question in that either/or way reveals that we are separating what Jesus holds together. Matthew, for instance, tells us that Jesus "went throughout Galilee, teaching in their synagogues, preaching the good news of the kingdom, and healing every disease and sickness among the people" (4:23).

Teaching, preaching, healing—in Jesus' ministry they are never separated. Why? Because each activity participates in the same reality — the kingdom of God, which is breaking in upon the world. The kingdom of God is all about restoring broken people to harmony with God, with others, with the self, and with the created order (see Genesis 2). According to Mark, Jesus' gospel had "come near." Jesus went about announcing this gospel (preaching), explaining its nature (teaching), and bringing it into being (healing).

The King's Model

Evangelism or social service? We may need to consider which is most needful at any given moment, but choosing only one or the other must never become the starting point for a philosophy of ministry.

Jesus met folks who were tormented by evil and delivered them. He turned water into wine. He fed a whole crowd with a few loaves and fish. He called a hated tax collector into personal discipleship. He died on a cross and then rose from the grave. All these marvelous actions demonstrated that the kingdom of God was invading and transforming the world.

The reason we end up with the either/or is that we have separated the kingdom from the King. Since the kingdom is wherever Jesus Christ is King, he could say "Lose yourself for the *kingdom*" and in the next breath say "Lose yourself for *me*." The power of the kingdom cannot be separated from the presence of the King.

The kingdom of God invades and pervades every sector of life — the private and the public, the religious and the secular. We enter and participate in the kingdom of God only through relationship with Jesus the King, so the gospel is personal encounter. When we have a relationship with the King, we enter the kingdom — a new order of life — so the gospel is social transformation.

E. Stanley Jones put it best in *The Word Made Flesh* (Abingdon): "An individual gospel without a social gospel is a soul without a body; and a social gospel without a personal gospel is a body without a soul. One is a ghost and the other is a corpse. Together, they make a living person."

Be Like Jesus

Evangelism or social service? We serve in Jesus' name, and we speak his name as servants in his kingdom. In one instance, people may need bread desperately for their stomachs. Another time, people may be open to accepting the Bread of Life into their souls.

How do we know which way to go in a particular situation? We consider the circumstances — and we pray. What need stands before us? In the person of a robbery victim, the Good Samaritan faced a medical need. In the person of a Philippian jailer, Paul faced a spiritual need. In the person of a disabled man on temple steps, Peter and John faced both, and offered both: "In the name of Jesus Christ of Nazareth, walk!" (Acts 3:6).

Evangelism and social service go together in Jesus' ministry, and they must work together in our ministries, too. One missions writer, Tetsunao Yamamori, called them "functionally separate, relationally inseparable, and essential to the total ministry of the church."

Evangelism or social service? Yes.

—*Darrell Johnson*

The Pastor's Role in Missions Ministry

What can a pastor do to promote missions in the congregation?

Many church people tune out as soon as pastors or lay leaders start talking about developing a missions budget. They perk up, however, when missions ministry becomes personalized. The magic word is *involvement*. Consider these two practical ways pastors can help their parishioners experience the personal impact of world missions.

A Friendship Matchmaker

Pastors can help their parishioners develop deep and lasting friendships with missionaries. Nothing promotes sensitivity to, and concern for, missions like having a missionary for a friend. As God became physically personal in Jesus Christ, so missions becomes relationally personal when a missionary gets deeply acquainted with a congregation.

A church that traditionally schedules a Missionary Sunday may want to make it into a Missionary Week and invite a missionary to stay in a member's home, with someone likely to build on the relationship. Another idea is to plan a church supper, where many members can eat and converse with the missionary. In other words, having the missionary blow in, blow off (in the pulpit), and then blow out of town is not nearly as effective as helping people in the congregation develop a long-term relationship. A more relaxed setting gives people a chance to get to know the missionary and become friends.

Some pastors arrange rotating church-member housing for missionaries on furlough. Imagine a year-long exposure to missions for each of the church's fellowship and ministry groups! This happens when a missionary family gets "adopted" by a congregation during furlough. Most missionaries are eager to find free or moderately priced housing for furloughs, and they enjoy having a home base in their sending country.

Firsthand Experiences

Typically, the pastor visits a mission field and returns to report on the work. It's much more rewarding, however, to take a delegation of lay people along. Congregations having the resources to send teams to visit international missions often are large or affluent, but judicatories have found it profitable to collect individuals from smaller churches to visit mission outposts.

Smaller congregations may have the resources to visit sites of national mission work. Such work usually is no farther than the nearest inner city, where, frequently, the world's peoples have gathered in ethnic neighborhoods. Pastors who arrange such group contacts return home with a turned-on group of lay people who are ready to report their experiences and urge participation by others.

A great way to start is to take youth on a missions work project. Some pastors have forged a continuing relationship with national and international mission workers through such youth involvements. For example, a congregation I served attempted one international contact and three national and local contacts with missionaries for each generation of senior high students. Over an eight-year period, the teens visited Haiti and Mexico, and maintained highly rewarding relationships with missionaries in rural Mississippi and inner-city Chicago. Adult sponsors accompanying these young people came back excited about the church's mission involvement. When one girl began to weep as she reported her experience of worshiping with Haitians who were dressed in rags, the congregation wept with her.

However we try to inspire our congregations for missions, we need to remember the golden rule of missions promotion: The budget kills; personal involvement gives life.

—Dave Philips

9

Planning Missions Ministry

Have you ever had little children offer to help you with yard work? You knew what was coming when they asked if they could contribute. Visions of toppled-over wheelbarrows and spilled sacks of fertilizer danced through your head. Letting a young child help would probably hinder the process. The work probably would take a lot longer than if you did the work yourself. But for the joy of letting enthusiastic children help, perhaps you invited them to join you.

God has "yard work" to do, too. He has a plan for the whole world, that of restoring its men and women to a vital relationship with himself. For some reason, he has given his children, the church, the privilege of helping in the process of bringing people to the Savior.

Today, unfortunately, many of God's children have neither the desire nor the abilities to help out in the yard. They see worldwide evangelistic planting and harvesting as a burdensome chore rather than an exciting opportunity to work with and for their Father.

Making the Case for Missions Participation

The typical church member is bombarded with program opportunities—building-committee meetings, Christian aerobics classes, softball teams, singles programs, estate planning seminars . . . and the list goes on. Most members are overextended with too many meetings per week already. So why should your church become committed to missions, adding another program that pleads for time and attention, adding another expense item to the budget?

This question can be answered only when local congregations take time to explore another, more foundational question: *What is the ultimate purpose of the local church?* If the church exists merely to be a safe haven from secular society, a place to raise children, get married, and hold social events, then there really is no reason for a church to try to make an impact on the surrounding world.

According to Scripture, however, a church's purpose is to function as salt and light in its community. When this begins to happen, the church will start to realize that God also wishes to see the influence of his kingdom spreading out to places around the world where there is no church to act as a change agent. In light of Acts 1:8, the church is to move its witness into increasingly broader spheres of influence. The next logical step for many American churches is to look for places of need beyond its country's borders.

Once this foundational issue of purpose is settled and a church has decided to become involved in world evangelization to any significant degree, it will become either a *sending church* or a *supporting church.*

Harry Larson, a seasoned missions pastor, has noted some key differences between these two types of churches. The supporting church focuses on funding workers who are already actively ministering. Church members have little personal involvement with the missionaries and can claim only the minimal ownership of any of its field workers. The sending church focuses on calling forth candidates for missions ministry and helps them prepare for the work. Like the church at Antioch in Acts 11:19–30 and Acts 13:1–3, it sees its missionaries as living extensions of itself, its members deployed around the world to advance God's kingdom.

In both kinds of churches, prayer and strong pastoral leadership must be at the center of all missions activity. Effective prayer for missionaries is informed prayer. Information comes best through consistent, caring contact with the missionaries and through research into the political, cultural, and social trends that are shaping the missionaries' lives and defining their work.

Missions will never reach its full potential in a local church without the enthusiastic participation and support of the pastor. The pastor must perceive missions as having a direct, personal benefit for the church. He or she may need to seek out opportunities for exposure to missions projects in order to generate personal enthusiasm for the mandate of world evangelization.

Organizing a Missions Leadership Team

It may be called a committee, team, or task force, but whatever the name, the local church needs a lay group to do more than just administer the missions program. The missions team should be a catalyst for involving the entire congregation in missions, responsible for putting feet on the philosophy of missions ministry and discipling individual members in missions.

Some qualities of an effective committee would be: (1) it is well-organized; (2) it aggressively recruits talented people to serve; (3) it fully orients new members; and (4) it gets the whole church body involved. The work of the committee should not be done in haste or by only following tradition. A simple, yet workable structure of subcommittees should carry out the work. Meetings should be regularly scheduled (at least monthly) and should include reports of work accomplished.

A subcommittee structure might look like this:

- *Strategy committee.* Determines the church's missions strategy and recommends action.
- *Sending committee.* Focuses on selecting, training, commissioning, and evaluating missionaries.
- *Support committee.* Sets up systems of personal and financial care of the missionaries.
- *Stimulation committee.* Develops plans for missions education within the entire congregation.
- *Serving committee.* Mobilizes the congregation for outreach in local areas and in other nations by developing specific strategies.

For a missions leadership team to function at peak performance levels and maintain continuity, it should set a minimum of three years for service commitment. Many teams involve both husband and wife together. If at all possible, members should be encouraged to make this form of service their primary—if not only—responsibility within the church.

Developing a World-Outreach Strategy

The process of setting goals for a church's missions outreach begins with writing a purpose statement that expresses the primary reason for the church's existence. Such a statement may be part of the church's existing by-laws. If not, perhaps the leadership of the church or an ad hoc committee might draft such a reason for existence and present it for congregational discussion, revision, and adoption.

Once an overall purpose statement is in place, the church is ready to develop a missions policy. Having a clear missions policy is the key mark of a missions-minded church. The Association of Church Mission Committees' *Church Missions Policy Handbook* describes in detail the process of writing a policy statement. The statement should cover the following areas, answering key questions related to each:

- *Statement of purpose.* What does your church mean by the word *mission?* What parts of the church life will be included in outreach activities?

- *The structure of mission.* What specific methods will you use to develop your outreach goals? What is your mission team's functions, and what are its limits? When should it meet? To whom does it report?
- *Strategy for missions.* What kinds of outreach work will your committee consider? What are the priorities used to evaluate support for each potential project?
- *Strategy for missions education and support.* Whose responsibility is missions education? How will you recruit missionary candidates? What part should the church have in short-term missions?

Financing Missions

The cost of sending missionaries has skyrocketed during the last decade. One mission agency reported increases of as much as 123 percent. In 1983 it cost that mission $26,458 a year to send a missionary couple with one child to Peru. By 1993 the figure had risen to $59,032. Sending them to Japan would cost almost $72,000. If the same couple were to serve in the Philippines, they would have to raise $42,928.

Alarming figures such as these raise at least three big questions.

Raising Money

How should missions money be raised? Churches use several common approaches. *Divided giving* allows members to allocate a portion of their overall giving to missions. *Faith promising* involves a periodic commitment of giving over and above existing levels. *Special appeals* raise funds that go to the purchase of equipment and supplies or to programs of limited scope and duration.

These three options have several advantages. They do not divert funds already allocated to church programs, and they tend to generate a relatively high degree of personal interest. However, in the event of financial stress, potential givers may abandon these "extra" commitments in order to meet immediate personal needs.

Some churches allocate a fixed percentage of the church's general budget to missions. This simplifies the process and does provide a higher level of stability. However, given the many programs competing for limited funds, there is no guarantee that missions will receive its fair share. In fact, this approach may be nothing more than a convenient way for members to avoid the challenge of a personal commitment to missions giving.

Still other churches send their missions funds to a denomination or a mission society for allocation. This tends to dampen personal interest, however.

Other churches support individual missionaries, either directly or through an institution. Since people relate to people better than they

• *Standards of accreditation.* What are the requirements for partnering with a particular agency? How will you handle exceptions that may arise?

• *Standards of acceptance for missionaries and projects.* What educational and training standards will you require? How will you measure training effectiveness?

• *Support principles.* What percentage of support will your church cover for each missionary? What specific conditions would necessitate termination of support?

• *Reporting policies.* What types of reporting should you expect? How often should you receive reports, and what requirements do you have for personal visits to your church?

---

do to agencies, this approach heightens interest. One potential danger is that the particularly gifted or eloquent missionary is likely to get the lion's share of available support.

Protecting Money

How should missions money be accounted for? Church members want to know missions funds are being used effectively and as designated. The path of accountability usually runs through the agencies that channel the funds.

Evaluating the effectiveness of such investments presupposes considerable knowledge. Church leaders can obtain information on host-country conditions, spiritual needs, and appropriate methods and strategies from experienced missionaries and missiologists. An informed approach enables a church to develop a wise giving strategy. This could involve deliberately channeling funds to unevangelized areas of the world while withdrawing support for wasteful programs. Such an approach also challenges exorbitant mission-agency overhead costs.

Having accurate and detailed information can also help local leaders respond wisely to the "cheap" solutions sometimes being proposed today. Money-saving plans such as tentmaking, send-money-not-missionaries, and some short-term programs may end up being more costly long term.

Giving Money

How can a church establish its giving priorities? Financing missions is not, at its most foundational level, just an organizing and promoting task. Since giving to missions is a direct expression of the importance a church places on world evangelization, congregations must grow together in their understanding of the theological and humanitarian beliefs that impel them to give. In order for that to happen, leaders must lift up the church's missionary responsibility by providing adequate, up-to-date information about the progress of the gospel message in the world. Then church members will have to make hard choices, such as having to abandon some worthy local projects in favor of other projects in remote places.

—*Edward Rommen*

• *Evaluation procedures.* How will your church evaluate its missionaries, projects, and programs?

Planning an Annual Missions Conference

In many churches the quickest way to empty the pews is to announce a missions speaker. Sadly, we have allowed missions presentations to seem less exciting than the evening news. Yet a missions conference need not be a two-week marathon of meetings at the church. Many congregations are proclaiming a month of missions emphasis. Others have two or three mini-conferences annually focused on world evangelization.

Here are a few basic guidelines for holding an exciting missions event: (1) Begin with prayer; (2) establish a purpose for the event; (3)

Promoting Missions

Missions ministry in the local church is not what it used to be. Even ten years ago, we could count on dozens of people showing up on a weeknight for a missions speaker scheduled to show slides of an overseas assignment. In these days of double-income families, competing outside interests, and a barrage of stimuli from all quarters, it is difficult to draw people to a specially scheduled missions event. Even missions fairs do not seem to draw. Therefore, we need to develop creative alternatives in order to maintain missions interest.

Creative Promotion

The most effective way to promote missions is through sending people of all ages on short-term, cross-cultural missions trips. Besides offering opportunities to contribute through team projects, these missions trips provide ideal environments for learning about missions. Volunteers should be commissioned during a Sunday worship service prior to departure, symbolizing their going on behalf of all the members of the congregation. Short-term missioners become our best advocates upon their return to the church. Some ultimately sense the call to become full-time missionaries themselves.

Beyond sending people to view the work of missions firsthand, what else can we do to promote interest in the local church? Here are three other alternatives to the standard "missionary and slides" meetings on Wednesday night:

• *Establish a "missions prayer partnership" program.* To do this, publish a brochure listing the missionaries your church supports and ask members to adopt a missionary family. Members promise to correspond with and pray for that particular missionary family. Any time the missionary comes home on furlough, those who have adopted that individual or family will serve as hosts, providing hospitality and

begin planning at least 11 months prior to the event; (4) promote the event as special, and then make it special; and (5) evaluate thoroughly, and then adjust next year's plan as needed.

It's best to include all major groups within the church. Early in the planning stage, leaders should start communicating with key group leaders to gain cooperation and input. Then the committee can work with them so the missions event does not conflict with regular ministries but rather complements them.

Maintaining Missionary Care

Missionaries should not have to beg to be remembered. A missions-active church cares for its missionaries, both by maintaining consistent, compassionate, direct contact with them, and by doing big and

friendship. In addition, those who are receiving more detailed information can lift up special needs to the missions committee for appropriate action. Church families could even plan a vacation to visit their adopted missionary families on the field.

- *Schedule a minute-for-mission during worship.* This moment during every worship service could sometimes include a word from a visiting missionary on furlough. Most often, it would highlight the country and ministry of one of the missionaries. A volunteer missions reporter might tell a little about what the missionary does and suggest specific prayer needs. Some churches use this weekly opportunity to highlight the financial support they provide, so that this becomes a valuable stewardship tool as well.
- *Infiltrate already-scheduled meetings.* It is challenging to add yet another evening out for many families. Therefore, a strategic technique that provides forums for missionaries to speak is to utilize already-scheduled Sunday school classes, evening meetings, and regular fellowship groups. This strategy gives quality time with smaller groupings. It also helps missionary speakers establish personal friendships by bringing them into contact with people in settings that encourage lively give-and-take dialogue.

Good Resources

Several agencies can assist leaders in the local church as they promote missions interest. Discover the World, Inc., of Pasadena, California, has developed a highly effective and interesting five-week seminar. A more academically oriented training program for teaching missions in the local church is the popular "Perspectives on the World Christian Movement," developed by the U.S. Center for World Mission (also based in Pasadena). Advancing Churches in Mission Commitment (ACMC) of Wheaton, Illinois, can provide tremendous resources to assist in a variety of missions-promotion ideas.

—David A. Dolan

small behind-the-scenes things that increase their ministry effectiveness. The church at Philippi provided continual support for missionary Paul, giving us an excellent scriptural pattern to follow.

Here are a few ways to maintain high levels of care and concern for missionary families:

• *Pray for them regularly.* Many churches have abandoned the traditional Wednesday night prayer meeting, but if you do have groups that meet regularly for prayer, here are some suggestions from George Verwer, international director of Operation Mobilization: (1) Mobilize as many people as possible to present short, specific requests at intervals during the prayer time; (2) read aloud "hot" items from the newspapers—relevant political news or items about religious oppression—to lend a sense of urgency; (3) use visual aids to focus on prayer needs; (4) if you have a guest speaker, communicate clearly that the bulk of the meeting time is for prayer; (5) emphasize different forms of prayer, especially praise, thanksgiving, worship, and intercession; and (6) use small groups to pray, introducing fresh requests every five to ten minutes.

• *Keep up with them through regular, live contact.* With today's wonderful technologies, there is little reason for poor communication. Make full use of modern tools that are far superior to the standard prayer letter that used to be distributed six weeks after it was written. For example, use the telephone to contact your missionaries on a regular basis. Use the fax machine to send and receive communications, or investigate whether your missionary already uses an electronic-mail system with his or her personal computer. Consider sending and receiving video clips for sharing in prayer gatherings on both sides of the relationship. Also check with your mission agency or board to see if they offer an 800 number that could function as a prayer hot line. When implementing any of these suggestions, plan to supply the equipment or pay for the cost of the communication as part of your ministry to the missionary family. As much as possible, make live connections *during* your meetings for prayer.

• *Invite church members to write them personal letters.* Many churches have pre-addressed mailgrams near the missions display, but are they used? Use creative ways to get your church members to write to your missionary family.

• *Take on special projects on their behalf.* Be sure to coordinate with their supervising agency. Provide tools to make their tasks easier or more effective. Or, on a more personal level, consider "adopting" the missionary's children as a special project. One of the most significant hindrances to new recruits is the fear of what might happen to their children. Ask what you can do to help alleviate that fear.

Yard work duties for the Lord don't have to be boring. If viewed as key purposes of the church, working in the harvest field, planting seed, cultivating, and harvesting, will bring great satisfaction. The task for the missions leadership team in the local church is to provide an environment in which each member of the body finds a way to contribute.

—*Kenneth W. Campbell*

Resources

Borthwick, P. 1987. A mind for missions: Ten ways to build your world vision. Colorado Springs: NavPress.

Church missions policy handbook. 1987. Wheaton, Ill.: ACMC, Inc.

Cultivating a missions-active church. 1988. Wheaton, Ill.: ACMC, Inc.

Duewel, W. 1986. Touch the world through prayer. Grand Rapids: Zondervan.

Lovering, K. 1984. Missions idea notebook. Charlotte: SIM International.

Local Missions Projects

The bumper sticker that says "Think Globally, Act Locally" can be a helpful challenge to mission-minded churches. Yes, it is important to pray for, contribute to, and go to the ends of the earth as we were instructed by our Lord in Acts 1:8. Yet, in this same passage, we are also challenged to go to our Jerusalems, Judeas, and Samarias.

Sometimes it is easier to go halfway around the world on a short-term mission trip than to work diligently in our own backyards year after year. Yet we may find increased local mission work generates more interest in global mission.

Getting Started Locally

The way to begin in local ministry is simply to go out into the community and see what we can see. We can drive and walk the streets of the community, go to local coffee shops and hear what people are saying, and talk with local officials to find out what they are concerned about. We can talk with the homeless, the disadvantaged, and others, and ask them what they are concerned about. It is amazing how many social projects are started without any consideration of the concerns of those being served!

When we find out what other churches are already doing, instead of reinventing the wheel, we may be able to enhance already-existing programs. Another way to begin involvement is to establish a partnership with another congregation. This congregation may be located in a different section of town and represent a different cultural background. Cooperative projects can be developed that foster deeper relationships and understanding among the cultures. It is important that such partnerships be coequal, avoiding a paternalistic situation by growing into a healthy sister-church relationship.

Deciding What To Do

As we ponder potential local-ministry projects, we should consider the priorities Jesus Christ lifted up in Matthew 25 when he singled out the hungry, the thirsty, the stranger, the naked, the sick, and those in prison. This list represents some of the greatest needs in contemporary society.

The parable of the Good Samaritan (Luke 10: 25–37) serves as a model for appropriate holistic ministry. As we remember Jesus' admonition to make disciples of all nations (Matt. 28:19), which includes people residing in the city, we can strive to keep a balance between evangelism and social action in our priorities. *The Lausanne Covenant* is a helpful guide to balanced ministry, locally and globally.

Some possible projects to consider include setting up homeless shelters, soup kitchens, and food banks; scheduling rest home visitations; sponsoring Boy Scout or Girl Scout troops for disadvantaged youth; or running a Meals on Wheels program, a Young Life Club, or a health clinic. Some churches have launched into gang-prevention programs or creative forms of street evangelism.

A book that can help us determine what ministries to focus on is *The Urban Christian* (InterVarsity) by Ray Bakke. It contains exercises and directions to assist church leaders as they evaluate their community, its needs, and how to implement local ministry. Robert C. Linthicum has written a helpful biblical perspective on urban ministry, titled *City of God, City of Satan: A Biblical Theology of the Urban Church* (Zondervan).

Several organizations support local-mission projects with resources, conferences, and opportunities for networking. These include International Urban Associates and their related Leadership Foundations (Chicago), the Seminary Consortium for Urban Pastoral Education (SCUPE, Chicago), World Vision International's Office of Urban Advance (Monrovia, California), and the Christian Community Development Association (Pasadena, California).

—*David A. Dolan*

National Missions Projects

From the start of the Christian era, *mission* has referred to more than just the ministry carried on in someone else's country. Jesus told his disciples that although their witness was to extend to the "uttermost parts of the earth," it would begin in their own national territory (see Acts 1:8).

What was true in Jesus' home country is true for us, too. Though we usually think of missions as crossing the boundaries of cultures, language, religion, and geography, there are pockets of considerable need within our own boundaries at home.

The Challenge at Home

Pastors and Christian workers must take the lead in awakening the church to spiritual concern for an increasingly multicultural America. Congregations need to see the foreigners in their midst and develop new, positive attitudes that will issue in creative outreach strategies. Consider just three of the groups with whom we can express Christ's love and share the gospel on this continent:

• *Legal immigrants.* About 700,000 legal immigrants from all over the world arrive in America each year. Over 50 percent of these arrivals come from areas designated by missions as "unreached." Peoples from the Muslim, Hindu, and Buddhist world are becoming our next-door neighbors in great numbers. Immigration of the Chinese alone has increased 107 percent in the last decade, and there are now 23 million Hispanic persons in the United States. A language other than English is now spoken in 20 percent of American homes.

• *International students.* Yearly, over 500,000 international students study in America. Some of these students attend the college or university near any of us. They are the cream of the intellectual crop of their countries, clearly future influencers of life and policy around the world. Do we know how to reach out to them?

• *Native Americans.* America's original inhabitants still constitute a mission field. Nearly five hundred tribes—speaking 250 languages—are now larger in number than they were before the Europeans ever arrived. Indians today struggle to keep their identity, even as the majority of them live in our larger cities alongside other minorities waiting to be reached.

We have countless churches and media ministries in North America, but this does not mean all persons have the opportunity to worship in ways relevant to them. Local churches need to work hard to ensure that all North Americans can hear the gospel—in terms and conditions that do not in themselves constitute cultural barriers to communication.

Existing Ministries

A number of ministries enable believers and churches to have a missionary impact right in North America. International Students Incorporated has a staff of 148 workers reaching out to internationals on 1,263 campuses in 73 cities. Staff members teach local churches and families how to reach out cross-culturally in their home towns. They currently have about nine thousand volunteers working with them to reach international students.

Some concerned denominations and churches are targeting newer minorities and effectively forming churches and ministries among them. For example, one church hosts a multicultural center, with "one-stop shopping" for various social and spiritual services for local Vietnamese, Cambodians, Laotians, and Hispanics. First Baptist Church of Dallas houses congregations of five different language groups and has started numerous foreign-language churches.

Other ministries worth investigating:

International Students
Incorporated
P.O. Box C
Colorado Springs, CO 80901
(719) 576-2700

SIM Ethnic Focus Ministry
P.O. Box 1251
Wheaton, IL 60189
(708) 653-4221

Multi-Language Media
Box 301
Ephrata, PA 17522
(717) 738-0582

The Intercultural Press, Inc.
P.O. Box 700
Yarmouth, ME 04096
(207) 846-5168

American Missionary Fellowship
P.O. Box 368
Villanova, PA 19085
(215) 527-4439

—*Michael Pocock*

World Missions Projects

Hardly anything energizes a church and expands its vision as much as a tangible involvement with world missions. Yet, a congregation is often so preoccupied with what happens within the four walls of the church that it forgets about the exciting things God is doing around the world, even though the local church is God's primary method of world evangelization.

To encourage greater involvement in world missions, we must constantly define and prioritize. We must have a clear understanding of exactly what missions is and exactly where to invest our greatest efforts.

Defining Missions

Church members can be confused about the term "missions." The tendency in the North American church is to call everything we do missions, and this diminishes the true meaning of the word. The "mission" of the church does refer to everything the Lord has called us to do. In light of this, we are to witness to our neighbors, preach the Word, feed the poor, and carry out a score of other ministries. "Missions," however, has a much narrower focus and definition. When we speak of missions, we are talking about those activities that reach beyond the regular ministries of the local church. Missions usually involves crossing cultural barriers in an attempt to share the gospel with people who have little or no opportunity to hear it. Although we are all commanded to evangelize our neighbors, the work of missions calls the church to reach out to the world, to cross barriers of culture and language, and to develop specialized ministries to win people for Jesus Christ.

Because "missions" is an action word, any church considering involvement in world missions should be pro-active in its strategy. If we only respond to those who come to us with their requests, we soon will find most of our budget and personnel going to local concerns. Many churches have found it helpful to set guidelines concerning how much of their missions budget will go to local, national, and world missions. This allows them to guard their resources for those projects and ministries that are of the highest priority.

Determining Priorities

How do we decide priority? The majority of missionaries currently work in areas already penetrated by the gospel to some extent. On the other hand, a relatively small percentage of missionaries are working among the three largest unreached groups: the Muslims, the Hindus, and the Chinese. Simple fairness would tell us we need to invest more of our future missionaries in reaching these people who have little or no opportunity to hear the gospel.

Geographically, most of these groups live in well-defined areas. From North Africa through Central Asia to China, we find nearly three billion people, most of whom belong to one of these three large, unreached groups. One way a church can focus its world-missions program is to set aside a certain percentage of resources to support candidates and projects ministering in these areas.

We must also define our priorities in terms of the ministry activities themselves. Although every job in the mission field is important, no church wants to have its entire missions budget going to home-office support! Missions groups employ dozens of strategies to communicate the gospel, and most have some degree of validity. The highest priority, however, must be that of church planting. Only by planting indigenous churches within the target culture can we provide an authentic, biblical witness capable of reaching its own culture for Christ and then discipling the converts to maturity.

—Robert L. Schneider

Mission Study

For many years, those passionate about the subject of missions have argued that the Bible is the very basis for missions. More recently, those teaching on the subject have gone further and contended that missions is the basis of the Bible. Both are right.

For our people to have a proper understanding of God's plan for missions, they must know its biblical and theological foundations. But to truly understand the message of the Bible, we must see that missions is at the heart of all that Scripture communicates. Thus the need to study missions in the church.

Motivate and Educate

Well-known missions educator Ralph Winter has said that to understand the subject of missions properly, we need to study both the Bible and the great eras and people of missions history. The question facing our churches is how to motivate Christians to pursue such studies and then be able to integrate the biblical and historical materials in a dynamic and stimulating way.

Both the motivation and the instruction must be done with excellence if we are to make an impact on our people and help them develop as world Christians. By giving current, accurate, and dynamic information to our congregations, not only do we nurture their growth as world Christians but we also enable them to make better decisions concerning how they will use their spiritual gifts and what vocational paths they will choose.

Throughout the year church leaders can provide missions updates to keep the congregation current on what God is doing around the world. A monthly missions forum on a weekday night allows missionaries on furlough to talk about their ministries abroad. Or churches can set aside an evening service once each quarter so that more people from the church can be exposed to the world of missions.

The annual missions conference can be an excellent time to educate a congregation about missions. Often churches send missionaries into existing group meetings for women, youth, seniors, and children, rather than try to create and promote new events. Special events work best when they are fun and lively, such as children-parent pizza parties or a youth sports night with the missionaries. Whatever the event to provide missions motivation and information, we should do it with excellence and enthusiasm.

Ready Resources

Churches can take advantage of a wide variety of educational resources today. Bulletin inserts, such as *The Church Around the World,* are available from many organizations. To educate the missions committee, many churches use the fine publications *Pulse* and *The Evangelical Missions Quarterly* from the Evangelical Missions Information Service.

Many churches simply do not know where to begin to educate their children and youth about missions or how to have a missions conference. One fine organization dedicated to helping churches in these areas is Advancing Churches in Missions Commitment, in Wheaton, Illinois. The group provides a wide variety of materials and manuals, and trains local lay leaders through regional conferences and consultations.

An adult course, *Perspectives on the World Christian Movement,* developed by the U.S. Center for World Missions, has been taken by over 100,000 people throughout the United States. It covers nearly everything a person would want to know about the world of missions today. Another helpful seminar in this vein, *Destination 2000,* is produced by Bob Sjogren of the Frontiers mission agency.

—Robert L. Schneider

10

Sending Missioners

Some church leaders say the age of Western-dominated, Western-based, and Western-directed missionary work is over. Does the North American church have a sending and supporting role in the future of world missions?

The answer has to be a resounding "Yes!" based on both the scriptural commands and the intense spiritual needs evident around the world. The future of Western church missions support rests on how well these churches work hand-in-glove with both sending agencies and the established churches and mission agencies overseas.

Becoming a Sending Church

Jesus did not make obedience to his great world-evangelizing command (in Matt. 28:19–20) contingent upon changing political, economic, religious, and ecclesiastical conditions. The evangelistic, church-planting fervor of the early church must be maintained at all costs. This means the vitality of world outreach depends upon the vitality and enthusiasm of pastors and their congregations.

Under ideal conditions, each church should grow its own potential missionaries; guide them into productive ministries with reputable agencies; and maintain their spiritual, emotional, and financial stability through the years. This means local believers would learn—from early childhood on—through every part of the church's program that world needs and local resources must always be linked.

This will not happen if the church relegates world missions to a minor committee, a women's prayer circle, or a few special events each year. The goal is to put world missions at the center of the church's life. If the pastoral staff and each church department can find both a natural fit and a spirit of enthusiasm, world missions will be as integral to the church's life as the cylinders are to an automobile engine.

The sending church will want to consistently reinforce its members so they can clearly articulate answers to the basic question: *Why send missionaries?* Yet, since every church agenda is stacked with many worthwhile endeavors, priorities must be established, based on both Scripture and needs in the world. The preaching and teaching programs of the church should include ample biblical evidence that God's love is universal and that, from the beginning, both Israel and the church were to be lights to the nations. To be God's instrument of salvation, righteousness, and peace, the church must be critically informed about millions of people who have never heard the gospel, about the religious and ideological conflicts competing for the souls of millions, and about the spiritual strength and wisdom needed by Christians and missionaries around the world. A healthy church, then, one that will both grow and attract missionaries, will take the initiative to have both biblically taught and world-sensitive members.

These goals can happen when the church's leaders make both short- and long-range plans. World missions must figure in all planning and scheduling sessions relating to preaching, praying, choosing curriculum, and organizing special events. In multistaff situations, each leader could develop means of accountability for a missions emphasis in his or her particular area of church life.

Deciding Who to Send

When the church becomes solidly convinced that sending missionaries is its God-given duty and therefore must have priority in its program, the next question is: *Who shall we send, and how?* Should we send everyone who wants to go, long-term or short-term? Who should we link with here in the States and on the field? What will be our responsibilities once we send our people out?

Generally, churches find missionaries to send not only from their own ranks but also from mission boards. Denominational boards may or may not assign specific missionaries to the churches. Some denominations assign their missionaries to regions rather than to local churches, giving the missionaries a wider exposure to various congregations.

Independent boards maintain lists of appointed missionary candidates who are looking for local-church support. Churches are welcome to invite these candidates to come and speak and to present their needs. At that time, church leaders can interview them and ask them to stay in the homes of church members.

What should the church look for in the people it intends to send to the field? Here are some things to inquire about and evaluate:

- *Spiritual maturity.* Candidates should reflect a warm walk in faith with Jesus Christ. The mark of God's hand upon their lives, their families, and their ministries should be clearly evident.
- *Current ministry involvement.* Are candidates using their spiritual gifts right now? Whatever they propose to do overseas should match what they are doing now: Helping people come to faith in Christ, teaching Bible classes, helping new Christians to grow, pitching in with work projects, caring for hurting people, counseling, helping neighbors, visiting shut-ins, and so on.
- *Academic qualifications.* Requirements vary according to ministry and mission board stipulations. Apart from specialized training, candidates should at least have a thorough grounding in biblical studies, theology, missions, anthropology, and linguistics. Language-acquisition aptitudes can be tested in advance.
- *Doctrinal compatibility.* Each church should make sure its missionaries agree with the church's theological perspectives. Again, depending on the church's stance, there may be some room for variance on certain issues. For instance, how important are eschatological views for the missionary teaching English as a second language in Russia?
- *Personal integrity.* Candidates for missionary service should be able to show that honesty, truthfulness, and integrity have marked their lives.
- *Missionary vision.* Missionaries should be able to explain why they want to serve overseas and how God has led them in that direction. What do they hope to accomplish for God? What are the biblical roots of their convictions?
- *Positive peer evaluation.* Again, character is the issue. Others ought to be able to testify to the potential missionary's commitment to Christ and to godly living.
- *Commitment to the church.* The church is the proving ground for service in God's kingdom. Out of a vital church life come prayer and financial support. If the candidate came to faith in Christ later in life, without roots in a local church, the church may well require one or two years of service and fellowship within a local congregation.
- *Sacrificial spirit.* Sacrifice is at the heart of missions, and the overriding spirit of missionary service is that of a servant. Would-be missionaries need to show this spirit before they leave for the field. A church can only gauge the willingness to sacrifice if there is time to

develop a strong relationship with the potential missionary in the context of practical ministry work.

• *Healthy family life.* Many new missionaries carry scars from previous family problems. Churches and boards need to probe candidates' past histories frankly and find out what is being done to maintain strong marriage and family relationships. In some cases, church leaders will ask candidates to spend some time in counseling. Churches cannot assume that just because people want to be missionaries, they have solid marriages and families.

• *Willingness to grow home-based partners.* Although financial-support policies vary from board to board, all of them insist that their missionaries build a strong prayer-support team at home. Therefore, the church should encourage new missionaries to build strong relationships among the people in all their supporting churches.

Roles of Missionaries

Jesus told his disciples to go into the world and make disciples of all nations. This may sound like a singular task, but if we imagine missionaries all doing the same thing, we are mistaken. Most missionaries would say they are trying to glorify God by witnessing to the life-changing power of Jesus Christ. The God they serve, however, is a God of great variety.

A Diversified Ministry

Far from acting out the old stereotyped image of pith-helmeted, khaki-shorts-clad workers marching through swamps, today's missionary may be found doing mime on the streets of Amsterdam or showing the *Jesus* film in Uzbekistan. He or she may be producing radio programs that will air around the world from superpower stations as widely scattered as Ecuador, Monte Carlo, or the Seychelles Islands.

Plenty of rural workers are still needed, but even in remotest Irian Jaya, a translator's face may be lit by the glow of a computer screen. High tech and a close touch often characterize missionary work today. A relief worker in Somalia cradles a feverish, dehydrated baby and administers the latest antibiotic, while worlds away another teaches English to Japanese university students in a totally different environment.

Contrast and variety mark what missionaries do today, yet each one tries to apply an age-old gospel message with the latest technology that fits the situation.

A Biblical Impetus

Can all these various roles be traced to the Bible? Certainly! Consider the apostle Paul's ministry as an example. Paul said his main aim was to preach the gospel to those who had never heard it. Such groups are called *unreached peoples.* Stretching beyond our existing limits to reach them must be a priority

Throughout the process of preparation, application, and approval, the church seeks to build strong ties with its missionaries before they go overseas. Some require a year or two of internship on the staff, or in the pastorate, or with some form of home-based ministry among students, internationals, or the urban poor, for example. The goal is to assure that once the missionaries leave, they will be more than just a name on the church's support list or a picture on the world map.

Providing Support

Churches provide missionary support in various ways. Traditionally, missions giving is lumped under "benevolences" and assigned to the denomination's budget. Even so, it helps if the church receives current reports from the field, disseminates those reports from the

focus today. It is the only basis on which we can finish the task of world evangelization. Yet we can have focus and balance at the same time. Paul also taught *newly reached peoples* in person and through his epistles.

Paul reached out to *misled people,* too: those who had their Scriptures, leaders, and meeting places but no spiritual reality. They were the Jews. In our time, these misled people may be nominal Christians, of which there are vast numbers in Europe, Latin America, Africa, and North America.

In addition to these ministry targets, Paul was involved with helping *unfed peoples.* He conducted an ongoing relief program for famine-plagued Palestinians, demonstrating that this kind of work is truly a part of missionary endeavor. Paul was a man of both focus and balance, and that's what's needed on the mission field today.

A Challenging Future

Missionaries at the end of the twentieth century face a wide spectrum of needs among over 6,000 language groups. They will continue to evangelize, train leaders, establish churches, and distribute Bibles and Christian literature, yet new challenges will bring new roles for missionaries.

For example, who would have dreamed that with the collapse of Marxism around the world, missionaries would be asked to provide educational systems to impart Christian values and morality to entire nations?

Churches now support missionaries doing a wide range of ministries. This means there is a place of service for a variety of people in any given congregation. Some tasks can be done in a matter of weeks; some on a short-term basis of one or two years. Still others call for a lifetime commitment.

Variety of roles means breadth of opportunity. The task of the Christian missionary, then, is to keep the single gospel message central while meeting multifaceted needs with a variety of methods.

—*Michael Pocock*

pulpit and in Sunday school classes, and makes sure the missionaries are prayed for regularly. People will respond to these needs if the information they receive is fresh and personal.

As noted above, many churches build their own missions budgets around support for missionaries, missions projects, and relief and development needs. It helps if a special committee looks at these needs and then promotes them effectively, so the people can tie their giving to specific people and projects. When new missionaries are invited and need support, their needs can be considered as well, so that the church's missions giving increases annually. At the same time, the missions budget should be increased annually for each missionary to keep pace with inflation and to insure that these workers do not have to return from the field with deficit accounts.

Deputation and Furlough

Deputation is the time-honored word for what missionaries do to raise financial and prayer support prior to going to the field. *Furlough* refers to the year in which missionaries return home, usually every three or four years, to report back to their supporting churches and agencies. Supporting congregations need to consider carefully their role with and ministry to missionaries who are either raising funds in preparation for the field or returning home on furlough.

Help with Deputation

Once a missionary candidate is appointed by a board, the board assigns specific sums to be raised, usually in two categories: monthly support and outbound, or launch, funds. (Missionaries who belong to denominations that pool funds from local-church missions budgets do not have to travel among churches to raise individual support.) Many missionaries spend one or more years raising sufficient funds to go overseas.

Churches can help these people in many ways. For example, the congregation can: (1) Take on a significant amount of the support initially, either by drawing from the church's missions budget or by asking individuals to contribute; (2) provide housing, transportation, jobs, and child care while missionaries are on deputation; and (3) offer the names of other churches and individuals who would be likely prospects for the missionaries to visit.

Deputation is a time of intense faith stretching. Missionaries doing deputation work need much encouragement and prayer during these months or years. They must be delivered from feeling like beggars as they go from church to church raising funds for the worthy purposes of kingdom work around the world.

Some churches also encourage their members to take on additional support of missionaries beyond the church's budget. So when missionaries are invited to come and present their work and their needs, they may receive not only support from the church but from specific individuals as well.

Beyond building financial support, the church must also work to develop daily prayer support for its missionaries. Of course, prayer for missionaries must be included at the worship services and midweek services, as well as in men's, women's, and youth prayer circles. Missionary prayer cards and letters work well for this purpose. Many churches also establish telephone hookups with missionaries during regular services in order to receive fresh news from the field. In addition, members may divide up the responsibility for writing to each

Furlough Encouragement

Furlough is now often called the "home ministry assignment," because some mission boards think "furlough" sounds too much like scheduled relaxation. Missionaries do have heavy responsibilities during furlough. They need to arrange for physical check-ups. They must find housing, transportation, and schools for their children. They will attempt to visit all of their supporting churches. If their support funds have fallen behind or the cost of living has gone up where they serve, they have to raise more money.

Many missionary families find the furlough experience particularly demanding and draining as they begin readjusting to life back home. Churches can help alleviate some of this stress in a number of ways. Consider these suggestions:

- *Offer free housing.* Some churches keep apartments and houses available for their missionaries. In other places, special agencies do this.
- *Provide transportation and clothing.* Missionaries coming from tropical climates will need warm clothing if they furlough in the north. Church families often have a spare car that missionaries can use.
- *Set up meetings.* Be sure the missionaries have one or more meetings with church leaders to give them firsthand reports. The missionaries should also be able to schedule informal times in the homes of various church members. As soon as possible, the missionaries should be given prime time to speak to the entire congregation and answer questions.
- *Plan and conduct review sessions.* Church leaders should review the missionaries' work over their last term and discuss their goals and assignments for the next term. It's also important to review future support needs. The missionaries may also need guidance from the church as they think through their next steps, in consultation with their sending board.
- *Encourage down time.* Hard workers need rest! The church might want to pay for a vacation somewhere. If the missionaries desire some refresher courses, the church can offer to pay the tuition.

—*James W. Reapsome*

missionary at least once a month. Sending quarterly "care packages" and special remembrances at birthdays and anniversaries brings added encouragement to overseas workers. Of course, as time and finances permit, church leaders should visit their missionaries on the field. Church members who travel overseas on business or vacations might also include visits to missionaries.

Evaluating Missions Agencies

To be effective and to exercise wise stewardship, the church needs to look not only at its missionaries' financial packages. The church must also evaluate the actual ministries to be carried out and the agencies with which the missionaries wish to serve. One of the best ways to begin mission-agency evaluation is to determine if the agency belongs to one of the major associations of mission boards: either the Evangelical Fellowship of Mission Agencies or the Interdenominational Foreign Mission Associations. These associations require stiff entrance tests for members and keep them maintaining high standards. Of course, not all reputable boards belong to these groups, for one reason or another. Another association giving financial credibility to charitable organizations is the Evangelical Council for Financial Accountability. A complete directory of mission agencies is published by MARC Publications (919 W. Huntington Drive, Monrovia, CA 91016).

Of course, it is important that the church invite someone from the mission to come for a visit and to bring all the necessary documents: financial audits, doctrinal statements, annual and five-year goals, reports from the field, the board's principles and practices, and names and addresses of other supporting churches. At this time the church can also go over the board's proposed support package for the missionaries, so that every dollar is accounted for. The church should also be clear about ministry assignments, conditions on the field, supervision on the field, and annual evaluations. For example, the church should expect a report of progress after the first year of language school.

The church and its missionaries should also look at strategic needs around the world. Simply because some people volunteer to work overseas and pass all the mission board's requirements does not necessarily mean the church should line up for support. For example, some countries are overloaded with missionaries, while others have relatively few Christian workers. Hundreds of tribal groups have no witness at all.

The church should also seek a balance in missionary vocations, too. Relatively few people volunteer to do pioneer evangelism and church planting, compared to the number who want to work at discipleship, church development, teaching, and so on. The task of training believers seems to attract more people than the challenge of starting new churches, either in urban high-rises or jungle villages. Since the church sees world missions as partnership, it should raise questions about assignments and about working with existing churches and the new mission agencies springing up overseas.

To get a feel for needs and opportunities around the world, a church might ask specialists to do research on both agencies and countries. Choose a number of agencies and ask to receive their magazines. Write to denominational headquarters for information. If the church is near a Christian college or seminary, the library will have numerous missions periodicals. The Evangelical Missions Information Service (Box 794, Wheaton, IL 60189) publishes *Evangelical Missions Quarterly* and *World Pulse Newsletters* to help churches and missionaries stay abreast of trends and needs.

Many churches gain valuable information and help from an organization called Advancing Churches in Missions Commitment (Box ACMC, Wheaton, IL 60189). This group publishes an excellent series of handbooks designed to help churches develop a vital missions program. It also sponsors regional training conferences across the country, encouraging churches with strong missions programs to help neighbor churches just getting started. Another organization devoted to helping churches start and maintain vital missions programs is World Thrust (Box 450105, Atlanta, GA 30345).

World evangelization is nothing if it is not partnership. Churches will find that most agencies are eager to help them launch successful, satisfying missionary-sending and support programs. Churches, missionaries, and boards are not antagonists. During their years of preparation and training, most missionaries begin to develop specific ministry goals and discover certain affinities for countries and people groups. They also begin to explore agencies that seem to offer both doctrinal and ministry compatibilities.

Here's a summary of what to look for in a mission board:

• *Doctrinal harmony*. Examine the published doctrinal statement carefully. Be sure it fits with the church's overall convictions. While talking with mission-board representatives and member missionaries, determine whether the agency is broad or narrow in its doctrinal convictions. Does it require strong internal consistency on such things as baptism, eschatology, church government, and relations with other churches and missions? Or does it have a broad latitude of acceptance?

An agency may say it is interdenominational, but over the years it may have developed some firmly held convictions that closely resemble those of a particular denomination. Ask what churches and denominations are represented among its missionaries. Ask what traditions have been elevated to doctrines. Read books and articles written by the board's leaders.

• *Compatible goals and policies.* Find out what the mission's purposes are. Why does it exist? What is it trying to accomplish? How well has it reached its own goals?

After examining both short- and long-range goals, decide if the emerging destination is where your church wants to go. Would the church risk everything to reach those goals? Do the church's goals, temperament, and ethos fit those of the mission board?

Ask whether the mission periodically reexamines its purposes and goals. Is there a regular review process in place? What new goals and strategies have appeared recently to show that the mission adapts to changes overseas and at home?

After hearing about policy positions, ask deeper questions about items the church doesn't agree with or understand. Such questions might relate to financial-support policies, field administration, agency government, rules of conduct, children's education provisions, health insurance administration, retirement practices, housing provisions, or furlough procedures.

Some boards are quite authoritarian, others less strict. Churches should try to find the best fit for their missionaries, as they assess candidates' gifts and temperaments. Church leaders should not give in to missionaries who want to work with a mission board that the church does not totally agree with, just for the sake of getting someone overseas.

• *A broad vision.* Does the mission's planning approach reflect creativity? Do the leaders constantly search for new ways to become more effective? Or does this agency give the impression of being tied only to traditional ways of doing things? The sending church should look for fresh ideas and broad vision, for "new worlds to conquer" enthusiasm.

• *Significant past accomplishments.* As the church's missionaries head for a specific field and ministry, they should look for the mission's track record there. Are the people already on that field encouraged by what has already happened, or are they giving up and coming home? Does the field show evidence of the Holy Spirit at work in measurable terms?

The church needs to ask about relationships and partnerships on the field among missionaries, between missionaries and the national church, and between the mission and other missions, home and international. Do these relationships reflect harmony or contention?

• *Agreeable lifestyle perspectives.* Probably the most difficult matter to probe is the mission's general attitude toward lifestyle issues. This attitude is shaped over the years by the agency's veterans, and it grows around unwritten codes. Key questions to ask are: Does the mission have a warm, family spirit? How do missionary wives or husbands, single-women missionaries, and children feel? How does the mission treat women and singles who may not fit the customary mold? Do any women have places of significant leadership? What are the attitudes about certain gray areas of Christian lifestyle, such as the use of tobacco or alcohol, or forms of entertainment?

• *An enthusiastic staff.* Most missionaries are attracted to a board because someone on the staff has ministered to them and because they sense top-quality people all around. That's the most impressive recommendation for a board—happy, satisfied, fulfilled staff people who know what they're doing. They reflect confidence in God's call and are excited to be part of his world mission. They are culturally aware, sensitive, and professional in every sense of the word. Candidates would consider it a great privilege to work with such staffs.

—James W. Reapsome

Resources

Borthwick, P. 1988. Youth and missions. Wheaton, Ill.: Victor.
Borthwick, P. 1991. How to be a world class Christian. Wheaton, Ill.: Victor.
Church missions policy handbook. 1987. Wheaton, Ill.: ACMC.
Cultivating a missions-active church. 1988. Wheaton, Ill.: ACMC.
Dayton, E. 1979. You can so get there from here. Monrovia, Calif.: MARC.
Johnstone, P. 1993. Operation world. Grand Rapids: Zondervan.
Missions education handbook. 1990. Wheaton, Ill.: ACMC.
Pirolo, N. 1991. Serving as senders. San Diego: Emnaus Road International.
Watkins, M. 1987. Missions resource handbook. Fullerton, Calif.: R.C. Law.
Watkins, M. 1987. Seven worlds to win. Fullerton, Calif.: R.C. Law.
Your church series (brochures). (No date). Wheaton, Ill.: ACMC.

Short-Term Mission Trips

After a commissioning service for youth mission teams, an elder asked about the group bound for Kenya: "Is that the capital of Africa?" While not every church member is this uninformed about foreign matters, most would benefit greatly from the kind of mission trip we send our youth on.

Preparing for the Trip

First, a church needs an appropriate place to go. One way to choose a place is by writing the missionaries supported by the church to inquire about possibilities. Some may be too busy to host a group; others might enjoy such a visit but have nothing for the group to do other than tour, and most churches want their groups to contribute something.

Still other missionaries or agencies may be looking for help and be able to use the services of a team. A limited project, such as painting a hospitality house, often works well. Better still, is the opportunity to work side by side with missionaries from one's own church — people committed to educating others about missions.

Next comes the question of finances. Keeping costs within the reach of volunteers is imperative. Sometimes missionaries can help arrange inexpensive lodging and meals. Cooperative travel agencies can use their expertise to cut travel costs, such as booking tickets for midweek flights rather than at peak times. In addition, the missions committee may earmark funds for volunteers needing aid.

At least six months before the trip, team leaders need to be recruited. Look for people who have overseas travel experience, administrative ability, and the willingness to go through a leader-training program. These leaders can, in turn, recruit team members. Everybody, then, prepares for the trip together, planning, working on projects, and building skills as a team.

Maximizing the Trip

A nine-day itinerary often works well to expose a team to the missionaries and their work. It gives time to actually accomplish something, but it also accommodates people who cannot take off two full weeks. It's wise to allocate time for visits to local churches, sightseeing trips for interest and exposure to other cultures, and lots of fellowship with the missionaries. Since adults often want to travel on their own (*following* the team project is advisable), it's good to allow that travel flexibility.

Nine days—including travel—pass quickly. How can leaders make sure those days contribute to the team members' growth as Christians committed to the Great Commission? One method is to debrief the team upon its return, helping members better understand their experience. Team members can also complete a follow-up evaluation, and often they want to hold a reunion.

A church can visibly affirm the team by featuring them in a service, holding an informational meeting, setting up a display booth in the fellowship hall, and reading about the trip in church mailings. The team needs to understand that their church is proud of their work and is interested in the many things they have learned. This public praise also plants seeds for future missions trips.

Following such trips, it is not uncommon for team members to become more active in the church's missions ministry. Some may join the missions committee; others may even pursue vocational missions service or become involved with agencies or ministries locally. Taking adults overseas often results in enlarged hearts and broadened vision for both participants and observers.

—Paul Borthwick

Youth Mission Teams

The summer work-and-ministry project had ended. The youth team had successfully painted the camp buildings—and alienated the resident missionaries. The evaluation was blunt: "They seemed more interested in pairing off with each other than in having significant contact with Indian students."

Service projects can be an eye-opening exposure to missions for teens. The projects can also benefit those on the receiving end. But young people need to go for the opportunity to serve, rather than the adventure.

The success of most summer missions trips is largely determined before the bus ever leaves the church parking lot. One key to success is implementing stiff requirements for team members, making the rules clear from the beginning. Interestingly, youth respond to such challenges with increased interest.

The requirements fall into two categories: personal preparation and team preparation.

Individual Preparation

What can individuals be held accountable for?

- *Application forms.* Have students answer questions such as "How do you know you're a Christian?" and "What are the strengths and weaknesses you will bring to your team?" Students can be required to furnish references who can describe their witness at school and their ability to work.
- *Writing assignments.* Given after acceptance onto the team, these assignments may include doing a book report on a missionary biography or a report about the climate, customs, language, and religion of the area where the team is going. Each team member can receive copies of the reports for his or her notebook.
- *Fund raising.* One workable system is for participants to be responsible for their own finances, including a $50 deposit two months before the departure date and the balance six weeks before the team leaves. Those needing aid can write letters to friends and relatives, or they can apply to the church missions committee for a subsidy.
- *Prayer support.* Have each student recruit three prayer partners, at least one of whom should come from outside the immediate family. This is a great way to involve students unable to go on a team.

Team Preparation

To prepare a mission group as a unit, the team must be formed no less than two months in advance. Team requirements may include:

- *A team retreat.* For kids to learn to work and pray together, required attendance at a training weekend is necessary. If other subgroups are to be formed, they ought to be given the opportunity to function together, too. Groups can develop a team covenant, which describes the Christian community they want as a team. Such a covenant should have at least four parts: team vision, team goals, team structure, and personal accountability.

• *Team meetings.* In addition to the retreat, three or four other meetings can be held with each team to give information, address the parents, answer questions, and cover everything from what clothes to pack to how not to insult a native. Team meetings also provide wonderful forums to draw a team together in prayer, thus building a spiritual base.

• *Team notebooks.* Everyone can receive an orientation manual, which includes instructions on cross-cultural adaptation and teamwork training, and space to organize notes, handouts, and team covenants. The notebook creates a seriousness within the team, giving teens a healthy sense of being professionals.

• *The team commissioning.* When most of the preparations are done, a church can set aside a special service to commission the teams. The youth can explain the work they will do and recite their team memory verses. The pastor may want to preach on servanthood. A highlight of the service is having the team members kneel as the elders and pastors lay hands on them and pray for their ministry.

—*Paul Borthwick*

Christian Travel

A minister and his wife collapse in their Jerusalem hotel room, happily fatigued by their day's tour of religious sites. Three Christian couples linger over coffee on board a spacious ocean liner steaming for Alaska. A retired couple dozes on a 747 returning from Nigeria, where they had visited their church's missionary. All these people have at least one thing in common: they're enjoying Christian travel—travel whose purpose is edification of faith.

• *Pilgrimages.* A pilgrimage to the Holy Land is the classic form of Christian travel and has been undertaken by millions of Christians since the days of the apostles. Naturally, Christians—whose faith is grounded in history, whose God "became flesh and dwelt among us"—are anxious to visit the places our Savior walked. Although most are interested in following the footsteps of Jesus, many also want to follow the travels of Moses, Isaiah, and Jeremiah, among others.

• *Recreation and fellowship.* Sometimes Christians simply want to enjoy a vacation in the fellowship of other believers, perhaps in the form of a cruise. The big advantage of a cruise is that everything is paid for in one fare: transportation, recreation, food, and lodging. Popular destinations for Christian cruises include the Caribbean, Alaska, the Greek islands, and Mexico. When groups sign up together, the group's devotions, dining, recreation, shore excursions, entertainment, and worship are planned by the Christian travel company.

• *Missions.* Christians also find their faith edified when they take mission trips to some needy environment and perform a service in the name of Christ. This usually means visiting a mission or missionary on location. Such a trip exposes people to new customs and cultures, and concretely demonstrates the need for Christ in all the world.

Planning Tips

Wise travelers need to think about many things. Here are a few items to keep in mind when planning a trip.

• Use an expert travel agent. Unless you're a true adventurer who likes to do research, write letters, and make myriad phone calls (and you don't mind taking chances during a trip), you will want a travel agent to plan for you. Modern international travel is complicated, and travel agents are in the business of overcoming the obstacles for you. If your travel is to an obscure mission station, look for a agent who specializes in *mission* travel and will know about more than typical tourist hot spots.

• Make sure your agent is reputable. How do you do it? Start by asking for friends' recommendations. Also check a potential agent's years of experience and make sure he or she belongs to the American Society of Travel Agents. The diligent traveler, however, will phone the prospective agency and ask for names of people who have recently used them. A reliable agent will quickly give such references.

• Plan at least six months in advance. Travel agents list this first when asked for tips. Some advise giving them nine to twelve months' advance notice.

• Don't merely jump at the cheapest trip package. For each package, compare items such as which side trips are included, how much transportation will cost, whether visas and airport taxes are included, and what is meant by "first-class accommodations." Any of these features can greatly affect the price of a trip.

• Include rest in your daily calendar. This not only gives elbow room to a crowded schedule that could go awry, but it also will help you enjoy the busier days of a trip. As one seasoned traveler put it: "Never run when you can walk. Never walk when you can stand. Never stand when you can sit. Never sit when you can lie down."

—*Mark Galli*

Part III:

Social Involvement

If Christianity means anything, it must have meaning for *all* parts of life—for culture, for politics, for ethics, for economics, for medicine, for science. We long ago decided against the notion of a dualistic God, one who affects souls but not bodies, minds but not hearts, prayers but not pocketbooks. No, our God is one whose kingdom is permeating all of life and eventually will rule it.

But we live in in-between times. The Adversary makes many aspects of life in the present less than kingdom quality. The world to come will be just and right, but in *this age,* the unborn are sacrificed, babies are malnourished, children are orphaned, young people are abandoned, adults are made victims of hate, and old people are left in despair. We live in a broken and hurting world, with vast needs and great inequities. Christians retain a monumental role to play.

We Christians have two avenues to continue this work that Jesus pioneered and then transfered to us to advance: social compassion (giving the cup of cold water) and social action (changing oppressive structures). It's not a matter of *if* we will do these ministries—Jesus didn't leave any other plan—but *how* we will perform them, and how faithfully.

The following articles offer plenty of practical advice from those who do the things they write about. They also present a theology of compassion and demonstrate a heart for service, both of which are necessary for the church wanting to make our world a better match with God's intentions.

11

The Purpose of Social Compassion and Social Action

Social concern and evangelism form the heart of the church's mission. Unfortunately, some Christians have viewed evangelism as the church's exclusive mandate, while others have emphasized only social concern. But biblical teaching, theology, and church history all advocate a mission that embodies both.

Social concern encompasses two primary forms: social compassion and social action. Social compassion involves direct, concrete ministry to existing social, physical, and emotional needs. Church-sponsored hospitals, prison ministries, food banks, shelters, soup kitchens, and educational programs down through the centuries have expressed this Christian social compassion. While usually remedial in nature, social compassion allows for personal expressions of love and often builds bridges for verbal proclamation of the gospel.

Social action, by comparison, focuses more on political, social, and institutional change. Preventive in nature, it seeks to keep social ills from developing in the first place. If ministry to prisoners illustrates social compassion, working to change laws and policies regulating the penal system denotes social action. The church uses political-interest groups, prophetic pronouncements (from both the pulpit and organized church bodies), and educational programs to raise sensitivities and provoke action on the part of Christians. The evangelical church in the twentieth century has been most at home with social compassion, but in recent years has again ventured into the arena of social action.

Theological Foundations for Social Concern

There are many theological themes that lend support to Christian social compassion and action. The most foundational doctrines are creation, fall, redemption, and eschaton (or consummation). These are essential stages of the biblical drama and provide a significant theological foundation for the church's mission, including both evangelism and social concern.

• *Creation.* At the heart of creation is an all-powerful, loving God creating human beings (male and female) in his image (Gen. 1:26–28). While theologians have long debated the meaning of the image of God, one implication is clear: all humans possess dignity and worth before God. Though the image of God was marred at the Fall, it remains intact. Thus, Christians must always be concerned about social policies, institutions, and human actions that deface the *imago Dei.* When Christians in eighteenth- and nineteenth-century England and America worked for the abolition of slavery, they usually did so with the rationale that all people, regardless of color, ethnicity, or even creed bear the mark of God's image. In our own time, the dignity of human life is a powerful ethical principle informing a whole range of issues from abortion and euthanasia to economic justice and racism.

Creation theology also provides a foundation for social concern through the cultural mandate that God gave to men and women at creation: "God blessed them and said to them, 'Be fruitful and increase in number; fill the earth and subdue it. Rule over the fish of the sea and the birds of the air and over every living creature that moves on the ground' " (Gen. 1:28). Being his image bearers, humans beings have received from God the task of caring for the physical, temporal earth. Though we as sinful creatures have abused that role by exploiting those resources (human and natural), we are nonetheless charged with the awesome task of trusteeship on earth.

• *The Fall.* The second stage of the biblical drama was the Fall. With the entrance of sin into the world, God's good earth became corrupted, human relationships were distorted, and social and cultural realities gravitated from peace, justice, and freedom to violence, injustice, and bondage. The fall of Adam and Eve in Genesis 3 produced alienation at four levels: from God, from self, from others, and from nature.

Sin, therefore, must be understood not only as encompassing individual actions and attitudes that transgress God's way but also as corporate and structural realities. The Old Testament decries civic laws that do injustice, while the New Testament denounces those principalities and powers that abdicate their God-given role. Sin extends to those cultural norms, political policies, institutional patterns, and societal practices that circumvent the will of God.

Corporate realities, though never totally divorced from human action and thinking, do tend to assume a life of their own. Therefore, when Christians in the nineteenth century became sensitized to abuses in the factory system, they sought not only to change the human heart but also to revise the legal code. Similarly, many contemporary Christians who engage in the cultural battle over abortion seek not only to influence personal decisions (as exemplified by crisis pregnancy centers) but also to change civic laws to restrict the practice of abortion on demand in society.

• *Redemption.* The third part of the biblical drama is redemption. Some Christians view social transformation itself as a redemptive process, but many would prefer to reserve salvation language in this world to personal redemption. This, however, does not negate redemptive implications for social concern.

In redemption, through personal faith in Jesus Christ as Savior and Lord, a person is justified before God. But redemption through Christ's forgiveness and the entrance of the Holy Spirit into one's life brings personal renewal that affects all domains of life. As the apostle Paul put it, "Therefore if anyone is in Christ, he is a new creation; the old has gone, the new has come" (2 Cor. 5:17). Newness in Christ leads not only to inward change or outward practice of personal piety but also to new expressions of love and justice, growing concern for social abuses, and highlighted sensitivity to cultural degradation. Christians are called to a life of spirit-empowered holiness that is not only inward but also outward and social in nature.

Commitment to Jesus Christ brings one into his body, the church, which is God's new community on earth, the first fruits of God's coming kingdom. As such, it is called to embody a new quality of relationships and commitments. It is called to live out God's love, mercy, and justice, and so to become salt, light, and leaven within the world. Its prophetic voice and its deeds of social compassion and action demonstrate that redemption through Jesus Christ makes a difference in this world.

• *The Consummation.* The fourth part of the biblical drama is the consummation, or eschaton. Manifestations of redemption in the present world are incomplete, but Scripture teaches that just as God inaugurated human history, so he will bring it to its culmination.

Christians throughout history have developed different interpretations regarding Christ's return and the end of time. Some eschatologies have propelled believers to great action in the present world, while others have engendered quietism and passivity. Whatever one's interpretation, several things are clear. It is indeed God who will bring about the consummation of history and the ultimate triumph. But Christians are to long for this "blessed hope" with actions that reflect its coming reality.

Though perfect peace and justice will ultimately be realized only in the eschaton, God's people are called to bear witness to that reality by their own lives and commitments. The coming of Christ in the New Testament is never portrayed as an occasion for crystal-ball gazing or passive waiting. It is rather a call to action that anticipates God's ultimate reign.

Creation, fall, redemption, and consummation—these form the foundations that give perspective for the church's social compassion and action in our world. Without this framework our actions in society can easily be reduced to mere humanistic moralism on the one hand or hopeless passivity on the other.

Social Action or Social Service?

Throughout history, Christians have come to differing conclusions about how the church should relate to the world, such as:

- *The church is separate from the world.* Those who practice this view tend to form themselves into Christian countercultures. They feel their responsibility is to set up alternative communities where they are free to show forth what they interpret to be signs of God's kingdom.
- *The church controls the world.* Sometimes called "Constantinism," this position holds that the signs of the kingdom should be legislated by the governments that control the world.
- *The church is a servant of the world.* This option, adopted by contemporary theologians of liberation, holds that the church should take its agenda from the concerns of the world and participate in movements that will best liberate and humanize the largest number of individuals.

While each of these options captures some facets of the complex relationship of the church with the world, the following option is preferable.

- *The church and the world are in creative tension.* The church must go into the world, not remain aloof. Jesus commanded his disciples to do so. Creative tension exists because the church recognizes that it is separate from the world and that its lifestyle is different.

Two Avenues of Ministry

As the church moves into the world to fulfill the cultural mandate, two general avenues of potential ministry open up: *social service* and *social action.*

- *Social service* is the kind of social ministry geared to meet needs in a direct and immediate way. If a famine comes, social service will provide food for starving people. If an earthquake or tidal wave devastates an area, social service will provide food, clothing, blankets, and medical supplies, as well as resources to rebuild. If agricultural

Biblical Examples of Social Concern

The Bible is full of exhortations and examples regarding social concern.

• *Old Testament.* The Old Testament books of the Law echo a strong concern for social justice. Laws regulating property, the use of land, and the treatment of other people (i.e., Exod. 21–23) helped control violations of human dignity and ensure justice. Allocations and uses of land were of particular significance, since the very existence and identity of the Hebrew people were bound up with land. Thus, God directed them not to harvest the corners of their fields or go back over

---

production is low, social service will introduce new crops, livestock, and farming methods so that food production will increase.

Within social service there is a further technical distinction of terms: *relief* and *development.* Relief treats the symptoms. It comes after the fact. Development treats the causes. Development would include establishing medical and dental clinics and training local people how to staff them, digging wells where the water supply is inadequate, setting up cottage industries, providing hoes. Both relief and development are social service; they are not social action.

• *Social action* is the kind of social ministry geared toward changing social structures. Like development, it treats causes, but the scope is much broader and the effects more far-reaching.

Social action, by definition, involves socio-political changes. If a government is mistreating a minority group, for example, it involves whatever is necessary to correct the injustice. It might mean picketing the legislature; it might mean organizing an electoral campaign to unseat a senator or even a president; it might mean supporting guerrilla bands that will overthrow the whole government and rewrite the constitution.

Social action might or might not involve revolution, violence, or civil disobedience in some degree. The goal of social action is to substitute just (or more just) for unjust (or less just) political structures.

The Results

Research has shown that when churches are involved in social ministries, the churches that specialize in social *service* tend to attract more new members than the ones specializing in social *action.* So since the church has no option about *whether* to be involved in social ministries and the Bible does not set forth exactly *how* to be involved, individuals and churches must make choices about their involvement. These choices will affect not only those helped, but also the health and evangelistic effectiveness of the church.

—*C. Peter Wagner*

their vineyards a second time, so that the poor among them would have food (Lev. 19:9–10). And every fiftieth year, the Year of Jubilee, land was to be returned to its original owner to ensure a measure of distributive justice (Lev. 25). God's law, then, stipulated not only acts of mercy for the downtrodden (Deut. 15:10–11) but also structural changes that limited exploitation and promoted justice in an agrarian, peasant society.

The balance of the Old Testament echoes a similar support for social concern. In the historical books, God condemns acts of social evil, such as when King Ahab and Queen Jezebel ordered Naboth killed to confiscate the vineyard that was his inheritance and means of livelihood (1 Kings 21). In 1 Samuel 2, Hannah prays to God who "raises the poor from the dust and lifts the needy from the ash heap" (v. 8).

The poetic books similarly portray Yahweh as a God of justice, compassion, and holiness. The psalmist gives praise to God because "he upholds the cause of the oppressed and gives food to the hungry.

Maintaining a Christian Focus

In defining the purpose of Christian social action, churches are faced with questions such as: What makes our work Christian? How does it differ from secular-humanistic work? As we attempt to right social wrongs, what is a proper emphasis of the gospel component of our message?

Each of these questions probes at a deeper question: What is the eternal significance of the church's social ministry? The task of changing our world for the better—of upholding moral values and reaching out to the disenfranchised—can exhaust the strongest Christian. Burnout, discouragement and frustration are common to many who passionately care about making a righteous difference in society. Workers sometimes wonder if they are accomplishing anything or if they are merely delaying the inevitable moral disintegration of society.

If we are to keep small irritations from becoming major problems and if we are to spare our workers from discouragement, finding a Christian focus for humanitarian ministry is imperative—something that lifts the work beyond the temporal and invests it with spiritual meaning.

Truly Christian Work

How do we develop and maintain a Christian focus?

• *Preserve a clear understanding of the gospel.* Social advocacy will save no one. Salvation is the result of faith in Jesus Christ and faith alone. Social action expresses Christian compassion and introduces Christian principles but does not, in

The Lord sets prisoners free, the Lord gives sight to the blind, the Lord lifts up those who are bowed down" (146:7–8). The Proverbs call for people to express that same character: "He who oppresses the poor shows contempt for their Maker, but whoever is kind to the needy honors God" (14:31).

It is with the Old Testament prophets that we find the most explicit calls to social compassion and action. In calling the people of God to a renewal of their spiritual covenant, the prophets challenge them to turn away from idols that destroy both their relationship with God and each other. They call for repentance from sin, including such social sins as apathy toward the poor, mistreatment of workers, greedy accumulation of land, and injustice in the courts. Amos, prophesying in the eighth century B.C. amidst great opulence and social unrighteousness, decries those who

> hate the one who reproves in court and despise him who tells the truth. You trample on the poor and force him to give you grain. Therefore,

itself, get people to heaven. Social programs earn a platform from which a Christian can speak, but they aren't the message.

• *Serve with proper motivation.* People serve God for a variety of reasons, including guilt, power, recognition, and personal psychological needs. Anything less than a desire to bring glory to God is faulty motivation, leads to frustration, and ultimately distorts the gospel. The foundational reason for social action is not to change the world but to please the Master.

• *Maintain a personal devotional life.* We can't run on an empty emotional or spiritual tank. A personal quiet time gives perspective when the demand for limited resources outruns the supply. It's a daily retreat that nurtures the love and forgiveness necessary for handling tension and frustration.

• *Guard against passionate overwork.* When we care, it is easy to immerse ourselves in the task so much that physical health and relational needs suffer. We have to realize the job will never be completed. Changing our world is an overwhelming assignment for which we need to pace ourselves for the long haul. Jesus did not attempt to right every social ill of his day. Instead, he prioritized his agenda and was not sidetracked into secondary issues.

• *Build ministry on a sound theological framework.* Our task is not to bring the kingdom of God into fullness on earth, but rather to bring a taste of the coming kingdom and to maintain an environment where the church can function freely until the Savior returns. The church is not dependent on a favorable political environment to conduct its basic business. The Christian gospel can flourish even in an hostile environment and can even ameliorate some of its sting.

—*Calvin C. Ratz*

> though you have built stone mansions, you will not live in them, though you have planted lush vineyards, you will not drink their wine (5:10–11).

Most of the prophets resonate in one way or another with the oft-quoted words of Micah: "He has showed you, O man, what is good. And what does the Lord require of you? To act justly and to love mercy and to walk humbly with your God" (6:8).

• *New Testament.* The New Testament further develops the themes of social concern seen in the Old Covenant, and nowhere is this more explicit than in the life and teachings of Jesus Christ. One day at the beginning of his ministry, Christ read from the prophet Isaiah, claiming that this Scripture was fulfilled in him:

> The Spirit of the Lord is on me, because he has anointed me to preach good news to the poor. He has sent me to proclaim freedom for the prisoners and recovery of sight for the blind, to release the oppressed, to proclaim the year of the Lord's favor (Luke 4:18–19).

Though Jesus never engaged in social action of an overtly political nature, his own ministry and teachings were deemed a threat to conventional societal norms, as evidenced in his arrest and death. His teachings trumpeted a clarion call for love, mercy, and justice, often in ways that broke ranks with the expected mores, as seen in his story of the good Samaritan (Luke 10). His healing miracles, while clearly an evidence of his deity, are examples of social compassion and demonstrate that Christ ministered to the whole person, not merely the soul.

The New Testament church sought to flesh out the ways of Christ both within the Christian community as well as the larger world. These early Christians felt their first responsibility was to fellow Christians, as evidenced in the selling of possessions to meet others' needs (Acts 2:45; 4:32–35) and in the offerings for economically distressed churches (2 Cor. 8–9; 1 Cor. 16:1–4). But as the apostle Paul made clear, Christian compassion was to extend beyond the walls of the church (Gal. 6:10, 2 Cor. 9:13) and was to be rooted in both love and justice.

Social concern in the New Testament is the outworking of God's grace in a person's life; without it, one's salvation can be questioned: "If anyone has material possessions and sees his brother in need but has no pity on him, how can the love of God be in him?" (1 John 3:17).

Social Concern in Church History

Throughout the history of the church, believers have demonstrated diverse forms of social action and social compassion. The greatest divergence, and controversy, has been lodged in the social action arena, where the church has long debated such foundational issues as the relationship of Christianity and society and the appropriate mechanisms for effecting societal or cultural change.

While the early church seemed most at home with social compassion, it also made a dent in certain socio-cultural practices. Its social ministries were set in a larger context of animosity and persecution, with the church being a distinct minority. The church viewed the state with great suspicion, rejecting the notion (which would become commonplace by the fourth century) that the state or any social institution could be counted on to reinforce Christian morals and belief.

Despite its minority status and tentative attitude toward society, the church made an impact through preaching-teaching and moral example in such social practices as slavery, gladiatorial fights, and infanticide. In contrast to the classical world, which displayed little concern for the needy, early Christians were filled with mercy and compassion, as evidenced by this description from Aristides:

> They love one another, and from widows they do not turn away their esteem; and they deliver the orphan from him who treats him harshly. And he who has gives to him who has not, without boasting. And when they see a stranger, they take him into their homes and rejoice over him as a very brother. . . . And if there is among them any that is poor and needy, and if they have no spare food, they fast two or three days in order to supply the needy their lack of food (Webber 1986, 56).

The church of the Middle Ages stood in stark contrast to the early church. In the fourth century under Constantine, the church was officially recognized and soon became the favored religious body, exerting great power over all of society. While the medieval church continued its ministries of compassion, it relied increasingly on social action and its influence over politics, economics, education, and the entire cultural fabric. While the church achieved unprecedented power and influence, it also came to be ruled by society and its norms.

With the Reformation came renewed but diverse visions of social concern. Lutherans, with their strong two-kingdom theology, granted the state temporal rule, while the church was in charge of the spiritual realm. In Calvin's Geneva, the Reformed church exerted such influence in economics and politics that it has often been branded a theocracy (rule by God's law). On the other hand, Anabaptists called for separation of church and state and were skeptical of the state's ability to uphold Christian beliefs or ethical norms. All three Protestant movements addressed social concern but expressed it with great variation.

This diversity of approaches has continued in the modern era. One of the most powerful expressions of social concern in this period came in the aftermath of the First Great Awakening in England at the end of the eighteenth and the beginning of the nineteenth centuries. A group of evangelical Anglicans (called the Clapham sect) under the leadership of William Wilberforce, spearheaded in Parliament the abolition of slave trade and eventually brought about emancipation. They, along with later evangelicals, also initiated reform in prisons, educational institutions, factories, and child-labor laws. The reforms clearly were rooted in the great "Evangelical Revival" and the preaching of John Wesley.

In nineteenth-century America, much the same story can be told. Revivalism had a profound impact on the antislavery movement, women's suffrage, and ministries of social compassion in industrial, urban centers. Great preachers like Charles Finney called people to walk the sawdust trail to receive Christ as well as to join the abolition forces.

During the first half of the twentieth century, many conservative Christians abandoned their commitment to social concern. However, in recent decades social compassion and social action have been reclaimed by evangelicalism. And yet not all is well. In the attempt to impact society, some Christians have become highly politicized, failing to grasp the complexity of Christian social action in a pluralistic society. Theological foundations have given way to pragmatism; emotional reactions have sometimes replaced prayerful wisdom.

Social compassion and social action in the midst of a secularized society are part of the church's mandate. But they must be grounded in Scripture, guided by theology, and informed by the church's prior involvements. Above all, Christian social concern must seek the glory of God, the compassion of Jesus Christ, and the empowerment and discernment of the Holy Spirit.

—*Dennis Hollinger*

Resources

Keller, T. 1989. Ministries of mercy. Grand Rapids: Zondervan.

Mott, S. 1982. Biblical ethics and social change. New York: Oxford.

Stott, J. 1990. Decisive issues facing Christians today. Old Tappan, N.J.: Revell.

Webber, R. 1986. The church in the world. Grand Rapids: Zondervan.

12

Planning and Operating Ministries of Social Compassion

A desire to minister to the community doesn't automatically translate into effective community ministry. In approaching our neighborhoods, we don't want to do something foolish or insensitive, but rather to bring the healing and saving love of Jesus Christ effectively into our spheres.

Churches that seek to do this should begin by asking two fundamental questions: "What should we be doing?" and, equally important, "What should we *avoid* doing?" Here are some principles to help answer those questions.

Attitude Check

Effective community outreach requires more than polished techniques. Meaningful outreach begins with a healthy attitude toward mission and the community around us. Consider these three essential approaches.

• *Serve others' needs, not our own.* As they mature in faith, Christians feel increasingly compelled to reach out to others. Sometimes, however, in our efforts to help, we end up merely satisfying our needs to serve rather than the community's needs.

For example, some time ago a young man came to me for advice about becoming an evangelist, knowing I had worked in interdenominational crusades for years. As we talked, it became evident that he was more driven by his need to do evangelism than an interest in the people who needed Christ. So I recommended that he first become a pastor and get to know and think with a congregation. I felt this would teach him to think first of others' needs, not his own.

A church that wants to serve people effectively will need to get to know firsthand the community in which it will minister. Church leaders can meet with other local church leaders. They can introduce themselves to the thought makers of the community and join various community organizations. It is important to get acquainted with neighbors, to discover both how to encourage them and what we can learn from them. This not only builds bridges of understanding, it also allows us to learn community needs from the people in the community.

It's important to remember that we cannot serve people without becoming concerned about *all* their needs, both spiritual and physical. When church leaders ask the question "How can we carry the love of Christ into our neighborhood?" they come to realize they have to do it with words of witness and deeds of compassion. That is the model Jesus gives us, a necessary model if our evangelistic words are to appear sincere. The old social gospel unfortunately reduced the Christian faith to good works only. But the true gospel message does call us to meet people's everyday as well as eternal needs.

• *Have a marketplace mentality.* Sometimes a church cannot offer formal programs that operate out of church facilities or are subsidized by church money or personnel. That doesn't mean the church isn't reaching out to the community. Often, its members are doing so individually and significantly. They initiate and sustain their individual ministries because of the encouragement and strength they receive at church.

For example, one successful business executive in our D.C. congregation was a model of stewardship and witness. Although our congregation could not take credit for his faithfulness, he nonetheless was an extension of the church's ministry in the community. In fact, he asked to be commissioned for his witness in business, as others are commissioned for other forms of service. By broadening our understanding of what constitutes church outreach, we get a better picture of the impact our church is having on the community.

• *Don't dump expertise; offer it.* The temptation for educated Christians working in poor neighborhoods is to haul out their arsenal of knowledge and expertise to fix the problems. But when we do that, we slap other people in the face with our privileges. On the other hand, to hide our knowledge and connections under a bushel would be selfish; such expertise can help them.

We can solve this seeming dilemma by *offering* our expertise and letting the people to whom we minister decide if and when and how they want to use it. If we are going to a place of social ministry because we truly care, we can use the benefits of our training, expertise, and experience to help the community as the people there desire.

Three Keys to Effective Outreach

If our attitudes must be checked regularly, so must our actions. There are dozens of techniques toward more effective outreach to the community, but three stand out as key.

• *Target the right community.* For example, there are three "cities" in Washington, D.C.: First, the federal government, made up of the people who work in the offices of Congress, the White House, the cabinet departments, and other federal agencies. Second, the several thousand business people who commute to the city during the day. Third, the Washington from 6 P.M. until 6 A.M., composed of the people who struggle to survive. Each of these cities has its own network and interacts only sporadically with the other two Washingtons.

When we went to Washington, we had to decide which "city" we were going to minister to. In our case, located as we are in the inner city, it was not a difficult choice. We chose to reach out to those who lived and worked in the city, not primarily the daytime commuters or the ever-changing federal work force.

Choices like this have to be made in order to focus energies and intelligently evaluate the work. In our case, when people asked, "Are you making an impact on Washington, D.C.?" we didn't have to apologize for not getting more bills passed in Congress, or for not having senators join our congregation. That was never our target community. Instead, we could talk about our work in the inner city and the community being formed among young professionals.

• *Allow outreach programs to trickle up.* Often concerned church members will feel called to meet a particular need. They form groups to focus on a concern and then take steps to meet the need. That is a process churches need to encourage. In fact, it is only then that the congregational boards (elders and deacons) become involved in the program with true enthusiasm.

Some churches, instead, wait for the administrative body to act first. Committees are assigned to carry out something the board has decided should be done. Or the pastor tells the congregation the six or seven things they ought to be doing in the community. Time and again, such projects go nowhere. That is because, first, the people have little ownership of the projects, and, second, the ideas, often generated by those away from the front lines, may not meet the needs of the people they seek to reach.

Consequently, it's usually best that elders not initiate outreach programs but rather pray and wait for a concern to emerge from a group within the church. One person with a burden is not enough, but when others begin to show an interest in a ministry, the church structure can encourage them to develop a plan, recruit the people needed, and launch the ministry.

For example, the church in Washington has a learning center with computers, and about forty neighborhood children drop in to use them every week. The learning center evolved from the vision of a church couple who began thinking about how neighborhood children could be tutored. First, they enlisted people from our church who would be willing to tutor the children. Then, they went to the local school and asked for a list of the underachievers and started tutoring them during evenings at the church. When these underachievers started achieving, the demand increased. At that point, a businessman gave twenty thousand dollars, and with that, the church bought the ten computers.

- *Know thyself.* A church that sincerely seeks to meet community needs is faced with a unique temptation: to do too much. Sometimes,

Maintaining Motivation for Compassion

D. L. Moody, the great evangelist, was said to have prayed often that the Lord would "keep him from ever losing the wonder." We are filled with wonder when people we serve respond with joy to Christ's love. But the same ministry that *fills* us with wonder sometimes *makes* us wonder. We can become disheartened, and then ministry gets mired.

Naturally, we want to do more than respond to discouragement and burnout. We want to avoid it, or at least minimize it. Our goal is to make the most of people's motivation, to build healthy momentum for social compassion and action. Here are two main ways I've found to maintain motivation.

Spread the Load

If overwork or mismanaged work is causing discouragement, then spreading the work load becomes a logical way to overcome discouragement. Specifically, that means:

- *Diversify.* Set up a number of commissions that will do the work of the church. For example, in a church I served, the number was five: worship, Christian nurture, fellowship, stewardship, and mission. Our very structure, then, assumed that about one-fifth of our time and energy would be spent on outreach.
- *Give people a break.* Not only can we spread the work load, but we can also spread the time load. Give people permission to take a break from a ministry — perhaps a year or two — to spend more time with family or to recharge spiritual batteries. The attitude to foster is not "This person just couldn't handle the job," but "People have the right and freedom to take a Sabbath rest in ministry."
- *Know when to say when.* Another key to spreading the load is limiting the number of tasks mem-

even when a group has banded together for a particular ministry, it is best not to give them the go-ahead, even if the need is pressing. The ministry may become overextended and ineffective, or it simply may not have the funds to support the group's ideas. At other times, a project may not be able to maintain a staff over the long run.

In Washington, for instance, the church put its desire for a youth coffee house on hold. It was conceived to benefit young people in both the church and the neighborhood. It was to be a safe place for them to gather on weekend evenings, and if designed well and adequately staffed, it could have been popular, meeting a community need.

After having gone so far as to check out facilities and locations, the church decided to wait, feeling it could not give it their best effort. They didn't want to end up with an inadequate facility and a poorly

bers take on. An average member shouldn't take on more than two significant jobs at a time. For most people, one is enough.

Help People Help Themselves

Since a minister can't be with people in their every ministry situation, it only makes sense to help people help themselves in ministry. In this respect, consider doing the following.

• *Let members do the talking.* Members need encouragement not just from their pastor, but from their peers. For example, in one church we let that happen during a time called "Windows of Service." Once a month in worship, different individuals talked about how they were sharing Christ's love in their workplace or neighborhood.

• *Enable laity to minister.* Enabling means encouraging others to reach out and evangelize instead of doing it all ourselves. It also means teaming up people in the congregation. Experienced people can work with those less experienced, and no one should be sent out alone.

In addition, enabling means training people. For example, a church can run a seminar for members who want to know how to rehab a building, teaching both carpentry skills and how to relate to the people they meet. It's well worth the effort to offer training in areas where people want and need training to do effective ministry.

• *Support small support groups.* Every person needs a sense of fulfillment, achievement, and worth. When people in ministry become independent and cut themselves off from mutual encouragement and guidance, they become susceptible to discouragement.

As pastors, we can use small groups to model how to handle discouragement. We can talk about a number of things in small-group settings that show people we struggle and need their encouragement and prayers. This gives the message that discouragement does come with the territory of a challenging social ministry, yet it can be handled effectively in the context of mutual Christian caring.

—*Myron Augsburger*

staffed, poorly funded ministry. The church and the community could do without that.

So, every time the community says "Jump!" the church needn't ask, "How high?" If it is sincerely reaching out to the community in significant ways, it can say no to things it can't do well.

The Pastor's Role: Prod and Praise

Even when a commitment to a mission project arises from within the congregation, it doesn't happen automatically. As pastors, we are not able to do all of the outreach, but we are key encouragers. For

Ministries with Transients

Most churches, and especially downtown churches or those near main highways, receive a steady stream of people in need. Many pastors thus inherit the responsibility to dole out the social assistance funds the church provides for people in need. These people often come equipped with a variety of dramatic stories, and amid the more spurious appeals come a number of genuine claims from persons who, for one reason or another, find themselves to be in desperate circumstances.

Often it becomes the pastor's job to distinguish legitimate needs (true stories) from professional con jobs (false stories). While most of us would prefer to err on the side of compassion rather than to turn away a legitimately needy person, we are also responsible as pastors to use our slim resources to accomplish the greatest good.

How Con Artists Operate

With experience in handling such people comes the ability to discern typical characteristics of the con artist's style. Here is a checklist meant not to replace the compassionate judgment that must enter into every decision, but rather to inform it. Con artists are known for:

- Volunteering irrelevant documents, such as hotel receipts, bus ticket stubs, or applications, to bolster their stories and create an aura of credibility.
- Offering an abundance of details not necessarily related to the main thrust of their stories.
- Name dropping—pretending to be familiar with well-placed persons or with persons you know remotely.
- Forgetting or being otherwise unable to produce a key fact, which

outreach in social compassion, we are the primary enablers in three ways.

First, preaching is an integral part of the process of finding a church's niche in the community. It's not that we just tell our people what they should be doing: "Open a food pantry" or "Establish a drug clinic."

Instead, we present God's Word and speak about the community in such a way that people begin to ask, "What should we be doing for Christ in this community?"

Second, we encourage people by pointing them in the right directions. When people or groups come to us with an idea for outreach, we

is the missing link necessary to corroborate their story.

• Inhibiting the verification of the story: "This must be dealt with in absolute confidentiality" or "Don't say anything to this person."

• Partially answering questions. Attempting to shift the subject or seeming not to hear a key question.

• Stressing the urgency of the request, which leaves no time to verify the story: "I must have the money tonight, or it will be of no use to me."

• Manipulating suggested solutions back to their terms. Usually this means they must have immediate cash; no other solution will do.

• Attempting to produce a sense of guilt in you for doubting their honesty.

• Appealing to your desire to play an important role in a significant story.

How to Avoid Being Taken

People legitimately in need usually exhibit few, if any, of the typical con-artist ploys. There are, in addition, specific precautions ministers can take to preserve funds for the genuinely needy and to keep from falling victim to the trickster:

• Follow through. Check the story, despite the pressures put on you. The honest person will do everything he or she can to help verify the story.

• Delay responding to a request until you have had time to think. Is the story plausible? Do you sense the person using any of the above tactics? Could you convince someone else of the legitimacy of the request?

• Vigorously pursue every alternative to giving cash. You can offer to arrange directly with lodging facilities for a room, or with restaurants or a grocery store for food. Be aware that con artists often try to circumvent your caution with the excuse that they need to travel somewhere, so be especially leery of giving money for travel. Also be aware that bus and train tickets can easily be converted to cash.

• If you conclude that giving money is the only possible solution, decide firmly how much you will allocate to this particular situation. Do not allow yourself to be swayed from your original intentions.

—Scott Campbell

can help them find resources, encourage them, and pray with them.

Third, as pastors, we give public support to outreach ministries. There are dozens of ways to do this without dominating the process. For example, instead of having a pastor announce the progress or needs of a particular ministry, it's much better if that sort of thing comes from the people involved in the ministry, itself. Following the announcement, however, we may thank the presenter and affirm the project. It helps the congregation support a project when their pastor supports it.

When and How to Work with Caesar

Sometimes as a church ministers to its community, it will run into the government. Either the government is not adequately providing justice as it should (civil rights is a classic example), or the church needs the government's help to provide a service (for example, permits or funds needed to open a food pantry). In either case, the church has to work with the governing authorities to meet a human need. How do we do that effectively?

Naturally, a great deal of the answer depends on one's theology of church and state. Yet there are some basic practical principles that most Christians can agree on.

First, the church does not serve the state; it serves Jesus Christ. Therefore, we will not compromise our ethics or principles just to get a few dollars. The dollars aren't as important as our integrity. Groups may expend great effort to get a grant and then have the shape of their programs determined by that grant. Some groups are then tempted to do unbiblical or unethical things in order to keep the funding.

In working with the Christian College Coalition, we once waited through countless delays and red tape to receive permits to renovate a building. Some of our people speculated that a little payola would have greased the wheels of the bureaucracy. After all, other organizations had walked their projects through without the problems we encountered, and they may have made sure "a certain expense was covered" to help in processing the permit. There may have been other reasons for our delays, but the fact that we didn't play this game may have been one. In the end, it cost us a great deal of time, but we maintained the integrity of our ministry.

Second, we can develop relationships and encourage dialogue with people who have political power. Our temptation is to depersonalize government with labels and titles, to distance ourselves and stand back in judgment. But government is made up of people, and the better we know these people, the better we understand the constraints with which they live. Likewise, the better they know us, the more genuine our interchange becomes. Many people in government struggle to do what is right, so we shouldn't criticize them carelessly.

Third, sometimes we do need to confront officials. We hold convictions on justice and peace that sometimes compel us to speak. But when confronting officials, we must not do it just to get the state to do what we want. We simply want the government to honor and respect the consciences of those who hold different views.

For example, as a pacifist I was opposed to the war in Vietnam. Yet while the war raged on, I didn't write angry letters or publicly denounce the government. But along with seven others, I did visit senators and Secretary of State Henry Kissinger to tell them our views about war. We made no impassioned speeches; we simply explained our position and quoted some passages from Scripture. We wanted them and President Nixon, who were talking about "peace with honor" at the time, to see that there was a higher honor yet. We also tried to show them that we spoke for a good number of the governed they represented.

We were not trying to create a pacifist government; the government has a right to have an army and protect its shores. If, however, our government is to be a government of all the people, it needs to understand the convictions of all of its people.

Some Seeds Fall on Good Ground

In our outreach ministries, we often don't see the results of our efforts. We may not know what has happened to the family of six that came to the food pantry last month. We don't always know what a pregnant teenager finally decided about the birth of her child. Sometimes we're tempted to give up because we see the needy taking advantage of the church's kindness.

It helps, in such times, to remember the example of our Lord, who gave with no thought of return. We can remember that much of our ministry involves merely planting seeds. As in Jesus' parable, some of those seeds are going to fall on stony ground, and some will grow among weeds, but the sower continues to sow. Every once in a while, we see the seed sprout and grow and bear fruit, and that reminds us that God, indeed, is at work in our ministries of social compassion.

—Myron Augsburger

Resources

Augsburger, M. 1983. Evangelism as discipling. Scottdale, Pa.: Herald.

Augsburger, M. 1990. The Christ shaped conscience. Wheaton, Ill.: Victor.

Emergency Benevolence for Church Members

Even the most affluent congregations have members who may need emergency financial assistance. The loss of a job, a medical emergency, or some other extraordinary event in a church member's life can bring that person to the church office with the plea: "Pastor, can the church help me financially right now?"

Historical Precedents

From the earliest days, the church has aided its members in need. The Old Testament speaks of helping the poor, who are God's chosen people. For example, they are allowed to glean the fields and vineyards (Lev. 19:9–10), and every third year they are to be given the tithe all Jews were to offer to the Lord (Deut. 14:28–29). Jesus, himself poor, told a rich young man to sell what he had and give to the poor (Matt. 19:21).

In the early church, Paul carried a money collection from Macedonia to Jerusalem for the needy in Judea. The church held property in common so that no one would be needy (Acts 2:45; 4:34). All were to be at work, however; idleness and handouts were not to be known. Anyone who was unwilling to work should not eat (2 Thess. 3:10–13).

Modern Procedures

To aid members when a crisis hits, congregations often set up benevolence funds. The most frequent method is the pastor's benevolence fund, directed and controlled by the pastor or other designated person. Some churches support this fund by appropriating the loose offering one Sunday each month. Other churches have a line item in the budget specifying a set amount each month. The advantage to this method is that the pastor can know what to expect in order to pace disbursements. In a few cases, the interest from a modest endowment might support this fund. For example, one pastor of a historic congregation has more than $20,000 in interest income available to him each year for benevolence.

Generally, only the pastor or perhaps one other member knows about disbursements. This approach guards the needy person's privacy while relying upon the pastor's discretion. If the pastor has sole discretion over the use of the funds, however, it may place the pastor in a difficult situation in relation to the IRS. Such funds may be counted as personal income by the tax authorities.

A small committee, including the pastor, may be charged with discerning true needs and disbursing the funds. What is lost in privacy is made up in accountability.

Handling Funds

Policies differ among congregations. Consider, however, these basic guidelines:

- *Set limits.* Consider limiting the amounts given at one time, the frequency of gifts to members, and the purposes for which the gifts may be used.

• *Have a membership requirement.* Clearly specify the length of time one must be a member in order to receive help. Nonmembers can be helped through other means.

• *Expect evidence of self-motivation.* Ask for some form of service in return for funds. This also benefits the receiver in terms of self-esteem and the avoidance of depression.

• *Don't make loans to members.* Especially avoid loans with interest, due to the legal and tax problems the church could encounter. Nevertheless, a member can be told that, as soon as he or she is able, repayment would be appreciated in order to help the next person in need.

• *Don't commit to indefinite support.* Benevolence funds should meet emergency rather than chronic needs, unless specified otherwise. Those with chronic financial need may have other problems that continued benevolence could aggravate rather than alleviate.

—*John Throop*

Food Pantries and Clothes Closets

We pastors can be overwhelmed by the human need that shows up at our doors. We want to respond to the Christ in the faces of our brothers and sisters, yet we are often frustrated by a lack of resources and plagued with uncertainty about the effectiveness of our help. Though our individual responses wear thin, an organized community effort can miraculously turn our five small loaves into a feast for thousands.

Should you begin a food pantry in your congregation? First do some research by asking key questions: Are food pantries or cooperative ecumenical efforts already in place for our congregation to support? Have we asked low-income people about their needs and included them in our planning? Do our church members have a heart for this kind of ministry? Can we identify the lay leadership needed for this demanding project?

Key Considerations

If you discover your congregation is ready to meet the challenges of a pantry, here are a few hints to keep in mind as you begin:

• *Responsibilities.* Key volunteers should gather donations, publicize the pantry and its needs, set policy, handle legal and liability issues, supervise operations, and schedule volunteers. It's good to include low-income people in these positions of responsibility. Without a rotating core group sharing responsibilities, chaos or burnout will soon take over. If the program grows, a paid coordinator may become necessary.

• *Donations.* In agricultural communities, many farmers allow gleaners onto their fields. This practice offers great opportunities for service projects. For instance, a church could do a Bible study on Deuteronomy 24:19–22 while picking fruits and vegetables. For other sources of donations, contact farmers' markets. Local grocery stores often give away day-old bread and dated dairy products. Ask local schools, service clubs, and businesses to sponsor food drives. One church asked its members to tithe their weight in food. They gathered two thousand pounds of food on one Sunday!

Churches can bring their resources together to form a central food bank to receive donations, coordinate volunteer efforts, and make referrals. Second Harvest (116 S. Michigan Avenue, Ste. 4, Chicago, IL 60603), a national network of food banks, receives large donations from the food industry and distributes to smaller church pantries. A full-sized pickup truck or van is useful for gathering donations.

• *Distribution.* Adequate distribution facilities include a clean space for sorting food and preparing bags, a waiting room, an interviewing area, storage areas, refrigeration, tables, files, desks, and chairs. In order to set up, clean up, and be kind to your volunteers, open only once a week for two hours. You can share space in the church, but be sure to coordinate the pantry with other church programs.

Keep a record of what you give away. You may be amazed by the large number of people who come to receive food, but with organization, most churches can serve them.

Clothing distribution requires a large room dedicated to this function, with racks or shelves, hangers, a washer and dryer, and lots of volunteers giving their time to clean, repair, and distribute the clothes. You can set up a counter and take requests for sizes and types, or you can allow people into a "store" in which they can "shop" for a set number of items.

• *Eligibility.* Determine eligibility based on level or source of income, identification, the reason for need, and how often people will be allowed to come for help. Devise a record-keeping and interviewing process. Make referrals to government-sponsored social agencies when appropriate. Through not only distributing food and clothes but also through relationships and counsel, your volunteers can discover the best ways to help and restore hope in Christ's name to many in desperate situations.

—David C. Hacker and Sheri L. Noah

Feeding Programs

Unlike the old "soup kitchens" of the past, today most feeding programs offer a ministry that provides hope as well as sustenance to guests. Some feeding programs provide as many as three meals a day. Others provide only one meal a day or a combination of breakfast, lunch, and dinner, scattered across a given week.

A food bank or food pantry differs from a feeding program in that the former provide packaged goods that are distributed to the community, while feeding programs prepare ready-to-eat meals at a specific location. Some churches combine the two, but this is usually a difficult undertaking.

Most cities or counties have a major food bank that can give considerable guidance to a church interested in establishing a food ministry. A food bank also can be a prime source of free or inexpensive food products to cook and serve in a feeding program.

Getting Started

As you consider establishing a feeding program, first assess the need by researching the number of hungry in your own congregation, neighborhood, and expanded community. Contact municipal or state departments of human services, or your local food bank. These agencies can give you valuable guidance and advice.

Questions of staffing and facilities must also be resolved. Many volunteers are needed, to keep the burden from being too great on a few, and specific leadership is essential for day-to-day operation. Volunteers can serve in various capacities: food solicitors, preparers, and servers, and clean-up crews. The church kitchen and eating area must be adequate to meet the needs of food preparation and serving.

It is essential that you involve the local the board of health and zoning board to make certain your site will not violate any codes. The board of health can guide you as to the permits that may be required for food service.

Meals should be as nutritional as possible, but nothing is wrong with soup for dinner if it has something in it other than broth. Stews and casseroles are also easy to prepare and can be nutritious. Add bread or rolls, and maybe a cookie for dessert or a gelatin with fruit salad, and you will have a relatively inexpensive and balanced meal.

Utensils for preparation should be heavy-duty and practical. For instance, use heavy, wooden-handled ladles for soup and hot stews. They are strong but heat-resistant and won't burn volunteers' hands the way metal ones might.

Working with Other Churches

One way to make a feeding program easier to implement and even more effective is to share the responsibilities with several churches in your community. With this approach, dinner could be available on Tuesdays at the Baptist Church, Wednesdays at the Presbyterian Church, and so on. This not only allows for the development of a cooperative venture but also creates political leverage should your neighbors begin to object to a long line of strangers in front of your church at mealtime.

Even in communities with many hungry people, neighbors may deny the problem exists or resist accepting its reality, fearing so many poor gathered in one location at one time. In some communities this can be a serious concern.

Many who come to feeding programs travel for several miles, often by foot. Churches usually see guests who are not residents of their immediate neighborhood. Hunger is a great motivator, both for those in need and for those attempting to put Matthew 25 into action.

—Richard A. Roberts

Shelter Ministry

An overnight shelter for the homeless is a difficult social ministry to implement. The church, in effect, becomes a 24-hour-a-day administrative operation, at least on those dates the facility is open as a shelter.

Steps to Shelter

Though this ministry can be challenging and even divisive, it is also one of the most spiritually rewarding programs a church can operate. Here are the steps to get started.

• *Needs assessment.* Survey the church membership and neighborhood for answers to questions like these: Are there homeless people in the immediate community? How many? Is the need for shelter year-round or only in the winter? Contact the municipal or state department of human services for some of this information. Local advocacy groups working with the homeless can give invaluable advice, too.

• *Committee formation.* Once a decision is made to proceed, establish a shelter committee, drawing mainly from church members but also including interested neighbors. Responsibility for running the shelter should not fall on just one or two persons. Once the committee is formed, however, it is important to have a primary decision maker on site each night shelter is offered. Committees are not effective at making day-to-day decisions.

• *Facility preparation.* Next, decide how many people can be handled and in what area of the church facilities. Will you offer shelter only to men, or will the shelter be open to women also? What about children and families? These decisions will determine the sleeping arrangements. Since you must provide adequate washroom facilities, you'll need to contact the appropriate city departments for guidance about building specifications and permits before opening the shelter.

Provide washable mats or cots, each of which should be covered with a sheet before anyone sleeps on it. Towels will allow your guests to wash up before retiring each night. Sheets and towels are not a luxury but a health prerequisite to help prevent the spread of lice and disease. You may also decide to open a free used-clothes closet.

• *Staff training.* Many people can do volunteer work in a hospital or children's home but are not suited for work with a street population. Ask a representative from a well-established homeless shelter to visit and talk with your committee about essential volunteer qualifications.

Reasonable Guidelines

Once the strategic planning is complete, the tactical efforts begin. Here are some key guidelines related to running a shelter day-to-day:

• *Post strict rules for the guests.* These rules should outline the required behavior for all shelter guests. Regulations might include a smoking and drug policy, the time for entry and leaving, the prohibition of violence, the limits of access to other parts of the building, and the use of washrooms and telephones. Consequences for infractions need to be communicated.

• *Establish clear guidelines for the volunteers.* At the least, volunteers would be required to keep confidential the home addresses of all volunteers. Other guidelines might include protocol for interaction with the guests, rules about lending money, and steps to take in an emergency.

• *Don't neglect tight security measures.* Lock doors to prevent access to restricted parts of the church. In addition, have the backup security of a volunteer whose duties include keeping an eye on where people go upon entering the church.

• *Contact your neighbors.* Inform the community of your plans. A special mailing or an open house can help assure their cooperation, or at least make you aware of any opposition in the immediate neighborhood.

—Richard A. Roberts

Battered-Women Shelters

Out of three women, the odds are that at least one will be physically abused by her spouse during her lifetime. The Bureau of Justice's National Crime Survey verifies that a wife-beating incident occurs every fifteen seconds in the United States and that 70 percent of all assault cases handled in emergency rooms involve battered women. What can be done to help alleviate this problem?

A battered-women shelter can be one effective response. A shelter is a building designed to house a woman and her children as she flees domestic violence. A shelter is different from a safe house, which is usually someone's private residence with space for one or two women; a shelter serves as an immediate place of refuge for many women and their children. A woman who really wants to escape the cycle of abuse must have a safe place to hide while she pulls her life back together.

Why can't a woman just go to the police? For numerous reasons, police departments are still relatively ineffective. Ninety-five percent of all police interventions conclude with the woman being sent back into the abusive relationship. Shelters are usually more helpful.

Setting Up a Shelter

There is much to do before a church can establish a shelter. Church leaders must ask some tough questions, such as: Are we the right group to do this? Do we have the support of the congregation? Are we willing to work with the community and government agencies?

This last question may evoke a strong emotional response from church leaders, but no shelter can establish itself successfully if it tries to ignore community support. For example, a shelter must secure guaranteed police protection. A shelter must also establish relationships with local women's advocacy groups and crisis centers, which are often the first points of contact for women in domestic crises. Turning-Point, a Wisconsin-based agency, even suggests consulting the local city planner from the beginning in order to avoid some of the eventual red tape. At any rate, community agencies play an important role in a shelter's existence and success.

After gaining congregational support, shelter leaders need to search for a suitable building. A church may decide to build the shelter, but existing buildings usually are cheaper and just as functional. A shelter must have a location close to community services, a fenced-in yard, separate apartments for families, and a security system to warn personnel of possible break-ins. The shelter must also keep its location anonymous.

It is wise to contact human-resource agencies to inform them of your intentions and to garner their support. A church may want to seek the advice of other shelters in the state that have already journeyed through the jungle of government jargon and rules.

Shelters need to maintain stringent rules. Most organizations regulate their affairs with at least these minimum guidelines:

- Specific statements about length of stay (the average is 30 days).
- No contact with spouse.
- Mandatory counseling and support sessions for mother and children.
- No alcohol or drugs.
- No spanking ("time-out" is more effective in shelters).
- No going to work or school (since the spouse often will patrol those areas to reestablish contact and control).

The most valuable way a church can contribute to this ministry is to help each woman build a support network before she leaves the shelter. The woman's family is the first line of support, but even secular agencies recognize the church as the best second source of support. The goal is to get the battered women involved with empathetic church volunteers who are trained to help.

—*Michael E. Phillips*

Crisis Pregnancy

The vows some congregations take in infant baptism apply to crisis pregnancies. Those promises represent the commitment of the people of God to welcome children and to extend the means of grace to their parents. The church has an essential role to play not only in providing for the safety and nurture of the unborn child but also in meeting the physical and spiritual needs of the mother and other family members (see James 2:14–17).

Church Resources

Because Christian churches reach into every corner of our nation, they can carry both the message of redemption and practical help to women and families affected by crisis-pregnancy decisions. Though over a million abortions now take place in the U.S. every year, not all women choose abortion, and many who do, say they would not have had an abortion if they had thought there were alternatives.

Working in cooperation with other churches and the network of secular crisis-pregnancy centers (which now number in the thousands), churches have resources to meet virtually every need that arises in a crisis pregnancy. Women who need a temporary home, a sympathetic friend, or a wise counselor can find them in the church. Women who need a doctor, a lawyer, a social worker, or a teacher can find these in the church, as well. Transportation, baby clothes and furniture, maternity clothes, help with adoption, or help finding long-term housing or a job—all these, the church can help provide.

What to Do

It is not easy to start a crisis-pregnancy ministry. Consider these suggestions as you assess your church's potential for such a ministry:

- *Don't start without in-depth planning.* Start with a well-reasoned philosophy of ministry and a clear mission statement. Then develop a written statement of purpose, expressing both the purpose of and the biblical and theological premises for the ministry. These initial statements will inform church members and the community about the reasons for your ministry and eventually will help the ministry group screen potential helpers and referral sources.
- *Delegate the ministry's management.* Just as ministry was delegated in Acts 6, assign the organizing of crisis-pregnancy ministry to an accountable body in the church. The group may be the deacons, the women's association, or another special committee set up just for this purpose.
- *Help women feel welcomed.* Many women are reluctant to make their needs known where they think they will meet with a judgmental response. This is a sensitive area that makes essential a good preaching and teaching ministry in the church for both adults and youth. Those with physical and spiritual needs must feel welcomed by the body. They also must be taught the biblical standards of morality and be assured that the church body desires their full restoration.
- *Seek broad-based involvement.* The ministry should be an integral part of the church's whole approach, both to practical ministry and to imparting the gospel message. This can be accomplished in a variety of ways: by actively involving the pastor, particularly in meeting the spiritual needs involved; by soliciting the participation of many members; and by teaching church members the pastoral implications of this particular social concern.
- *Don't neglect the soul.* The ministry should not allow the obvious physical needs of women in crisis pregnancies to obscure their spiritual needs. The group needs a strong pastoral component that is as eager for the spiritual restoration as it is for the physical. Every woman or man who needs it should have opportunity to be led gently toward repentance and restoration (2 Tim. 2:25).

—*Terry Schlossberg*

Caring for Latchkey Children

Children between the ages of 6 and 12 are often left home alone while their parents are away at work or school. The parents, typically isolated from the help of an extended family, earn a very moderate wage and cannot afford private day-care programs. Therefore, latchkey ministry can be an effective outreach to families outside of the church. It provides us a wonderful opportunity to develop relationships with families as we support them in meeting a most pressing need.

Family-Support Ministry

A church launching into latchkey ministry needs to understand that the most important component will be the loving attitude of staff members. This love has the power to heal sagging self-esteem, establish lasting friendships, and open the door to fellowship within the church.

Here is a six-step plan for developing this ministry:

• *Form a committee.* Bring together a group of interested and talented people for an initial informational meeting. The mandate is to research the situation and recommend a course of action. Strive to incorporate the parents in the program, including all interested parties in some capacity in the structure of your formal committee.

• *Discover the needs.* Use a neighborhood survey to conduct a needs assessment among parents. Also interview teachers, pastors, apartment managers, and leaders of service organizations. Try to uncover the greatest needs.

For example, will transportation be a problem? Can families afford to pay a fee? Will the children be hungry when they arrive? How are they doing in school?

Be sure the program will respond to the felt needs of those it is designed to help. For example, a club activity meeting one afternoon a week may be a great program, but it does not meet the needs of a family with latchkey children. Many latchkey children have remedial academic needs, so you will probably want to explore an educational component, one that at least checks on homework completion and offers basic tutoring by volunteers.

• *Establish goals and objectives.* Here are four possible goals: to provide adult supervision for latchkey children, to increase the children's self-esteem, to improve academic performance, and to offer Christian education.

Each goal should have detailed objectives. For example, the first goal could have the following objectives: to provide care five days a week, to do so for up to fifty children who are 6 to 12 years old, with a priority on low-income households in the immediate neighborhood.

• *Design the program plan.* Before making any decisions, the committee should visit the sites of existing programs and do some research into state regulations governing children's programs. Then, along with developing a budget, the committee needs to describe in detail your basic child-care policies, the services to be provided, the available transportation options, the facility to be used, and the job descriptions and qualifications of staff members. Include a plan to evaluate the program, as well.

• *Do a feasibility study.* The feasibility study should raise and answer key critical questions: Is the facility available? Does it meet program requirements, and is zoning approved? Are staff and volunteers ready to begin? Will our financial prospects provide the income necessary to meet expenses? The answers to these and other questions will either move the plan forward or force the committee to reevaluate and change the plan, based on available resources.

• *Implement the plan.* If the program is ready for implementation, a management committee needs to be commissioned and a director secured. From this point forward, the director implements the program with all the financial and personnel resources at his or her disposal.

—*Chris Ellerman*

Substance Abuse

Victims of substance abuse are among us in the church. Many such people, feeling trapped, wounded, and ashamed, are waiting for an outstretched hand from their pastors and other church members. When a wise pastor and compassionate congregation recognize that a primary duty is to bear the burdens of their struggling brothers and sisters, they will stretch out their hands with the offer of Christ's healing power.

Filling the Emptiness

A substance-abuse ministry can be one of the most gratifying and effective programs in the church's outreach plan, because it speaks directly to the emptiness of soul that Jesus came to fill when he promised us "abundant life" (see John 10:10).

Here are some suggestions for reaching out to those who have tried to fill that emptiness with mind-numbing chemicals.

• *Confront congregational denial.* It is surprising how little awareness of substance abuse many congregations have. Because of addiction's hallmark—denial—it is so easy for congregations, like individuals, to cry, "No addiction here!" Yet forms of substance abuse exist within virtually every congregation.

In some appropriate way, then, we must let the congregation know the leadership of the church is launching a new program to meet a newly recognized need. We can gently inform the people that a raging problem in our society will be addressed by this congregation and invite them to participate. We should approach this ministry as we would look after other hurts that call for the Lord's healing.

• *Thoroughly educate the volunteers.* Expert training for ministry volunteers is a must. Search the community's resources for agencies and individuals who are thoroughly equipped to provide education to members who will guide this new ministry. At the least, volunteers must know what addiction is, where it comes from, what the addictive personality is like, how to recognize symptoms, and how to teach family members about the destructive effects of enabling and co-dependency.

• *Take a holistic approach.* We minister best when we address all the victim's problems together—the physical and mental as well as the spiritual. We should make full use of the Christian Twelve-Step Program and its *Serenity Bible.* Also, most large cities have a Council on Alcoholism and/or a Drug Education Center. Agencies like these can provide excellent resources.

• *Team with other churches.* Church members must bear one another's burdens in this ministry. Since the ravages of addiction in our day comprise one of the weightiest burdens in history, whole congregations can increase their effectiveness in ministry by working together. In Charlotte, North Carolina, for example, churches have formed a Ministry of Recovery, which has encouraged several churches to collaborate in this vital Christian enterprise.

• *Recognize the ultimate source of all healing.* The eleventh chapter of the Gospel of John captures the clearest picture of Christian rehabilitation when the victory giver, Jesus, calls to the one in bondage to death: "Lazarus, come forth!" Then Jesus instructs his helpers to loose Lazarus from the graveclothes.

In light of Christ's vivid demonstration of his power to release from bondage, we might say an explicitly Christian treatment approach involves two basic steps: (1) introducing the addicted to the Great Physician and (2) helping them remove their "graveclothes"—the remnants of the old lifestyle.

In my own dark years of being hooked on drugs, I came under the care of several psychiatrists, two private sanitariums, and many other forms of treatment. Each medical professional and therapy gave valuable help and support, but my rescue ultimately depended on the love and grace of my healing Lord.

—*Gordon Weekley*

Prison Ministry

Prisoners often go unnoticed by the general church population. However, Jesus spoke about extending ministry to his followers who may be imprisoned (Matt. 25: 31–46). In fact, he said that showing compassion to those who are hungry, thirsty, or imprisoned is showing compassion to him. The writer of Hebrews also reminds us to pray for those in prison as if we are there with them (Heb. 13:3).

All a church needs to begin a prison ministry is two or three Christians who have a heart for those incarcerated. These Christians can arrange times to meet together to begin praying specifically for inmates and their families. From that point, the church can plan a quality ministry representative of our great Lord and King.

Planning the Ministry

Here are some suggestions for beginning and conducting prison ministries:

• *Go first as a guest* with an established ministry group. This helps a group gain experience and decide on the type of ministry they may be able to provide. Churches often serve by offering a Bible class, holding a short worship service, or counseling with individuals.

• *Meet with the chaplain and other prison officials.* It is important to explain ministry goals, learn the institution's requirements, and gain permission to begin. This is a good time to arrange a given time each week for visitation.

• *Use the Scriptures as the central focus.* Since rehabilitation — a change of heart—is one of the major purposes for the incarceration of law offenders, the Word of God is our greatest tool for prison ministry (Acts 2:37; Rom. 1:16; Heb. 4:12). Prisoners are not excluded from the gospel message; nevertheless, some, like Jonah, must be captured by God before they learn to accept it.

• *Visit frequently.* Most prison officials agree that frequent visits from the Christian community help improve inmates' behavior. Since prisoners are used to having their days highly structured and regulated, visitors need to be prompt and consistent with their scheduling.

Wise Practices

Seasoned visitors learn to be prepared for a few problems. Here are some dos and don'ts in response to the inevitable problems:

• Don't be discouraged by either small attendance or little verbal response. Few inmates are church oriented, and the results of our work may not be obvious in terms of radically changed lifestyles. However, the visitor and many others will be blessed by the ministry, and God's kingdom will increase.

• Don't be surprised by shallow professions. Some inmates use a profession of faith as a method of gaining special favors. It's best to just keep assuring inmates of God's impartial love and his complete forgiveness. This involves being patient and refusing to try to force decisions. We may only plant the seed; God may call someone else to be the harvester (see 1 Cor. 3:5–8).

• Do prepare for criticism at home. It's wise to secure enthusiastic support from the church leadership before starting a ministry. One big reason is that some inmates, upon release, may begin attending the church. Since a few members may feel uncomfortable with former inmates sitting next to them, a united church leadership can best deal with criticism of outreach to these unpopular folks.

• Do set up a support system for ex-convicts. The sad fact is that many released convicts eventually return to prison, and it's good to plan how to prevent that occurrence from the first day of a prisoner's release. Effective approaches get released prisoners involved with others in clear, consistent forms of accountability.

—James E. Martin

Helping People with Disabilities

Just as Jesus ministered to the whole person, we are called to care for the physical as well as spiritual needs of people. For people with disabilities, this coupling of the spiritual and the physical is essential if we truly are to make a difference in their lives.

Where Do We Start?

As we look to minister to those with disabilities, a few practical steps can get help us begin:

• *Conduct a survey.* Often, a church is unaware of who has disabilities in the congregation or community. Develop a survey to determine who is coping with a disability and what that disability is.

• *Develop a strategy for outreach.* Few people with disabilities attend church (about 1 in 20). Yet it is estimated that 10 to 17 percent of any given community is disabled. Many would attend church if they were invited and made to feel welcome. A team of volunteers can be assembled for outreach and ministry to those with disabilities.

• *Don't forget the family.* Often families are the primary caretakers of a person with a disability. Stress takes its toll on these families, as seen in their unusually high divorce rates (over 85 percent) and incidents of physical, emotional, and sexual abuse. Alienation from church and community are common in these families. A night out or an offer to do the grocery shopping can be a welcome relief.

• *Support the ministry from the pulpit.* This is not a ministry that can survive without support from the pastor. It's tough and unpopular. A pastor who promotes and models a warm response to people with disabilities will gain the congregation's support.

• *Start with disability awareness.* Even with a committed pastor, a team of trained volunteers, and an accessible building, the church may not be a pleasing environment for disabled people and their families. Recent studies indicate that "attitudinal accessibility" is more critical than physical accessibility. Planning a Disability-Awareness Sunday and using a disability-awareness study guide, such as *Hearts in Motion* (Agoura Hills, Cal.: JAF Ministries), can help the congregation understand the disability world and what the Christian's response should be.

• *Create an annual ministry plan.* The plan should reflect goals and objectives for the year. Avoid focusing on a single disability, as it tends to exclude people with other disabilities. Instead, build a ministry that crosses disability lines, such as respite care and support groups. The plan should promote inclusion, which simply means participation in the usual activities of the able-bodied community. The only real need for segregating any disability group is for educating those with mental retardation.

Tips for Workers

In fostering the personal side of the ministry, we should observe certain relationship principles:

• When meeting a person with a disability for the first time, treat that person like you would any other person you might meet.

• Establish eye contact when speaking with the disabled person.

• Ask questions regarding the disability when appropriate, not out of morbid curiosity.

• Deal with a person on an age-appropriate basis.

• Treat the person with dignity, respecting his or her space (and equipment).

• Admit it if you don't know how to help, followed by ". . . but I'd like to try."

• Avoid labeling a person by his or her disability; use "person with a disability" rather than "the disabled" or "the handicapped."

• Listen, even if it's difficult and tedious.

• Be persistent; sometimes their "no" means only "I don't want to bother you."

• Maintain a sense of humor.

—*Conrad Mandsager*

Tutoring and Educational Enrichment

After-school and evening tutoring programs are a low-cost, high-impact way to make a difference in the lives of young school students. Programs usually involve many of the church members. Since most churches have members that are already school teachers, these people can be encouraged to use their skills and talents to help organize and implement the tutoring program. This leads toward some excellent interaction and role-modeling for the youth.

Education Is Ministry

Fundamental to beginning an educational ministry is an understanding of its context within the church's broader mission. The concept of "Sunday school" was begun years ago to assist poor children in developing their reading and writing skills. Yet many churches have moved away from that wonderful ministry approach to viewing Sunday school as providing exclusively religious instruction. However, youth programs can be organized to meet both educational and spiritual needs.

One way to start a ministry is to follow this sequence:

• Explore the idea with the church as a whole, allowing broad input and capturing the interest of as many people as possible.

• Identify a coordinator who will carry the major leadership responsibility.

• Start a dialogue with the local schools, identifying ways the church can supplement their programs in students' lives.

• Plan a date to begin the program as soon as possible while also allowing time for adequate preparation and team building.

• Begin the program on a once-a-week schedule, meeting for approximately a half hour.

If the tutoring program becomes successful, the next step is to develop a learning center. This facility usually includes computers, textbooks, and desks—all similar to what might be found in a school classroom. Depending on the size of the program and financial resources, the center may be staffed either by volunteers or paid professionals. Many learning centers begin in Sunday school rooms before they move into new facilities used mainly for tutoring.

For further information on creative educational ministries from around the country, contact the Christian Community Development Association (3848 West Ogden Avenue, Chicago, IL 60623; phone 312/762-0994).

—*Wayne Gordon*

Job Training

Economic changes and problems produce a significant stream of newly unemployed persons to join the hard-core unemployed. Corporate downsizing, combined with a shrinking industrial factory base, has created an opportunity for congregations to help the unemployed. Churches can assist both their own members and those in the greater community by utilizing resources they might not know they possess.

A Vocational Second Chance

Job training does not necessarily require a vocational training school method of operation. Rather, an emphasis on developing interview skills, increasing literacy, gaining practical experience, and receiving technical assistance can offer people a second chance at a new or rejuvenated career. Here is one way to launch this ministry.

• *Set up a job-training committee.* The committee first decides which parts of the unemployed population in the community are in most need of help. Will it be unskilled workers, partially skilled workers, skilled workers, or management people? Once the target groups are identified, the next step is to decide how large a program to undertake and what resources are available. Then the committee can decide if the project will use volunteers only or hire a full- or part-time director.

A volunteer appointed by the job-training committee could address inquiries from a "command central" either at the church or at a member's home, offering information about the job-training project. Many deacons and elders are leaders not only in their communities of faith but also in the business or academic worlds. Their advice and counsel within the committee can be invaluable.

• *Announce a regular schedule of daily activities.* Offer the ministry during normal business hours. This encourages people to function during the day just as they would if they were still employed, helping to avoid one of the first casualties of unemployment—damaged self-esteem. Establishing a team of volunteers who will be available during business hours and who can hold regular meetings with the unemployed to listen and offer emotional support is essential. Volunteers should also begin offering classes in job-search and interviewing skills.

If literacy skills are lacking, a cooperative venture with a local high school or junior college will produce outside volunteers who are happy to offer classes in a church basement. Should your church have access to an unused computer or two, classes in beginning word processing can be part of the program.

• *Offer unpaid work during training.* A church is a ready-made repository of practical job experiences. A part of the job-training project could include having participants work alongside church-maintenance people in repairing the roof or fixing an electrical problem. The custodian might teach someone how to use a floor buffer or clean kitchen facilities and equipment properly. A cooking class that prepares food for church special events is another excellent practical job-training project. You might even find someone you or another church could hire full- or part-time.

• *Get church members networking.* Invite your members to post job openings from their employers on a special bulletin board, and ask representatives from various companies in your community to visit your job-training program to see it firsthand.

Naturally, it's wise to avoid promising anyone that you will find them a job. In the best of times, job hunting is difficult. Offering support is essential, but false promises only create false hope, more despair, and feelings of failure.

—Richard A. Roberts

Immigration and Refugee Work

In the parable of the Good Samaritan, Jesus calls us to demonstrate the power of the kingdom by crossing all social and cultural borders to assist a fellow traveler in need. This poignant parable forever redefines the concept of neighbor and directs us to act in the face of need. We must constantly ask ourselves, "Who is our neighbor?" The answer obviously includes immigrants and refugees.

A Welcome-Mat Ministry

All newcomers to the U.S. are *immigrants. Refugees* are those who have fled persecution and have been accepted by the American government for resettlement. Ministries to refugees and immigrants differ from other ministries in that they are designed to meet the unique needs of people who are new to the culture, the structure, the language, the customs of life in the United States.

How can your church get involved? Allow refugees and immigrants in the congregation to help define the opportunities. If the church is isolated from the immigrant community, contact immigrant churches or the county government to obtain demographics on the new arrivals in your community: How many immigrants arrived last year? Where did they come from? What languages do they speak? What agencies are working with refugees and immigrants? What services are missing? Then consider the forms of ministry your church might be able to offer in Christ's name.

Here are just some of many opportunities:

• *Resettle a refugee family.* There is a partnership between the U.S. government and the private sector that most Americans know little about. All U.S.-bound refugees arrive through U.S.-contracted agencies. There are five Christian agencies: the United States Catholic Conference, Lutheran Immigration and Refugee Services, Episcopal Migration Ministries, Church World Service of the National Council of Churches, and World Relief of the National Association of Evangelicals. These five agencies have a network of offices that cover almost every community in the United States.

A participating church assists in the care and maintenance of an arriving family for up to 90 days. This may include providing housing upon arrival, registering children for school, taking the family for medical checkups, stocking the refrigerator, collecting furniture, and—most important—making friends.

• *Maintain a clothes closet.* Refugees and other newly arrived immigrants may find themselves needing clothes for a new climate. A local church can collect, sort, repair, and maintain clothes for new arrivals. Coordination with the community will bring the church into the mainstream of service providers and will allow other agencies that work with immigrants to refer them to the church's clothing resources as well as to its other ministries.

• *Schedule ESL classes.* Immigrants need to learn English. Even those who find jobs upon arrival will need to acquire language skills to achieve advancement. Often, state funded ESL (English as a second language) programs offer classes during the day when many immigrants are working. An evening program for adults, with child care available, is a good ministry option for a church.

• *Start an after-school tutoring program.* Children of newly arrived immigrants often have difficulty doing schoolwork and homework because of language limitations and cultural differences. A church can coordinate with schools to provide after-school tutoring for immigrant children.

• *Create an employment network.* Immigrants need jobs, good employers, and benefits. Churches networking within communities can prepare job listings, teach newcomers how to complete applications, assist with transportation to and from interviews, and teach job-interview skills.

When churches stand shoulder-to-shoulder with new arrivals, the whole community will know that in Christ's kingdom the welcome mat is out.

—*Peggy Gilbert*

Respite Care and Hospice

Most pastors would give their right arms to have a person like Stephen in the local congregation. Stephen was Spirit filled, Scripture saturated, and steadfast unto death (Acts 6 and 7). But how did the apostles utilize this wonderfully gifted disciple? They appointed him to design the first outreach to home-bound widows in Jerusalem (Acts 6:1ff). The apostles must have sensed that half of the equation for "pure religion" meant taking care of those who could no longer take care of themselves (James 1:27).

If we hired Stephen to be a twentieth-century church consultant, this creative leader would likely draw our attention to the 30 million Americans who are 65 years of age and older. Most of them are healthy, living independently in their own homes. However, 20 percent do need some help with daily living, and 5 percent require the services of a hospital, hospice, or nursing home. What can we in the local church do to help?

Offer Respite Care

When a person needs help in daily living, a family volunteer usually offers some of the following "cups of cold water" in Jesus' name: *direct care,* including bathing, helping to the toilet, feeding, dressing, or walking; and *indirect care,* consisting of cooking, house cleaning, driving, banking, or dispensing medications.

But what happens when the family volunteer isn't available, undergoing surgery, for instance, or going on a business trip or caring for a sick child? Or what if the helper just needs a vacation? That's where respite care comes in. When the family caregiving gets temporarily interrupted, church-sponsored respite care can fill the gap.

During daytime hours, families can find respite from their caregiving duties through an adult day care center headquartered at the church. For longer periods of time, a family might engage a nursing home to secure a few days or weeks of respite care. The difference between family care and respite care is that the latter may cost money, occurs away from the family home, and provides a nurse on duty around the clock.

Though families must guard against "granny dumping," even the Good Samaritan paid the innkeeper two silver coins to provide substitute care during his absence (Luke 10:35). Joseph, too, had others helping keep the 17-year bedside vigil for his father, Jacob (Gen. 47:29; 48:1–2).

Support Hospice Ministries

When a person enters into the final stages of a terminal illness—and knows it—hospice can help. With its two trademark features, hospice helps people to: (1) remain as pain-free as possible, and (2) die at home, close to their family members. If we had entered a hospice during the Dark Ages, we would have been in an overnight resting place for weary travelers. Today, however, entering a hospice means preparing to depart this world for the next (2 Tim. 4:6).

While dying patients wait for "that final, quiet hour," hospice volunteers encourage them to deal with their unfinished business. Though this sacred business is often emotionally and spiritually rich, hospice volunteers are strongly discouraged from viewing their patients as captive audiences, ripe for coercive evangelism. Instead, clergy volunteers who have made themselves available to the hospice team can respond to the terminal person's request for spiritual nurture.

In light of the opportunities for ministry offered through respite care and hospice ministry, the church with its good news can continue to offer God's grace and nurture throughout every stage of life. Getting old and getting sick need not be the final word.

—Jeffrey A. Watson

Health Care Services

Although churches normally do not involve themselves in the direct delivery of health care services, they do have an appropriate role to play in supplementing the existing systems. Traditionally, for example, churches have set up support groups for the terminally ill and their families, provided hospital visitation, and offered counseling and chaplaincy programs. In addition, some churches are developing referral programs, while others are becoming more involved in advocacy and organizing for public-policy changes.

These are all important efforts that increase sensitivity for the infirm and provide avenues for ministry. But what should a church do if it finds itself in a community that lacks basic health services?

Fostering Health

Here are a few steps for churches to take as they consider working with community leaders to develop a health center:

- *Assess existing health care providers.* The barriers to health care in the community need to be brought to the surface, perhaps for the first time. Where are the gaps in the area's health care provisions? Do existing services care for the uninsured poor?

It is important to survey local providers, because they quickly can identify the barriers to providing quality and affordable health care, factors such as slow public-aid reimbursement, a high rate of uninsured citizens, and the high cost of malpractice insurance.

Accurate data is necessary to build a solid case for developing a health center. The survey should include local residents, too; people in the community need to give their opinions and air their grievances.

- *Identify key health professionals who have the same vision.* Look for health professionals who might be willing to spearhead the effort. These people need to own the ministry from the beginning, since they ultimately are the ones who will implement the services.

Many health centers attempt to open without the direct involvement of doctors or nurses, which is a mistake. It is essential that health professionals be involved in the planning; they need to take ownership of the plan. The most successful health centers are developed by doctors and nurses rather than by social service workers or ministers.

• *Form a business plan for the health center.* Know your game plan for launching health care. Unlike many church social ministries, health care is very expensive. Without proper business planning and forethought, it is doomed to fail.

Thus, it typically isn't prudent to begin by planning to build a new health center. Rather, it's often better to begin small, finding out what the needs are and responding to them as resources allow.

A good starting point for many churches would be to begin with a few basic services. Or consider offering a "health service night" or a health fair, during which volunteer doctors and nurses could provide free or low-cost care for area residents.

• *Talk with other groups involved in health services.* Some groups—such as Lawndale Christian Health Center, Circle Care, and Westside Holistic Family Center in the Chicago area—have many years of experience and can provide an accurate and honest assessment of ideas and plans. A church can also contact the Christian Community Health Fellowship (P.O. Box 12548, Philadelphia, PA 19151-0548; phone 215/877-1200), a coalition of church-based community health centers providing services in poor areas in the United States.

—Wayne Gordon

Recreation

Recreation ministries reach whole communities for Christ, but a church doesn't need to excavate for a new building in order to start a recreational outreach program. It can begin small and grow into the ministry as the financial and personnel resources become available.

For instance, our community had almost no recreational facilities when we first began reaching out through recreation, and we dreamed of a gym for over ten years before we were able to build one.

Grow into Your Program

It's good to start with research by surveying the community for what athletic and recreational needs are not being met. For instance, our first endeavor was to purchase a weightlifting machine, because the local high school did not have such equipment. This was a great way to invite high school students into our church building. More important, it let the community know our church was concerned about the needs of the whole person.

After identifying community needs, a church can look for ways to facilitate existing programs. Low-cost, high-visibility options might include starting or supporting a softball league (not necessarily a church league, but one that gets the whole neighborhood involved), a Little League team, or a flag football league. These options all require substantial administration and supervision but are excellent ways to reach out to the community.

Churches could also explore renting park-district facilities for family-recreation nights. Church members might be required to bring non-Christian friends as tickets to get in. This type of night of fun goes a long way toward helping people feel good about the church.

Should a church sense the need to build a recreational facility, a gym is an excellent option that typically meets important needs in the neighborhood. A gym can house volleyball and basketball leagues and after-school clubs, and provide for numerous other recreational activities. For example, our church invites the public schools to use our gym for their junior high basketball tournaments and allows the high school to use the gym for practice during the holidays when their own gym is unavailable.

More than Evangelism

One caution regarding recreation programs: We shouldn't view them only as opportunities for evangelism. We certainly can offer short devotionals that point people to God before or after they play. However, we want to be careful not to give people the feeling that this is simply a way to increase church membership. Instead, recreational activities should be seen as ways to build relationships.

A church will grow through these ministries, but many participants may go to other churches or remain uninterested in spiritual matters. Recreational ministry is a seed-planting ministry; others may well water and reap the seeds of the gospel that have been planted. In this way, even through fun and games and a little sweat, the kingdom of God grows.

—Wayne Gordon

13

Planning and Operating Ministries of Social Action

Called to be salt and light in the world, churches and their members are increasingly launching into the waters of social action. By attempting to shape social policy locally and nationally on such controversial issues as racism, poverty, the environment, abortion, and pornography, Christians have greatly increased their visibility in the public-policy arena. While this deepening involvement has proven unsettling for many churches, we should not be surprised that God's people, having witnessed the power of Christ's transformation in their personal lives, desire to affect their communities in a similar manner.

Although most evangelical church members have heard countless sermons on personal righteousness from the Sunday pulpit, few have the same depth of familiarity with the call to be witnesses for righteousness and justice in the public arena. In the eyes of many, both within and outside the church, it is one thing to call one's congregation to refrain from sin and quite another to suggest a policy for a whole community or nation.

How a church's involvement in social action will be received in the broader community is a function first and foremost of the attitude believers bring to their efforts. A desire to serve, born of genuine humility before God, will bear good fruit even in the midst of hostility and opposition. On the other hand, a transparent attempt to assert raw power will publicly identify the church as one more interest group merely concerned with its share of the social and political pie. Christ is not honored when we foster such an impression.

Knowing Where to Start

Churches that want to make good things happen in their communities and nation need to decide where to direct their resources of personnel, time, and money. These three general rules can guide a church beginning to survey specific community problems and issues:

- *Begin where competent leadership already exists.* Focus on problems for which committed lay people have already demonstrated both concern and expertise. Look for people who not only have the basic leadership skills but who also demonstrate a Christ-centered character. Such people must have made mature and thoughtful choices over an extended period of time. This is important, since leaders in social-action ministries will have their character weaknesses tested, both in the context of the church and more forcefully in the broader community in which the church desires to witness. Pick well and strive for excellence.
- *Focus where people agree on the issues.* Choose community problems for which some degree of consensus exists in the church. If a congregation's leaders and most members cannot agree among themselves on the significance of a problem and the appropriate action to take, seldom will they make an impact on the community surrounding them. Explore where consensus exists and then plot a clear biblical course of action.
- *Labor where the perseverance will stay strong.* Become involved only with those problems you are willing to stay with over the long haul. Social change is a slow process that usually involves as many setbacks as advances. There are always at least two sides to every issue, and we can be sure our calls for change will encounter opposition. If churches truly desire to serve as the conscience of their communities, they need to pick issues for which their commitment has staying power. They'll need a stick-to-it attitude that can transcend the discouragements of the next election, the next adverse policy decision, and the next inevitable setback.

Spreading the Word

Having chosen an important social issue to address and called forth mature leaders to help carry the message, the congregation then faces the rewarding and difficult task of communicating its message to the public. In our experience of combating sexual violence and pornography, we have found it advantageous to allow a diversity of strategies and methods. We should not assume we have the one true way of solving a particular problem.

Yet several general principles do apply to the most effective social-action planning done by churches:

• *Do your homework.* Clear information presented in a compelling manner wins respect. For instance, if we want to draw attention to the relationship between pornography in the community and an increase in sexual violence, we need to know whether such a relationship actually exists and what studies document the connection. Our credibility in the community on any social issue is a function of having done good homework.

• *Educate to motivate.* Communities seldom act without understanding why something is a problem and knowing exactly what they can do about it. Our responsibility is to educate and motivate the community to action, honestly but passionately.

This usually requires a good measure of creativity. With the growth of the media and communications technology, we are increasingly inundated with images of pain, injustice, and suffering from every corner of the world. These constant images have a desensitizing effect on many people.

• *Organize concerned citizens.* Organization makes the difference between an effective movement and an unfocused concern. Develop communication networks, task forces, and other structures that will allow you to mobilize people and resources quickly and effectively when action is needed.

• *Build partnerships and alliances.* By joining with others who share our desire for action on a particular issue, we bring additional insight to our cause and numbers to our ranks. In a pluralistic democracy, diversity is an asset when confronting social issues. Joining with others also helps hold us accountable to wise action, as our zeal is tempered by a variety of opinions.

Many people who may not be a part of the church community do share our concern for reduced violence, freedom of worship, or ending racism. One note of caution: If we ask others to be a part of our team, we must be prepared to respect their opinions and allow them to function as full partners in the decision-making process.

• *Seek cooperation before confrontation.* Civic or business leaders may disagree with a course of action we feel called to follow as we address a social problem. That doesn't lessen our responsibility to seek dialogue, cooperation, and understanding. By demonstrating respect when principled differences arise, we earn respect for our approach. Sometimes confrontation in the form of a rally or boycott will be necessary. Such action, however, should only follow sincere, repeated attempts to have dialogue and collaboration.

• *Utilize national expertise.* Don't reinvent the wheel. In almost every area of social importance, there are national organizations attempting to make good things happen. Find them and then utilize their expertise, assistance, resources, and counsel. Never be shy about asking for help.

• *Stay focused on your issue.* With issues of importance pressing on every side, it is easy for social-action ministries to lose focus and become involved in every hot issue of the day. Invariably, this dissipates energy and impact. In the worst instances, it can lead to attempts to preserve a ministry for the sake of the ministry, rather than solving the problems the ministry was chartered to address. There's no shortage of sin and injustice permeating contemporary society. Difficult choices need to be made if deep and lasting impact is our goal.

Being Taken Seriously

We all want to be taken seriously, particularly because we believe Christ has given his people constructive insights into many social problems. Yet speaking, being heard, and being taken seriously are three different matters. The first is far easier than the second or third. A few basic guidelines can help ensure that we are taken seriously.

First, the church should diligently practice actions and policies it asks others to adopt. Those who have attempted to address a problem over time will have more respect when they advocate a public policy

The Legality of Social Involvement

Participation by religious leaders in public debate over social and moral issues is an ancient tradition. In modern-day America, participation such as this may jeopardize a church's exemption from federal income taxation, since section 501(c)(3) of the Internal Revenue Code prohibits tax-exempt organizations (including churches) from engaging in any intervention or participation in political campaigns or in substantial efforts to influence legislation.

The Campaign Limitation

Churches are prohibited from engaging in *any* intervention or participation in political campaigns on behalf of or in opposition to any candidate for public office. This is an absolute prohibition; there is no requirement that the participation or intervention be "substantial." The IRS and the courts have stated that the following activities are inappropriate: (1) the endorsement of candidates, (2) making donations to a candidate's campaign, (3) engaging in fundraising on behalf of a candidate, (4) distributing statements, (5) becoming involved in any other activities that may be beneficial or detrimental to any candidate, and (6) "voter education" activities (such as publishing the voting records of candidates on various topics) that manifest a bias in favor of particular candidates or ideologies.

The IRS also has clarified that any statement made by a pastor from a church pulpit "at an official

to solve it. For instance, as one of the nation's largest providers of private hospitals, Roman Catholic officials have offered many respected insights related to health-care policy.

Second, we should choose our rhetoric carefully, being sure of a prophetic call before assuming one, and always matching our actions to our words. When necessary, threatened actions (such as letter-writing campaigns, political accountability, and boycotts) are better understated than overstated. Leaders in any field are taken seriously when they can fulfill their promises.

Third, focus on building relationships of trust that will last. Policies on every social issue are made by individuals, not institutions. Those individuals will listen to the voices they trust and respect. Sincerity, honesty, consistency, conviction, and a proven track record are keys here, as they are with any good relationship.

Participating in the Public Square

As we noted earlier, those called to operate ministries of social action usually face intense public scrutiny, particularly on controver-

function" of the church will be attributed to the church itself and will not necessarily be deemed the individual opinion of the pastor. Similarly, any statement made by a pastor in an official church publication will be attributed to the church.

On the other hand, the IRS has acknowledged that the prohibition against political activity will not prevent pastors (or other church leaders) from being involved in a political campaign "so long as those ministers or officials do not in any way utilize the organization's financial resources, facilities, or personnel, and clearly and unambiguously indicate that the actions taken or statements made are those of the individuals and not of the organization."

It is reasonably certain that a church is free to have political candidates address the congregation, so long as (1) overt campaign activities (enlisting campaign volunteers, etc.) are avoided, (2) the same opportunity is afforded all other qualified candidates, and (3) the congregation is informed before or after the speech that the church does not endorse any candidate for public office.

The Lobbying Limitation

To be exempt from federal income taxation, no "substantial part" of a church's activities can be the "carrying on of propaganda, or otherwise attempting to influence legislation." Many churches and religious denominations have lobbied actively for or against specific legislation concerning such causes as civil rights, peace, nuclear disarmament, and abortion. Such activities do not threaten a church's exempt

Continued on page 182.

sial issues. At the same time, one of the best communication vehicles for our social efforts is the media.

• *The role of the media.* For the most part, reporters have a natural suspicion of all those who claim to offer the community a better way. Some of their skepticism is understandable, given the number of broken promises, inconsistent lives, and misstated facts they encounter daily.

In order to work with the media effectively, we must think first and speak second. Words in print or on audio- or videotape are difficult to rescind.

Second, we must always tell the truth. We shouldn't exaggerate or pretend to know something we don't. Both errors will weaken our integrity and credibility over the long run.

Third, we should choose and train spokespersons for our issue. Effective media communication is a learned skill, requiring training and practice.

On many issues, a lay person will make a better spokesperson than the pastor, whose "audience" is usually the church. In our communication with the broader community, we need to use terms that will be understood and applied to the whole community. Few of us fully understand doctors or lawyers when they use their own complex terminology. The church also has a language of its own, which seldom translates with the same impact and depth of understanding to the rest of the world.

• *The role of the pastor.* The pastor does have a pivotal role to play in enabling effective social action. He or she can lead the church by

Continued from page 181.
status as long as they are not a substantial part of church activities.

Unfortunately, the critical term *substantial* has not been defined by the IRS or the courts. Whether or not particular efforts are substantial will depend upon a balancing of the facts and circumstances of each case. Accordingly, churches have no clear standard to guide them.

Nevertheless, it is clear that certain activities would be insubstantial, such as the circulation of a few petitions each year addressing legislative issues. Also, it ordinarily is the exempt organization itself that must engage in the legislative activities, not individual members. The income tax regulations specify that an organization's exempt status is not jeopardized if it, in carrying out its primary purpose, "advocates social or civic changes or presents opinion on controversial issues with the intention of molding public opinion or creating public sentiment to an acceptance of its views."

Serious Consequences

To be sure, there have been massive violations of both of these prohibitions, particularly during presidential election years, with little response by the IRS. Nevertheless, in recent years the political activities of churches and religious or-

teaching the importance of being salt and light, in calling forth the gifts of interested lay people, and in drawing attention to their efforts. Church members will also need lots of encouragement as they confront injustice and evil around them. Changing the system is difficult and requires big doses of courage and perseverance, which the pastor can help provide.

In addition, pastors also have the powerful opportunity to help their members who are a part of the system understand the ways in which they can be agents of transformation from the inside. Many of these Christians feel lonely and isolated in their responsibilities.

Some pastors are understandably hesitant to lend their names and reputations to the vagaries of the public-policy and social-action arena. Their congregational members often disagree on the most effective course of action and hold distinctly varying political and social philosophies. While social-action ministry is never a substitute for preaching the good news of redemption, it should be viewed as a proper response to our message of salvation for all believers. If being salt and light is to have any meaning, we will have to take some difficult risks in these areas.

Avoiding Pitfalls

Ministries of social action come with a distinct set of pitfalls to avoid. By being aware of these pitfalls from the outset, we will find it easier to avoid serious mistakes.

Here are a few:

ganizations have been scrutinized more aggressively by the IRS, Congress, the public, and various special-interest groups. As a result, the lobbying limitation, like the campaign limitation, must be taken seriously.

In evaluating campaign or lobbying activities, church leaders must consider the consequences of a loss of tax-exempt status. Among other things, loss of exempt status would mean a church would pay corporate income taxes on its net earnings, no member could deduct contributions made to the church, the church would lose its eligibility for preferential mailing rates, staff members would be ineligible to participate in tax-sheltered annuities, and the church property tax exemption would be jeopardized. Such results are sufficiently undesirable to suggest caution and conservatism in interpreting the limitations on campaign and lobbying activities.

One final point: The United States Supreme Court has suggested that 501(c)(3) organizations desiring to engage in substantial legislative activities should establish a 501(c)(4) exempt organization, which can engage in legislative activities but cannot receive tax-deductible contributions.

—Richard R. Hammar

• *Ignoring unethical behavior by staff or workers.* It can be incredibly painful to receive a call from a media representative asking for comment on the local leader of a crusade against a social ill caught indulging in the behavior he or she was seeking to stop. No substitute exists for personal integrity and accountability. Social action often means combating sin, and we do well to remember that sin is seductive for the believer and unbeliever alike.

It is a deeply serious responsibility to attempt to speak on behalf of the church for a given social action. We represent Christ to the world in everything we say and do. Correspondingly, we damage not only ourselves but also the entire witness of the church when our personal behavior does not reflect the cause we advocate in the public forum. Those who lead and operate ministries of social action should surround themselves with strong partners who can provide oversight and who won't hesitate to point out inconsistencies or dangers that may appear in their life or ministry.

• *Using methods that don't match our witness.* We do not honor God by "winning" with methods or tactics that are not consistent with our role as his servants in the world. For Christians, the means to an end are as important as the goal itself.

Particularly in the political forum, it is easy to lose sight of the subtle and not-so-subtle ways our methods reflect on Christ. We do not have the option of inappropriately and unfairly vilifying those who oppose the objectives we are advocating. In a like manner, we must avoid the temptation to speak ill of believers or churches whose approach differs from our own. Many churches don't agree on *where* action is appropriate, much less on the methods to use. We must demonstrate respect for differences.

• *Supporting personalities over principles.* Avoid supporting individuals, bright personalities, or political parties rather than principles. In civic leadership, few—if any—candidates or parties can lay exclusive claim to being God's chosen representatives for a position. When we support principles of justice and righteousness that will benefit a community, we offer all those in responsibility the opportunity to participate in their achievement and benefits.

• *Confusing the kingdom with politics.* The government is not a substitute for the church, nor vice versa. Politics will not institute the kingdom of God, just as the church is not the appropriate institution to govern society. For some citizens, political or social victory is a means of control. Our responsibility remains consistent in the midst of the many battles that are a part of social action: first, to be of service to our communities, and second, to remind our governing leaders of their promises, commitments, and standards of justice. The church is painfully compromised when it functions merely as an extension of a secular party or individual.

• *Being careless with funds.* Maintain impeccable financial integrity, with outside checks and balances in place. Asserting communal benefit in public while privately cutting corners or seeking personal gain will destroy most ministries, including those involved in social action.

Making a Lasting Difference

In attempting constructive social action, we take risks in order to call forth positive change. While it is easy to become discouraged in the process of being witnesses for righteousness and justice in societies filled with far too much injustice and darkness, we should never lose hope. Just as we often see remarkable personal change after a lifetime of pain or sin, so too can we witness similar transformations in policies that don't reflect the glory of God.

Two examples of Christians who have attempted change in social policy illustrate the attitudes that can characterize our own efforts. The first example involves a government official working inside the system as a member of a powerful national commission. Asked to express the reasons for his optimism in the face of so many losses on policies he was seeking to change, he noted: "The civil rights battle was an uphill battle. The battle against slavery was an uphill battle. All the battles that are worthwhile probably have, at one time or another, seemed like uphill battles. The question is whether you want to be remembered as having played a constructive role in those uphill battles or having avoided the fight altogether."

The second example involves a retired Christian grocer in Oklahoma City who decided one day that God had called him to do something about pornography, sexual violence, and the safety of children in his community. Encouraged by their pastor, he and his wife started a ministry of social action named Citizens Concerned for Children and enlisted the support and sponsorship of local churches.

Initially, as is often the case, they were met with deep skepticism and hostility. Public officials didn't believe their claims and hesitated on taking action. Even as the officials hesitated, they noticed the broad-based coalition, the reasoned approach, and the accurate statistics assembled by the group. The citizens involved also had a long track record of compassionate work with children in the community.

Five years later, officials in the city were vigorously enforcing their laws to the point where over 150 peep shows, adult bookstores, and other sexually oriented businesses either closed down or chose to leave town. The county's rape rate plummeted by over 25 percent, and prostitutes were offered employment training. George Harper, the grocer with enough courage to attempt making a difference in his community, went to meet the Lord after a long bout with cancer. He left a powerful legacy of positive social change for the church and an honorable witness for his Lord.

Not all of us will experience the blessing of seeing quick fruit from our ministries of social action. Yet, our Lord reminds us again and again to be diligent in overcoming evil with good. Martin Luther King, Jr., once noted, "The time is always right to do what is right." Ministries of social action are one powerful means to shine Christ's light before the world.

—Jerry R. Kirk and H. Deen Kaplan

Resources

Colson, C., and E. Vaughn. 1992. The body. Dallas: Word.

Neuhaus, R. 1984. The naked public square: Religion and democracy in America. Grand Rapids: Eerdmans.

Pornography

Pornography has inundated American communities during the last three decades. There are now more outlets for hard-core pornography in the United States than McDonalds restaurants. Unfortunately, studies demonstrate that the explosive growth of pornography contributes directly to child molestation, sexual violence, addiction for men, the spread of sexually transmitted diseases, and a demeaning, destructive attitude toward women. Sexual sin, which pornography directly encourages, has brought pain and suffering to millions of lives and thousands of churches.

Smut Can Be Stopped

Yet, at the time of this writing, Cincinnati, Ohio, has no commercial outlets for hard-core pornography. There are no adult bookstores, peep shows, massage parlors, or local video stores that carry *any* hard-core pornography. All soft-core pornography (which is legal) is shielded from the view of minors. Why? Because citizens and churches formed a team, insisted on high standards for the community, and supported law enforcers in making that standard a reality.

Pastors and churches can make the same difference in their own communities to help ensure a safer neighborhood for everyone. However, it takes lots of perseverance, a knowledgeable, committed team, and a willingness to deal with a distasteful subject.

An Action Plan

Specifically, what can we do to help win this battle? The most important action we can take is to educate and recruit members of our community to combat the problem with us. Public officials, law enforcers, and even many store owners respond to the public and its concerns. Here are the first steps to take:

• *Educate yourself.* Obtain information from one of the organizations involved in combating pornography. Few people, particularly in the church, fully understand the depth of the problem and its relationship to dozens of other social ills. Since dozens of myths and misconceptions about pornography have taken root, you'll need to clarify your concept of exactly what you can do to help combat it.

• *Utilize existing expertise.* In talking with the experts, ask what works and what doesn't. By doing this, you'll not only avoid many common mistakes but also provide additional opportunities for your church members to be encouraged by victories in other communities.

• *Build a team.* Call forth those in your congregation who are gifted for the task—gifted with a great deal of fortitude, perseverance, and patience. Focus on building a broad-based team, including representatives from a wide cross-section of the community. Rape-crisis centers, PTAS, and women's organizations can become natural partners. The goal is to demonstrate that the whole community has an interest in addressing this problem.

• *Choose your targets.* Start with one or two establishments and call for appropriate social and legal action. This takes lots of planning, but dozens of communities have begun the process of total city clean-up by starting small. In many cities, a handful of interested citizens from local churches have mobilized entire communities and eliminated hundreds of pornography outlets.

• *Apply community pressure.* The battle against pornography is often complex, involving the legal system, a focus on the First Amendment, and a well-entrenched and well-financed opponent. Yet the bottom line for most pornographers is economic. When pornographers understand that concerned citizens in a community are organized and will not relent until the problem is addressed, they leave.

Pornographers routinely attempt to dissuade citizens from taking appropriate action by applying derogatory, inaccurate labels—such as "censor"—to the activists. These labels won't define your team if its style and actions reflect a willingness to encourage *legal* action only against illegal materials and *social* action against materials that are legally protected.

—Jerry Kirk and H. Deen Kaplan

Hunger

One out of five children live in poverty in the United States, and approximately twenty million Americans are hungry for at least some period each month. Though we have an enormous welfare bureaucracy in place, private food banks channel millions of pounds of food to millions of Americans who cannot get the food they need any other way.

Throughout the world, it is estimated that one billion people are hungry. One child in ten dies before its first birthday. Forty thousand children die each day. Yet there is enough grain grown worldwide to provide every person on earth with plenty to eat every day.

What response can the church give to the disparity between the abundance of God's creation and the vast numbers excluded from that abundance? What can the church do in the face of such great need?

Four Actions

• *Study the Scriptures.* From a simple desire to let the poor glean crops after harvest to the elaborate system of the sabbatical and jubilee year, the biblical concept of a healthy community has always required the proper care and inclusion of the most vulnerable in society. Christ walked with the poor, called the rich man to see the suffering Lazarus, and inspired Zacchaeus to give away half his wealth. He declared the jubilee year fulfilled in himself and proclaimed the kingdom of God, calling us to seek it first above all things. Thus, the Scriptures support efforts to alleviate the ravages of hunger.

• *Get to know the hungry.* Frances Moore Lappe speaks of knowing the emotions of hunger. Hunger, she says, is the anguish of having to make choices no person should ever have to make. It is the grief of watching loved ones die, the humiliation of poverty, and the fear of oppression. There may be poor and hungry people in our own congregations. We can volunteer our time working at a food pantry or become a sister church with another congregation in a poor neighborhood or in a third-world country. By building relationships in this way, we break down many barriers between people and discover firsthand the struggle of poverty.

• *Use political processes.* Many denominations have hunger education and advocacy departments. Bread for the World, a Christian lobbying group, works on the national level to influence hunger legislation and asks congregations to join them in an annual offering of letters. Church World Service sponsors local CROP walks to raise funds for the hungry. Some states have an active Council of Churches that lobbies their legislature and educates their affiliated members.

Churches can publicize the needs of hunger agencies and speak on behalf of the poor at city hall. Some groups have written food policies adopted by their communities that insure "food security" for all citizens. In all such efforts, we must listen to the people most affected by poverty and help them work for their own solutions.

• *Include the hungry at special celebrations.* We can have people bring a can of food for a local pantry, and when we meet for worship, we can challenge each other to live more simply. We may want to try a simulated hunger dinner: divide the food among people based on the actual distribution in the world of the haves and have-nots, and let everyone try to get a decent meal.

As congregations begin to see the vision of the kingdom of God, the walls of Jericho may not come tumbling down immediately. We are called to be faithful, not necessarily successful. Our hope remains in the Lord, the One who fed the five thousand because of his heartfelt compassion for people in need.

—David C. Hacker and Sheri L. Noah

Racism

In many parts of our society, the problem of racism still persists. We still live in separate neighborhoods. We still go to separate churches. We send our kids to separate schools. But rarely do we consider ourselves to be racist. The good news is that Christians are beginning to take the call to racial reconciliation more seriously.

Although Sunday morning is still America's most segregated hour, Christians understand that if anyone has the mandate to do something about the problem of race, it is the followers of Christ. A major part of our witness to the unbelieving world lies in our ability to demonstrate a message powerful enough to cut through our racial baggage and present to the world a body where Jew and Gentile, male and female, slave and free can all drink from the same cup.

Perhaps, then, it is not so important whether we categorize ourselves as racist or nonracist. Maybe it is time we begin asking ourselves a new question: What are we doing to bring about racial healing?

A Minority-friendly Church

One practical way for Christians to begin to eliminate racism is to focus on the positive. Instead of trying to determine if our churches exhibit racist tendencies, here's a better question to ask: Is our church minority friendly? That is, do minorities of all kinds feel welcome and comfortable in our midst?

The answer to this question can be difficult to hear. Thus, it is more important to make sure that our churches are intentional about creating an atmosphere of openness and acceptance. Here are some ways to help accomplish that purpose:

- *Find out how your church is being perceived by minority groups.* Churches need to make sure that although they are saying "Everyone welcome," minorities are not hearing "Whites only." It matters little the message we think we are giving if it is perceived as something radically different.
- *Understand the difference between integration and reconciliation.* Integration was a legal struggle. It forced people to change their actions but not their hearts. Reconciliation, on the other hand, is spiritual. We *can* force people not to discriminate on the basis of race but we *cannot* force those people to love regardless of race. Because this new struggle is a spiritual one, the church must take the point position in showing the way.
- *Fellowship regularly with minority churches.* For most churches this will take significant commitment. Church members and leaders will be challenged to go out of their way to befriend people who may be skeptical of their motives. Yet one "picture" of cross-cultural friendship exhibited by two leaders will be more effective than a thousand sermons.
- *Maintain personal contact with the poor.* It is difficult to talk about racism without mentioning its first cousin, classism. The poor are close to the heart of God. We can hardly

read God's Word without feeling his deep compassion for these members of society. Every individual and church, if they are to follow Christ, must respond in this area. As leaders, we can be sure we are following in the footsteps of Jesus when we are directing our followers toward the oppressed and disenfranchised.

• *Demonstrate the gospel's power over racism.* The fact that homogeneous churches grow faster does not necessarily mean they are best. It's tempting to justify our weaknesses rather than reach out effectively. What kind of witness is a large, homogeneous church whose gospel is not strong enough to lead people to work to overcome a human weakness as obvious as racial prejudice?

—*John Perkins*

Abortion

The number of medical students refusing to learn abortion techniques became so large that the National Organization of Women began demanding the training be made mandatory at medical schools. When the President made abortion available to the military, many military doctors refused to perform them. The National Abortion Federation has found it necessary to provide workshops for doctors, nurses, aides, counselors, and even trash collectors employed at abortion clinics, in order to help them deal with their nightmares.

Abortion is legal, but these examples demonstrate that moral conscience maintains a powerful effect on behavior. And the proper development of moral conscience is the church's job. The church's primary role in opposing abortion is to change the cultural perception of what determines right and wrong, showing people how to make good moral decisions in difficult circumstances. Without the church's help to shape the values of a culture and combat the false ideologies of a society, even good lawmaking will have little effect.

A Prophetic Role

Ezekiel 33 emphasizes the prophetic role of God's people with respect to a culture that has fallen into evil practices. God assigns us as "watchmen," and our job primarily involves issuing a warning. Here's what we can do:

• *Go public.* Be bold in taking a public stand from a moral perspective. We can work to keep abortion visible as a moral and spiritual issue, being as public as possible about abortion in our speaking, publishing, and personal outreach. Give leadership in applying moral pressure to civic organizations, and encourage members of your congregation to challenge pro-abortion stances held by their professional organizations.

• *Preach and teach.* The word *abortion* isn't in the Bible, but Scripture has plenty to say about the unborn and about the obligation of both Christians and civil governments to protect and care for the innocent and needy. We can strive to show our church members how every major doctrine of Christian faith applies to abortion.

Teaching children and adults the high standards and blessings of sexual purity and commitment to family will foster biblical attitudes about abortion. Investigate local school sex education curricula and get involved in changing them where necessary, or in providing alternatives.

Convictions against abortion among Christians often run much deeper than their knowledge, leading them to become easily frustrated in discussions with those who disagree. So we can help our church members become knowledgeable about all aspects of the issue.

• *Use a soft approach.* Because so many churches are divided on abortion, we'll want to acknowledge a range of views among Christians. Teaching and discussion sessions should avoid treating truth and falsehood as equals; nevertheless, allow for an exchange designed to lead by gentle persuasion and honest application of biblical truths, in the spirit of 2 Timothy 4:1–5. A winsome, caring, and loving attitude goes a long way toward convincing people of the truth.

• *But don't be soft.* In some cases, we may need to exercise church discipline, particularly with members of the church who routinely perform "abortions on demand." Make it known that those who support a cavalier approach to abortion put themselves outside of Christian orthodoxy.

• *Guard against becoming politicized.* Churches should guard themselves against taking on a role that belongs within the political arena. Our strength lies not in dictating the law but in influencing moral perceptions and behavior. If we are effective, we will see an aversion to abortion spread—from doctors who have direct exposure to the procedure, to other members of our society for whom abortion is only an academic question.

—*Terry Schlossberg*

Homelessness

Just east of a famous Los Angeles freeway stands a luxurious hotel, complete with limos, butlers, and crystal chandeliers. Immediately behind the hotel lies the city's skid row. On an average summer night, hundreds of people live in discarded cardboard boxes along the sidewalks. These people on the street, as well as their wealthy brothers and sisters in the hotel, were created in God's image. Thus we are compelled to work within the systems of our society on behalf of the homeless.

Only One Gospel

Ironically, many of the difficulties complicating our efforts to help the homeless come from within the church. Most grievous is the unbiblical separation of the gospel into a social gospel, which concerns itself with humanity's physical needs, and a personal gospel, which concerns itself with humanity's salvation. In contrast to this artificial separation, the apostle Paul insisted in his letter to the Galatians that there is only one gospel. That this gospel has implications for humanity's spiritual and physical needs is made clear by such texts as 1 John 3:17 and James 1:27.

While we may logically and biblically assign a higher priority to humanity's need for a relationship with Christ, we are not free to separate the one kind of need from the other. A tendency to indulge in this separation, ignoring either spiritual or physical need, may indicate an unhealthy willingness to let political ideology dictate one's theological stance.

Church and Society Together

If we agree that the physical needs of humanity are a proper focus of the church, how should we go about meeting these needs? At the congregational level, that process ideally starts from the pulpit. The Old and New Testaments have much to say regarding our direct, practical provisions for the poor and homeless, and these texts must be proclaimed. The process cannot stop there, however, since the congregation must consider how to be an advocate within society's social, political, and economic institutions.

Work at the institutional level is complicated. When a church attempts to influence a body of politicians or members of the financial community, all sorts of accusations surface. Chief among them is the charge that such activity is a violation of the separation of church and state. The logical and scriptural fallacies inherent in this position need to be exposed. Jesus offers us some critical guidance in this regard in Matthew 10:16, where he says, "I am sending you out like sheep among wolves. Therefore be as shrewd as snakes and as innocent as doves."

Christ's advice is twofold. First, he calls us to innocence. The leadership of the church must be held accountable for what it attempts, and the means of accountability must be highly visible. We must work hard to insure that there are no hidden agendas behind the effort and that no immoral or unethical behavior occurs. Clear, consistent communication is essential. All financial matters should be handled according to standard accounting practices, and any financial records should be open for public inspection.

Second, Christ calls us to be shrewd. The body of Christ has limited resources to use on behalf of the homeless. To avoid ineffectiveness, we must take the time to understand the value system operating within each institution approached. For example, the media are interested in how many people are watching their program or reading their publication. A politician is interested in getting reelected. A bank wants to show a healthy profit. Proceeding with biblical shrewdness means recognizing that if a plan for helping the homeless can be ethically aligned with the value system of a given institution, that plan has a greater chance of succeeding.

—John Hambrick

Peacemaking

Jesus said, "Blessed are the peacemakers, for they will be called [known as] sons of God" (Matt. 5:9). Again he said, "All men will know that you are my disciples if you love one another" (John 13:35). In every social context, the community of faith is called by her Lord to be agents of reconciliation, to transcend the racial, ethnic, class, gender, and national lines that separate us.

Practical Peacemaking

We, as a people of God in our identity with Christ, are the one movement that ought to include all peoples of the earth in God's peace. Theologically, we know we are his agents of peace, but what must we do in order to be peacemakers in the practical business of everyday living? We need to:

- *Develop an ethical Christology.* We must begin with an understanding that Jesus as our Lord and Savior is also our mentor. As our Lord he enables us by his transforming grace to live by his love, to walk as he walked (1 John 2:6). We should relate our ethics to Christ in the same way we relate our salvation to Christ; we are *saved* in relation to him and we *behave* in our relation to him.
- *Commit to righteousness.* This commitment requires a right relatedness to God and to all people. The New Testament word for "righteousness" could literally be translated as "justice-righteousness." This means that we as Christians promote justice for all people, even as our secular order affirms "that all people are created equal." We should remember that it was to a Gentile, Cornelius, that Peter spoke of the gospel of peace (Acts 10:36). Again, Paul writes of Jesus that he is our peace, having made the Jew and Gentile to be one new humanity (Eph. 2:14). Our peace ministry must cross all racial lines to truly incorporate the family of God.
- *Confront economic difficulties.* We must find ways to remove the impasse between the "haves" and the "have nots" in a constructive manner. One example is the success of Robert Lovell of Pittsburgh. As president of a savings and loan, he helped many poor people with loans and extensive counsel, enabling many to achieve and to gain hope for the future.

In the inner city of Washington, D.C., our congregation arranged with a credit union to be security for needy persons we would recommend, enabling them not only to get a loan but to build up an invaluable credit history.

- *Approach violence redemptively.* "Turning the other cheek" is not a surrender but a strategy of operation (Matt. 5:39); it is saying to another, "Your treatment of me doesn't determine my treatment of you. I can decide by other principles."

We are called to love our enemies, both when our government engages in war and when the enemy is across the street. Peacemaking requires exercising the active initiative of love. As peacemakers, we need an evangelistic spirit, loving others with a love that invites them to know and walk with the God of love. As evangelists, we will seek to make even our enemies brothers and sisters in Christ. We cannot destroy a person for whom Christ died.

• *Exercise freedom within a culture.* As disciples of Christ, we need to exercise greater freedom in a given culture, rather than be determined by that culture. We should place emphasis on diversity within the membership of our congregations. And as we share Christ's mission in the global community, we need to network with the people of God in all countries in our mission of meeting human need.

—Myron Augsburger

Ecology

Some pastors report that their biggest environmental task is convincing their members that it is Christian to care about God's handiwork. Too often we appear to be faced with the options of either loving the Creator or loving the created. This dilemma is unfortunate—and false.

God's Masterpiece

Perhaps our first response to the problem could be to invite our members to contemplate with new awareness the marvel of creation itself. It bears all the fingerprints of a rather extravagant Being. God spared no effort and delight in crafting this magnificent piece of work we call his creation. Not one of us has the ability to craft a single flower and make it live, yet God designed millions of petals, leaves, and stems, and threw in countless colors. That was just the beginning. There are fish, animals, stars, galaxies, and—the crown of it all—people. We cannot find any "utility" in all this; apparently God simply loves to create.

As a result of such contemplation, we'll find we have no reason to fear involvement in the environment; it has always been the work and possession of our God. When we show our respect and love for all that God has created, we demonstrate our love and admiration for God and his stunning masterpiece. Conversely, to trample creation is to walk over the personal handiwork of the One we claim to love.

Our Work

Once people are convinced, theologically, that environmental activism is properly Christian, what can we suggest for those who want to get more involved? Here are three practical possibilities:

• *Green the church.* Interested church members could begin taking inventory of church practices that relate to waste. A simple program might recycle materials that come out of the church office. Creative thinkers could develop alternatives to the use of bulletins and other handouts that usually create a lot of waste unnecessarily. For example, one church uses the overhead to make all service announcements.

• *Green the members.* How about turning one Sunday morning a year into a "Save God's Creation" event? A couple of motivated members could set up a regular means of collecting newspapers, bottles, and cans from church attenders as they drive into the parking lot. Green arm bands would mark the volunteers who collect the material as people drive up. Money gained from the recycling could go toward any number of worthy environmental causes, from buying up plots of rain forest to supporting a river clean-up project.

- *Green the outreach.* Every year on Earth Day, hundreds of thousands of Americans participate in environmental parades and celebrations. There is no more natural bridge to evangelism, since these folks already respect the handiwork of God. Why not attend these rallies and, while celebrating along with all the others, look for opportunities to help connect these people with the One who is really behind Earth Day, the Creator of every day that earth exists?

One Christian organization that serves other Christians who want to do something about the environment is The Christian Environmental Association (P.O. Box 25, Colfax, WA 99111). This group can provide first-rate resources, newsletters, ideas, and even travel opportunities to environmental projects operated by other Christians.

Everything we do to increase our church members' awareness that God is the Creator of the environment will enhance our efforts to save it. Above all, we can seek out practical ways to stay on the cutting edge ourselves, so that our members will be able to witness our deep admiration for the handiwork of our personal Savior.

—*Gordon Aeschliman*

Part IV:

Pastoral Care

What image would we use for the Good Shepherd in today's society? The Good Executive, who practices "management by walking around" and cares for every one of her employees? Or the Good Programmer, who understands every single line of code in his software and doesn't quit until each one is bug-free?

We could be more prosaic and use the term *pastor,* which derives from the word for shepherd in the first place. The parish pastor cares for his or her flock every bit as much as the agrarian shepherd watched his flocks. Learning the role from Jesus, today's pastors pray for their flocks, protect them from harmful influences, feed them well and build them up to withstand difficulties, give them meaningful activities, and place them in good company, watching out for their sense of belonging. They make calls on individuals and expend their time on their parishioners.

It's not easy being a pastor today—as if it ever was. But today, pastors must lead sophisticated congregations with high expectations. Pastors today retain much of the responsibility but have lost much of the authority—and even the respect—enjoyed by previous generations. People are so busy that even the shut-ins are hard to find at home! Members' commitment to institutions of all kinds is waning, yet they seem to demand ever more program options.

How is the pastor to cope? Certainly not by relying on personal stamina, not by mere talents or techniques. And definitely not solo. The wise pastor—the one who not only will tend the flock well but will be doing it joyfully for years to come—will exercise pastoral care with spiritual strength derived from God and with ample help provided by church members exercising their spiritual gifts and calling. Such is the counsel of the following chapters.

14

The Purpose of Pastoral Care

The goal of pastoral care," said Manfred Seitz, "is becoming whole through helping conversation in acknowledgement of faith." Those who do pastoral care help people through the situations of life from the perspective of the gospel. Such care is focused on the brokenness of humans in their alienation from God and emanates from the point of view of the healing of humanity offered in Jesus Christ. "The goal of pastoral care," Seitz continues, "is the person becoming whole, becoming an ordered person, becoming a coping person, becoming a person at peace" (Seitz 1978, 73–79).

If we were to survey the biblical and historical roots of pastoral care, would Seitz's descriptions of its purpose emerge there and still ring true for us today? Let's find out.

Pastoral Care in the Bible

• *Old Testament roots.* Pastoral care in the Old Testament is primarily concerned with the political and religious guidance of the people of God. Moses, the Egyptian prince turned herder, is the first pastor in the Bible. As deliverer of the Israelites and preacher of God's revelation, Moses was also the shepherd of God's people. He was an encourager who reminded his people of God's promises in the face of onrushing Egyptian chariots (Exod. 14:10–14), a priest who led their celebrations of praise and worship to the God who had rescued them (15:1), and a mediator of the conflicts among the people (18:15–16).

David, the shepherd-king, is the other great pastor of the Old Testament who serves as a model of godly leadership. The prophets Ezekiel and Jeremiah, in particular, saw him as the good shepherd who tended to God's flock, in contrast to Judah's apostate religious elite who neglected the people (Ezek. 34:23–24; Jer. 23:1–4).

Various pastoral figures with different means of shepherding God's people can be found throughout the Old Testament, including the priests, the prophets, the wise men, and the scribes. The functions of Levitical priesthood, outlined in Leviticus 8–9 and 21–22, focused primarily on Israel's public worship. The pastoral significance of this liturgical ministry, however, should not be discounted simply because of its ritual nature. Priests were also personal counselors who offered moral and spiritual guidance to pilgrims visiting Jerusalem for the festivals. The prophets, known for their public calls to national repentance and obedience, also gave personal counseling and guidance to both the nation's leaders and ordinary folk.

The pastoral guidance of the wisdom tradition came to have a significant influence in later Judaism. The wise men were "practical counselors of the soul, proclaiming reverence for God and justice to man, and making plain the path of right conduct" (McNeill 1951, 9). While the wisdom tradition of the Bible (Job, Proverbs, Ecclesiastes) was conservative and traditional, it distanced itself from both the rituals of temple worship and the radical obedience of the prophets.

The pastors of Judaism in the time of Jesus were the scribes or rabbis, whose roots went back to the rebuilding of the temple under Ezra. They were experts in the Law (Torah) and its application to the daily lives of the Jews. Most villages had a synagogue with a rabbi who served as worship leader, teacher, counselor, and conflict mediator. Trained in one of several rabbinical schools, the rabbis were generally respected for their knowledge of the Scriptures, spiritual guidance, compassion, and practical wisdom.

• *New Testament developments.* Pastoral care in the New Testament focuses on building up the church as the body of Christ and the people of God. This care has its roots in the ministry of Jesus and in the dynamic activity of the Spirit, given at Pentecost. Jesus utilized the position of rabbi in his teaching and his personal encounters, often with surprising results, though traces of the prophetic and wisdom traditions also emerged in his ministry. While Jesus often spoke to large crowds, his preferred means of ministry was one-to-one dialogue, in which personal spiritual needs would arise and be addressed.

The Gospels record numerous personal encounters in which Jesus heals (Mark 10:46–52), teaches (Luke 7:36–50), encourages (John 8:1–11), casts out demons (Luke 8:26–33), and offers spiritual renewal (John 3:1–21). Jesus seems to have reserved his most extensive pastoral care for the disciples, who were with him constantly for three years. He offered them spiritual guidance and training, teaching them how to preach, teach, heal, and cast out demons.

Pastoral care in the early church took its form from the Jewish synagogue, out of which the first Christians had their religious formation. The position of elder, pastor, or bishop is thus parallel to the synagogue's ruling elders. Elders were responsible for the spiritual and physical needs of Christians in the community. The appointment of Stephen and six others as deacons (Acts 6:1–7) seems to be a response to two needs: the need for the presence of Hellenistic Jews in the leadership of the Jerusalem church and the need for a more efficient organization of local relief efforts.

The transformation and maturity of the whole person into the image of Christ is the basic aim of pastoral care in the early church (Eph. 4:11–16; 1 Pet. 5:1–4). Its basic message of salvation is a proclamation of whole-person healing as well as spiritual deliverance. Repentance (*metanoia*) indicates a fundamental orientation to Christ as the result of a personal encounter with him. Growth in Christ (*teleis*), on the other hand, is the outworking of that orientation under the guidance of the Spirit in the context of the Christian fellowship. The apostles' ministry was aimed at guiding and directing persons, through conversion, into spiritual maturity in the Christian community (Acts 2:41–47).

The primary modes of pastoral care in the New Testament consist of mutual edification (*oikodome*), encouragement (*paraklesis*), and a mutual discipline (Matt. 18:15–17). The work of pastoral care is here recognized as the work of the whole people of God. The ministry of pastors, elders, and bishops encourages, rather than prevents or controls, this "one another" care ministry.

On the other hand, the New Testament also recognizes the unique calling of pastors, elders, and bishops, who are given a ministry of oversight and supervision. Shepherding is the primary metaphor for this kind of pastoral care (Oden 1983, 49–63). Along with giving spiritual direction, the shepherd engages in a wide range of functions, from leading worship and teaching to providing food and caring for widows and orphans.

So Christ's ongoing caring ministry takes place in the context of the Christian community. The church offers human community through spiritual communion, that is, through the work of the Spirit who unites believers to Christ and to one another in him. Thus Christian community is not simply the fellowship of kindred hearts, but the product of divine activity. In this way people can achieve a sense of personal identity through belonging, being "in Christ" together with others. This mutual belonging is the only enduring foundation for the ministry of mutual caring.

Pastoral Care in Historical Perspective

• *The patristic and medieval eras.* The pastoral care of the church in the pre-Constantinian era focused on supporting and encouraging Christians during times of persecution and in the expectation of the imminent return of Christ (Clebsch and Jaeckle 1965, 14–23). During this period, however, post-baptismal sin and restoration to the fellowship of the church was a central concern. As a result, pastoral care became increasingly focused on discerning and dispensing the appropriate penance for sins. Later, church leaders would specify the forms of discipline to be borne by those who had lapsed into paganism under the pressure of the persecutions.

Many pastoral functions became formalized in the work of a hierarchical church as Christianity became the dominant religion of the Roman Empire. As the moral and spiritual guide of the Constantinian

Enrolling People in Ministry

The best measure of a New Testament church is how many people walk out of church on Sunday to be the royal priesthood on Monday, Tuesday, and Wednesday. If the basic "product" of the church is people in ministry, then central to pastoral care is putting people in ministry and supporting them there. Consider these four distinct kids of ministry for lay people:

• *Material ministry.* Lay people can give money and goods to bless and heal and help people. Material ministry might involve digging wells in Haiti or painting a local shelter for battered women. It's people providing material goods for others.

For example, two retired executive women had a special concern for the down-and-out on Seattle's skid row. One night a week, these women took sandwich fixings to the First Avenue Service Center, where they made sandwiches while dispensing care and conversation to the street people seeking food. Over the years they have dispensed a lot of love and dignity as well as more than a million sandwiches.

• *Spiritual ministry.* This involves introducing people to Jesus Christ and to life in the Spirit. Our churches, unfortunately, may be full of unconverted believers who ascribe to all the right doctrines but don't allow those beliefs to affect their lives. They need to move into vital ministry for their professed Lord. Getting involved in a small group is one way they can do it.

I recall a deeply unhappy woman who, over a ten-year period, endured assorted illnesses. Although she was only 40, she was already frail. The final blow came when her husband divorced her. When that happened, I thought she might die.

However, she was part of a small group of ordinary Christians who ministered to her in wonderful

empire, the church supplied needed social stability through preaching and catechetical instruction. The concern for spiritual discipline waned during this period, however, as church membership and Roman citizenship became increasingly synonymous.

From the fifth century, the Western church increasingly confronted the new populations moving into northern Europe. During this period of missionary expansion, pastoral care often took the form of civilizing the "barbarian hordes." At the end of the sixth century, Pope Gregory the Great wrote a treatise entitled *Pastoral Care,* which described the basic pastoral work of the priest: to offer moral and spiritual guidance to the unchurched and to administer the sacraments.

By the eleventh century, the Roman church had thoroughly shaped western civilization. Church and society formed a mostly seamless fabric. The pastoral care of the church, based on the administration of the seven sacraments by the "secular" clergy, stood at the center of

ways. They helped her come to grips with how she would handle life with her husband gone. They encouraged her to return to school to obtain job skills. She got her driver's license and became more independent. Increasingly, by means of this group's spiritual ministry, the Lord moved into this woman's life, and she became a new person.

• *Wholeness ministry.* After he raised Lazarus from the dead, Jesus told those standing by to unwrap him. There are countless church members who have been raised from the dead but have never been unwrapped. They're alive and walking, but they're still bound with fear and guilt. Jesus gives them new life, and it is the job of those around them to do some unwrapping.

Lay people can't do brain surgery, but some of the key words used to explain illness are stress, loneliness, resentment. Healing comes when those negative emotions are replaced with love, purpose, and hope. The staff at the Menninger Foundation believes that if you get hope, you get well. Dr. Viktor Frankl connected healing to purpose. Norman Cousins wrote a book on the healing effects of joy. Lay people have all of those to offer in a ministry of healing and wholeness.

• *Prophetic ministry.* This kind of ministry changes the way people live within the structures of society. Those practicing prophetic ministry look at the structures and ask, "How can they be changed for the better?"

One man I know is working to find new ways to provide low-cost housing for the poor. He contends that churches don't have the money to underwrite housing on the scale that is needed, and Housing and Urban Development won't. His plan is to approach businesses and say, "Let me show you how you can build low-cost housing for the poor and make a reasonable profit." He's a prophet in the profit sector!

—*Bruce Larson*

the citizen's life. The monastic orders supplemented this ongoing sacramental work with monks and nuns who offered personal spiritual direction and counseling, as well as itinerant preachers, healers, and counselors (some of whom were sincere and godly, while others were frauds and quacks).

Despite the contributions of gifted and profound spiritual guides like Francis of Assisi and Bernard of Clairvaux, much pastoral care in the medieval churches was appallingly inadequate. Most priests were poorly trained and underpaid for their work; bishops were frequently more concerned with political intrigue than with the spiritual welfare of their parishes.

• *The Reformation and post-Reformation eras.* Pastoral care in the Reformation churches reflected the newly recovered emphasis on justification and the forgiveness of sins. The Reformation began with criticisms and reforms of many questionable pastoral practices intro-

Leadership Training

Who sets the spiritual tone of a church? Most new graduates from seminary would probably answer without hesitation: the pastor. After all, who is more visible? Who takes up most of the time in the pulpit? What better way is there for a visitor to ascertain the pulse and direction of a church than by zeroing in on the pastor?

That is what I would have said. Now I'm not so certain.

Lay Leaders Set the Tone

To be sure, we pastors play a major role in charting the theological course of our churches. We have the constant and awesome duty of lifting up biblical models and divine priorities. We learn that we can affect the temperature of a room simply by the way we conduct ourselves. People watch us to see whether we are goofy or grave, pious or playful, self-effacing or self-serving. It doesn't take long for parishioners to form their opinions about us.

Even so, the longer one has been in ministry, the more he or she will likely come to believe that the prevailing tone of the church is set by the lay leadership. After all, pastors are *expected* to be cheerleaders for Bible study and spiritual growth. If we did not believe in those things, we probably would not be pastors. Far more remarkable for the congregation are lay leaders who display an insatiable hunger for spiritual growth and an irrepressible enthusiasm for serving Christ. In other words, pastors can jump up and down and wave their arms, but a congregation will not warm up to spiritual growth until its lay leaders catch the vision and get excited about Christian discipleship.

For that reason, many pastors have found it helpful to gather their elders and deacons (as soon as possible after their election to office)

duced by the church, in particular the sale of indulgences that offered remission of sins for the buyer or whomever the buyer designated. The Reformers contended that the gospel offer of forgiveness was the unconditional gift of Christ and could not be sold by the church. The abuses of private confession also came under scrutiny. Appealing to the doctrine of the priesthood of all believers, Luther argued that anyone, not just a priest, could hear confession and pronounce God's forgiveness.

The Reformers devoted much attention to improving the quality of pastoral care and spiritual direction in the regions under their influence. Two important documents from this era are Zwingli's *The Shepherd* (1524) and Bucer's *On the True Care of Souls* (1538). Zwingli offered a biblical theology of the pastor and a thorough critique of the false prophets and shepherds occupying clerical offices. Beginning with Paul's "one another" statements, Bucer developed the concept of

for a weekend retreat. The first thing these pastors tell their lay officers is that by electing them to office, the congregation has asked them for spiritual leadership. Their brothers and sisters in the faith are counting on them for spiritual support and guidance. Parishioners need someone other than the pastor, someone who lives in the same 9-to-5 world they do, to show them that an authentic Christian life is really possible and that ordinary, everyday people can bear a powerful witness to Jesus Christ.

Credible Examples

A congregation rarely will exceed the spiritual reach and depth of its lay leaders. If lay leaders think Bible study is important, if they show up at advertised church events, if they exude an honest enthusiasm for ministry, service, and prayer, then (and only then) will the rest of the congregation begin to take lay leadership seriously. In short, if something is actually happening spiritually in the lives of lay leaders, their credibility as leaders will go through the roof.

So developing spiritual leadership among the members of our ruling boards begins with encouraging their individual growth in discipleship. We can provide Bible studies and yearly Bible-reading schedules. We can steer them toward books that will increase their theological understanding and sharpen their spiritual vision. We can take them with us on home and hospital visits and give them meaningful roles in worship services.

Why not encourage lay leaders to organize Bible studies or to say the grace at the next church potluck? While we ask for their best efforts, we need to leave room for imperfections. We let the congregation see we take lay leadership seriously by not trying to control everything ourselves. As leaders are allowed and encouraged to lead, they will.

—*Brent Mitchell*

mutual care (*aedification mutua*) in the local church.

Pastors in the Reformation era were encouraged to focus on preaching, teaching, visitation, and spiritual discipline. As Calvin put it: "The office of a true and faithful minister is not only publicly to teach the people over whom he is ordained pastor, but as far as may be, to admonish, exhort, rebuke and console each one in particular." In the Presbyterian Church of Scotland, Knox's *First Book of Discipline* delegated certain pastoral duties to elders, such as visitation, private counseling, and discipline.

Baxter's *Reformed Pastor* (1656) is the best known and most enduring statement of Puritan pastoral care. For Baxter, pastoral care consists of seven basic functions: converting the unconverted, giving advice to inquirers, building up the believers, shepherding the families in the parish, visiting the sick and dying, reproving the inpenitent, and exercising discipline. This approach to pastoral care was highly directive; that is, it depended upon the intervention and guidance of the pastor. The pastor was the expert on appropriate behavior as well as correct doctrine. Puritan pastoral care primarily addressed the individual's conscience and moral conduct. As a result of these features, the Puritan approach could fall into excessive casuistry and legalism.

As early as 1738, Wesley emphasized lay pastoral care in the Methodist class meetings and societies, in which Christians could confess their faults and temptations and receive encouragement and constructive criticism in return. These class meetings heralded the contemporary small-group and lay pastoral-care movements. In North America, the Methodist circuit rider and the Baptist lay preacher represented a new form of pastoral care on the frontier, where the parish-church system of Europe and the Atlantic seaboard was not yet established.

In the nineteenth century, revivalism and liberalism both made their marks on pastoral care. Frontier camp meetings and urban revivals focused the purpose of pastoral care on the process of conversion and the assurance of pardon. The holiness movement's emphasis on Christian perfection led to concern for eliminating "known sin" from one's life and attaining the "second blessing" of entire sanctification. Pentecostalism, an offshoot of the holiness movement, also sought a second blessing, which would be confirmed by speaking in tongues. Pentecostals also advocated the use of other supernatural gifts in pastoral care, such as healing and exorcism.

The rise of liberalism had a significant impact on the shaping of pastoral care in the nineteenth century. Reacting against the legalism of the Puritans and the perceived excesses of revivalism, liberalism encouraged a form of pastoral care suited to the temperament of the "modern era." Instruction in faith, for example, was no longer merely doctrinal instruction but an exploration in religious self-awareness. Discipline in the Reformation and Puritan sense virtually vanished in the mainline churches. As early as the 1840s, some Methodists were lamenting the disappearance of the class meetings. On the other hand, pastors spent more time visiting the sick and dying, and calling upon parishioners in their homes, offering personal encouragement and an inoffensive mixture of common-sense advice and religious insight.

Ahead of its time, Bushness's *Christian Nurture* (1847) suggested long-term Christian education beginning in childhood as preferable to leading adults into a crisis conversion experience. In a different vein, Rauschenbusch's *Pastoral Theology* (1908) offered a perspective on pastoral care fueled by the social gospel, which was born out of his ministry amid urban poverty and suffering.

• *Recent developments in pastoral care.* The twentieth century has witnessed several significant developments in pastoral care. First, an unmistakable feature of contemporary pastoral care has been the professionalization of ministry. Like other professionals, clergy have sought degrees and other credentials as benchmarks of competence in ministry. This trend has also led to the specialization of pastoral care. At the turn of the century, all pastors were generalists who could presumably do everything required of a church leader. Now many large churches have developed specialized care ministries staffed by specialists. Several pastoral theologians have warned of the "professional captivity of pastoral care," in which the biblical call for mutual edification gets replaced by the medical model of the therapist-patient relationship.

The discipline of psychology has made a significant impact on pastoral care in the twentieth century, from preparation for ministry to the methods of caregiving. In 1900, for example, students received little or no training in psychology. By the mid 1960s, however, clinical-pastoral education (CPE) and counseling were standard features of seminary education.

Another trend has been the proliferation of Christian counselors trained in graduate psychology programs. Some are affiliated with local churches, while many others are in private practice. Often thought of as pursuing a profession within a profession, Christian counselors frequently adopt techniques employed by their secular counterparts. Many larger congregations have established counseling centers, staffed by certified counselors and marriage and family therapists. Professionally led groups sponsored by local churches or by nationwide organizations have become an option for many unable to afford traditional psychotherapy. Smaller congregations have established referral networks with Christians working in secular, private, and public mental-health agencies.

A third trend, paradoxically, is the increasing role of the laity in providing pastoral care. Since the 1970s, lay-counseling training programs have equipped many lay men and women for primary pastoral care. Greeted initially with skepticism on the part of pastoral-care professionals, lay pastoral care continues to grow as believers discover their gifts and calling to ministry.

Small groups known as covenant groups or care groups are another type of lay pastoral care. The charismatic renewal movement lifts up prayer, the miraculous, and inner healing in pastoral care. In many churches prayer ministries serve as part of a comprehensive congregational-care strategy.

More recently, the Christian recovery movement has responded to the epidemic of abuse and addiction in North America society. Lay-led support groups utilize explicitly Christian versions of the now-famous Twelve-Step philosophy pioneered by Alcoholics Anonymous.

Transformation and Maturity

This survey of both the biblical and historical roots of pastoral care suggests a primary, two-fold purpose for Christian pastoral care, which is most explicitly conveyed in the New Testament writings: (1) transformation (*metanoia*) and (2) maturity (*teleis*). Transformation and maturity are both goals *and* processes, means *and* ends.

As a goal or end, transformation refers to a shift in one's fundamental life orientation toward Christ. *Metanoia* is a real change in a person's psychological and spiritual functioning brought about by the activity of God. Personal transformation is possible because of freedom in Christ, rather than because of a general human potential for change. Ray Anderson calls this the "therapeutic intervention of the grace of God" (Anderson 1990, 103–120). Christian pastoral care may thus affirm conversion as a turning toward Christ and an embracing of new life in his Spirit. It further aims to encourage and guide persons to and through this event.

As a process or means, *metanoia* indicates an ongoing evolution in which the person is always being transformed by the renewing of the mind (Rom. 12:2). Ongoing conversion is thus a process of reorientation to the source of wholeness, that is, to Christ himself. Like the event of conversion, the origin of the lifelong process of transformation is outside the self. Anderson comments: "Conversion as the saving work of the sanctifying Spirit of Jesus Christ is a work of grace which promotes mental health in healing the estranged and narcissistic individual" (Anderson 1990, 116). In view of this, pastoral care aims at sustaining and guiding others through an ongoing conversion, a life of personal transformation and change in the community of Christ.

Maturity (*teleis*) is similarly both a goal and a process. Paul writes that the ultimate criterion of maturity is Jesus Christ (Eph. 4:13). Thus growth in grace is not growth for its own sake but movement toward a specific goal or end. One comes to the point of being ordered, or integrated, in the various dimensions of human life. The Spirit works in and among believers to build them up corporately and individually toward this goal of completeness in Christ. We might say that wholeness, health, and integration are eschatological realities for the Christian. In the consummation of creation, human maturity will be fulfilled as we fully bear the image of Christ, who is the Whole and Complete One.

As a process, maturity implies continuous growth. It is the growth of the whole person—social, personal, sexual, psychological, and spiritual. Pastoral care offers guidance and direction to those seeking growth in understanding themselves, their relationships, and their meaning and purpose in life. Yet it is helpful to distinguish between therapeutic gains and growth goals. Progress in overcoming loss and grief, coping with depression, or communicating more effectively with a spouse, for example, are therapeutic gains, which may or may not contribute to growth and integration as a Christian person. Caregivers are growth promoters who guide and direct the growth process for another (Anderson 1990, 44–77).

This transforming and maturing movement in the believer's life appears to describe the results, or the practical outworking, of Manfred Seitz's definition of pastoral care, stated earlier. Such care can be judged effective as it actually succeeds in helping each member of Christ's body along the path of "becoming whole, becoming an ordered person, becoming a coping person, becoming a person at peace."

—Robb Redman

Resources

Anderson, R. 1990. Christians who counsel. Grand Rapids: Zondervan.

Baxter, R. 1982. The reformed pastor (1656). Portland: Multnomah.

Campbell, A. 1981. Rediscovering pastoral care. Philadelphia: Westminster.

Clebsch, W., and C. Jaeckle. 1965. Pastoral care in historical perspective. Englewood Cliffs, N.J.: Prentice-Hall.

Firet, J. 1986. Dynamics in pastoring. Grand Rapids: Eerdmans.

Haugk, K. 1985. Christian care-giving—a way of life. Minneapolis: Augsburg.

McNeill, J. 1951. A history of the cure of souls. New York: Harper.

Oates, W. 1982. The Christian pastor, 3d ed. Philadelphia: Westminster.

Oden, T. 1983. Pastoral theology. San Francisco: Harper & Row.

Seitz, M. 1978. *Praxis des glaubens*. Gottingen: Vandenhoeck and Ruprecht.

Finding and Using Spiritual Gifts

In some congregations, people call the minister for even the slightest pastoral need, and sometimes pastors themselves have created such a dependency among the church members. For many pastors, however, Scripture study reveals that God has endowed every member of the church with spiritual gifts. When pastors help church members discover and use their gifts for mutual ministry, they properly share the burden of pastoral care that is so often relegated only to the "professional" clergy.

Uncovering Spiritual Gifts

The apostle Paul says that all gifts "are the work of one and the same Spirit, and he gives them to each man [and woman], just as he determines" (1 Cor. 12:11). When one is born again, the Spirit bestows the gifts. Like colorfully wrapped presents, the spiritual gifts are waiting for each individual to open, appreciate, and use.

Paul says the Holy Spirit gives spiritual gifts to prepare his people for doing works of service, for maintaining unity, and for encouraging spiritual maturity among the members of the body of Christ. Finding and using spiritual gifts spurs each member to mature adulthood in the body, helping them discern right teaching and sound ministry. Use of the gifts greatly expands a church's ability to offer pastoral care and ministry (see Eph. 4:11–16). There are at least 19 definite spiritual gifts listed in the New Testament (some find up to 27 gifts). Some are considered "sign gifts" (tongues, prophecy, and discernment, for example), while other gifts are not accompanied by signs and wonders (liberality, administration, showing mercy).

Often people will be using their gifts, unaware that the Spirit empowers them. When the gifts come into full use, however, people and churches are transformed and renewed. The church becomes what God designed it to be: a center for spiritual growth and training for ministry in the body and in the world.

Jobs Become Ministry

Two barriers can hinder the release of spiritual gifts. First, many congregations are too clergy centered. In such cases, it appears that all ministry derives from the pastor. Second, there may be a mistaken belief that spiritual gifts belong only to theological charismatics and that gifts must always be spectacular in operation. A renewed appreciation for the person and work of the Holy Spirit opens churches to the reality of spiritual gifts and helps overcome these barriers.

The pastor leads by helping members find and use their particular gifts as part of an overall ministry plan. As members become aware that they are exercising Spirit-given gifts, they begin to see their "ordinary" jobs and tasks in the church as vital avenues of spiritual *ministry*. Ministry-oriented members become bolder in evangelism and service in the community, too.

The pastor, then, is chief teacher, trainer, and coach for all-member ministry.

One way to introduce spiritual-gifts discovery and ministry is to have church members take a spiritual-gifts inventory. Assessment tools include the Houts Inventory of Spiritual Gifts, in the Baptist tradition, listing 16 gifts (no sign gifts). Peter Wagner of Fuller Seminary has modified the Houts Inventory (thus the Wagner-Modified Houts Questionnaire) to identify 25 gifts, including sign gifts. For those from the Wesleyan tradition, there is the Wesley Spiritual Gifts Questionnaire, modeled after the Wagner-Modified inventory. For liturgical churches, there are 17 gifts to discover (no sign gifts) in the Trenton Spiritual Gifts Analysis. Any of these inventories can be obtained through the Charles E. Fuller Institute of Evangelism and Church Growth, P.O. Box 91990, Pasadena, California 91109-1990; phone (800) 999-9578.

—John R. Throop

Prayer and Healing

Jesus "went through all the towns and villages, teaching in their synagogues, preaching the good news of the kingdom and healing every disease and sickness" (Matt. 9:35). Preaching, teaching, and healing—in Jesus' ministry the three are never separated. The reason is that each involves the same reality—the kingdom of God, which is breaking in upon the world in and because of Jesus. Where King Jesus is present and reigning, there is preaching, teaching, and healing.

That healing can come through many means. One of them is prayer.

Biblical Precedent

In chapters 8 and 9 of his gospel, Matthew gives us ten examples of the healing work of Jesus. In five of these examples, someone prays, that is, asks Jesus for help. The man with leprosy prays for himself: "Lord, if you are willing, you can make me clean" (8:2). The Roman centurion prays for another: "My servant lies at home paralyzed and in terrible suffering. . . . just say the word, and my servant will be healed" (8:6, 8). The blind men cry out, "Have mercy on us, Son of David!" (9:27). It seems that Matthew wants the church to know that our Lord is moved by the real hurt of people—and responds to heartfelt prayer.

So how do prayer and healing go together? We pray with all the faith we have, and leave the answer to the Healer. Ours is not to anticipate the answer. Ours is simply to pray, to do like the friends of the paralytic did (Matt. 9:1–8). They carried the man up on top of the roof of the house where Jesus was teaching, broke a hole through the roof, and lowered him to Jesus.

We do whatever we can to get others (or ourselves) to the feet of the Healer. We then let him do what he, in his compassion and wisdom, chooses for us.

How to Pray

Specifically, we can approach prayer for healing through these six movements:

- We begin by acknowledging who Jesus is, the Creator and Redeemer and Re-creator, the Good Shepherd who lays down his life for his friends. We affirm his love and power.
- We then acknowledge that we are in no position to tell him how to run his kingdom. "Lord, we do not pretend to be able to tell you what to do with this need. You are Lord and are therefore free to do what you will."
- We tell him what we desire: "We cannot tell you what to do, but *this* is our heart's desire. O Lord, please . . .".
- We acknowledge that the real problem may lie elsewhere. Much physical sickness is not structural; it is due to unresolved internal turmoil or to thought processes gone awry. So we say, "Lord, if something else is the problem, please let us know. And grant us courage to face it and bring it to you."
- Then we leave the request with our Healer. This is the hardest aspect of prayer. "Lord, to the best of our ability today, we trust you with this. We trust your love, which *wants* the best for us; we trust your power, which can *do* the best for us; we trust your wisdom, that *knows* the best for us."
- Finally, we give thanks that our request is heard and felt by the Healer. We give thanks that he has now made our concern his. If the answer is "not yet," we can go on, knowing that we are not alone in the brokenness.

—*Darrell W. Johnson*

Confession and Absolution

Confession has been a part of the church's ministry from earliest times. In 1 John 1:9 we read, "If we confess our sins, he is faithful and just and will forgive us our sins and purify us from all unrighteousness." The word "confess" (*homologeo*) means to avow frankly, to admit, to declare openly. In James 5:16 we are advised to confess our sins to each other so that we may be healed. Early church practice included individual and corporate confession, so that the individual Christian's relationship with God and relationships in the church body could be healthy, open, and free from deceit. Gradually, the practice of confession became private and priest centered.

The Reformation sought to correct medieval abuses of priest-centered confession and to reemphasize grace over works for forgiveness. While the Reformers recognized the need for confession, the practice of personal confession fell into disuse. General confession, a formalized confession to God and one another, has become a part of the liturgical worship in many Protestant churches, while the Roman Catholic Church has also continued the practice of personal confession to a priest. Protestant churches today may include a general confession in worship but typically do not make face-to-face sacramental confession a part of normal church life.

Confession as Pastoral Care

People in every stage of spiritual development tend to rebel against admitting their sins. Yet even mature Christians admit to a constant struggle with sin. Therefore, a ministry of reconciliation begins with teaching about this common struggle with sin and the need for regular confession.

Liturgically, the use of a general confession in worship can introduce such a ministry. Here are three additional ways pastors can regularly use confession as a means of pastoral care:

• *Use confession in the counseling room.* Pastors in nonsacramental traditions will readily see a logical need for confession in counseling. We can make it an intentional element of counseling, then, to assure a repentant sinner of God's pardon and mercy, and to suggest ways to amend one's life and resist the sin. We may decide to refer psychological problems to a counseling professional but minister to those with guilt and brokenness.

For example, sometimes people admit to adultery in counseling: The marital issues need competent marriage counseling, but the adulterous behavior is a spiritual issue to be confessed. The pastor acts as priest, assuring the counselee of forgiveness and reconciliation.

• *Train lay confessors to expand your ministry.* We may want to look for members with the spiritual gifts of discernment and compassion who can be trusted to keep confidentiality, and then training them to serve as lay confessors. Confessors must be people of unquestioned integrity and discretion, always accountable to the pastor. Through lay confessors, a pastor can encourage a more general ministry of confessing to one another within each of the church's small groups.

• *Offer sacramental confession during special seasons.* If your church is open to a sacramental approach, consider setting up formal appointments for confession, particularly during the liturgical seasons of Lent and Advent. Retreat or camp settings provide opportunities, too, especially for nonliturgical churches.

A good setting is a private and quiet place, preferably in the church or chapel. The confessing person comes to describe what troubles the conscience or burdens the heart. We need to isolate the specific sins to be confessed and then use a liturgical form, such as "The Reconciliation of a Penitent" in the Episcopal *Book of Common Prayer,* to proclaim absolution. It's important to remember that *we* are not doing the absolving but simply declaring God's promise of pardon to all who sincerely repent.

—John R. Throop

15

Calling Ministries

Pastoral visiting thrusts us into a great variety of interpersonal situations. In fact, pastors must be able to read family situations as quickly as a professional quarterback reads defenses. Yet for all the skill required, visitation isn't nearly as glamorous as professional sports. Directors don't make movies or television shows about routine pastoral visitation. There are no songs immortalizing it.

But maybe there ought to be, because pastors across the world put in long, heroic hours visiting the people in their churches and communities. They gently teach. They give assurance. They offer prayers. They keep families together. They comfort the grieving. They rejoice with the joyful. In their words and especially with their presence, they communicate to an increasingly impersonal world of mass media and teleconferencing that God cares for individuals, one by one, day in and day out.

Visitation: At the Heart of Ministry

Every pastor has strengths, gifts, and interests. Some may emphasize preaching, others administration, others teaching. Not all pastors, of course, will make visitation their top priority. Nonetheless, personal care for members remains a vital part of every pastor's ministry for three reasons.

• *It's central to our call.* To some degree, the words we use to describe our calling determine the nature of that calling. We call ourselves *ministers,* so we serve our people. We call ourselves *preachers,* so we proclaim God's Word. If we call ourselves *pastors,* that means we will also shepherd the church flock.

As a shepherd spends time with the sheep, being with people is the heart of the pastor's responsibilities. In his book *Pastoral Theology,* Thomas C. Oden says, "The pastoral office is by definition a shepherding task. . . . Shepherding cannot be done at a sterile distance, with automated telephone answering services, computerized messages, and impersonal form letters. By definition there cannot be an absentee shepherd. There can be no mail-order or mechanized pastoral service, because pastoring is personal. It is not just public talk but interpersonal meeting where richer self-disclosures are possible."

Once when I visited a schoolteacher in our community, she told me of a child in her school. The child's mother is twice divorced. While the child was visiting her father in another state, the mother moved in with a new boyfriend and his parents. One morning after the child returned, the mother and boyfriend fought, and the little girl assumed the blame for it. She was brokenhearted, feeling out of place in a strange house.

I grieved for the child and admired the teacher, with whom I then prayed. In such situations we really can't preach or evangelize; we can't administrate, delegate, or plan. But we can perform essential Christian ministry: spending time with a member of the congregation, learning from her experience, and encouraging her in her faith.

• *It's something people really need.* Those who analyze our culture and business world underscore the value of personal contact for leaders. John Naisbitt, in his book *Megatrends,* says that in a high-tech society people crave high touch. Effective management happens best through personal contact, the personal touch.

Likewise, in the church, research shows that lay people consistently think pastoral calling important, even more than ministers may. Routine pastoral calls, during which we don't talk about anything urgent, are the most important ones to church members. Such contacts say clearly, "Your pastor cares for you—not just about spiritual things, but about you."

When asked what he appreciated about his church, one man wrote, "A pastor who takes time with his flock, to lift them up out of the stony places, to encourage them, to uphold them in prayer on a continuing basis." People do need pastoral contact.

• *It's a primary way to love incarnationally.* As one minister put it, "Pastoral visitation is incarnational: The Word became flesh and visited among us."

Consider a grandmother I know who lives with one of her daughters. The older woman's husband divorced her years ago, leaving her to raise the children, including one handicapped child. Her grown sons got into drugs. Her married son and his wife neglect their children. She also dislikes her job and feels detached from her community because she and her daughter have had to move several times over the years. I always feel her anguish.

The grandmother is powerless to do anything except love and pray. Many times she is heartsick and weary. Yet as her pastor I stand in awe of her, as does the community and church, because she is a model of strength and integrity. When I call on her, we join hands for prayer before I leave, and I usually pray that God will embrace her with love and strength. Yet somehow I feel that, as her pastor, I'm one who can literally embrace her.

Most members don't have the time or ability to visit someone like this woman. We pastors do. It's an awesome opportunity and responsibility, but we can be, for many people like her, an extension of Christ for them, an expression, albeit imperfect, of God's love.

Misconceptions Reconceived

We can line up the witnesses for visitation's defense—professors, business consultants, even the Bible—yet it continues to be dreaded or neglected by many pastors. That's partly due to bad experiences. But sometimes it's due to misconceptions. In particular, three misconceptions need to be cleared up.

• *Visitation is an inefficient use of time.* With so many to minister to, the pastor may feel that time spent with individuals is not as effective as time spent with a group. That's not necessarily so. An advertising journal once explained a hierarchy of communication effectiveness. The least effective method for influencing people's attitudes, it said, was mass advertising—newspapers or the TV. The article progressed up a half-dozen steps to describe, finally, the most effective method: personal time with an individual. A well-timed conversation with an unchurched person or a growing member, then, can be the most effective time we spend. In a personal conversation, a pastor can respond to another's specific situation.

Mr. Kilmer was my fifth-grade teacher. He was popular at Eugene Field Elementary School; all the kids wanted to be in his class. No wonder: he spent time with kids. I still remember the Saturday afternoon Mr. Kilmer invited me to his house to watch baseball on TV with him and his family. Wow, was I impressed! And I was more apt to attend to his lessons after that.

• *Visitation is too difficult to schedule.* In most places in our country, life speeds by at a hectic pace. Some people drive an hour or more to work; others work late shifts until all hours. Who knows when they'll be home or in bed grabbing a few winks? Everyone is busy these days, even laid-back country folks. It may be difficult to schedule visits in the home, but that doesn't mean it's impossible or unimportant. If visitation powerfully enhances ministry and our church's health, perhaps we should be willing to put up with some of the obstacles and try to overcome others.

Many pastors can work toward scheduling several afternoons and evenings each week for visitation. With such a plan, mornings, Tuesday through Saturday, are designated as study times. But around 2 P.M., two or three afternoons a week, they head out to see people.

Sometimes we might want to make appointments, but usually we can just drop by, being sensitive to family schedules—work shifts, dinner time, bed time. Naturally, we will want to try to work visits around people's schedules. Congregations become used to the pastor dropping in, and pastor and people learn to work with the occasional

Shut-in Calls

In a frantically busy world, who has time for shut-ins, or more accurately, the housebound? While all members of Christ's body ought to take time, a pastor *must* make the time. Even a little pastoral care, love, and time brings much blessing in both directions.

How to Call

Consider these suggestions for making ministry to the housebound more nurturing and effective:

• *Find out the reason for the person being housebound.* People become housebound for many reasons. The *recuperating* have had surgery or serious illness and will return to the church body in due time. The *chronically ill* are unable to leave their homes except for outings to the doctor. The *dying* require the church's ministry to prepare them for death and life eternal.

• *Determine the pastoral purpose of the visit.* In all cases, basic pastoral care — especially listening — is our principal task. In some traditions, anointing, blessing, or serving Communion to the housebound person will be an essential part of a visit. Lay teams can visit to provide company to the lonely and to help with errands and shopping. In any case, a clear purpose in mind improves a visit.

• *Develop a ministry plan for use of time.* The recuperating person usually wants a brief visit, especially when he or she has just returned, all energy spent, from the hospital. As healing progresses, visits should continue to be brief, in order to encourage a return to corporate worship and life. For example, one parishioner who had back surgery enjoyed my visits and personal attention. When she resumed going to her small-group meetings, it was

awkwardness visitation sometimes entails because they appreciate the difference it makes.

• *Visitation is risky and scary.* Facing individuals on their home turf can be unnerving. However, dreading pastoral visitation is not a 1990s development. Early in this century, J. H. Jowett dealt with the pastor's home calling in one of his Yale lectures on preaching, published in *The Preacher, His Life and Work:* "The difficulty of delivering a message is in inverse proportion to the size of the audience. To face the individual soul with the Word of God . . . is one of the heaviest commissions given to our charge. . . . It seemed as though I could preach a sermon and never meet a devil. But as soon as I began to take my sermon to the individual, the streets were thick with devils."

This anxiety is aggravated if pastors think poorly of themselves or

time to end the visits and encourage her full return to normal routines.

The chronically ill person needs predictability and continuity in our visits. He or she may want to visit longer, since we may be the day's (or week's, or month's) only visitor from outside. With the dying, we more directly assume the role of priest, gently guiding people toward God and helping them bring meaningful closure to fundamental life concerns. Depending on the lucidity and strength of the dying person, such a visit may be lengthy, encouraging in-depth conversation.

• *Call ahead to make an appointment.* We must respect people's care schedules. The person may need to rest or may need plenty of time to get ready for a visit. For example, one woman I visited had severe arthritis and could not move easily. In scheduling an appointment with me, she had to allow herself time to bathe, dress, unlock the door, and get into a chair—at least a full hour's work.

• *Assess the pace of recovery together.* Each time we visit, we function as guides to God in priestly ministry, assessing with each person just what is needed for personal and spiritual growth at the moment. The recuperating person needs encouragement to become active once again in the community. The chronically ill person often feels isolated and cut off, hoping for news from church and friends. The dying person needs to say good-by and to begin separating from this world. We can also provide assessment on the person's condition to family members and home-health-care workers.

• *Brainstorm ways for the housebound to minister.* What better words can anyone hear than the Lord saying, "I was sick, and you visited me"? The housebound can experience that blessing by becoming "visitors" from afar. Though weak, shut-in members of the body are ministers, too. One person I know sends get-well cards to others. Another has become a faithful intercessor as she sits physically alone but in spiritual communion with the other members of Christ's church.

—John R. Throop

fear rejection. A pastor may fear that professional credibility may be seriously jeopardized in personal conversation. At some point we will no doubt be put on the spot to explain tough points of theology, such as the classic: Why would a good God allow evil to exist? Someone might have a grudge against the church or Christianity and find the visiting pastor a convenient target.

There's another side to this experience, however. Certainly, some of the most uncomfortable moments in the pastorate will come in a family's living room. But we will have unique opportunities to minister to people directly, immediately, personally in those contexts. While sometimes after a difficult experience, we'll crawl home feeling whipped, a failure, we will mature through those experiences. And we'll be able to turn many of those awkward moments into growing experiences for others, too. In sports they say, "No pain, no gain." In the pastorate, it's "With pain comes much gain."

Hospital Calls

Several years ago my own surgery taught me a few things about how to make a hospital visit. Calls can be made for a lot of reasons, but a call that a minister makes aims for the healing of the patient's soul. Here are some suggestions for the next time you reach out to comfort a friend or parishioner.

• *Determine the patient's emotional need.* Major-surgery patients go through at least three basic emotional stages or time periods: First, the night before and the early hours of the surgery day. Second, the three days after surgery, when people typically are under pain-killing drugs and the vital signs are slowed. Third, the four or more days that comprise a return of strength and mobility.

During these periods we can expect to find at least three or more basic moods: Fear is almost surely a part of the presurgery hours; loneliness is common during the first six or seven days of recovery; depression and impatience with the rate of recovery are common during the fifth or sixth days. Try to determine, therefore, the patient's mood in order to minister appropriately.

• *Visit at the right time.* Be sure to visit the patient the day before (or in the early hours before) surgery for the maximum ministry. Like telling a joke or giving a kiss, timing is everything here. Six visits during the week following surgery will not recover the lost ministry opportunity of those hours before the unknown. As a professor, I am grateful for those students who recognized this truth during my last class before I headed to the hospital. They insisted that we pause and pray just prior to my walking out the front door, alone.

Visitation Builds Better Ministry

Haddon Robinson talks about the "halo effect" in ministry, the extraordinary regard church members sometimes accord their preacher, and the positive effect it has on ministry. One factor that contributes to the halo effect is the deepening relationship between pastor and people, especially as the pastor visits people through the years. Specifically, pastoral visitation enhances ministry in the following ways.

• *Preaching is enriched.* Many pastors put in long hours to study the Word. But preaching is better still if we also invest ourselves in a thorough study of our people. Pastoral visitation gives us a handle on the questions people are asking and the issues they are facing.

For example, Bob wanted to get together because he was in a quandary about a new job opportunity; he just couldn't bring himself to

• *Recognize the value of pure presence.* This is especially true during the mood of loneliness. Sometimes presence is much more meaningful than words. For instance, on Saturday night a friend came to see me in the hospital. I had gone three days without a shave, a tube was stuck down my nose, and I was only half conscious. It was more than he could handle. He paced the floor saying, "I had no idea. I had no idea." I think he thought I was about gone.

After about three minutes he mumbled something and left. But as he walked out the door, I smiled. Why? Because he had come. His simple presence broke through my isolation.

• *Use therapeutic touch.* During a brief visit, don't hesitate to take the patient's hand firmly, or gently touch in other appropriate ways, depending on the patient's physical condition. Touch communicates empathy, concern, strength, and companionship to the patient.

• *Minister to the patient's family, too.* We have ministry opportunities in the waiting room during surgery. That is the time and place when so many questions and fears arise in the minds of loved ones. My wife was grateful for two friends who had experienced the terror of their own husbands' surgeries. They remembered and came to be with her while I was in the operating room.

• *When appropriate, share select portions of the Psalms.* The Psalms convey tremendous openness of the soul toward God: "God is our refuge and strength, an ever-present help in trouble. Therefore we will not fear, though the earth give way and the mountains fall into the heart of the sea, though its waters roar and foam and the mountains quake with their surging. . . . The Lord Almighty is with us" (Ps. 46:1–3, 7a). We will never improve upon that—the Word of God for the cure of souls.

—*Bruce Shelley*

make a firm decision on the matter. I'd known Bob and his wife for a couple of years. He was likable, enthusiastic, and well-meaning, but he was obviously agitated. Bob and I began talking about a subject we had discussed before: his boyhood relationship with his father. His father had been quick to hand out orders but not to give praise. His father always found something wrong with the work Bob had done. Instead of saying, "Nice job" after Bob shoveled the walk, for example, his father would say, "Come on, Bob. The shovel hangs on the wall. Can't you do anything right?" As we talked, slowly he made some breakthroughs. He was finally able to see that God loves him in spite of tough decisions.

Many people struggle with decisions, as does Bob, and many times the root of their struggle lies in childhood. With Bob's permission, I preached a message that raised such issues. It touched a chord; many were in tears by the end.

"One of the most palpable benefits that most pastors will realize from visitation," writes Thomas Oden in *Pastoral Theology*, "is the kindling of the homiletical mind. Let us assume that due confidentiality will be maintained. Pastoral conversation will furnish the mind of the preacher with a full train of ideas and kernels of insight. Biblical subjects will be animated by rich experiential vitality."

• *Administration is made easier.* If the pastor develops a feel for people's spiritual states, the church's program can be planned more accurately and sensitively. For example, I once counseled with a young couple, Martin and Connie. Their problems were many: They hadn't spent time alone together in months, their preschool children were demanding more attention, money was tight, and each was ready to walk out on the other.

My heart went out to them, but I recognized they were not alone. Indeed it was the problem of many young families. How could our church help? As I thought and prayed, I finally came up with an idea: What if we matched up a younger family with a family whose children were older or gone from the home?

At the next Sunday morning service, I left the pulpit and walked down the center aisle. I began talking about the pressures that families with young children face day in and day out. I suggested the idea of a family with older children adopting the younger family for support, encouragement, and childcare a couple of times a month. Applause broke out.

After the service the congregation was buzzing about the idea. Martin told me several people approached them after the service and offered assistance. Visitation, then, led to a church program targeted to meet genuine needs.

• *Crises are averted.* By continual circulation, dropping in from time to time, we often can detect a crisis in the making. It might be that seeds of conflict, explosive anger, or despair lie just below the surface. Often, through an extended time of personal ministry, we can help a person get a grip on the problem.

For example, once when I visited Sally, a woman I had counseled often over the years, she told me about the latest troubles of her daughter and son-in-law. When she was through explaining the latest episodes, she said, "I know there's nothing anyone can do, but it's frustrating. I feel so alone with this problem."

"No, there's no one who can actually solve the problem," I responded. "But there are some friends who could help you bear the problem, some friends who could listen, understand, and pray with you about it." She appeared puzzled momentarily. Then she began to recite the names of numerous people in the church she thought could understand and help.

That conversation was pivotal for Sally. She had been discouraged, feeling increasingly isolated. Aside from providing the suggestion that she talk with friends, the pastoral visit alone averted a crisis of deepening depression.

• *Ministry is affirmed.* An effective pastoral visitation ministry can give the pastor a sense of accomplishment. Pastors work with a lot of intangibles. Often success or failure is measured by an ill-timed comment mumbled by a disgruntled member on his way out of the Sunday service. Let's face it: pastors could do with a regular dose of satisfaction and achievement.

I'd known George and Maggie for nearly ten years. I'd sat with them in my study and in their living room on numerous occasions. However, George, while warm, had always held me at arm's length. While Maggie had attended church regularly with the kids for eight years, George found something else to do on Sundays. He acknowledged his intention to develop his relationship with Christ, but he did little about it.

Then he began facing some business problems that weren't yielding to his usual efficiency, and business stress was adversely affecting his family life. Although I knew about his problems, on this night I had just happened to stop by on a routine pastoral call, intending no more than a friendly visit.

After greeting me warmly, George quickly plunged into describing his frustrations. I empathized with him about his pain and confusion. When it seemed appropriate, I mentioned that at certain crisis points it's helpful to step back and consider the whole of life. Once in a while a man must ask hard questions such as, "What am I living for?" "What am I accomplishing?" "Am I investing my energies in what will bring a deep sense of accomplishment?"

George had been asking himself just those questions, so he was eager for wisdom. I suggested some ways he might effectively analyze his problems—spiritual, vocational, and marital. My words fell like rain on parched earth. Sometimes his face brightened; other times his brow furrowed, indicating deep thought. He commented several times that he wished he had his tape recorder running so he could save the conversation.

He then talked about his wife. He acknowledged that her life of constancy had been an inspiration to him. Her deeper relationship with the Lord had impressed and attracted him. As a result, he felt he could now more readily give himself to Christ. His wife was beaming and crying. Her prayers of many years were being answered.

—*Doug Self*

Resources

Bolton, R. 1979. People skills. Englewood Cliffs, N.J.: Prentice-Hall.

Engel, J., and W. Norton. 1982. What's gone wrong with the harvest? Grand Rapids: Zondervan.

Hudnut, R. 1986. This people, this parish. Grand Rapids: Zondervan.

Noyce, G. 1981. The art of pastoral conversation. Atlanta: John Knox.

Oden, T. 1983. Pastoral theology. San Francisco: Harper.

Nursing Home Calls

For the first time in our country's history, there are fewer teenagers than citizens over 65. The fastest-growing age group in America is people over 85. Such facts should focus our attention on the growing ministry opportunities to be found in the nursing home. Since our once-young citizenry is rapidly growing older, and geriatric ministry is quickly picking up pace, pastors will be making more nursing home calls. Here are four suggestions for making visits effective.

• *Be positive.* Our ability to love as Christ loved is in direct proportion to the depth of our relationship with Jesus Christ. We need to bathe our visits in prayer and be positive about what we have to offer in Christ's strength. A positive attitude goes a long way in any ministry but especially in a nursing home ministry.

In visiting the nursing home, we're often called to love the unlovely. Our ministry needs to reflect the graciousness that comes from the Spirit's influence in our lives. Older saints need just as many affirming hugs as our younger saints. Appropriate touching goes a long way toward showing genuine concern, acceptance, and positive regard for the one we're visiting. We want to communicate to each person how important he or she is to the body of Christ.

• *Be faithful.* Maintaining a regular visitation schedule is crucial. We must not make promises we cannot keep. People look forward to visits and will schedule their activities around our arrival.

A regular service is an important event in the lives of our senior saints. The opportunity to sing and hear a short devotional from God's Word is often a highlight of the week. We also want to include everyone in the celebration of the Lord's Supper.

• *Be creative.* A creative ministry generates interest and gives people topics for conversation during the entire week. Nursing home patients respond especially well to brightly colored attire and unusual events. The mere presence of children in nice clothes or in brightly colored costumes, singing or presenting a program, will bring hours of enjoyable talk.

Your senior citizens will cherish holiday parties with festive decorations and special gifts. Flowers, tapes of the morning message at church, or the prayer list from a regular service are special to these folks. Pictures and pets are always a hit. We can be creative and have fun. If we stir things up a bit, people will love it.

• *Be patient.* Nursing home ministry also requires a lot of patience. We must beware of falling into some of the typical traps. Watch out for the myth of senility or the tendency to infantize the patient. When a person grows into old age, some inhibitions may break down, but we need to respect each person's privacy and sexuality. We want to love and value all as Christ would.

Nursing home ministry can be fruitful. Residents gain so much joy from even the little things we can bring into their lives. May we work hard at nurturing their minds and bodies while encouraging their spiritual vitality.

—Douglas M. Cecil

Emergency Calls

Emergencies don't come at convenient times. The question is not *if* a crisis will come but *when.* We may not be able to plan for a specific emergency, but we can decide ahead of time what steps to take once a crisis presents itself. Here is a plan:

• *Offer presence.* People in pain want to withdraw, like a turtle into its shell. But isolation intensifies the pain. So those in crisis first need others to be with them. Meaningful touch helps pull crisis victims out of isolation. Sufferers can dismiss our words, but touch—the language of crisis—has innate authority.

In the midst of a suicide tragedy, one woman from my congregation went to the victim's family home and just sat on the couch with her arm around the shoulder of the grieving mother. For the entire afternoon, she said less than ten words. But the mother later told me, "I drew more comfort from her than from anything." Presence is powerful.

• *Listen attentively.* It's a mistake to prescribe answers and solutions in the initial stages of a crisis. At this stage, crisis victims need description, not prescription. We can let people fully describe what has happened, what they're feeling, what they're going through. Few things communicate compassion and concern more than unhurried listening.

This means resisting the temptation to offer even good advice. We all know that cliches usually cause more pain than comfort. When crisis victims hear pat answers, they feel we don't understand the depth of their trauma.

• *Clarify the situation.* Medical crises require quick decisions about procedures to be done, organs to be donated, life-support systems to be used. One such decision alone is stressful. Add many together, and it's bewildering. Tack on emotional shock, and it's crushing.

Not surprisingly, decision making can cause people in crisis to freeze. They desperately need someone who can identify the issues objectively, sort the priorities, and clarify values. In helping a family deal with doctors, funeral directors, and lawyers, remember: If these professionals are not making sense to us, they almost certainly are not making sense to the crisis victim, who is normally too intimidated to ask many questions. So we need to ask questions on the victim's behalf and help interpret the technical language, procedures, and decisions.

• *Do damage control.* Most people can deal with only one emergency at a time, but every crisis has the ability to spawn other emotional, financial, occupational, and family crises. Victims can quickly lose hope.

Consider marital crises. A couple came to me right after the wife learned of her husband's three-year adulterous relationship with his secretary. I knew I wasn't going to save their marriage in one session, but I did need to contain the forest fire. So in that first session, I determined only to listen to their story, trace how the adultery developed, and let her initial anger and his defensiveness blaze in a place where they couldn't incinerate each other.

• *Suggest the next step.* People in crisis tremble before a dark future; they need light shed on the next step. They need to look forward to care and attention in the immediate future. So a wise way to conclude an initial call is with "I'll call you tonight" or "We'll meet at my office on Tuesday at three." That specifies what we're going to do next, and it's not set too far in the future. We can tell them, "We're going to take this one step at a time." Most crisis victims can't see much beyond the next step, anyway, and are relieved we'll be with them.

—Gary Gulbranson

Grief Aftercare

The memorial service isn't the place to terminate ministry to the bereaved. It is the place to begin a different but no less important one. As one grieving church member observed, "The pastor saw me right after my husband's death, and he met with me before the service. He said a few words at the funeral. But I never saw him again in regard to my husband's death. My real struggles didn't begin until two weeks after the funeral, and by then, everyone was out of sight."

Most churches want to do a better job than that. To minister more effectively to grieving families, a program of grief aftercare can help people deal with their grief in a fuller and healthier way.

Early Aftercare

Grief aftercare can begin before the funeral service, when we tell the family it will take perhaps a year or longer to work through their grief. Occasionally family members say: "As soon as this funeral is over, we can put our lives back in order," or "Just a few more hours, and we can get on with life." Here we can offer a gentle reminder that death affects us longer than a few short days.

The second step is a series of phone calls and visits. A week after the funeral, it is good to visit the family. The extended family members usually have returned to their homes and jobs, and friends and neighbors have turned their attention back to their own struggles. The rush of funeral preparations is over, life is quiet, and the family is alone. Often this is when the reality of their loss hits them. A visit provides the family with an opportunity to express new grief questions or to rethink the old ones.

Extended Aftercare

Wise pastors often plan a second visit or phone call about three weeks later to assure the family they have not been forgotten. They are still in the pastor's thoughts and prayers, and also those of the congregation. Another purpose of this visit is to stress our availability.

Often this is the watershed visit. Perhaps three weeks after the loss is simply the point at which people begin to deal with the deeper issues. For example, people hit me with theological questions at this time: "Where is God in the death of my loved one?" "Did God cause this death, did God allow it, or did he have no control over it?" "I'm afraid I'm losing my faith. How do I hang on?" "I'm not sure I believe in life after death. Is there some way I can be sure?"

A third visit about three or four months after the funeral furthers the aftercare. By this time any significant difficulties in the grief process are apparent. We may want to encourage the individual to seek additional professional help if symptoms include chronic depression, suicidal tendencies, or eating and sleeping disorders.

Expanded Aftercare

Ministry to grieving families shouldn't fall only upon the pastor's shoulders. A few weeks after the funeral is a good time to contact someone who has gone through similar circumstances to ask that member to visit the family. Having endured a similar situation, the visitor usually understands acutely which words hurt and which heal.

Once I asked an elderly widow to visit a recently widowed woman. Through this woman's intervention, the new widow was given needed training in budgeting and bookkeeping. Since the visitor had gone through a similar situation, she could assure her charge that God does help and that his strength would carry her through.

—Kevin E. Ruffcorn

New-Prospect Calls

Who makes house calls anymore? It's rare for a physician, and when plumbers call, it costs more than a physician. After all, we're busy people. Leaders can't be expected to spend valuable time knocking on doors, can they? Isn't that an unproductive use of time?

Not if the leaders are pastors, and especially not if the people being called on have shown interest in the church.

What Is Accomplished?

Just what can we accomplish with new-prospect calls? At least three agendas:

• *Provide individual attention.* During a home call, a pastor's complete attention belongs to the one being visited. In a society that feels increasingly impersonal, such a lavish gift of time is gratefully received.

• *Become acquainted.* It's hard to pastor a stranger. A pastoral call on a church visitor can build rapport, giving each person a glimpse of the other's personality.

• *Offer a personal invitation.* When the pastor says, "We'd like to see you often!" visitors feel welcomed indeed. No longer the strangers, they feel like they are noticed, appreciated, special. The next Sunday, someone they *know* is leading worship.

Productive Calls

While pastoral calls on church visitors can provide great benefits, they remain costly in terms of the time and attention invested. We must propel ourselves into the unknown territory of strangers' lives. No doubt, *trite* will describe some of the conversations, and *unproductive,* others.

So how can we make the most return on our investment?

• *Make appointments only as a last resort.* Appointments tend to formalize the call, casting it into the category of "important event" rather than "friendly visit." People will feel the need to clean up the place, fix some refreshments, and entertain the pastor properly. The activity becomes a burden rather than a treat.

Some people are practically impossible to find at home, and others, such as people with disabilities, may need time to prepare themselves for a visit. In such cases, we can make appointments.

In some communities, 4:30 to 5:45 can be a good time to find people at home. They have arrived home for the day but aren't involved yet in evening activities. Midday on Saturdays or Sunday afternoons also may prove fruitful.

• *Dis-invite yourself readily.* Since people aren't expecting a visit, we may arrive at an inopportune time. Favorite TV shows, other scheduled activities, meals to prepare—all can make a surprise call less than welcome. We need to keep our senses attuned to any circumstance—or even body language—that says, "This isn't a good time," and be quick to excuse ourselves, cheerfully offering to return at another time.

• *Focus on them.* The person being called on needs to feel special, and so we should spend the brief call talking more about them and their needs than about the church and how much we'd like people to swell our ranks. Certainly the church is an interesting subject and has much to offer, but we want to make the new attender feel more appreciated than recruited.

• *Leave an informational brochure.* An attractive flier can help people understand and remember the church. Again, the brochure should center on how the church can meet people's needs. "What First Church Can Offer You" will be better received than "Spotlight on First Church."

• *Keep it light.* These calls typically wouldn't be considered evangelistic. When the purpose is to greet and welcome visitors, the pressure is off. Newcomers don't feel pounced upon.

Some people, however, are spiritually hungry, aching to hear the Word of Life. A sensitive caller will know when to be a friendly visitor, pre-evangelizing people by inviting them into church life that can transform their lives, and when to be an evangelist, offering people life itself.

—*James D. Berkley*

16

Church Membership

Many Christians today do not view membership in a local congregation as significant or even necessary. The popular attitude is: "I'm a member of Christ's universal church, and that's all that matters. I don't need to belong to one particular local church." Even believers who regularly attend and financially support a congregation often feel no need to become official members of that group.

We live in an era of noncommitment. Many hesitate to become members of anything that might require a long-term demand on time and energy. Whether considering a social club or a community service agency, people want benefits with few responsibilities. Unfortunately, the church is feeling the impact of this attitude.

Why Is Membership Important?

We do need to rethink the importance of church membership. Though membership is not specifically mentioned in the Scriptures, the principle of joining together with people of like faith to work together for the cause of Christ is certainly well-established in the New Testament. Luke tells us that "those who accepted [Peter's] message were baptized, and about three thousand were added to their number that day" (Acts 2:41).

A brief look at the New Testament church indicates there must have been some form of organization and recognition of those who were believers. The new churches had specific doctrinal standards, along with a list of believers who at times were disciplined. We know church leaders were careful about who participated in the Communion services (see 1 Cor. 11:17–33).

In some way, New Testament church leaders kept track of who was inside the fellowship and who was not. This accounting became important for them when administering Communion and providing care. Keeping track of members became even more important as external persecution, first from the Jews and then later from the Romans, threatened the fragile church enterprise. Membership also protected believers from false teachers and those who twisted the apostles' original teachings. Letters of recommendation, based on church membership, became a way of authenticating character.

Today, however, being a church member has lost its value in the eyes of many. There is even a growing trend for people to consider three or four different churches as "ministry centers" for their families. These folks might attend one church for its wonderful music and praise experiences, another for solid biblical teaching, another for its thriving small groups, and still another for the ministries it offers to their children. For such people, commitment to a single church is an anachronism, an unnecessary irritant.

Yet church membership is still critically important. Christians clearly contradict New Testament teaching when they think it is possible to be a follower of Jesus Christ without making a commitment to the body of believers who make up a particular congregation. To remain unattached is to fail to grasp the basic implications of biblical Christianity for the congregation, corporately, and for the individual, personally.

• *Benefits for the congregation.* Membership offers security, protection, and continuity. While forms of church government vary greatly, the establishment of an official register of members in a congregation establishes a safeguard for the ownership and maintenance of real estate, facilities, and equipment. Church assets today frequently are valued in the millions of dollars. Membership provides a secure way to care for church property, because it designates the owners specifically and legally.

Membership also establishes a legally protected way to administer church discipline. When someone applies for membership in the church, he or she agrees to live in harmony with the statement of faith and the established standards of behavior in that congregation. Because the choice to become a member is voluntary, the church has the right to discipline members within the parameters of the church's constitution and doctrinal statements.

For example, one church used a nonmember in its Sunday school program. It was later discovered that the nonmember was a practicing homosexual. Though the church's position on homosexuality was clear, legal counsel indicated that because the man was not a registered member, the church put itself in a dangerous position when trying to remove him from teaching. Had he been a registered member, the board would have had a clear right to exercise discipline.

• *Benefits for the individual.* Membership offers participation and belonging. Membership should be a welcome haven in a rapidly changing, hectic world. It confers the privilege of participation, with church members being entitled to serve in the various positions of leadership and ministry within the congregation. Membership offers the privilege of fellowship, opening up the opportunity for a deeper level of *koinonia* within the church family.

Membership also provides individuals with a statement of credibility and connectedness when they move from one city to another. A letter of reference stating one's previous membership and good standing in a congregation offers immediate entrance into the fellowship of another congregation.

What Should Churches and Members Expect?

To confront the growing trend toward detachment from the structured church, membership must be reaffirmed as legitimate and important. It can't be cheap; it must be deeply meaningful and relevant. It must do more than offer convenience; it must require commitment. Growing churches make becoming a part of the local body a step of supreme significance.

This significance is based on the premise that membership should offer a fair exchange of commitments. There must be something in it for the church and something in it for the member. Churches cannot expect just to receive from their members; they must give something in return. That is why vital membership has both its privileges as well as its responsibilities.

The key word is *commitment.* When a person is received into membership, the church makes a commitment to that person, and that person makes a commitment to the church. Since the biblical concept of the church proclaims that believers are members of one another (see 1 Cor. 12), the entrance of new members is akin to the marriage ceremony, when a bride and groom vow to commit themselves to each other for mutual growth and benefit.

Consider, for instance, these benefits that members might appropriately expect from their church:

• *Pastoral care.* When members suffer sickness, tragedy, or bereavement, they have a right to expect pastoral attention and the involvement of other members of the church family in providing loving care. Members should expect pastoral assistance with weddings, baptisms, dedications, and funerals. They can expect tangible expressions of concern and the counsel of pastors and church leaders in a variety of situations and predicaments.

- *Solid biblical teaching.* Members should be able to look to the church with confidence for balanced, practical instruction from God's Word. They also have a right to look to the church for meaningful corporate worship. Part of the joy of the Christian life is joining with brothers and sisters to express adoration and praise to the Lord.
- *Opportunities for ministry.* The church ought to be a recruitment center, a training institution, and a mobilizing agency to coordinate the ministries of the individuals within the body of Christ. Members can look to the church to coordinate local evangelistic efforts and to

Deploying Members in Ministry

As we seek to incorporate members into our church ministries, we must work from two assumptions: (1) God has entrusted to each believer the necessary resources to do ministry, and (2) God has given each church the people necessary to do what he has called the church to do.

To discover the untapped resources already within our congregations, we can do a spiritual planning process to help people see how God has especially prepared them for ministry. Three phases make up this process.

Phase One: Inventory

One method to take inventory is to have people attend four sessions with a spiritual planner. The first three sessions focus on a personal-inventory questionnaire that must be completed prior to the first session. Questions include:

1. Describe your personal, spiritual pilgrimage. What led to your conversion to Christ? What formal and informal training has contributed to your growth? What crises have you weathered? What have been your experiences in ministry?
2. Is God cultivating a concern in you for ministry? What specific needs, issues, or situations particularly touch your heart?
3. Up to now, what concrete steps have you taken to address these needs or get involved in these issues?
4. What do you believe is the general purpose of this spiritual-planning process?
5. Identify several things you expect to accomplish through this process.
6. Assume you had all the resources you wanted and needed, and that God would guarantee your success in anything you wanted to do. Describe what your life would look like ten years from now.
7. Identify several resources God has entrusted to you (spiritual gifts, natural talents, acquired skills, experiences).
8. What is your greatest strength?
9. Describe any present barriers keeping you from living up to your

mobilize the members for worldwide missionary outreach. New members should expect information from the church leaders related to ongoing ministry needs in the community. And they should expect those leaders constantly to encourage members with the appropriate spiritual gifts to meet those needs in vital ministry efforts.

• *A network of supportive relationships.* As the church provides acceptance, friendship, and love, membership should offer an antidote to loneliness, along with the opportunity to be a part of something eternally significant.

Working in partnership with people of similar values, members should expect to find a deep sense of fulfillment.

God-given potential.

10. Where do you need to grow the most?

Phase Two: Possible Ministries

During the first session, the spiritual planner goes over responses to the questionnaires, asking people to clarify or expand answers. At session two, information on spiritual gifts (based on Romans 12, 1 Corinthians 12, Ephesians 4, and 1 Peter 4) is provided. People then take a couple of weeks to work through assigned exercises on spiritual gifts. They talk to other Christians who know them, and think through what they have enjoyed doing or have done well. All these activities move them closer to identifying their spiritual gifts.

During the third session, they discuss the homework they have done on spiritual gifts. It appears that most people have more than one spiritual gift—often three or four, called their "gift mix."

Phase Three: Action Plans

At the end of the third session, participants are provided printed descriptions of the church's ministries. In addition, they are encouraged to imagine ministries they might like to be involved in that do not yet exist.

Participants leave session three with two assignments. First, based on what they have learned, they pick three or four ministries they might try. Second, they prepare a written action plan.

The action plan is a specific, written blueprint for spiritual growth and ministry. It lists detailed goals for the next twelve months in seven areas: worship, instruction, fellowship, ministry, stewardship, family and friends, and personal development. That action plan then forms the basis of discussion at session four.

Action plans reflect individual uniqueness. One artistic woman I know presented her written plan in the form of a beautiful collage, while an engineer came in with a four-page computerized printout. Whatever the form, the church can then help the people realize their goals as they channel their energies into ministry.

—*Ron Oertli*

The church also has a valid set of expectations from its members. Membership is not cheap; it has a price tag. Here is what the church, at a bare minimum, ought to expect from its new members:

• *Live in harmony with the church's doctrines and purposes.* Seldom, if ever, will every member in a given church be in total agreement on how to interpret every passage of Scripture. When it comes to the daily practice of the Christian faith, even more differences will surface. Standards of behavior differ within each congregation, as do expectations for the worship and evangelistic services of the church.

A church can expect, however, a general unity among its members when it comes to the basic foundations of Christian orthodoxy. A church has a right to expect its members to promote unity within the body and to work actively for the dissemination of the gospel message.

• *Attend church services regularly.* It hardly makes sense to be a member of the church and not to share in its worship, fellowship, and ministry. We might join a golf club and not use the facilities, but we cannot be a member of a church and not participate in its life.

Transfer of Members

In a simpler era of American life, it was quite common for a person to be born, raised, employed, and buried in the same community. People worked at carving out a career that would move them up and through—but not out of—an organization. The "fifty years and a gold watch" ideal mirrored a reality common to a less transient American culture.

So, likewise, many Christians spent their entire church-going life in one home church. Within that one place, they were baptized, nurtured in the faith, married, and finally memorialized.

Pastoring Our Pilgrims

Times have changed. The average working American now changes his or her vocational direction five times before retiring. Extended families span one end of the country to the other. Not surprisingly, pastors find themselves wondering how long it will be until even new members are pulling up stakes and heading for the next stop on their journey through life. Because we have become pastors to a pilgrim people, we need to find ways to provide continuity and spiritual support for our gypsy joiners. Consider these three suggestions:

• *We will seldom gain a new member or family "for keeps."* When the time comes for these folks to make a move, like pastors, they will. In the meantime, we are wise to nurture the idea that in joining a local church, a new member has joined a worldwide family of faith, the body of Christ. As that idea takes root, church members who find themselves moving to a new lo-

• *Support the church's programs financially.* Regardless of a church's approach to financial stewardship, every church expects its members to participate in meeting the financial needs of the congregation and its ministry budget. Giving cannot be coerced; it should be voluntary. It is not to be a drudgery, but a delight; not demanded, but expected.

• *Have a personal ministry.* The biblical principle is that every member of the body function as a minister, a servant of others. That means members should be expected to serve in and through the programs and ministries of the church. To be a member means to contribute to the spiritual health and growth of fellow members in an ongoing process of mutual edification.

How Do People Join?

Depending on denominational traditions and theological perspectives, churches have used a variety of approaches to initiate members into the fellowship of the church. Some churches in the Reformed

cale will start to realize that leaving town doesn't mean leaving behind their family of faith. They are card-carrying members of a family that has its arms open around the world. People in transition need a sense of stability, and a church can provide that sense of family in a meaningful and biblically authentic way.

• *The church can extend care.* It can do for its members what a family does for a student leaving for college: phone ahead to make contacts to ease the transition. Most pastors have access to current church listings in their denominations. If not, a brief 411 phone inquiry should enable us to find the nearest affiliated church for the transferring member. If all else fails, local Chambers of Commerce love to send lists of churches that welcome newcomers. For the few minutes invested in a long-distance call, we can send the reassuring message to transferring members that (1) we care about what happens to you, and (2) there is help up ahead; they will "keep the light on for you."

• *We can use the networks available to us in our denominational circles.* If phone or personal contact with a distant pastor is not possible, a simple postcard saying a member of our church is moving to their area and would appreciate the extended hand of hospitality will serve the same purpose. We may want to include other helpful information, such as ages of their children, how long the family has been in membership, and any offices family members held in the church.

If we are fortunate enough to receive such a notice, we won't want to waste any time arranging for a visit to take the family information about the church. We can let them know the welcome mat is out for them.

—*Brent Mitchell*

tradition automatically count as communicant members the children of adult members. Other churches link membership with the conversion experience or with the act of baptism, making membership a distinct activity that follows the experience of salvation and requiring a specific choice by an individual believer. Regardless of the theological understanding of membership, pastors should set up an entrance process that elevates membership to a high level of significance. Many churches accomplish this by establishing membership classes.

Membership classes provide several safeguards and are generally considered a wise requirement. The very act of requiring attendance in the classes says to the candidates that the church treats membership as vitally important—and so should they.

What should membership classes do to promote the initiation process? Consider these basic functions:

- *They should provide crucial teaching.* Naturally, a membership class should begin by clarifying the meaning of salvation and what it means to be a follower of Christ as Lord. The pastor (or other class leader) should see that the prospective member has personally experienced the forgiveness of sins and has cleared up misunderstanding about the implications of water baptism for personal faith.

Second, the membership class should outline the moral and ethical standards of behavior expected of members. Many candidates, products of our post-Christian secular society, are new to the faith. They need to appreciate that, as members of the congregation, they are "advertisements" for Christ and his church in the community. They should therefore maintain a lifestyle consistent with biblical principles.

Third, the class should thoroughly explain both the statement of faith and the constitution of the church. These should be provided to prospective members in writing, so they enter the church with eyes open, fully aware of what they are joining.

Fourth, the class should explain how the church functions, how it elects leaders and officers, and how it chooses its pastors. The logistics of administration need to be explained, so the new member knows how to participate in the life of the church.

In our church, for instance, we fully explain the mission statement of the congregation, expounding on the main biblical principles that form our philosophy of ministry. We want new members to feel from the beginning the same desire for renewal within the church and outreach to the community that we do.

Of course, the classes should provide many opportunities for questions. Often these questions will form a significant portion of the agenda for each session.

A senior pastor may not always be able to attend membership classes. However, it is wise to attend at least one of the sessions to answer questions and get to know people. In addition, some pastors provide audio- or videotapes to contribute to class sessions.

• *They should clarify the terms of commitment.* During the last class session, students may formally apply for membership. A written application, signed by the prospective member, can be kept on file in the church office. The application indicates a potential member's commitment to the Lord and to the church. It's a commitment to be involved in ministry, to support the budget, and to live in harmony with other believers in the congregation.

One such form includes the following statement: "It is my earnest prayer that God shall keep me true to him, but if for any reason I shall depart from the faith or absent myself from the church or cease to live a godly life or change my doctrinal beliefs, I shall consider it just to be released from my membership in this church." This statement strengthens the hand of the board in dealing with any members' actions that might detract from the church's witness.

In our church, the membership applications are initially processed by the leader of the membership class, who passes on his or her recommendation to the pastoral staff. The application is then taken to the board of deacons for approval. The minutes of the board of deacons approving the membership application make the membership official. The minutes of an official board are necessary to meet the legal requirements.

• *They should give new disciples public recognition.* Following the official board approval of the membership applications, it is good to recognize the new members in a public service, usually on a Sunday morning, extending the right hand of fellowship. Why a public ceremony? It puts both the church and the new member on record. A commitment has been made and now must be kept. When a new member stands at the front of the sanctuary, he or she says, "This is my church; this is where I belong."

A public declaration of intent generates staying power through appropriate peer pressure. For example, I once announced to the congregation that I was going on a diet. I had a reason for publicly declaring my intention. From that moment, I knew everyone was watching me. I had gone on record, and that became a powerful incentive for me to keep my commitment.

What about Records?

It is absolutely essential that a congregation keep an accurate record of membership, because membership has legal implications. If a church is challenged in court for any reason, its records must be accurate. The process of adding and deleting names must be done legally and constitutionally. Some churches appoint an official membership secretary, often an office secretary. Legally, however, membership accounting is the responsibility of the secretary of the board of the church.

Computers make the task easier than ever. Database programs can now help a church build a profile of each member. These programs can track all types of data, including attendance, giving, ministry involvement, and spiritual-growth milestones.

Many constitutions require an annual review of membership. The official register of members is to be brought up to date in relation to attendance standards, stewardship patterns, and lifestyle issues. Keeping the membership list current makes it easier to have a quorum for congregational business meetings.

Often a church must take the time to remove names from the membership rolls. The purpose of the review process is not to punish anyone or to push people away from the church. Rather, it is to restore stray sheep to active fellowship.

If names must be removed, this must be done prayerfully, with patience, gentleness, and kindness. The door should always be left open to allow the dropout to return. While a letter to the person being removed is usually legally required to cancel membership, church leaders should vigorously attempt to restore the individual through personal contact.

Once I regularly walked by a construction site in the inner city where a new brick building was slowly emerging. I noticed, one day, that a truck had delivered a fresh load of bricks for the new building. However, when the bricks were delivered to the lot, they were carelessly dumped and spread in a loose pile. Day after day, I watched the pile get smaller, not because the bricks were used in the building but because looters were carting the bricks off for themselves. Each night a few more bricks disappeared. I began to realize that only when the bricks were cemented together with other bricks would they be safe and able to accomplish their true purpose.

Church membership, too, locks building blocks together—the people-blocks of God's kingdom. Membership protects believers from doctrinal thieves and enables them to be "built on the foundation of the apostles and prophets, with Christ Jesus himself as the chief cornerstone. In him the whole building is joined together and rises to become a holy temple in the Lord" (Eph. 2:20–21).

—*Calvin C. Ratz*

Promoting Membership

They tell others, "This is my church." They brag about your programs, give glowing reports about the pastors, and buy tapes of your sermons for their closest friends. Yet "they" haven't joined your church. Is it possible to convince them to join without being heavy-handed or conniving?

People join more readily when they advance through the following stages:

Awareness

Whether a person is buying a car, choosing a real estate agent, or joining a church, he or she will not move to the action stage before first becoming acquainted with the organization. We need to make it easy for newcomers to learn the inner workings of the congregation.

We can practice several awareness routines with new people. On pastoral visits with new attenders, we can take them memorable written materials that explain the church's ministries. Full-color brochures, pamphlets, or cassette tapes can help explain the details of weekly church life. A videotaped tour of the church facilities and ministries works wonders.

Within the next few months, we can follow up the initial visit with several more informational approaches. One church holds a Meet-the-Pastors Night every few months for new attenders and reaches a dozen people or more at a time. The pastors individually outline their areas of ministry and preview coming events.

Interest

Experts in advertising tell us that a good advertising campaign moves the prospective buyer from awareness to personal interest. The casual attender is looking at the church with awareness. What can the church do to stimulate interest in joining?

We can constantly show casual attenders the people who *are* joining. We don't need to wait for twenty new candidates before scheduling a Membership Sunday; we can bring them in by twos and threes. Bulletin features can showcase new members by highlighting their life stories.

Another way to move people from awareness to personal interest is to involve them in public services. People will join a church where they are allowed to be involved. The testimonies of members whose lives have been touched by God since attending your church are effective in attracting others. Nothing raises interest in potential members like satisfied new members.

Desire

We can begin to move interested attenders to the desire stage by asking ministry leaders for lists of entry-level ministries—forms of ministry that do not require extensive training or commitment. We can also provide a list of interested attenders to each ministry team and encourage them to contact these people. When an attender feels ownership in a piece of the church's ministry, he or she will desire more intimate involvement.

An individual church mailbox for regular attenders helps them feel a part of the team, and we should make sure they are on every mailing list applicable to their family. Surprisingly, good-natured references to the church's—and the pastor's—shortcomings can actually work for a church. Many prospective members are sinners seeking change; they often desire to join a church that seems "real" to them.

Action

We can't rest on the assumption that awareness, interest, and desire will automatically move people into membership classes. We need to present at least three invitations to join the church every month. Bulletin inserts, special role-played announcements, mailbox hints, or notices of membership classes on bulletin boards can give the person desiring membership the push he or she needs.

When people do indicate the desire to join, three immediate steps are wise: (1) making an appointment without delay, (2) delivering a statement of membership requirements *before* the interview begins, and (3) calling for a specific decision at the close of the interview.

—Michael E. Phillips

Conflict Management

What should we do first, after conflict explodes into the open? Agree on the *process* before trying to agree on solutions. That is, before discussing the viewpoints themselves, members need to agree on a fair way to discuss the various viewpoints and come to a decision. It is much easier to agree on procedure than on issues.

Discussing procedures first lays a foundation for cooperation. It usually is not difficult to gain the broad support of a congregation if a proposed procedure is fair and impartial. When a process has been agreed upon, there is a better chance of gaining support for a solution. Many people who once strongly opposed a given solution will be more apt to support it later if they become satisfied that their viewpoint was heard.

How to Proceed

A pastor who initially is caught off guard by conflict can prevent damage by moving the group to this important first step. One way is to note the different opinions, summarize each empathetically, and then say, "I propose we lodge this issue with the church council and ask them to take leadership in resolving this disagreement." Placing the conflict on the official agenda of the church prevents further avoidance and allows careful planning of succeeding steps.

The church council can then form a group to develop and propose a decision-making process for congregational approval. Such a committee should represent the various viewpoints on the issue. This means, however, that everyone will be tempted to engage in little power games to "win" at the expense of others. The best way to reduce this temptation is to take half an hour during the first committee meeting, and occasionally in later meetings, to discuss the issue openly. Encourage members to view their jobs not as advocating a particular solution but as setting up a process by which each view will be heard.

The process committee should outline—in writing—a proposed process, sometimes known as the "Agreement on Procedures." This "Agreement" is then submitted to the congregation for approval before discussion of the issue, itself, begins.

A Full Agreement

In their book, *Church Fights,* Paul Kittlaus and Speed Leas suggest four items that should be included in the Agreement:

- *Issues:* Specify the issue that needs to be decided. In the opening stages of discussion, people often disagree on what the real issue is. It is important that people agree on what they are disagreeing about before trying to seek solutions.
- *Goals:* The Agreement should also state what the group would like to happen as a result of this effort. Surely one goal would be to understand the viewpoints of each group better. In many situations, another major goal would be to develop a specific recommendation that most of the congregation can accept.
- *Time line:* The Agreement should lay out what will happen when. Probably the first event in the time line will be congregational approval of the proposed Agreement. The second event could be gathering viewpoints from all corners of the congregation. It's good to specify how this will be done — questionnaires, interviews, group discussions, or all of these. Normally the third event is a specified group tabulating and reflecting on the congregational viewpoints. The fourth event is the group presenting for congregational approval a resolution they believe will be acceptable to the majority.
- *Decision rule:* The Agreement should specify the rule by which the final decision will be made. Is a simple majority vote adequate? Or must there be greater support? A decision supported by 75 percent of the congregation is much easier to live with than one supported by 53 percent.

—Ronald S. Kraybill

Church Discipline

Most churches have a predetermined system of disciplinary steps to be taken in cases of a member's moral, ethical, spiritual, or doctrinal failure. A pastor or ruling board can follow such procedures with considerable confidence when a member has an adulterous affair, for instance, or an elder espouses false doctrines. For every clear-cut discipline decision, however, there may be ten fuzzy problems crying out for creativity, diversity, and grace. The following guidelines can help a pastor who faces these gray areas of church discipline.

Prayer Confrontations

When someone needs confronting but the facts are muddled, or the issue seems more severe than it first appeared—any situation where delay seems appropriate—prayer is the most effective first step. Here are some goals to accomplish in the prayer closet:

- Ask the Father to reveal and clarify the problem to the offender.
- Ask God to bring a solution without the need for direct, personal confrontation.
- Ask God to adjust your attitude so you'll react properly in this complex situation.

After praying this way, allow the Lord time to work on your requests.

Partnered Confrontations

The Bible advocates confronting a backslidden believer one-on-one. The one-on-one approach generally helps the person being confronted to overcome any natural embarrassment or defensiveness. In the case of more serious sin, especially when the consequences of discipline may be quite unpleasant, it is better to confront with two people. The presence of another person lends a stabilizing factor to a potentially explosive meeting, and the additional person can act as a corroborating witness in the event of future counteraccusations (or even a lawsuit).

Homework Assignments

Church leaders who are called to administer discipline need to be tutorial, not vindictive. After all, "discipline" and "disciple" are cognate words.

For those who have sinned and have voluntarily agreed to a regimen of discipline, we can give assignments such as attending therapy sessions, going to specified retreats or seminars, joining a support group, doing work for the church, keeping a devotional journal, or demonstrating regular attendance at church functions.

We can help protect the church from lawsuits in these cases by following two crucial rules. First, discipline committees should maintain a detailed written record of all proceedings, with the person being disciplined and the discipline committee having the only copies. Second, leadership should adhere strictly to church by-laws. In test cases, these two simple procedures have protected most churches from liability.

Temporary Suspensions

Temporary suspension is always preferable to permanent expulsion. Suspension can proceed in stages, perhaps in this order: suspension from regular duties in the church, from elected offices, from all ministries, and from membership privileges.

As several legal scholars have pointed out, except when people are disturbing the assembly, it may be unlawful to bar them from church attendance. We need to be wary of going to that extreme. We should once again write down all judgments and keep all records confidential.

Disputes among members have

embroiled churches in lengthy legal battles. Thus it is wise to avoid arbitrating in private disputes unless the procedures for doing so are clearly specified in the church's bylaws and all parties agree in writing to the ground rules.

In addition, when adults in church leadership are found to have abused children under their care, those in charge of discipline must take three immediate steps: (1) notify the police or other authorities, (2) remove the offender from any contact with children while the case is pending, and (3) write down the details of all discipline hearings from the beginning.

—*Michael E. Phillips*

17

Small Groups

The small-group movement has come of age. After fifty years of trial and error, the small group is now recognized as a primary vehicle for growing the church spiritually and numerically. However, the movement must be kept from veering off balance, as it can so easily do and has done sometimes in the past.

What can we do to keep from making the mistakes of the past? First, we need to understand the history of the small-group movement in order to recognize the roots of its contemporary strengths and weaknesses. Second, we can become familiar with the five basic types of groups and consider diligently how to encourage them within our congregations.

As people become available for small groups and willing to join one, they need to be offered a meaningful place to fit into Christ's body, a group within which they can "together with all the saints . . . grasp how wide and long and high and deep is the love of Christ" (Eph. 3:18).

How the Movement Began and Grew

The Mississippi—definitely a large river—is made up of many smaller streams. Likewise, the small-group movement today is a large movement composed of many small streams that have come together over the last fifty years.

• *1900–1950: Origins.* In general, we could say the movement started out in the student world as an attempt to get back to primitive Christianity. It was driven by a missionary passion to reach the world for Christ, and the strategy became the ever-multiplying "cell." North American tributaries included the Student Volunteer Movement, with Robert Speer and John Mott; the YMCA movement; and the spillover from England of the Oxford Group and the Keswick "Deeper Life" movements. Biblical Seminary in New York (with its emphasis on inductive Bible study) and the experimental studies on group dynamics from Sara Little at Union Seminary were major influences.

• *1950–1960: The period of the prophets.* During this period, North America emerged from the Second World War as the major world power. Revival broke out at Wheaton, Asbury, Baylor, and other Christian schools. Campus Crusade for Christ and the Navigators went after the secular campuses. Billy Graham crusades led thousands to a personal faith in Christ and introduced them to ssmall groups for fellowship.

The small-group movement in the fifties was largely a parachurch movement. When a church did embrace small groups, the groups were an appendage to the program. Bible study was the focus, and the requirements for group membership eliminated all but the highly committed. It would be another thirty years before the church learned how to manage groups and provide a menu for all levels of commitment in the church.

Some of the most influential leaders during this period included: Sam Shoemaker (Faith at Work), Elton Trueblood (Yokefellows), Glenn Clark (Camps Furthest Out), Dawson Trotman (Navigators), C. Stacey Woods (InterVarsity), Bill Bright (Campus Crusade for Christ), E. Stanley Jones (Ashrams), and Frank Buchman (Moral Rearmament).

• *1960–1970: The movement takes off.* In this decade, the major denominations began to embrace small-groups as a technique for evangelism. They were heavily influenced by the Organizational Development movement. Some of the most influential seminaries turned to the American Psychological Association for group-therapy techniques and introduced CPE (clinical pastoral education) to seminary students.

Leaders during this period included Bruce Larson (Faith at Work), Samuel Emerick (Yokefellows), Ben Johnson (Institute of Church Renewal), and Don James (Pittsburgh Experiment). There were several church renewal "watering holes," where pastors went for training and personal renewal (Dayspring Retreat Center of the Church of the Saviour, Washington, D.C.; Laity Lodge in Leaky, Texas; Kirkridge in Bangor, Pennsylvania; and Yokefellow Institute at Earlham College in Richmond, Indiana).

The sixties were exciting years, but the influence of secular ideas may have set back the explicitly Christian small-group movement. The therapy model of closed groups (for reasons of confidentiality) crippled the cell-multiplication system. Also, the social-action focus in the mainline denominations tended to go overboard. Elizabeth O'Connor warned in her book *Journey Inward, Journey Outward* that "any group that neglects the journey inward for the journey outward will burn out." By the end of the sixties, the small-group movement had burned out. It would be another twenty years before the movement's leaders learned to keep the balance.

• *1970–1980: The period of excess.* Political idealism was shattered by the war in Vietnam, and the church was burned out on social action. A new crop of leaders emerged that were more attuned to personal growth, such as Carl Rogers (Human Potential), Fritz Pearls (National Training Labs), and Ira Progoff (Journaling Workshops). Some of the retreat centers and leadership-training ministries moved away from Christ-centered small groups to form human-encounter small groups.

So after going overboard on Bible study in the fifties and social action in the sixties, the small-group movement went overboard on personal growth in the seventies. Books demonstrating this trend included Thomas Harris's *I'm OK, You're OK,* Sam Keen's *To a Dancing God,* Ira Progoff's *At a Journal Workshop,* Charles Schultz's *Joy,* and Scott Peck's *The Road Less Traveled.* These were primarily secular books, but they reflected the spirit of this decade, when the small-group movement turned to personal introspection and human interaction. Often psychological tests were promoted as kick-off materials for starting groups. The church on the whole followed the humanistic education model for personal growth in small groups. It would be another ten years before the small-group movement learned how to keep a healthy balance between psychology and theology.

• *1980–1990: The integration period.* Church growth studies demonstrated that the fastest growing churches in the world (particularly in Third-world countries) were cell churches. Church-planting agencies adopted small-group techniques, and the church turned to church growth technology. Leaders in this movement were Donald McGavran, Peter Wagner, and Eddie Gibbs (Fuller Theological Seminary); Carl George (Charles E. Fuller Institute of Church Growth); and Win Arn (Institute for American Church Growth). The influence of David (formerly Paul) Yonggi Cho in Korea was also significant.

Tough times in the eighties caused the church to deal with the survival instincts of people. This has brought about a greater balance of the three basic needs of any Christian small group: Bible study, caring, and multiplication. By the end of the eighties, a number of churches had demonstrated a workable model for "growing the church through small groups." There remained only the need for an effective management system for keeping groups healthy.

• *1990–Present: The expansion of the church through* small groups. Three basic survival systems of society have collapsed: the extended family, the guaranteed job, and the secure neighborhood. By the millions, people are turning to the church for help. The small group is a primary vehicle for the church to minister to this broken world.

Leadership for the movement emerged from pastors in churches trying new models: Dale Galloway (New Hope Community Church, Portland, Oregon), Rick Warren (Saddleback Community Church, Mission Viejo, California), Bill Hybels (Willow Creek Community Church, South Barrington, Illinois), John Wimber (Vineyard Chris-

Disciplemaking Groups

"None of us will ever forget this man who was totally committed to putting God first, a man whose humble life combined muscular Christianity with radiant godliness." That's how David J. Michell described Eric Liddell, the missionary to China whose life was dramatized in the award-winning movie "Chariots of Fire." Liddell died in a Japanese prison camp in 1945, but his legacy of muscular Christianity and godliness far outlasts the vapor that was his earthly life.

Producing Muscular Christians

Disciplemaking groups should aim at producing Eric Liddells—men and women of spiritual muscle, who learn personally from the Master as they walk daily with him. Such disciples live by the Word, contribute to the work of the church, and influence the world for the cause of the gospel. To develop successful disciplemaking groups, take these four steps:

• *Create a vision for disciplemaking.* The vision you hold out to your group members must be worth significant sacrifice in time and energy. "Changing the world, one life at a time" or "Turning ordinary people into extraordinary disciples" would make good goals, for example. We light fires in people's souls when we find a slogan, theme, or logo that captures the passion of disciplemaking and then use it to impart a world-changing vision.

• *Set up a structure that serves.* A disciplemaking vision must be accompanied by a ministry structure that serves people; otherwise we have fuel without a rocket. Leaders must be given appropriate spans of care (from four to ten people) to avoid burnout. In addition to discipling members, leaders can multiply their ministry by mentoring an assistant or apprentice who will

tian Fellowship, Anaheim, California), and Ralph Neighbour (Touch Outreach Ministries, Houston, Texas).

Some of these churches are radical, but they must not be discounted. Every movement begins by painting outside the lines. The challenge in the nineties is to find a way to equip lay people for caring and to provide an administrative system that keeps the small groups healthy. The senior pastor is the key.

Five Groups to Help Churches

In the 1920s, General Motors discovered the art of segmenting and targeting the desires of buyers with different kinds of cars to meet

one day lead a group. To prevent abuses of power, we must model servanthood and avoid hierarchies (for example, do not make the apprentice role a "promotion").

• *Develop a process that produces your product.* Drawing on insights from the Scriptures, each church must define what it means by a disciple and then develop a process that helps produce such a person. For example, we can ask about our disciple-products: Are they using their spiritual gifts by serving in a meaningful ministry? Do they regularly support the work of the church? Are they growing in grace and learning the Scriptures? Have they begun to walk with Christ without being externally motivated? Are they growing more obedient to Christ as they learn more about him?

In light of such questions about our discipleship goals, homework assignments should emphasize quality devotional times and personal spiritual disciplines. Praying, journaling, meeting with unchurched friends, and serving others make excellent homework and directly fulfill the Great Commission.

• *Equip leaders and release them for ministry.* Disciplemaking groups face two main challenges: the support and care of leaders, and the potential for groups to become ingrown. To support leaders, we can hold regular meetings for encouragement, problem solving, and training in areas of group process, listening skills, caregiving, leading dynamic discussions, developing apprentice leaders, and mastering spiritual disciplines.

Fully equipped leaders can keep groups from becoming ingrown by making sure their groups add new members at strategic times throughout the group cycle, until a group reaches the maximum size of ten members. At the completion of the cycle, the apprentice can begin a new group.

As Eric Liddell reminded us, it is not willingness to know but to *do* God's will that brings glory to God and lasting spiritual growth. Liddell demonstrated a life of muscular Christianity and godliness. This is a powerful combination and a worthy target for every disciplemaking group member.

—*Bill Donahue*

different kinds of needs. In the same way, the church today is discovering the value of segmenting and targeting the needs of people inside and outside of the church and providing a variety of groups to meet those needs. Here are five group types that need to be offered.

• *Covenant groups.* Target audience: Active church members who are open to further commitment. Purpose: To build long-term relationships. Biblical basis: The Old Testament covenants. Key leader: Roberta Hestenes.

The covenant group begins with a short-term commitment—seven to twelve weeks—with a group agreeing to common ground rules for Bible study, prayer, and mutual support. At the end of this period, the group can renew the covenant and continue for another specified time, such as the rest of the school year.

The primary strength of this type of group is that it offers long-term support for participants. There are, however, some weaknesses with this model: (1) The required high-level commitment will rule out about 60 percent of the church members, (2) there is no built-in system for reproduction, and (3) there is a good chance the members will burn out by the third year of continuous meeting.

Task-oriented Groups

Setting up task groups is a great way to develop a growing number of faithful volunteers in almost any area of ministry. A task group is distinct in that it is not just a traditional fellowship-building group or a team of people simply fulfilling a task. By definition, task groups attempt to accomplish both fellowship and ministry at the same time.

Fellowship *and* Ministry

The principle mission of a task group is to set aside a 30–45-minute group time to develop the spiritual and relational life of each team member. People tend to join a group because of the task they want to work on, but ultimately they will stay because of the mutual caring among the group members. Being intentional about developing the sense of community through a designated group time strengthens and improves the overall health of the ministry.

Most of the principles used to develop effective traditional small groups can be transferred to working with task-oriented groups. However, several features will especially enhance the development of task groups:

• Encourage groups to meet before or after their serving time. No matter how frequent the serving opportunity (whether once per week or once per quarter), add a community dimension to each meeting.

• Monitor task-group curriculum selection and usage. To begin with, use simple, open-ended questions, such as those found in Nav-

These weaknesses can be overcome by promoting "reproductive policies" for groups and by instituting a management system. For example, the group administrator could require that every spring groups would "graduate" at a churchwide banquet. At that time participants would be encouraged to move to an "alumni" level and meet occasionally for reunions, but not on a weekly schedule.

This frees up the group members to put their energies into forming new groups. In this way, groups would multiply when small groups kick off in the fall. This principle could be written into the group covenants so that there would be no misunderstanding at the conclusion of the groups' annual lifecycle.

• *Integrated groups.* Target audience: The congregation that attends the Sunday-morning teaching service. Purpose: To link the teaching on Sunday (at the worship service or Sunday school class) to a small group during the week for Bible application. Biblical basis: The early church example found in Acts 2:46 and 20:20. Key leaders: David Yonggi Cho and Dale Galloway.

The pastor and group coordinator write Bible-application questions with the group leaders before the groups meet. Everything is

---

Press's *201 Questions.* Evolve to using an uncomplicated small-group curriculum. For instance, group members could respond to discussion questions after reading a short passage from a *Serendipity Bible* or *Life Application Bible.*

• Develop a sense of *teammates* versus *soulmates.* People who join task groups generally have a primary commitment to the task and a secondary commitment to the people. Creating a teammate atmosphere helps everyone recognize that this group is different from the two-hour women's or couples' Bible study. Task-group members should accept and enjoy the fact that they have gathered in order to *do* something.

• Make the task a means to a greater end. Ultimately, changed lives is our goal. Over 50 percent of those serving in a task group will never join a traditional fellowship group. Yet a task group is an excellent place to connect unconnected people. For this reason, encourage groups to form around any appropriate impassioned cause for which a qualified leader will emerge.

• Provide ongoing leadership development. Leaders of task groups need regular support, training, troubleshooting help, and encouragement in order to lead over the long haul. Also, leaving an "open chair" (for the potential invited newcomer) in task group meetings will serve as the principle means of gathering the next generation of volunteers and leaders.

The beauty of leading and managing volunteer teams through task groups is that people not only accomplish the important task but also ultimately grow in their walk with God, with each other, and with the church. These are goals worthy of our labor.

—*Brett Eastman*

tied together—the Sunday sermon, leader training, and small groups. This model works best when the church as a whole buys into the entire package.

The link of the integrated group means that the pastor-teacher is deeply involved in the groups, providing a safety net against doctrinal error. The integrated group has a built-in system for reproduction through an ever-multiplying cell. This model depends on teaching from the pulpit for generating excitement, so the groups suffer if the pastor-teacher moves.

This model appeals to the 40 percent of the church members who attend church on Sunday, but it has difficulty reaching out to church members who do not attend church. It seems to work best in a church with an authoritarian pastor and a highly integrated program.

• *Cell groups.* Target audience: The entire church membership. Purpose: To multiply the church membership. Biblical basis: Jethro, the father-in-law of Moses (Exod. 18). Leaders: Carl George and the Charles E. Fuller Institute of Church Growth "Meta-Church" consultants.

In this model, the church is organized (or reorganized) around an inverted pyramid, with the pastor selecting a leadership team who, in turn, recruit, train, and supervise leaders of groups. Every group starts off with at least three people—leader, host, and apprentice-in-training—and an empty chair to fill. As soon as the group reaches ten or twelve in number, the apprentice takes one or two people and starts a new cell.

When there are five groups, one of the leaders moves up to be the district pastor-coach of the five group leaders. When there are ten coaches, one of the coaches moves up to become the supervisor of the coaches, and so on—much like Amway. The system is tied together in a monthly or bi-monthly training event for the group leaders and apprentices, in which the pastor and district pastors-coaches pass on the vision to keep multiplying.

This model seems to work best in a church with an authoritative pastor who can sell the vision with passion. If the senior pastor does not get involved, this model will not work. It requires a significant restructuring of the church around groups, including rewriting the job description of everyone on the church staff. For a new church, this may be the best model. For an older, traditional church, however, this model requires a lot of work.

• *Support and recovery groups.* Target audience: Inactive church members and people outside of the church. Purpose: To meet people at the point of felt needs. Biblical basis: The healing ministry of Jesus. Key leaders: A few courageous churches like First Presbyterian in Colorado Springs (Deborah Mahan) or Church of the Open Door in Crystal, Minnesota (Jeff VanVonderen).

The support or recovery group serves as the entry point for hurting people on their way back to God. These groups start with a short-term, low-level commitment for seven to twelve weeks for wounded seekers. Participants may not be committed or interested in Bible study, but they are open to being in a small group if their needs are addressed. The issue that brought them to the meeting is the focus. Someone with life experience in this issue is the leader or group facilitator.

This is not a therapy group but a self-help or mutual-support group. Up front, before the group starts, the ground rules are carefully spelled out so that people know what they are getting into, including the termination date. If people want to continue after this date, the group must move on to one of the other kinds of group models or the group members filter into existing groups for ongoing spiritual growth.

The great strength of this model is that it can serve as a conduit into other groups. For instance, at New Hope Community Church in Portland, Oregon, recovery groups last for six weeks, with two weeks off for people to visit other groups before a new series of recovery groups is launched. A potential weakness is that group leaders need special training and ongoing supervision. Churches without a safety net for group leaders can be liable for problems that occur.

In spite of the risks, the church needs to get involved in ministry to broken people in the community. With other survival systems in shambles, people are gathering at the church door by the millions. Their needs are spiritual, but their immediate need is often personal. The support or recovery group can be the entry point for such people, helping them on their way back to God.

- *Discipleship groups.* Target audience: The highly committed church members—the 10 percent. Purpose: To build mutual accountability in the spiritual disciplines. Biblical basis: Jesus and the twelve disciples. Key leaders: Robert Coleman, Bill Hull, the Navigators, and Campus Crusade for Christ.

Accountability is the focus of this model. Like the Holy Club that John Wesley belonged to, the group starts off by agreeing to a set of spiritual disciplines in Bible study, prayer, and moral accountability. Then the group members meet to check up on one another, share their needs, and hold each other accountable.

This model offers a place in the church for the small core of people who are ready for a high level of commitment. Such groups can become staging areas for small-group leadership training, and they also provide a place for pastors and church leaders to belong to a special group that can be "closed" for confidentiality reasons.

Unfortunately, this model will appeal only to a few people in the church, and closed and confessional groups often turn into cliques.

Accountability can turn into co-dependency. Without some supervision and an agreed-upon termination date, these groups can get out of control. Yet, even with such potential weaknesses, the discipleship group is needed in the church today. A few people in every church are looking for a place where they can launch into a higher calling in personal discipline, confession, and accountability.

A Place for Everyone

For the last one hundred years, the Sunday school movement has served the church well. But now, the neighborhood church is gone. The time has come for a new paradigm, a new system that can bring spiritual pilgrims to the door of the church through support and recovery groups, into the fellowship of the church through cell and integrated groups, into the core of the church through discipleship groups, and into ongoing relationships through covenant groups.

These groups can work like a spiritual transportation system, a subway with regular switching stations where people can transfer from one track to another track for the next stage of their spiritual journey. The church that can see the big picture and the needs of an extended parish can offer a means for everyone—whatever one's commitment to Christ—to find a place to belong.

—Lyman Coleman

Resources

Arnold, J. 1990. The big book on small groups. Downers Grove, Ill.: InterVarsity.

Callahan, K. 1983. Twelve keys to an effective church. San Francisco: Harper.

Cho, P. 1981. Successful home cell groups. Plainfield, N.J.: Logos International.

Coleman, L. 1993. Basic training for small groups. Littleton, Colo.: Serendipity House.

Galloway, D. 1986. 20/20 vision. Portland, Ore.: Scott.

George, C. 1991. Prepare your church for the future. Tarrytown, N.Y.: Revell.

Gibbs, E. 1985. I believe in church growth. London: Hodder and Stoughton.

Gorman, J. 1993. Community that is Christian: A handbook on small groups. Wheaton, Ill.: Victor.

Hestenes, R. 1980. Building Christian community through small groups. Pasadena, Cal.: Fuller Seminary Bookstore.

Neighbour, R. 1990. Where do we go from here? Houston: Touch Publications.

Peace, R. 1985. Small-group evangelism. Downers Grove, Ill.: InterVarsity.

Schaller, L. 1992. The seven-day-a-week church. Nashville: Abingdon.

Care and Self-help Groups

Open any newspaper today and you will see a large number of notices for self-help groups, ranging from the traditional 12-step groups, such as Alcoholics Anonymous, to the more unusual, such as Incest Survivors. Groups now exist to address a full range of human problems and predicaments. What do they actually do?

Meeting Spiritual Needs

Early on, self-help groups emerged primarily to assist people with their addictions. Participation in these groups tended to be long-term. More recently, self-help groups have emerged to help people cope with myriad other life problems. A divorce-recovery group would be a good example of such a coping group. Participation in these groups tends to be short-term.

The 12-step formula, though not explicitly Christian, proclaims unmistakably Christian themes like grace, redemption, and sanctification. People who enter a 12-step group are asked to acknowledge powerlessness over their addiction and affirm their dependence on a Higher Power for recovery. During recovery, which is a life-long process, people attempt to make amends with others they may have harmed along the way.

Treating addictions in this unabashedly spiritual fashion has turned out to be successful where conventional psychology has often failed. Individual therapy, while typically an adjunct to a person's recovery program, usually does not provide what the spiritually oriented 12-step program provides. The founders of Alcoholics Anonymous made their most significant contribution by identifying the underlying spiritual need, which could be met best in a small-group setting.

Offering Mutual Support

Such explicitly Christian themes are not necessarily a part of every self-help group, however. Without the 12-step formula, groups rely primarily on mutual caring and support to help one another through difficult circumstances. Parents who have had young children die, for example, frequently discover that *only* other parents who have experienced the same tragedy can understand the depth of their pain and loss.

The internal dynamics and leadership of small groups are as varied as the life issues they address. Most groups do have a leader—or at least people who are assigned to be facilitators. In some cases, these leaders have training in social work or psychology, but most often leadership simply emerges from people who have experienced the particular issue of concern. The act of leadership itself can be part of the recovery process for these people.

Connecting with the Church

Churches are uniquely qualified to offer and sponsor self-help groups, not only because the church has space to make available but also because the church is equipped theologically and spiritually for the task of healing. Most churches enter self-help group ministry when they recognize a particular need within their membership or community. For example, recognizing a high number of widows and widowers, church leaders may encourage a group like THEOS (They Help Each Other Spiritually), which meets the needs of young and middle-aged widowers.

Sometimes churches can draw on the services of existing national organizations to help them start a self-help group. Other times churches must go it alone. In those cases, leaders should feel free to borrow from and adapt other readily available models.

Leadership is the key ingredient for success. Groups usually begin with a small core of highly committed people who themselves have a need for care and support. While pastors ordinarily do not lead the self-help group itself, they can and should equip and provide resources for the leaders. Churches need not discount what they have to offer spiritually, either; people who seek out self-help groups are usually quite open to the Good News of the gospel.

—Douglas J. Brouwer

Study Groups

We study Scripture to meet God, discover God's priorities for us, and learn how best to respond. This is why *group* study is so powerful. *Together* we can discover more and explore more options for creative response. Therefore, pastors want to be familiar with basic principles for starting and facilitating group studies.

Start with Inductive Studies

There are myriad ways to organize a study group, but each group should intentionally choose a definite plan. Here's a sample format: Meet once a week for two hours, with 15–30 minutes devoted to getting settled, perhaps catching up on everyone's week; use 45 minutes for inductive Bible study; and then spend 45–60 minutes in *either* sharing, prayer, singing, worship, or planning service projects.

New groups should start with inductive Bible study, aiming to discover truth from a Scripture passage with little or no reliance on other references. They can begin by *observing* the text, then *interpreting* their observations, and, finally, *applying* the truth they discover. In inductive study we base our interpretations on observations made solely from the text in front of us. So in a new study, a typical follow-up question by the leader might be: "How do you come up with that idea from this text?"

As we launch into inductive study, narrative texts are more accessible for study by newer believers than didactic or poetic texts. Also, Bible dictionaries help students look up background information as appropriate. Commentaries and study notes, on the other hand, can undermine the rewards of personal discovery.

Master Group Facilitation

A primary task of the facilitating leader is to help groups develop specific, short-range study goals. For example: "Let's study one chapter of Philippians during the next four weeks."

At the end of such commitments, groups can take a week or two to celebrate and to review, raising questions such as: What went well? What not so well? What group goals do we want to change? Do we want to take a break for a while? What shall we do next?

Once we get group members into an inductive study, we want to help them observe well, interpret soundly, and avoid jumping around to other passages. Participants will remember more with this approach, and everyone can participate, because practically everyone can contribute at least an observation when guided by good questions. As group members practice this approach they get better at feeding themselves from Scripture.

As facilitators, we can humbly acknowledge when a passage raises more questions than answers, but we can press members to identify what clear truths they do discover. We are not responsible to answer every question that arises in the discussion; God is infinite, our understanding finite.

Many good inductive study guides can help us practice group facilitation. Leaders who want to develop their skills further can study and prepare questions on their own and then compare theirs with those in the published guides. Regardless of how they use a study guide, leaders need to come to the group knowing what succinct main point they want members to grasp and how their prepared questions will support the group's discovery of that point.

God builds individual differences into every community and uses these differences to help us grow. Authentic relationships include conflict, and we miss the grace God desires for us when we avoid conflict or distort our personality differences into moral issues. We will more effectively address conflict when we strive to understand divergent views within the group and remember that our primary purpose is to meet and respond to God.

—Roger Razzari Elrod

Fellowship Groups

Church growth specialists tell us the establishment of strong friendships is one of the most important reasons people commit themselves to a church. Studies also show that a major reason people drop out of church is the feeling of not belonging. Though a church may have an overflowing sanctuary and dynamic preaching, members may still lack the meaningful fellowship they seek.

The Cell Group

Several factors in our society have contributed to the need for greater stress on fellowship in our churches, the greatest being the breakdown of the traditional family structure through divorce. No longer having the advantage of a nurturing home life, individuals search for support and strength from caring people elsewhere. The workplace, too, creates much loneliness and anxiety if there are no fellow believers there. In addition, we have become such a mobile nation that we hardly have time to establish meaningful relationships before moving to a new part of the country. Many people among us end up living far from relatives.

Church growth experts stress that each new member should have an average of six or seven new friends within the first six months of joining a church. Most agree that many new members are likely to return to their old friends outside the church unless they gain new friends quickly in the local congregation. Therefore, more and more churches, regardless of size, have recognized the need for building solid relationships among the members.

One method that promotes such relationships is cell group ministry. A cell group is a small, intimate gathering that intentionally brings people face-to-face on a regular basis. Members share common goals and seek to grow together in the grace and knowledge of Christ.

Cell Group Characteristics

Cell group ministries come in all shapes and sizes, differing according to each church's needs and limitations. However, three characteristics tend to be true of all such groups. The groups are:

• *Modeled after the New Testament church.* On the day of Pentecost 3,000 people received Peter's sermon and were added to the assembly of believers. The Bible says, "they devoted themselves . . . to the fellowship" and they "broke bread in their homes and ate together" (Acts 2:42, 46).

• *Organized by specific areas of need.* Cell groups may meet for a number of reasons, such as Bible study or special projects, but fellowship and social interaction in a Christian context are legitimate ends in themselves. People come to see that the life of the church is not in the building but in the cells. Although there is a weekly celebration in the church building, significant ministry takes place in the home groups.

• *Used as evangelism tools.* Unchurched family and friends may be more likely to attend an informal home gathering, viewing it as less threatening than a large worship service. As relationships build, these same people may begin to accompany cell group members to their church meetings. People sometimes make commitments to Christ through cell group involvement, which is sometimes referred to as "side-door evangelism."

• *Multiplied by division.* The pastor may start with a pilot group that agrees to meet for six to eight weeks for training. Those people are then asked to go out and start their own groups, each having an assistant leader. The groups then grow as members invite others to attend. As the groups enlarge, the assistant leaders can take three or four members and split off to form other groups. It is wise for the elders to evaluate the ministry periodically to make sure it continues to meet people's needs and the church's objectives.

—*James E. Martin*

Shepherding Groups

With today's emphasis on church growth and with the blossoming of larger churches, congregations must be ready to respond to the inevitable decrease in one-on-one contact with pastors. Personal pastoral care can come in other ways, such as through trained lay leadership in shepherding groups. This not only brings relief to overworked pastors, it also produces a caring, loving atmosphere that pervades the entire congregation.

Prior Questions

In setting up a shepherding program, planning committees should ask these key questions:

• *Who will be the lay shepherds?* It's best not to ask for volunteers. Some volunteers may subconsciously seek the position as a means of meeting their own needs. Since ministering to the spiritual and psychological needs of others requires people with particular gifts, it is best to screen potential lay ministers for any evidence of personal, familial, or emotional "baggage" they might unwittingly foist on a group. Lay shepherds must have plenty of emotional energy to give to others. They can't be takers.

In the church I serve, the deacons and their wives are elected to share in the care ministry of the church. Additional couples are carefully invited into what has become the Shepherding Board of the church.

• *What type of training will we provide?* A congregation can set up a weekly training program for nine months a year. Such a program typically combines formal teaching, on-the-job training, and a mentoring time with the head shepherd of the congregation. A sense of strong accountability, not only to the head shepherd but also to the team of shepherding leaders, results from such frequent sessions together.

• *How should we form the shepherding groups?* Some churches draw up geographical areas and assign each to a zone lay minister who lives in the area and exercises pastoral responsibility for each family in the assigned zone. Other churches design their shepherding plans on a relational basis, assigning people to homogeneous units or carefully selected heterogeneous groups.

Our experience indicates that natural relationships form more readily and people network better if the groups are homogeneous units drawn from adult Sunday school classes. About twelve households are represented in each group.

• *When should the shepherding groups meet?* This varies from church to church. For example, some groups might meet in homes on the third Sunday evening of each month in lieu of the regular Sunday evening service. Some groups may want to meet bi-weekly. Others may wish to have dinner together after Sunday morning worship and then spend time in fellowship for an hour or two.

How to Succeed

In spite of the variety of approaches, three critical requirements determine the potential success of a shepherding program:

• *Effective training.* A large number of churches recruit lay shepherds, assign groups, and then abandon them. Leaders need to offer at least twelve initial training sessions to train lay shepherding leaders adequately, and then follow up with regularly scheduled refresher courses.

• *Broad scope.* The tendency is to add just a few shepherding groups to the other small-group ministries in the church. In order to work, however, the program must encompass the entire congregation. Every church member should acknowledge the need for personal pastoral care and support its provision through lay shepherds.

• *Ongoing accountability.* A laissez faire approach to lay shepherding dooms the ministry to failure. Lay shepherds must report regularly to the authorized staff person about how things are going in their groups. When the leadership expects competency and accountability, it is more likely to happen.

—*Charles Ver Straten*

Part V:

Pastoral Counseling

Pastoral counseling as we know it is a relatively new phenomenon—a hybrid of classical spiritual direction and modern psychology, with a strong dose of theology thrown in. A labor-intensive service spent with an individual rather than invested in a group, pastoral counseling yet remains a major ministry for many pastors and a favored alternative for pastors moving out of parish ministry.

The reason isn't hard to determine: pastors can truly help the people they counsel. The couple that enters the office wracked with marital strife and leaves with hope, the adolescent struggling with self-esteem problems who eventually sees his life as God views it, the grieving widow who turns a page to face the next chapter of life—all bring the pastor-counselor great satisfaction. When counseling works well, such obvious and joyous results buoy counselors. Those who feel called to ministry precisely to help people find genuine fulfillment in the successes.

But counseling isn't always successful. Sometimes it's downright discouraging. Most often it's emotionally and physically draining. And the time it requires can eat a schedule alive.

That's why counseling, of all the pastoral activities, demands careful study and wise action. Some techniques do work better than others. Some systems make counseling go smoother. Some policies have proved to be prudent; some attitudes, more effective. For the pastor wanting to better understand and practice pastoral counseling, the following articles offer appropriate counsel in themselves.

18

The Purpose of Pastoral Counseling

In the mid 1930s, some Christian ministers became interested in counseling as an expression of their pastoral care of parishioners. In the past, religious leaders had given guidance for living, but this was a new dimension of pastoral care, incorporating insights and techniques from the emerging world of psychotherapy.

Counseling has traditionally involved giving advice and guidance about how the counselee ought to live. More recently it has typically referred to a full-blown psychotherapeutic process in which the counselor is engaged in a healing action, assisting a mentally distressed or maladjusted person to become more healthy or whole.

Many parish ministers are now learning brief counseling techniques (not more than six sessions) and crisis-intervention methods to improve their pastoral-care skills. Other ministers have secured advanced training in counseling, specializing in a psychological healing ministry. Nevertheless, regardless of the level of one's expertise or training in the area of pastoral counseling, the question remains: Why should counseling, when it is done within the bounds of the local church, be considered an act of Christian ministry?

A Brief History of Religious Counseling

Let's begin exploring possible answers to that question by briefly surveying the development of counseling in the church. Pastoral care of persons has been offered as ministry from the earliest days of Judeo-Christian history. Moses, for example, as leader of the Hebrew tribes interceded with God for them (Num. 14:11ff), and to settle disputes and maintain the people's welfare, he appointed judges. The admonition to confess one's sin is found in both the Old and New Testaments. In confession, the believer admitted guilt and sought God's blessing for personal wholeness.

Jesus, in the spirit of Moses and the other Old Testament prophets, healed physical diseases to demonstrate God's presence with and for people. Significantly, his statements directly related spiritual and physical health when he was challenged for healing the paralytic man (see Luke 5:17–26). Later, Paul's admonitions to the quarreling Corinthian Christians expressed his pastoral concern for their spiritual growth and interpersonal healing. The injunctions of the later epistles—in Timothy, John, Peter, James, and Jude—regarding proper living give us additional expressions of pastoral care for the well-being of early Christians.

Pastor is the Latin word for shepherd, and very early it was applied to Christian clergy to describe their care for the spiritual lives of individuals and groups. Though confession to a priest had begun to develop in the early centuries of the church, by the fifth century complete penitential manuals were being used. The priests used these to assign penance, which was to help the sinner express regret and keep from repeating the sin. Thus, pastoral care of parishioners became both supportive and corrective at an early time. This practice continued the mission of the Old Testament prophets, as pastors tried to bring people into greater obedience to God and wholesomeness in living.

The focus on pastoral guidance for daily living continued in the teachings of the early Protestant reformers. Much of Martin Luther's writing was directed toward how Christians should live out the practical implications their theology in daily life. John Calvin's leadership in Geneva constantly addressed the behavior expected of citizens as they grew more informed about Christian doctrine. The work of the clergy as caring for the sick came to full expression in the monastic orders that operated hospitals in the Middle Ages.

During the last part of the nineteenth century, the concept of psychological treatment for mental disorders gained attention. Moving from hypnotism into psychoanalysis, Sigmund Freud and his early followers developed a full-blown theory of neurosis and its cure. And the counseling movement, as distinct from Freud's mental-illness treatment, began in 1906 as a program of guidance for people making vocational decisions. These developments paved the way for Christian ministers to begin utilizing the insights of psychiatry and guidance techniques in their work with distressed church members. Charles Holmes wrote *The Cure of Souls: A Socio-Psychological Ap-*

proach (1932). *Pastoral Psychology,* by Karl Stolz, appeared that same year. John Sutherland Bonnell's *Pastoral Psychiatry* followed in 1938.

The development of Clinical Pastoral Education (CPE) gave psychological-oriented pastoral care a legitimate, technical standing among the secular counseling approaches. Begun in a mental hospital setting in Worcester, Massachusetts, in 1925, and in social-service agencies in Cincinnati in 1927, CPE brought theological students into immediate service to the ill and needy, adopting teaching methods from medicine and social work to evaluate the effectiveness of pastoral practice. CPE stimulated use of those methods to improve the pastor's service to others with a view to their personal and spiritual wholeness—salvation, understood in its broadest sense.

The experience of chaplains in the Second World War, as they provided religious services to soldiers suffering psychological disorders, helped focus significant attention on pastoral counseling in the fifties. The use of counseling as a psychological method of pastoral care became prominent in many mainline theological seminaries. Pastoral counseling centers in the United States proliferated rapidly in the sixties, extending their influence to the present.

Theological Support for Christian Counseling

The theological basis for counseling as a practice of professional religious leaders rests upon three major Christian doctrines: God as Creator, human beings as sinners, and Christ as Mediator.

- *God as Creator.* God's act of creation was an expression of divine love. We recognize life as a gift bestowed to us immediately by parents but ultimately by the Divine Parent. Biblical narrative and church tradition affirm that God created the universe to share love, and people would be able to respond with their own love and commitment.

Love combines three dimensions: an *awareness* of the other and her or his needs and wishes, a positive *emotional response* to the other, and a *commitment* to the welfare of the other. The level of investment and degree of commitment varies with the age and ability of each individual, but the characteristic found in all love relationships is the presence of two or more persons interacting in mutually satisfying and mutually growth-stimulating ways. This awareness-emotion-intention quality, which acts for the other's good, will result in creation. The physical human form of creation is the child, and the existence of children creates a family. Since families propagate new families, the extended families become tribes and cities and nations. In brief, creating love develops into community.

Humans as sinners. The actual human communities that exist do not consistently demonstrate the quality of love, either toward one another or within their own borders. Human existence is marked by strife and tension rather than harmony and mutual respect.

At the biological level of our existence, each individual seeks to survive. The infant, without awareness of parental needs, cries when uncomfortable and demands attention. All of us have a normal, created desire for self-maintenance. As we grow up, however, this self-maintenance need becomes spiritually self-centered. It keeps the protection and care of the self as the chief good. Sometimes in relationships this self openly demands to be first, but often it seeks priority more subtly.

This push to make my own welfare the goal of all my actions, begun before I consciously knew what "selfish" was, places ME at the center of my world. ME becomes the god whose will ought to be followed by others. ME resists the call to live with others in mutual respect and to

Prayer and Counseling

Prayer is no magic formula that causes problems to vanish. Some deep wounds in lives and personalities need long-term, sensitive care. We can never consider prayer a Band-Aid to patch a deep hurt, nor is it an easy way to disclaim responsibility and end an uncomfortable or unproductive counseling relationship.

Yet in prayer, God has given us a unique gift to draw people to him. Often prayer can become the most productive and comforting part of a counseling session, the means by which God enters into a difficult human problem.

The Power of Prayer

In all of us reside guilt and anger, sometimes growing out of past experiences and the imperfect child-raising practices of our parents. Some people project the human imperfections of their parents onto God. Some blame God for the difficulties in their lives, believing God is giving them trouble as a punishment for some unremembered wrong of the past. People may not realize consciously that they hold these attitudes, but their lives are infected by them anyway. Wounded spirits prevent them from fully receiving God's love or having healthy relationships with other people.

This is where the strength of prayer enters in. Prayer is powerful, as we know, yet don't we sometimes speak of prayer and counseling as if they were separate activities with different goals? We counsel, and then we pray that the counseling works. Suppose we came to see prayer and counseling as two strands within the single fabric of God's work? It's our job to weave the two together.

meet others' needs. ME substitutes modes of benefit-exchange (trade-offs) for love. ME thus denigrates the divine Creator, whose goal is to engender unconditional love, and replaces community with survival, seeking dominant-subordinate relationships rather than mutually enhancing ones.

All this is to say that sin is not only a spiritual reality but also has its roots in our physical and psychological development from the earliest moments of life. And that sin leads to problems of relationship among persons and among the various aspects of our inner landscape. There is an essential unity in the relationship of the physical, the mental-psychological, and the spiritual. When we are physically ill, we often become psychologically depressed and spiritually questioning. When our relationships are troubled, God may seem to be distant, and our resistance to infection decreases. Sin separates us from

Weaving Prayer and Counseling

The weaving process will go smoother if we keep in mind a few simple guidelines for using prayer in counseling. Consider these:

• Pray silently while listening. As the person tells his or her story, consciously bring God's presence into the counseling situation. Under my breath I may pray: "Lord, thank you for joining me as we seek to minister to this person. Please help me rein in my own ego and remember that though I may be a channel of your grace, healing is only in your power."

• Get the endorsement of the other person. Only as long as our words actually reflect the prayers from deep within the soul of that person will he or she give assent to our words. If we misread the situation radically, the person simply will shut out our prayer. He or she might *listen* to the prayer but will not *pray* it.

• Avoid moralizing manipulation. One sure way to undercut prayer is to forget that the prayer is addressed to God and not to the counselee. All of us have heard manipulative sermons disguised as prayers: "Lord, you know that Joe here has caused his own problems. Help him to shape up before he wrecks his marriage." Moralizing statements in prayer obstruct the effect of placing the problems into the hands of God.

• Don't hurry to prayer. It's best to prepare for the prayer through careful listening and probing that will help unblock the counselee's line of communication with God. For example, a woman who has just suffered a stillbirth may not be able to open herself to God's healing until she has been given the chance to vent her anger. We'd want to encourage her to talk about her feelings *before* we pray.

• We need to remember that God is already at work in this person's life. Each person has a past and a future that are known to God, so we need to resist the tendency to see only the factor that is presently troubling.

—*Nancy D. Becker*

God and others, and it contributes to illness, to unethical and destructive behavior, and to "a hell of a life."

This is hardly a full statement on the doctrine of sin, but it may be sufficient to support this key point: one cannot rid oneself of sin! Sin results in immoral behaviors, but, at a much deeper level, sin is a quality of the self's relationship to God and to the world. In other words, sin is present in each of us *before* we commit bad deeds. Our self-centeredness is a biological reality that expresses itself in psychosocial and spiritual aberrations as we mature. We simply *cannot* outgrow sin, or learn to behave in sinless ways, or become "good enough" to compensate for sin. Hence, we cannot, by our own willed action, build a loving relationship with God and others that will contribute

Legal Responsibility and Liability

"When you have a dispute," admonished Doug Llewellyn of "The People's Court," "don't take matters into your own hands . . . take them to court." Despite an opposite admonition concerning lawsuits between Christians in 1 Corinthians 6:1–9, even the church has gotten caught up in today's litigation explosion.

The suing of the church can be attributed to any number of causes: a lessened respect for religion in American society, the erosion of the charitable immunity principle, and the advent of professional malpractice insurance for clergy and Christian counselors. Whatever the causes, pastors and counselors today must develop an awareness of how legal issues affect the practice of their ministries.

Two Big Dangers

There are two actions that can result in a lawsuit for malpractice or negligence in counseling:

- *Doing* what we, as pastors or counselors, *shouldn't* do. For example, engaging in sexual conduct with a counselee (surprisingly, this is the most common lawsuit against pastors and counselors).
- *Not doing* what we *should* do. This includes not taking action to prevent a destructive act by a counselee, such as suicide or homicide, when we had an indication that such an act might occur.

Pastors also have the responsibility to take action in the event of child abuse, whether physical or sexual. Some states exempt pastors from reporting suspected child abuse if they learn of the abuse in the course of pastoral or penitential counseling. However, if a pastor also has a counseling practice separate from his or her pastoral ministry, that pastor is required in most states to report suspected child abuse cases, regardless of the source of information. The state reasons the pastor is acting as a mental-health professional rather than as a pastor.

Likewise, most states require

to community as the Divine Creator intended.

Christ as Mediator. Both the Old and New Testaments proclaim the message that the Creator has—from the very moment of creation—been reaching out to humankind. The ultimate form of this divine outreach was the Incarnation of the God-man, Jesus. Jesus' life, death, and resurrection became the climactic demonstration of God's love for us.

God had sought relationship with created beings through covenant (Law), through wisdom teaching (Proverbs, etc.), and through prophetic statements. Yet humans were mostly unwilling to meet God face-to-face. So mediators have been employed by God to reach the human race. Jesus was—and is—the supreme Mediator.

nonparish pastoral counselors (those who do not actually pastor a church) to report any suspected cases of child abuse. Since child-abuse reporting laws are established at the state level, it is important to learn the details of your state laws.

How to Be Safer

What determines whether we will be held liable for negligence? The general rule is that we will be held to the standard to which a similar practitioner in our role is held. That standard is largely determined by how we market our services. If we purport to be professional counselors, we will be held to that standard in a court of law. For that reason, pastors who do not have a graduate-level degree in counseling should avoid describing themselves as professional counselors, especially since an increasing number of states are passing legislation that defines minimum standards for professional counselors.

Likewise, it is important that lay counselors accurately represent the scope of their capabilities and do not purport to be professional counselors. Under the principles of *respondeat superior* (in which the principal is liable for the acts of the agent), any lawsuit resulting from negligence on the part of a staff counselor, lay counselor, Sunday school teacher, church bus driver, or any other person acting on behalf of your church may involve the pastor, the church, and the parent denomination.

The best medicine for avoiding lawsuits is preventive education, instead of corrective litigation. Few Bible colleges or seminaries currently offer courses in legal issues for pastors and Christian counselors. Fortunately, a number of books have been published that address legal issues in ministry from a Christian perspective, such as:

- *Pastor, Church, & Law* by Richard R. Hammar (Matthew, N.C.: Christian Ministry Resources).
- *Christian Counseling and the Law* by Steve Levicoff (Chicago: Moody).

The best time to read such books is *before* we find ourselves in a legal bind.

—*Steve Levicoff*

A number of theories explain how Jesus relates us to God. The specific doctrinal explanation a person holds is secondary to the agreement that Jesus, the Christ, does actually provide the only means by which humans can find complete acceptance with God. Our sin is understood and forgiven by our Creator. We can acknowledge our sinfulness—our use of others for our own desires and purposes—and receive that forgiveness. We can see our sin and that of others, and we can accept their limitations and our own.

But we do need a mediator. It is here that the human extension of God's love can come to our rescue. Someone must tell us of Jesus.

Counseling and God's Healing Love

For many people the mere act of telling is not convincing. They may have been reared in families in which they did not experience love. Others may have had educational experiences in which, by studying science or philosophy or comparative cultures, they have developed serious intellectual doubts about the truth and uniqueness of Christianity. Some have not been instructed in Christian history and doctrine, so their ideas about Jesus and his mission are sketchy. For these and other reasons, hearing about Jesus and the meaning of his life, death, and resurrection may seem unrelated to their lives.

The original tellers were the apostles and disciples, those who represented and carried on the teachings and ministry of Jesus in his place. Paul, for example, referred to himself as an ambassador of Christ, "as though God were making his appeal through us" (2 Cor. 5:20). This representative role has been extended to subsequent church officials down through the history of the church. Thus, the minister is the human stand-in for Jesus, both in carrying out the work of the church and in speaking to the world.

The learning and utilization of counseling or psychotherapy by the pastor, then, is intended to extend the minister's representation of God and of his healing, saving love to others. Counseling thus becomes an expression of the healing aspect of Jesus' ministry, going beyond verbal telling by demonstrating God's continued presence for human wholeness. It is also the implicit recognition that healing requires more than merely ridding the body of infection or injury. The work of physicians is affirmed, for it improves human life, but physical well-being, as important as it is, is much less than the redeemed relationship with God that divine love seeks and offers.

The minister, as official of the church, the physical body of Christ in the world, becomes the representative of Jesus. He or she does not claim the sinless quality accorded to Jesus, but the indwelling of the Holy Spirit, working through that clergyperson, *is* God's presence for the person in need.

Harold, 43 years old, grieving his father's death, asks, "Why did my father have to die of cancer? He was a good man. At 67, he was too young to die."

The pastor responds, "He didn't deserve that pain. You wonder if God is just." The minister acknowledges Harold's implicit anger without criticizing. This communicates acceptance of Harold and his questioning. The minister thus enacts God's understanding and care for Harold.

Healing as the Experience of the Gospel

The pastoral counselor combines knowledge from both theology and psychology for the growth toward wholeness of the counselee. The pastoral counselor cares for the sinner, the sick or maladjusted person. The care given is guided by psychotherapeutic skills to aid the person in making changes in his or her life that move toward a committed, loving relationship with the Creator and with other persons.

In actual practice it is in the experience of an accepting relationship with the pastoral counselor that the seeker of wholeness "hears" the gospel at an emotional, holistic, interpersonal level. The pastoral counselor "tells" the gospel by attitude, posture, and grace-filled responses that enable the seeker to know herself and to see her self-made distance from others. Judgment is given, just as surely as Nathan confronted David, but it is done in a manner that loves even as it clarifies the maladjustment (sin) that is present.

How does this work? Suppose Betty has learned that Frank had an affair. She is hurt and angry. Frank begs her to forgive him, and together they consult their pastor. In the first session, the pastor learns that Frank had been working overtime and that a secretary in his office had been assisting him. Betty and Frank had been married 19 years and have three children, with whom Betty is deeply involved.

In the second session, the pastor comments to Frank, "You seem to have been missing Betty's companionship." He agrees. In the third session, the pastor says to Betty, "You have told about all you do for your children. Tell me some of the things you have done together with Frank."

As she tries to think, Betty muses, "There hasn't been much togetherness the past two years. Have I been neglecting Frank?"

The pastor has voiced judgment of Betty's part in Frank's affair in a nonthreatening way. God's view of the Frank-Betty relationship has been shared in a way Betty may be able to accept. And Betty begins to realize that she has sinned, even as Frank has sinned. The pastoral counselor tells the gospel by living it in her relationship with these two fellow sinners.

At times in the counseling relationship, verbal telling will be helpful. There may be times when the use of Biblical illustration or specific instruction about religious doctrines or praying with a seeker is useful. We should not hesitate to employ this form of witness. Yet the decision to use a specific religious expression should be made in the light of the counselee's readiness for such intervention and the appropriateness of it in the person's growth toward health and wholeness.

Leonard had been an altar boy and active in his youth group. When he married, he left his Episcopal Church and joined a charismatic group. He came to the pastoral counselor because of depression; his work and marriage both were suffering. In the therapy it became clear his depression was related to his mother. She disapproved of his present church and had refused to attend his adult baptism. Leonard's depression lessened as he began to grapple with its roots, struggling with new awarenesses about past deprivation and seeking ways to heal the relationship with his mother. But he remained unhappy about his mother's rejection of his faith.

The pastoral counselor discussed with Leonard the different doctrines of atonement that Episcopal and charismatic theologies often hold. Leonard was then able to understand his mother's strenuous objections to his current belief. This made it possible for him to be at peace with her, at least in this area, even though he was still hurt by her refusal to come to his church.

Leonard's case demonstrates that as the love of God found expression in the healing work of Jesus, so the love of God is expressed today in the care that ministers provide. A focused form of that pastoral care is the counseling work that some religious professionals practice as their call from God to be living witnesses of the gospel. They tell of God's love by their actions and their responses. And those with whom they work "hear" the gospel and move toward healing and wholeness in their lives. Counseling, when done within this incarnational framework, is truly a masterwork of Christian ministry.

—*Quentin L. Hand*

Resources

Clinebell, H. 1984. Basic types of pastoral care and counseling: Resources for the ministry of healing and growth. Nashville: Abingdon.

Glaz, M., et. al. 1991. Women in travail and transition: A new pastoral care. Minneapolis: Fortress.

Hunter, R., et. al. 1990. Dictionary of pastoral care and counseling. Nashville: Abingdon.

Patton, J. 1983. Pastoral counseling: A ministry of the church. Nashville: Abingdon.

Maintaining Confidentiality

Confidentiality is probably the most thorny ethical issue in the pastor-counselee relationship. Trust is crucial in the counseling room, yet it is so easy to trip up and break that trust. We may find ourselves facing the dilemma of confidentiality in at least four ways.

• *Church matters.* Sometimes the ethical requirements of the counselor's role come into direct conflict with the requirements of the pastor's role. Say Pastor Warren knows that Michael Thomas is unfit to serve as an elder. How can he convey his knowledge to the elder nominating committee without breaching the confidentiality of his counseling relationship with Thomas?

There are no easy answers, but one tack that some pastors have found effective is to say something like this: "I know Michael Thomas very well, and I'm aware of some issues in his life right now that would make this a bad time for him to be involved in this role. Sometime down the road, perhaps we can put his name in consideration, but at this time it wouldn't be wise to burden him with this responsibility."

There need be no hint as to what those issues are, nor the fact that those issues surfaced during a counseling session. In this approach, any comments regarding Thomas's fitness for church office should be nebulous, nonspecific, and nonjudgmental. Someone may ask for more detail, but the pastor should not get drawn into any elaboration beyond the original statement.

• *Consultations and referrals.* There are some people, though, to whom we must speak professionally about counselees, yet we need to get the counselee's permission before doing so. Occasionally we will encounter a person whose issues and problems are beyond our abilities and training, so we need to consult with someone else on the pastoral staff or an outside resource person.

At the beginning of counseling, we can ask the counselee to sign a release that gives us permission to consult with other professionals. It is also good practice to inform the counselee when we need to consult.

• *Family counseling.* Some of the trickiest aspects of confidentiality arise in family counseling. Counseling may involve one or two parents and one or more children, each with personal issues, and each deserving our confidentiality. Even when such situations cause us great anguish as counselors, it is best not to betray a confidence.

For example, a son tells the pastor in confidence that he habitually uses dangerous drugs. The wise and conscientious pastor will do everything in his power to obtain the son's permission to tell the parents, but without that permission, the confidence must be kept, even if the counselee is a minor.

• *Inadvertent slips.* We may accidentally break a confidence, because there is often a fine line between public and private information. For example, say a parishioner enters the hospital for an operation. The fact that she is in the hospital is probably public information that can be announced from the pulpit so the congregation can pray for her. But the specific type of surgery should be kept confidential, unless the hospital patient indicates otherwise.

Sometimes, even with the best intentions, we may let slip information given to us in confidence. When that happens, we need to go to the injured party immediately with the sincere message: "I'm so sorry. This is really embarrassing for me, and I apologize for any embarrassment I've caused you." Chances are, people will be understanding once they realize it is an honest mistake and our rigid policy is never to betray privately shared information.

—Jim Smith

Counseling Effectiveness

By 1983 counselors and psychotherapists were using more than 100 different methods of therapy, everything from traditional psychoanalysis to pop approaches such as "est." Given the varieties of Christian counseling and new methods of secular counseling developed over the ensuing years, the number of approaches may now be well over 200. Because no approach has ever been discontinued for failure to live up to its claims, all coexist and are added to year by year.

The Therapeutic Triad

We ought not to be daunted by the sheer number of approaches, however. Researchers Truax and Carkhuff have observed that all effective counseling modalities have at least three things in common, which are often called the "therapeutic triad."

• *Accurate empathy.* The effective counselor is able to make the counselee feel that she is with him, able at both the intellectual and feeling level to grasp what the counselee is experiencing. It is called accurate because the counselor neither overstates nor understates what the counselee is experiencing. She hears the counselee, devastated by divorce, talk about the terrible sense of loss and says, "You have lost a great deal: your mate, your children, the status of being happily married, your personal sense of worth, to say nothing of the financial effects you have just begun to feel."

This spirit is exemplified by Jesus Christ, our Great High Priest, who was *sumpatheo* (able to "suffer with us," Heb. 4:15). The effect is to get inside the hurting individual and dispel the loneliness and isolation, the feeling that no one understands.

Accurate empathy sets the stage for the giving of information or advice. The person who truly feels understood will be much more open to advice from a counselor who shows accurate empathy. Conversely, we react negatively to those who don't understand our pain, thinking, *How can this person help me when he doesn't even know how I feel?*

• *Nonpossessive warmth.* The counselor must be able to provide a safe and secure atmosphere for the counselee to reveal himself. If the counselee feels that self-disclosure will be met with disapproval, he will not seek help. For example, when I was a pastor, people from other churches often came to me for counseling because they were afraid they would be condemned by their own pastors. It is quite possible that people from my own church did the same thing.

We often find it difficult to create a climate for the counselee to speak freely, because we don't want to appear as though we approve of wrong behaviors. But letting them speak freely without verbal or nonverbal hints of disapproval does not imply approval. Jesus' handling of the woman caught in adultery is a good example (see John 8:1–11). Grace offers forgiveness and deliverance without minimizing the truth.

• *Genuineness.* This is the ability to be authentic and congruent. Do our counselees sense that what we are saying is really how we think and feel? Though we may not be self-disclosing to the degree that we are with our families, our counselees must be convinced they are talking to a real person who is experiencing life as they experience it.

We serve as a model of how a human being can handle difficulties without being phony. The deity of Christ never got in the way of his being fully human. Likewise, our Christianity must never get in the way of our being genuine with those we would counsel. If we make use of the therapeutic triad in our counseling and bathe our work in prayer, the specific counseling style we may use will no doubt be more effective.

—*Andre Bustanoby*

19

Lay Counselors

Several years ago, Columbia University Press published a book titled *The Nonprofessional Revolution in Mental Health.* Lay people, it was argued, are becoming more and more involved in "people helping." This surely is a healthy trend, especially as lay counseling moves into the local church and becomes the responsibility of church members as well as Christian leaders. Such caring is not only part of a trend; it is a biblical requirement commanded by the Lord and taught by the biblical writers.

By his life and teaching, Jesus emphasized face-to-face contact and encouraged mutual caring among his followers. The writers of the Epistles used the words "one another" almost sixty times, usually in the form of admonitions to care, encourage, edify, teach, confront, and support. James defines "pure and undefiled religion" in terms of both holy living and compassionate service, such as caring for needy widows and orphans.

So people helping is taught in the Scriptures; it is required of all believers (not just pastors); and it is urgently needed in all congregations, whatever their size, as people struggle with today's stress, confusion, and anxiety. Recognizing this need and the biblical mandate to meet it is the first step toward developing a congregation of people helpers. Only then can we look at the practical, procedural questions.

What Is Lay Counseling?

Counseling involves a caring relationship in which one person seeks to help another deal more effectively with the stresses of life.

There can be a number of counseling goals: to clarify problems; to explore and express feelings; to cope with stress; to find freedom from spiritual, psychological, and interpersonal conflicts; to develop self-acceptance and God-awareness; to confront counselees with their sinful and self-defeating thoughts and/or actions; and to help them find a new or renewed willingness to live in accordance with biblical teaching.

Counseling also enables counselees to reach their fullest potential and to become involved in growth as disciples and disciplers for Jesus Christ. The process is summarized not so much by the Greek word *noutheteo,* which means to admonish, warn, and rebuke, but by the word *parakaleo,* which means to comfort, support, and encourage, as well as to exhort and admonish.

Counseling is often seen as a foreboding process involving couches, complicated terminology, and foreign-accented therapists with mind-reading skills. Such a stereotype is collapsing quickly, as it should. Although counseling can mean face-to-face discussions between sensitive, skilled professionals and their paying clients, the term *counseling* has come to mean much more. It may include, for example, the teaching and learning of skills, an involvement in activities that reduce personal and community pressures, or joining a group of people who work together to solve their problems. Counseling may occur in an office or clinic, but it also takes place in restaurants, shopping centers, homes, work settings, and churches. As defined in this broad way, counseling is "caring" or "people helping," and thus is an activity that should involve all Christians who are concerned about one another.

Are lay counselors effective? According to an impressive body of empirical research, the answer is *yes!* Lay people can and do help, often as capably as professionals. Regrettably, little of this research is brought to bear on the church. Nevertheless, many congregations are developing and emphasizing lay counseling programs.

Who Does Lay Counseling?

Psychologist Lawrence Crabb has proposed that lay counseling should take place on three levels. Level I is *counseling by encouragement.* It involves all believers of a local church, and its objective is to teach them how to be more sensitive and caring. An example is the covenant groups found in many churches. These groups are composed of believers who care for, support, help, encourage, and give account to one another.

Level II, *counseling by exhortation,* is more selective. It is implemented by a group of mature believers who learn helping skills through a training program of at least 35 to 40 hours. At Level III, *counseling by enlightenment,* a few selected Christians in a local church are given in-depth training for a 6- to 12-month period, being taught to handle the deeper, more stubborn problems that don't yield to encouragement or exhortation.

Although this three-level approach is not accepted by everyone, it emphasizes the widely held view that all church members should care for and help others, but only a selected few should be trained as lay counselors. In Romans 12:8 we read that *paraklesis* is a spiritual gift. Such gifts are distributed throughout the body of Christ as God wills and are to be used for the purpose of edifying the church. Not all members of the body have this gift of "coming alongside to help." But many do, and these people must form the basis of a lay counseling program.

In considering who should do the counseling, it is important to recognize that within any congregation are members who have no special counseling gifts or training but whose personal experiences enable them to help others in special ways. Widows, for example, can often help other widows, and divorced persons frequently can help those whose marriages are breaking up.

Once a teenager in our church lost her hand in an accident. Within a short time, another family in the congregation called to say that their son had experienced a similar tragedy several months earlier. Soon one family was helping another through the sharing of a common experience.

For those who show evidence of being gifted in "coming alongside to help," a formal lay counseling program is an effective way to meet the overwhelming needs of many congregations. Such a program can be successful if we give four key ingredients careful consideration: pastoral support, careful selection of counselors, effective training, and development of programs for using trained counselors. Let's consider each of these in turn.

What Is the Pastor's Role?

The pastor's encouragement, support (especially from the pulpit), and willingness to allow trained lay persons to counsel are critical if the program is to succeed. For a variety of reasons, some pastors are reluctant to let lay people counsel, and others seem to be threatened by lay counselors who might be more effective than they or their staff members. In churches in which the pastor believes all problems can be resolved by exhortation or is convinced that the church should avoid any appearance of being a therapeutic community, lay counseling programs are likely to flounder and eventually die. In successful lay counseling programs, the pastor is enthusiastic and clearly supportive.

How Are Lay Counselors Selected?

Churches will find a variety of selection techniques ranging from open invitation (where anyone who so desires becomes involved) to selection through a process of interviews and tests. To keep classes small and to be more carefully selective, some churches give training by invitation only.

Such a procedure can create resentment among people who want to participate but are not invited. Often, however, many—but not all—of these people are individuals with problems of their own. They come to the class subconsciously seeking solutions for their own needs or intent on helping others as a means of sublimating their own struggles.

Supervising Lay Counselors

Supervisors need two fundamental qualifications: First, they must be competent to do any of the counseling they are supervising. Second, they must be qualified to do the supervising itself, which takes the form of providing education, training, and consultation to lay counselors in the course of their work. Supervisors might be either ministers with special training in counseling, or counseling professionals. It is preferable for the supervisor to have administrative oversight as well as personal supervision of the counselor.

Overall Responsibilities

Counselor supervisors have three primary areas of responsibility. The first is to the person being counseled, insuring that the ministry to the counselee is accomplishing its stated goals. The next responsibility is to the lay counselor, making sure this person is not placed in a situation where he or she could be harmed, either physically or through false charges from clients. Finally, the supervisor seeks to protect the church from any liability, scandal, or division as a result of the lay ministry. In most cases, these responsibilities work together — what is good for the client is typically good for the counselor and for the church.

The supervisor sets up a system to review all of the cases regularly, checking on the progress of clients. Supervision and evaluation of counselors may be done in groups but should be one-on-one at least part of the time. In the review sessions, the lay counselor presents the facts of the case and describes recent meetings with the client. The supervisor directs the process and facilitates both client progress and counselor training by listening to audio tapes, by receiving periodic written evaluations from the client, and, in some cases, by personally observing the counseling sessions.

To recruit the right people, leaders first begin to publicly emphasize the importance of caring, while stressing that counseling is a gift that many believers may not possess, that a rigorous training program is required before the potential lay counselor will become active in the counseling ministry, and that completion of the program will not necessarily make one a qualified lay counselor. This helps discourage causal involvement in the program.

Second, it should be announced that there will be a selection procedure to enter the program. This may cause some resistance and criticism, but it helps prevent insensitive, immature, and otherwise unsuitable people from entering the program. If leaders are careful not to put down anyone, most people will see the value in some initial screening.

Supervisors work at maintaining oversight by constantly defining and restating the goals of each case. They scrutinize the methods used and discuss any evident biases of the lay counselor. They also give valuable encouragement, pointing out positive aspects of the counselor's work, providing opportunities for academic study, and directing counselors toward specialized training experiences.

Occasionally a supervisor will be faced with the need to discipline a lay counselor for failure to carry out commitments or for unethical conduct. Discipline should be handled simply and directly by clearly explaining the reasons for concern and pointing out the consequences.

Selecting Lay Counselors

Volunteer lay counselors want to utilize their gifts to help others, but such laudable desires do not automatically qualify someone for lay counseling. Some people may volunteer to gain status, control others, or avoid their own emotional problems.

The supervisor, in selecting lay counselors, should look for key indications of fitness, such as:

• *Formal preparation for the task.* Lay counselors should be trained in the overall counseling process as well as in the specifics of the cases they will likely handle (such as premarital counseling, marital support, parenting, etc.).

• *Self-awareness.* Potential lay counselors must be aware of their own deeper motivations and feelings—and be willing to honestly express these to the supervisor. It's great if the potential counselor has already progressed through his or her own psychotherapy.

• *Personal maturity.* Lay counselors should show emotional and spiritual maturity, as indicated by the supervisor's interactions with them and by the reports of their personal references.

• *Communication skills.* Lay counselors must have the ability to listen with great concentration and empathy, and then communicate clearly and directly.

—Randy Christian

Criticism will be reduced (and some personal needs will be met) if the church conducts a prior class on the ministry of caring and the discovery of spiritual gifts. This class could be open to everyone, followed by a more in-depth class open only to those who successfully complete the selection screening.

Screening might involve:

- A brief written statement acknowledging the applicant's adherence to the church's doctrinal positions, plus a testimony of personal Christian experience and the applicant's reasons for wanting to be in a lay counseling program.
- A letter of recommendation from two or three people who know the applicant well.
- An interview during which the class leader and another church leader begin to assess the spiritual maturity, stability, and motivation of the applicant.
- A psychological test or two. Many churches use the Taylor/Johnson Temperament Analysis, although research has demonstrated that a test known as the 16PF is the best predictor of counseling effectiveness. Such tests have to be obtained and interpreted by a trained psychologist or other certified person.

How Are Lay Counselors Trained?

Several programs have been developed for counselor training. Obviously, any training program will be more effective when the teacher has some familiarity with professional counseling techniques and counselor training, although such background information is not absolutely necessary. Typically, training will proceed in three phases: pretraining, training, and posttraining.

- *The pretraining phase* involves selection of materials, announcement of the program, and selection of the participants. If a church decides to do an initial course on caring and the discovery of spiritual gifts, it might want to discuss such books as my *The Joy of Caring,* Ray Stedman's *Body Life,* or Rick Yohn's *Discover Your Spiritual Gift and Use It.*
- *The training phase* should give students opportunities to learn by listening to lectures, reading, observing, and gaining personal experience. Most programs involve at least 40 to 50 hours of training (some of which may be completed at home), spread over a period of several months. It is best to keep the training groups small (12 to 15), to meet regularly, and to use at least some printed materials.

The training sessions should allow time for students to share about themselves and to express their own needs and insecurities as they discuss complex problems such as depression or homosexuality. The sessions should make use of student role plays—brief periods of practice counseling in which class members divide into pairs, counsel each other about some real or assumed problem, and then discuss the practice counseling with other class members who have been observing.

Ideally, all training should include basic biblical knowledge (especially that which relates to personal problems, helping people, and the person and work of the Holy Spirit); knowledge of counseling skills; opportunities to practice these skills; some understanding of such common problems as discouragement, anxiety, excessive stress, or spiritual dryness; an awareness of both the ethics and the dangers in counseling; and a knowledge of the importance and techniques of referral to other professionals.

• *The posttraining phase* is a follow-up time of further learning, discussion of cases, and encouragement. When posttraining is not implemented, lay counseling programs sometimes have difficulty surviving, although trainees may continue to apply the training to themselves or informally to others.

In one Wisconsin church, the second year of training involves periodic seminars by an outside resource person on such subjects as self-image, alcoholism, or understanding adolescent problems. At the end of two years, the graduates are available to talk with people who want counseling, but they also continue to meet weekly for a session with a psychologist, who gives guidance as cases are discussed confidentially and anonymously.

How Are Lay Counselors Used?

Lay counselor training brings help and benefit in three ways. First, the counselors are helped, themselves. Professional counselors sometimes talk about the "helper-therapy principle"—a belief that the people who get the most benefit from counseling are the counselors. This has been found repeatedly in lay counselor programs. People appear to mature spiritually and psychologically as a result of the training, even though such training may never be used to help others.

Helping other people informally is a second outgrowth of a lay counselor's training. Family members, neighbors, work associates, fellow church members, and others appear to benefit from the informal help given by lay counselors.

Third, there are the benefits that come from more formal, church-related programs. Some of these programs are highly organized; others are not. As examples, consider the following:

• A midwestern church broadcasts the morning service and invites listeners to call in to discuss personal or spiritual matters with trained lay counselors who answer the phones on Sunday afternoons. A similar outreach approach is used in Christian television.

• A church in Southern California has a training program for singles, who in turn are available to counsel with other never-married and formerly-married church members.

• A church in the West has a "reach out" program started by one of the lay counselors. The purpose is to find overburdened mothers in the church and community and reach out to them with encouragement, practical caring, and counseling help.

• A prominent Chicago-area church has a counseling service staffed entirely by lay persons. A couple of newspaper articles in major papers alerted the community to the availability of free counseling help. Now when people call the church to request counseling, they are asked to leave a telephone number and are called back by the lay counseling coordinator, who assigns callers to trained lay counselors from the church.

Such lay counseling is not limited to church settings. Mission organizations and parachurch groups such as Youth for Christ, Young Life, Navigators, and others have developed their own training programs or used published programs to train staff members and lay persons in counseling skills. At times, the church can work together with these organizations both in training and in lay counseling.

What Problems Might Be Encountered?

Counseling is emotionally draining work. It involves helping people at times of crisis, and often it is time consuming and schedule disrupting. Therefore, in launching a lay counseling ministry, we must be prepared for several obstacles, such as:

• In some places laws regulate the licensing of counseling centers. Although these laws often exclude churches or employees of religious organizations, they sometimes restrict use of the term "counseling," or raise requirements concerning malpractice. It is wise to secure legal advice about whether lay persons in your area could be sued for malpractice or for harming counselees through the giving of unsound advice or guidance.

• Lay counselor training programs often attract people whose own problems could interfere with effective helping. Included are the *rescuers,* who have a need to control other people's lives; the *pushovers,* who have a serious desire to help and are unable to resist the manipulative demands of counselees; and the *super-enthusiasts,* who cannot accept rejection or failure, so they quit whenever they encounter counselees who are not quickly getting better. Careful selection screening should discourage such people from lay counseling involvement.

• Some lay counselors are unable to handle the drain of counseling others and are unwilling to admit that the load is too heavy. Ongoing supervision of lay counselors, preferably by a professional, can help the counselors deal with their own tension or withdraw gracefully and without embarrassment if the emotional strain becomes too great.

• Some lay counselors may become overly involved with counselees both personally and, at times, sexually. Posttraining supervision can help prevent this, and so can training programs that emphasize the dangers of intimacy in counseling, the possibility of counselee manipulation, and the importance of referral.

One additional problem churches may encounter in setting up a lay counseling ministry: a lack of the pastor's time for supervision and guidance of the counselors. Several solutions to this problem are possible. An efficient lay counseling coordinator might be recruited to serve as a "clearing house" person who assigns counselors to counselees and monitors possible problems that should be referred to the pastor or to an oversight committee. A professional Christian counselor in the community might be hired to supervise lay counselors. If no professional counselor is available, look into the possibility of supervision by a psychiatrically alert physician or nurse, a school guidance counselor, or a vocational guidance counselor. If none of these is available, three or four lay persons might form a counseling committee that pools its understanding and gives direction and encouragement to the individual counselors.

—*Gary R. Collins*

Resources

Sturkie, J., and S. Tan. 1992. Peer counseling in youth groups. Grand Rapids: Zondervan.

Tan, S. 1991. Lay counseling: Equipping Christians for a helping ministry. Grand Rapids: Zondervan.

20

Planning Counseling

One of the most common questions asked by graduate students applying for internships with church counseling programs is: "Will I be ready to be a professional counselor when I'm through?"

The best answer: "When you are through with this training, you will be ready to begin *practicing* counseling."

Counseling is considered a practice for a reason—the more you do, the more you learn. Ministers and church leaders often have learned much, informally, about interpersonal dynamics that will help them in counseling sessions, but they rarely have the opportunity to learn the basics of management related to counseling. Here is some practical guidance in key areas of concern for those of us who counsel.

Choosing a Counseling Style

As pastors (or other church leaders who counsel), we possess a number of strengths we shouldn't ignore. Our most important strength is that we represent the Lord. Whatever else our counseling style reflects, we must communicate and utilize our special prophetic and priestly calling. For example, we have the Scriptures—direct revelation from God. A style that makes use of the Scriptures would likely emphasize cognitive approaches.

Another part of being the Lord's representative is the call to embody God's love. Counseling pastors are to show God's love in all they do. This means our counseling style should communicate a foundational acceptance of all counselees, based on the fact that God does love them and has already paid the price for their sin and foolish choices. We also represent a loving community, so our counseling methods should include the use of resources available through this community.

In further determining our style, we need to consider our personal values, training, personality, and areas of spiritual giftedness. However, we should all be careful of the idea that we can be eclectic. Counselors often get into trouble with this approach by assuming they know enough about many methods to use or blend them all. In reality, such people are rare. It is best to understand the various personality theories and choose a style that fits us personally, our situation, and the people we will be working with—not to mention our theological assumptions.

Providing Facilities

Counseling, even in church settings, should occur in a comfortable and professional environment. Whenever possible, the room should be an office with a desk, several comfortable chairs, a small table, and secure file cabinets. The desk should never be in the middle of the room, facing the chairs "principal style." This establishes an atmosphere of authority and dominance that hinders self-disclosure and vulnerability.

The desk should be placed against a wall, preferably perpendicular to the chairs, so we can use the desk without having to turn a back to the counselee. Chairs can be of any design, but those with arms and wheels work nicely. This allows flexibility in positioning and lets counselees move in relationship to each other and the counselor. These movements can be informative during the counseling session.

For reasons of confidentiality, it is best for the office to be located in an out-of-the-way place and to be as soundproof as possible. Unfortunately, the same factors that make the counseling room confidential also make it more dangerous for the counselor, who can become the target of accusations of impropriety. Yet there are ways to provide both privacy and some protection for both the counselee and the counselor.

Some counselors limit their hours to times when the building has other people going in and out. Others prefer to have a receptionist or other staff member close by during counseling sessions. (Some ask a receptionist, other staff member, or even a spouse to actually sit in on the session. This can add undue awkwardness to the situation and, if the other person is not a qualified counselor, would generally be considered unethical.)

A simple solution is to make sure the door of the counseling room has a small, vertical window, four to five inches wide—the kind many school classrooms have. This window should be positioned in such a way that the counselor can be seen from outside the office but not the counselees. This allows for confidentiality as well as accountability.

Scheduling Appointments

Many ministers like to feel they are available to their people at any time. Realistically, this isn't possible. People who need counseling need to know they can count on seeing the counselor at a specific time and place. Counseling sessions can be scheduled on a weekly basis, for either a certain number of weeks or indefinitely, with periodic evaluation of progress and ongoing adjustment of counseling goals.

For example, the Browns might be coming in for marital counseling. The counselor can see them on Monday evenings at 7 P.M. This time slot is reserved for them and scheduled at least two months in advance. Each month, the counselor determines whether the counseling is likely to continue beyond the period that has been scheduled. If so, sessions are scheduled for another month.

The typical counseling session lasts approximately 50 minutes. This allows a few minutes for wrapping up notes and stretching before the next appointment. However, some prefer counseling sessions to last longer. For example, I like to extend the sessions to 90 minutes when doing family counseling and shorten them to approximately 30 minutes when counseling younger children.

Counselees should be informed that it is their responsibility to call well in advance if they are unable to keep the appointment. If an emergency arises, counselees should notify the counselor as soon as the situation allows. Under no circumstances should counselees be allowed simply not to show up for appointments. Some counselors determine a specific time limit for cancellations, beyond which the counselee pays for the service anyway.

Each counselor must determine a policy to pursue if counselees do stand them up. I allow one such incident but clearly inform counselees they will not be allowed to continue counseling if another incident of this type occurs.

I also encourage counselees showing up late to work hard at arriving on time in the future. (This means, of course, that I should also be ready to begin on time!) If circumstances do not allow a counselee to come on time, we can negotiate a different time slot. If a counselee continues to come late for an appointment, we can handle it as we would if they fail to come at all.

If available time slots for counseling do not work for a potential counselee, we can refer him or her to another counselor. If we attempt to just "work them in," we will likely find our schedules become unmanageable.

Some pastoral counselors limit the number of sessions they are willing to meet with any individual or family. This is usually wise, since it allows for helping counselees when it can be done in a manageable period of time, preventing the counselor's time from being consumed with long-term counseling.

However, if we do limit the number of sessions, we should do it as a matter of policy, not on a case-by-case basis, We should explain the policy to counselees when they first make an appointment for counseling. During the first session, we can evaluate the situation to determine whether it can be handled within the given number of sessions. If the answer is no, we can always refer the counselee to another helper.

Boundaries and Safeguards

The question of ethics in counseling relationships has never been more important than it is today. The counseling room, once a safe haven where a pastor could simply counsel and pray with a troubled parishioner for an hour, has become a source of moral anxiety and legal liability. Since acting ethically is a key to developing the trust relationship with counselees, we have to build personal boundaries that will encourage ethical behavior.

Here are some of the broad boundaries to set around a counseling ministry:

- *Limit the counseling load.* The amount of available counseling hours will vary from pastor to pastor and church to church, but it's probably best for a pastor's mental health to devote no more than ten to twelve hours a week to counseling, unless this is one's primary responsibility. Pastors can become overwhelmed by their counseling loads because they fail to set limits. They can't get their sermon study done, and they rarely see their families. They become so busy trying to fix other people's problems that their own lives begin to fall apart.

- *Maintain the appearance of propriety.* For a pastor, the appearance of propriety—being "above reproach"—is crucial. For example, it's a wise policy in formal counseling situations never to be alone on the premises with the counselee. Don't sit down with a counselee unless someone else—a secretary or a member of the pastoral staff—is close by. On rare occasions when we may visit an opposite-gender counselee in the home, we can take a spouse or another party to wait in a nearby room.

- *Do formal counseling in the office only.* There are times when, in our roles as pastor, we're called to listen to someone's problems, to give a few words of counsel or ad-

Setting Fees

One of the most difficult questions facing ministers doing counseling is whether to charge a fee. Some feel their services should be provided free of charge. Others feel members of the church who are presumably giving to support the ministry should not be charged an "extra fee." Still others feel that charging a fee not only supports the ministry financially but also insures that counselees will be thoroughly invested in the process. Other considerations may enter into the decision, such as whether the church's insurance covers the minister-counselor for liability if fees are charged.

There are no clear right answers to this question. However, we may want to consider charging fees for several reasons: (1) Fees do encourage counselees to have more ownership of the counseling goals; (2)

vice, to offer an encouraging or comforting passage of Scripture. But these are not *formal* counseling situations. When we discover that the issues our church member wants to discuss at the funeral home or in the parking lot or over the phone requires more time and deeper consideration, we'll need to make a formal appointment at the office.

A formal counseling visit, with well-defined boundaries, creates a working environment for the counselee. There has been an appointment and an agreement to start on time and end on time. The counseling time is spent productively. A sense of being "put on the spot" lends just enough creative tension to help counselees bring real issues to the surface rather than just chat in generalities.

• *Consider a contract.* In some cases, we may want to develop a written "contract" between counselor and counselee. This doesn't need to be a long document written in legalese, signed, and notarized. It can simply be a memo outlining the times and dates of the counseling appointments and any special expectations, such as, "Mr./Ms. Jones will be expected to read *Solving Marital Conflicts,* keep a daily journal, and come prepared to discuss personal insights, feelings, and issues."

• *Graciously decline gifts.* Sometimes churches charge a fee for pastoral counseling, and thus people rarely offer the pastor money, since they feel they are paying for a service. Still, parishioners like to do nice things for their pastors, and within certain limits they should be able to do so. But when that parishioner is also a counselee, we must ask ourselves: *Suppose this person is giving that gift because of an emotional attachment?* Clearly, accepting a gift under such circumstances only promotes that unhealthy kind of attachment. The safest course is politely to refuse gifts of any kind from counselees.

—*Jim Smith*

fees tend to reduce the total number of sessions required, while discouraging long-term dependency; (3) fees can help cover the expenses of providing the ministry; and (4) fees encourage responsible behavior and can contribute to counselees' feelings of competence and self-esteem.

Many pastors feel uncomfortable with fees, not wanting to turn people away when they need help and cannot afford to pay. However, these policies can eliminate this problem: (1) Base all fees on the counselee's ability to pay; (2) turn no one away because of inability to pay; (3) provide the first session without charge so people can determine how much time and money they wish to invest in future sessions; and (4) provide any counseling required by church policy—such as premarital counseling—without charge.

Counseling the Opposite Sex

If you were hungry for love, wouldn't it be nice to find someone who was well-educated, mannerly, a good listener, respected in the community, unselfish, and willing to spend time alone with you for free? Numbers of counselees think so. They come to a church office and find themselves in the presence of the kindest, most receptive, admirable, gentle, wise person they've met in a long time.

The client may begin projecting feelings and desires into the counseling relationship that belong somewhere else. This problem is technically known as *transference.*

Dealing with Transference

The average pastor cannot afford the time and energy demanded by a counselee with a high propensity for transference. Training in dealing with transference problems requires extensive supervision. If this training is available, take advantage of it, but in the meantime:

- The safest way to deal with transference is simply to receive it as one would receive any feeling of a client. Help the client see that the feelings reside in him or her, not in the counselor.

The counselor may ask clarifying questions to increase the client's understanding of feelings: "You feel you're in love with me. Why do you suppose this is so?" In other words, the expression of feelings is allowed within the clinical boundaries without either condoning or rejecting the person.

- At a later stage, and only when it can be done without offending the client, the counselor then interprets the transference feelings directly. For example, "Sometimes when people share their innermost secrets with someone else, they feel drawn to that person. Do you think this is what is happening here?"
- Always stay professional. This doesn't mean we cannot be friendly and personable. However, we must keep to our appointment schedules

Keeping Records

Counseling records include case notes, personality inventories, information forms, messages, correspondence, receipts, and more. These must be treated with great care to safeguard the integrity of the information and the confidentiality of the counseling relationship. The best way to do this is to maintain a file for each counselee that includes all the material pertaining to the case. Also, the case file should include the reasons for counseling, the specific goals of counseling, and a record of each contact (session, phone call, etc.), along with a description of what occurred and the amount of time taken.

Counselors can take notes during the counseling session if they can do it without drawing undue attention, which can make a counselee

---

and avoid stepping out of our professional roles.

Countertransference Dangers

Another transference problem, *countertransference,* occurs when a pastor responds to the client with inappropriate feelings of affection. Since an intimate affair can develop almost unnoticed during counseling, it is crucial to recognize these danger signals:

- One early signal of countertransference is when a pastor begins to look forward to the counseling sessions with a particular parishioner. He or she ruminates about the appointment and cannot wait for the time to arrive.
- Soon the pastor begins to extend the session time and may even grant extra counseling sessions. He or she cancels other appointments to please the client.
- Hidden or oblique messages are sent both ways. The message, which on the surface is innocuous, means something more personal at a deeper level.
- Counseling sessions may focus an inordinate amount of time on sexual matters. The client may begin to share sexual history or previous affairs that are quite unrelated to the presenting problem.
- The pastor may begin to notice his or her own marital frustrations more, perhaps complaining about petty things, often because he or she is feeling guilty and can alleviate this guilt by transforming it into anger.
- The pastor begins to fantasize excessively about the client. Sexual fantasies may focus on the client exclusively.
- The pastor makes excuses to call and have extra conversations with the client. Luncheon appointments in a remote setting may then follow. These are rationalized as "additional counseling sessions."
- Then casual touching becomes more frequent, and the sessions end with embraces that become more prolonged or intense.

Before transference or countertransference gets out of hand, don't hesitate to make a referral to a trusted Christian psychotherapist. A mark of professional competence is knowing our limits.

—*Archibald D. Hart*

nervous. One caution: What we write could conceivably be read later by people we had not intended to see it. Because of this, notes should be concise and accurate, including only what is necessary and can be documented. A general rule of thumb is "Don't write what you don't want written."

Other items in the case file include background information forms, assessment forms, fee schedules (if used), and authorizations for release of information. Specific assessment forms should never be given to counselees. They become a permanent part of the case file, with copies being released, with consent, only to other professionals who have the appropriate training to interpret them.

Counselees must feel safe revealing information to us, so we must keep files secure at all times. The basic rule is to keep them in a locked file cabinet, which is, in turn, kept in a locked room. Access to the cabinet should be restricted to the counselor and possibly a confidential secretary. If a secretary is given access, the counselor remains responsible for the security of the information and the files themselves. We should keep records a minimum of ten years. However, many counselors recommend that unless storage is an extreme problem, records should be maintained indefinitely. Any discarded records (including phone records) should be shredded to the extent that they cannot possibly be reassembled.

Other security safeguards include locking up appointment books, receipt books, calendars, phone-message copies, and anything else that might include even the name of someone in counseling. Phone conversations, even for appointments, should be conducted where they cannot be overheard.

Secretaries and other staff should be trained in security procedures, such as not leaving messages for counselees which might reveal they are being seen for counseling. Under no circumstances should any information regarding the counseling process be revealed to anyone without the written permission of the counselees. In general, we need to remember that it is our responsibility to maintain confidentiality in *all* situations.

Beginning and Ending the Sessions

A counseling relationship is begun when a counselee seeks help and the counselor believes he or she is capable of providing that help. This relationship begins during the initial interview, during which we complete the paperwork, explain policies, and thoroughly describe our approach and possible goals we will be pursuing. We should document the general and specific goals of the counselee (agreed upon by both parties), and counselees should be given as complete an explanation as possible of the methods we will use to accomplish these goals.

Many counselors find it useful to inform counselees that approximately every six sessions they will be asking for a written evaluation of the counseling process from their perspective. Doing so gives counselees permission to provide feedback; they don't have to worry about whether the counselor will listen if they want to discuss the process itself.

When the goals have been accomplished or when it is clear they are *not* going to be accomplished, the relationship is ended. While this relationship is never purely a friendship, it can still be difficult to end. We need to be sensitive to counselees' withdrawal feelings and, when possible, prepare people in advance for the closure that needs to happen in the relationship.

If the goals have not been accomplished, we should make an appropriate referral. In either situation, we can help a counselee see positive gains and encourage him or her to continue working on growth issues after the counseling relationship ends. If a counselee resists termination, we should gently but firmly state our decision about ending the period of counseling: "I understand your hesitation, but as your counselor, I do not believe it would be in your best interest to continue because . . .".

Working Ethically

Most questions of ethics in counseling can be resolved by applying common sense and scriptural principles. However, every counselor should have a general standard of ethics to which he or she can refer for guidance in confusing situations.

Traditionally, counselors have begun with the principles of the Hippocratic Oath as a basic standard: Counselors will always practice with competence. Counselors will not exploit their counselees for personal gain of any kind. Counselors will treat people with respect. Counselors will protect confidentiality.

Counselors interested in a more developed set of standards can contact the Christian Association for Psychological Studies, which adopted an excellent set of ethical standards specifically for Christian counselors in 1992.

Regardless of how advanced we become in the practice of counseling, we occasionally will face situations that go beyond our abilities to help. In such situations, we need to consult with another professional. All pastors who counsel should have a working relationship (even if only by phone) with someone who can fill this role.

Since it would be unethical to take on a case we have little hope of resolving, we must ask ourselves several questions in potential referral situations: Is this a situation I have the training to handle? Do I have the time and energy to provide adequate care in this situation?

Am I the best resource person available for this counselee? Am I free of relationships (positive or negative) with this person or close family members that would make it difficult for me to work with him or her objectively?

If the answer to any of these questions is no, we should refer the case to another counselor. Failure to do so is not noble; it is unethical and will most likely hurt both us and the person who seeks—and deserves—the best help we can give.

—Randy Christian

Resources

Christian Association for Psychological Studies. 1992. Ethical guidelines. Temecula, Calif.: CAPS.

Collins, G. 1976. How to be a people helper. Santa Ana, Calif.: Vision House.

Hart, A., et al. 1992. Mastering pastoral counseling. Portland: Multnomah.

Wynn, J. 1982. Family therapy in pastoral ministry. San Francisco: Harper and Row.

Malony, N., et al. 1986. Clergy malpractice. Philadelphia: Westminster.

Regulating the Counseling Load

We may regularly find ourselves weighing the cry for pastoral care against the clamor of our other pastoral duties. Like a mother robin, standing worm in mouth before a nest full of gaping, chirping beaks, pastoral counselors often have a conflict of responsibilities. Who will get our limited supply of time and energy? There may be no tidy solutions, but we can do at least two key things to balance the demands better.

Teach the Church to Counsel

Certainly we must regard as our responsibility the hurting people who call on us. As Moses learned from Jethro, however, our responsibility isn't to counsel everyone but to ensure that counseling gets done. Since our churches likely understand this principle, we can seek ways to spread the load.

For instance, a church may offer an evening Circle of Concern in which people gather each week for a month to learn about a particular problem (child abuse, eating disorders, alcoholism, and the like). Helping skills can be taught at these meetings, and volunteer lay counselors can learn about proven helping agencies and counselors in the community to which they can refer people.

In addition, we can train lay counselors and invest in staff members with counseling gifts. For example, a church may want to pay for a youth pastor or youth sponsors to receive some formal training to augment their ministry with young people.

Preaching is a key time to equip people for counseling ministry, as well. We can prepare sermons to be useful not only to people in trouble, but also to those who will be helping such people. Such sermons might include point-by-point application: "Here are five things to do when you are depressed." "Here are six steps for getting out of financial troubles." We can encourage listeners to take notes and to share those sermon ideas with others.

At holidays pastors can say from the pulpit, "During special holidays, people expect more than ever that they will find some happiness. Instead of taking away some of their depression, though, holidays often make matters worse. During holidays I often have an increased counseling load. But there are some things that you can do to encourage others at this time of year." Then we can list some ways to help.

Get Counselees to Help

Counseling can feel like a lonely job, but the majority of callers will help us manage our schedules if we recruit them as allies. For example:

• *Offer clear orientation.* After a counselee's problems are on the table, I say, for example, "We'll meet for fifty minutes each week. We will need four sessions to get a handle on this issue. If we haven't begun to resolve things by then, we'll decide together whether we should refer you to someone else." People in counseling begin to understand that such plans are not arbitrary rules but boundaries within which we can work effectively. They then get down to business more quickly, saving our time.

• *Help people plan ahead.* Before their sessions, people can write an agenda and keep a record of areas in which they've been seeking improvement. Thus they arrive focused, mentally prepared, able to address problems more thoroughly. This increases the comfort quotient on both sides, since the counselor knows they won't waste time, and they know what to expect.

• *Consider sharing about emergencies.* When other pressing responsibilities intrude, we can sometimes enlist the help of counselees by telling them what's happened. Sometimes this changes the whole dynamic of the relationship as counselees offer to reschedule, pray with us, or help in other ways.

—*Gary Gulbranson*

Making Referrals

None of us can meet every need of those who come to us, but we can guide people to other qualified helpers. Making appropriate referrals can save us from overwork and provide the best resources available for those who need them. Each situation is unique, but these basic steps will help make a referral effective.

• *Ascertain what the real need is.* When we are approached for help, our primary task is to decide what help is needed and who is the best person to meet the need. This will usually mean at least one meeting with the counselee to ask enough questions to be sure we know what the need is.

A key decision concerns recognizing the differences between the needs for individual, marriage, or family counseling. For example, on the surface, the Johnsons' need might appear to be individual counseling for only one of the family members. The deeper need, however, might require family counseling to explore and heal the other family members' relationships with the so-called problem person.

• *Make the referral personal.* Once we know the need, it's best to refer to a person, not to an institution. The reason is simple: Counselors are not equally qualified, even within a counseling group. We may refer a counselee to a counseling agency and may even respect counselors at that agency, but if our counselee is seen by someone we don't know, we will be unaware of the level of care being given. We need to know the individual counselor, not just an agency, to be assured we are placing our counselee into competent hands.

• *Make the reasons clear.* As we make our suggestions to counselees, we need to be ready to explain exactly why we believe it is best to refer them to someone else. We increase the likelihood of a successful referral by answering all legitimate questions straightforwardly and by giving counselees time to think about the referral.

• *Insure communication with the new helper.* It is not good to refer people to anyone unwilling to communicate with us. In one community, an agency providing a wide variety of counseling services rarely got referrals from area ministers. The reason: When ministers tried to follow up on referrals, no one was willing to talk to them.

We don't need to know all the details of the new counseling relationship, but we do have a responsibility to be sure the counselee is truly being helped. A good tool to use here is a release-of-information form, a simple statement giving the parties named the freedom to exchange specific information. By having the counselee sign a release when we make a referral, we give the other professionals the freedom to communicate with us.

• *Specify to the new helper what his or her role is to be.* If we want a specific type of help to be provided, we should spell it out clearly. For example, when referring people to doctors or therapists for technical counseling, such as sex therapy or treatment of depression, we can request that questions related to moral or spiritual issues (about birth control or abortion, for example) be referred back to us.

• *Follow up on the referral.* It is good to follow up within a week after a referral and periodically thereafter, asking such questions as: Has the counselee made contact? How is the work going? How can I best support the process? How can my work as a pastor complement your efforts?

—Randy Christian

Group Counseling

Group counseling focuses on principles of communication and relational dynamics. It tracks the interpersonal behaviors of group members from moment to moment, with individuals learning about themselves by the way they function as *members of a group*. The group-counseling process offers the church an excellent means of promoting *koinonia*.

Promoting True Community

True communion and fellowship require that we understand one another's feelings and recognize how we affect each other on the feeling level. The group-counseling process avoids the rationalization and justification of feelings that hinder fellowship, because the discussion of those ideas is not the purpose of the group. The purpose is to discover how we really feel about each other and to promote a willingness to change any behavior that alienates others.

Participants should clearly understand that the counseling group is not another discussion seminar dealing with ideas taught and to be debated, and it is quite different from a sharing group in which life experiences are shared. Rather, the group is to be uniquely experiential, a process by which people learn to understand themselves and each other by the way they relate to each other at the feeling level when the group is together.

Making Groups Work

Group facilitators need special training, often available through seminars and workshops offered by universities and family institutes that train counselors. Those who conduct groups should keep four guidelines in mind. Effective groups should:

- *Deal with the here and now.* Avoid the tendency to lapse into discussing ideas or analyzing what is happening in the group. Stay with the feelings that are surfacing and keep before the group members what is happening at that moment to make them feel as they do. What is each member of the group experiencing at the very moment the group is together? How do participants experience the other members of the group right now? Do they feel comfortable? Uncomfortable? What is it about the others in the group that seems to generate those feelings?
- *Require individual honesty.* Encourage each member to be absolutely candid and honest. Dishonesty ought to be challenged. We usually can detect dishonesty in the incongruence between verbal and nonverbal cues. For example, someone may say he feels relaxed and composed, but the body language and tone of voice may betray tension.

Honesty does not mean individuals will be coerced into vulnerability. It is perfectly honest to say, "I don't trust this group enough to say how I feel." Finding out why that is so would be immensely helpful to the group.

• *Recognize the benefits of silence.* Let the group be silent, no matter how long. Silence builds tension, and someone eventually will break in with something very revealing of feelings. For example, someone may say, "This seems to be a big waste of time to me. I thought we were here to promote fellowship." The group members can then be encouraged to get in touch with the feelings behind that statement. If it is anger, then let the speaker talk about his or her irritation. This will no doubt lead to a disclosure of irritation about other things.

• *Accept the broad spectrum of feelings.* Let so-called "negative" feelings—sad, fearful, or angry feelings—be expressed. Usually people who are not in the habit of communicating feelings feel safest with the emotion of anger or feelings of shame and anxiety. For example, the angry person feels less vulnerable to attack when she is able to create distance with her hostility. Not everyone feels comfortable with loving, tender feelings, but enmity often can be turned to amity as we permit its expression.

—*Andre Bustanoby*

21

Distinctively Christian Counseling

A woman, whose problems stem primarily from abuse, comes for pastoral counseling. Throughout her life she has been physically and emotionally mistreated by various men, including her husband. In order to find personal healing and wholeness in her marriage, she desperately needs the spiritual resource of biblical truth.

In the early stages of counseling, however, we cannot simply read the blueprint for wedded peace in Ephesians 5, not because we doubt the validity of that passage in her difficult situation but because she would not understand those verses as God intends. For her the term *submit* has been perverted into *be abused*. Still, we need to offer her spiritual resources. The question is how.

Like a surgeon at a state-of-the-art hospital who employs the best technology can offer, a Christian counselor has powerful resources—spiritual resources—to draw on, but they are not automatically helpful. They can even be counterproductive. Therefore, a counselor must employ spiritual resources—prayer, Scripture, fellowship groups, worship experiences—with skill, sensitivity, and wisdom.

Use Prayer Intentionally

More than any other activity, prayer represents the spiritual side of counseling. Our prayers show we do not ultimately rely on our education, skills, or methods, but on God's Spirit to work in a particular situation. Prayer is a confession of weakness that allows God's power to prevail.

Yet prayer can be unspiritual, even a counseling cop-out. A counselor may simply use prayer to produce an emotional catharsis, or as a convenient way to bring ritual closure to a session—indeed to get rid of someone. Such tactics cheapen prayer and disillusion the counselee about its effectiveness. Needy people desperately need a model of authentic prayer.

Prayer in counseling can be legitimate. Here's how we can use it:

• *Pray before a session to prepare our attitudes.* Occasionally, we may harbor an adverse emotional bias toward a counselee. As the father of two daughters, for instance, I have a tough time counseling a man guilty of child abuse. In this case, I must pray for the compassion of Christ, for sensitivity concerning people's needs and what causes their behavior, for self-control so that I will not overreact.

• *Pray for guidance and insight.* Our best insights into the puzzle of an individual's problems often come from the Holy Spirit. We have likely been trained to draw information out of people, and God uses that information to help them, but he can also reveal things to us that we couldn't have known or figured out ourselves. More often than not, this will come in the form of an impression that suggests to us what trail to pursue.

For example, once a sporadic church attender requested an appointment for herself and her husband, saying, "We have some business and marriage problems."

Before the appointment I prayed for guidance: "Lord, I sense a lot of things need to be dealt with here, and I need to handle them in their proper order. I'm not sure what that order should be. I need insight so that we can make enough progress to keep them working on their problems."

As the counseling session began and we got better acquainted, I felt a strong impression to pursue the business problem first. Bringing that up was like popping open a well-shaken Pepsi can. The couple had gone into business with another family member, and along the way, they had compromised their integrity.

We called a lawyer and set them on a course to rectify matters. That brought relief, enabling us in future sessions to resolve their marriage difficulties. The business situation had been the powerful source of their conflict, and prayer helped us discover that.

• *Pray with the counselee at the start of the counseling session.* In praying, we are communicating to God and to the counselee that we will draw on our relationship with the Lord to help this person. In addition, the counselee gains some sense of God's presence; it is not just two people in that office. As Alcoholics Anonymous and the recovery groups have proven, people who feel helpless or short on control need their attention drawn to God.

Such prayer changes the tone of the session. Many counselees are tense. Never having been through the counseling process, they are uncertain and vulnerable. Prayer relaxes them, as Philippians 4:6–7 promises, giving them a measure of the peace of God, which can't help but facilitate communication.

• *Assign prayer as homework.* During marriage counseling, counselors can request that a husband and wife pray together at home. Prayer fosters an intimacy that cannot be produced any other way. In addition, a couple will get more in touch with their feelings in other facets of their lives. If they say they can't pray together, we can suggest they talk about what they need and then pray silently in each other's presence.

Prayer can be given as a homework assignment for the person who says, "I don't feel close to God. I just can't talk to him about this." Such an assignment can help people discover that we act our way into a proper way of feeling; we don't feel our way into a proper way of acting.

• *Pray to close the session.* This serves as a summary statement in God's presence, a reinforcement for the counselee that we've discussed this in God's presence, that he has heard what we've said, that he knows everything about them and the situation, that he cares more than the counselor ever can. Especially when major sin is involved, people need to sense this bonding with God after they have brought their problems and failings into the open. At this time it's good to specifically ask God to work in the situation, to provide what is needed, and to change what needs changing. This also conveys a message: we expect God actually to *do* something in their lives.

The nature of our relationship with the counselee determines who voices the closing prayer. Some people walk into our offices with such a feeling of isolation or pride that the furthest thing from their mind is the possibility of praying with others about their problems. For them it's daunting enough just to talk about them. With time, however, they usually see prayer as something in which they want to share.

• *Let counselees pray for us, too.* At the end of a session, some counselees may ask if they can pray for us, which is often a sign of growing health. Especially because we relate with most of our counselees in the church context as well, we want them to know this is not a one-way street; we are receptive to what they want to return spiritually. We can show people that we do not intend to stay behind a big desk or pulpit, telling them how to straighten out their lives; we'd rather share in ministry with them as members of the body of Christ. No matter how devastated at the moment, and despite the present feelings of impotence, they can still do something significant for others: they can pray.

In dealing with the weighty, sometimes crushing problems of counseling, some pastors find fasting helpful. We may not want to assign it to counselees, but fasting for our own sake can provide us an emotional and spiritual bath.

For example, I also use it as a prayer discipline when dealing with a host of problems that begin to affect my life when counseling, such as when I work with so many people in marital crises that I start to feel pressure in my own marriage. Fasting allows me to focus attention on some aspect of God's character and to simplify my desires.

Use Scripture Appropriately

In their confusion, hurting people desperately need and want wisdom and words from God. That means a pastoral counselor has an incomparable spiritual resource: biblical truth. Scripture is our greatest counseling source for answers, comfort, and guidance.

Assessment in Counseling

Every pastor has to diagnose, if only at a rudimentary level, a troubled counselee's problem: Does this person need to make a commitment to Christ and thereby experience the new life of regeneration? Does this person suffer a form of supernatural oppression? Or is this clearly a case for psychotherapy?

In all matters of discernment, the principle that should guide us is the "law of parsimony." In essence, this law compels us to understand a problem at its most obvious and fundamental level. Simplicity is the rule as we seek the most obvious and natural explanation *before* moving on to diagnose in more complex ways.

Here is how to apply this law to pastoral counseling:

- *Take a careful history.* This is vitally important if we are not going to miss an obvious cause of a problem. A thorough history should include details of family background, history of dysfunctional patterns in the family, history of mental illness in the family, history of the presenting problem, when the problem first occurred, how often the problem occurs, the changes that have taken place recently, history of spiritual experience and practice, experience of conversion, and patterns of spiritual development since conversion. A thorough history should provide a clear picture of what is troubling the person, how it started, and how it continues to be a problem.
- *Intervene at the most obvious level first.* Following the law of parsimony, we now try to explain the problem in the most obvious or natural terms. For instance, if there is a history of mental illness in the family and the person we are counseling is experiencing bizarre behavior or emotions, the most obvious cause is likely the familial pattern of illness. Genetic factors do strongly influence the severe mental disorders.

Like prayer, however, Scripture can be misused in counseling, and with greater harm. We can use the Bible in a way that short-circuits the counseling process. The counselee describes a few symptoms of her problem, and immediately verses begin popping into our minds. Before she can finish her story, we want to interrupt with last month's sermon on "How to Mend Your Marriage."

If we become trigger happy with Scripture, we will fail to hear counselees' true concerns. As a result we won't understand their problems' contexts and causes, and worse, we won't grasp how *they* understand the Bible. We can't hit the target unless we know what the target is. If we go too quickly to "thus saith the Lord" before we know what saith the counselee, we won't see what the real issues are. Thus, we need to be patient in drawing people out. That said, here are ways to employ the Bible in counseling:

Unless a pastor is trained in psychopathology, the most responsible action is referral to a trusted psychologist or psychiatrist for diagnosis. While treatment is under way, we may want to counsel the person in the steps of Christian commitment, encouraging a surrender to the claims of Christ. It is possible, however, that the professional treatment temporarily may need to take precedence over spiritual guidance, simply because the disease needs to be under control before the person can comprehend spiritual matters adequately.

• *Investigate the need for regeneration.* One of the great drawbacks of secular counseling or psychotherapy is that it may not deal directly with the core problem of human existence: our alienation from God. As Christian counselors we can prepare a person to be receptive to God's work. We can help remove the obstacles of childhood traumas or distorted God images so that God's grace can become effective.

Even explicitly Christian counseling does not do the work of grace; it merely aids it. It is nothing more than burden bearing as we are instructed by Bible passages such as Galatians 6:2. We are helping others rely upon the greatest burden bearer of all (see Matt. 8:17).

• *Consider supernatural causes.* At what point should one consider the possibility of supernatural or demonic causes for a problem and invoke deliverance as the remedy? Only when the more obvious causes have been eliminated.

If there is a history of severe depression in the immediate family of a troubled person, for instance, psychiatric treatment must be given first consideration. It is gross negligence to move beyond this diagnosis without thoroughly exploring whether the symptoms have physical causes.

Another word of caution: We should never try to diagnose supernatural causes by ourselves, but rather seek corroboration from others and hold ourselves accountable to the corporate discernment.

—*Archibald D. Hart*

• *Use Scripture not to condemn but to outline a new direction.* This is how Jesus used the Word as he ministered to those who were sincere. Christ's use of Scripture differed radically from the Pharisees'; they used Scripture to condemn people. They focused on the past—the sins already committed—and how God's commandments condemn such conduct.

Christ focused on the present and the future, on how a person can restore a relationship with God and how to maintain that relationship. With the woman caught in adultery, he refused to condemn but rather said, "Go your way and sin no more." Most people know when

Schizophrenia or Demon Possession?

Scores of emotionally troubled people every year are told they have an "evil spirit" possessing them, but demon possession is rarely the problem. The hopelessness such a false label engenders in the sufferer (especially after exorcisms fail to cure the problem) can often do more harm than the original problem.

Pastoral counselors need to be able to distinguish between demonic possession and serious mental disorders, such as schizophrenia. The first task is to make certain that no psychiatric or organic cause is being overlooked. Only after all possible natural explanations are exhausted should we consider investigating demonic possession.

Recognizing Schizophrenia

Schizophrenia is a physical disease. Because its sufferers exhibit such bizarre symptoms, it is sometimes labeled as demon possession. But just as we learned with epilepsy (another disease formerly labeled as demon possession), we now know that schizophrenia is the result of a defect in brain chemistry. Often medication can be the cure. Any delay in starting the right medication for treating schizophrenia can impact the sufferer's long-term recovery. So misdiagnosis here can have serious consequences. This is especially true for a form of schizophrenia that sometimes starts in late adolescence.

Some basic symptoms of schizophrenia include: extreme forms of social isolation or withdrawal; marked inability to function as wage earner, student, or homemaker; markedly peculiar behavior (collecting garbage, talking to self in public, hoarding food); extreme loss of attention to personal hygiene and grooming; digressive, vague, over-elaborate conversation, or lack of conversation, or lack of content in conversation; odd beliefs or magical thinking that affect the person's behavior (being superstitious, believing in clairvoyance, telepathy, or the idea that "others can feel my feelings"); unusual experiences (recurrent illusions, sensing the presence of a force or person not actually present); and marked lack of initiative or energy.

they are breaking God's plan. The resulting destruction eventually forces them to face the need for change.

Jesus was also sensitive to each individual. He understood people intimately and used Scripture in accordance with that insight. He helped people understand their motives and attitudes. Then he offered forgiveness, a fresh start, and a new discipline.

• *Back into Scripture.* People understand most terms, including biblical terms, based on their experience. Until we understand their reference points—their contexts and definitions—we easily miss the mark with Scripture. In fact, most of the time when we start handing

What might appear to be demon possession, then, usually will be some form of schizophrenia. This is important because falsely attributing emotional problems to demons has several dangers: It keeps the sufferer from recognizing and confessing *human* sinfulness, it emphasizes Satan's power inappropriately, and, most important, it delays the introduction of effective treatment.

Schizophrenia is a complex disease. If a pastor suspects it in a counselee, he or she should make the appropriate referral immediately. Delaying treatment for a problem like schizophrenia can significantly decrease the likelihood of the sufferer's return to normality.

Diagnosing Possession

If this is schizophrenia, though, what does demon possession look like? The characteristics of demon possession are not easy to discern. However, those who have extensive experience with possession look for such factors as:

• *A striking lack of human warmth.* The possessed seem barren and empty, and they lack empathy.

• *The presentation of a new personality.* The person's voice and expressions change, and he or she begins acting and speaking like a different person. (However, this is also seen in "multiple personality disorders," a severe psychological problem associated with childhood abuse.)

• *Marked revulsion to Christian symbols.* The cross, the Bible, and other Christian symbols often make the possessed extremely uncomfortable. (However, schizophrenics may also display this reaction.)

• *Strange physical phenomena.* Many observers describe an inexplicable stench, freezing temperatures, flying objects, and a "smooth, stretched skin" (see Malachi Martin's *Hostage to the Devil*).

• *Supernatural behavioral transformations.* For example, the victim may display "possessed gravity" — in other words, he or she cannot be moved physically, or can levitate.

Obviously, then, possession is not as common as might be supposed, and many so-called possessions have more natural explanations. Diagnosis of demon possession is a matter of eliminating all possible mental disorders as causes of bizarre presenting problems before proceeding to supernatural explanations.

—*Archibald D. Hart*

out biblical injunctions to "love" or "submit to one another" or "serve one another" without probing how they understand these biblical ideas, counselees end up feeling frustrated and condemned.

For example, several years ago a husband and wife came for counseling. The wife's biggest complaint was "My husband isn't romantic enough."

What he heard her saying, though, was "He's not good enough in bed." With such a narrow perspective on the term *romantic,* he was devastated, because he had been raised to take great pride in his ability to perform sexually.

I explored her complaint and discovered she was really saying, "He isn't attentive to me during the day."

In a similar way, after we discover what the counselee means by certain biblical phrases, we can explain what the phrase means in its context, using their understanding by way of contrast. Then we can help people discover the truth of Scripture for themselves by assigning homework, such as having them fill out worksheets on abuse, alcohol, or marriage and family.

Use Small Groups Strategically

A pastoral counselor can employ the home-field advantage: the church community. Pastors lead a group of people with the potential to serve and to love others into well-being. But since such groups can easily turn into quagmires of dysfunction, we need to lead the groups in strategic ways.

- *Supervise involvement.* We dare not just send people to support groups or ask them to get involved in Bible studies without watching over them as they get involved. Some people even need to be discouraged altogether from small groups, at least until they can participate in them maturely.

Some people hug their hurts. They try to wrest significance by drawing attention to their problems. In a small group, these people will inevitably plunder everyone's attention and energies, making their needs the centerpiece.

For example, one young woman I counseled came from a severely dysfunctional home. To get the attention she craved, she created crises, and these were the only times her parents would notice her. She developed a drinking problem and then a pattern of dating men who exploited her. She brought the same pattern into church. Every group she was in sooner or later had to turn its full energies toward her. She liked that; she didn't really want her problems solved.

We can try to help such a person understand the patterns she has gotten stuck in and teach her new behaviors. But it will be slow going, and it demands careful direction.

• *Help spawn small groups.* The key to small groups is intentionality. We need to know exactly what we want to accomplish and then make sure the people know what the group is trying to do in relation to the broad ministry of the church.

In the church I serve, our primary small-group format is what we call "Circles of Concern." For a month, on Tuesday evenings, we gather a group to discuss a particular problem, with the goals of: (1) providing useful information about the problem, and (2) encouraging interaction among those facing the common difficulty.

We designed one Circle of Concern for people making decisions about what to do with elderly parents. At the first meeting a geriatric worker talked to the group. The second week a nursing home supervisor discussed the legal and financial factors involved in placing a loved one into such care. The third week I taught a Bible study on how God perceives the aging process and our need to be sensitive toward the elderly. The final Tuesday, a panel of those who had made these decisions told their experiences and the lessons learned.

Other topics that lend themselves to this type of small group include life as a single, parenting children who grew up in church but are no longer walking with Christ, financial planning, retirement, long-term illness, specific emotions such as anger, and marriage enrichment (one for those married up to five years, another for those married five to fifteen years, another for those fifteen years and more).

Encourage Worship Attendance

Because people in crisis need all the spiritual input possible, many pastors insist that their counselees attend worship. The heart and mind can be healed in public worship in ways that cannot happen in the counseling office. In worship, desperate and lonely people can sense the presence and power of God. Such sunshine through the window proves especially vital for those who feel distant from God, separated from him by their problems. No matter what their counseling issues, people do need the support of the church body and the inspiration and renewal of church worship to stabilize them.

Counselees often need a nudge to get to church, however. A simple "I'll be looking for you on Sunday" helps. Sometimes we can introduce them to someone who has weathered similar troubles. Attending church with a friend like that can reverse the feeling that the church is threatening by making it invitingly familiar. To ease the transition into the relationship, pastor, counselee, and "sponsor" may want to sit down together to begin to build the church network for the counselee.

A counselee's involvement in church does present two hurdles. After a couple of sessions, we may want to tell a counselee, "A time will come fairly soon when you'll be sitting in the congregation on Sunday morning and you'll think, *He's preaching at me,* or *He's letting these people know about my problem.* But that won't be the case at all. In the normal course of preaching through Scripture, I unavoidably deal with problems many people in the congregation have. Be assured I won't put you at risk, and if you think I am, come and talk to me."

We may also need to tell counselees, "Then the time will come when you're past the crisis, and you'll think, *That man in the pulpit knows more personal things about me than anyone else in the world,* and you'll be uncomfortable with that. You'll feel like packing your bags, moving elsewhere, and starting over. But you need to resist that feeling. What I know about you should be the basis for trust and a strong relationship, not for running away." We must keep on guard for signs of detachment. When counselees pull away, we need to contact them immediately to begin to pull them back in.

Spiritual resources for counseling, though not automatically effective, are supernaturally effective. When used with wisdom, they pierce the very core of a person's being, as Scripture says, "penetrating even to dividing soul and spirit, joints and marrow," healing where other methods cannot touch. I would not want to counsel anyone without them.

—Gary Gulbranson

Resources

Bridges, J. 1978. The pursuit of holiness. Colorado Springs: NavPress.

Colson, C. 1992. The body. Dallas: Word.

Morling, G. 1987. The quest for serenity. Waco: Word.

Whitney, D. 1991. Spiritual disciplines of the Christian life. Colorado Springs: NavPress.

Wright, H. 1986. Self-talk, imagery, and prayer in counseling. Waco: Word.

Premarital Counseling

In the exciting time before the marriage ceremony, couples are open to building the best marriage they can; our aim is to coach them toward that goal. The following steps can help these sessions run smoothly while addressing the important issues.

• *Establish a relationship.* Begin by building a friendship with the couple through positive, easy questions: How did you meet? How did you decide this is the one you want to marry?

After establishing rapport, follow with questions such as: Which of you felt the most discomfort in coming to see me, and why? How do you feel when visiting each other's families?

• *Cover counseling expectations.* Couples respond well when given three or four topics to choose from. A list of options might include misconceptions of love and marriage, ways to increase friendship, practical issues in marriage, romantic love, and Christian marriage.

• *Uncover misconceptions about marriage.* One way to stimulate discussion in this area is to give a "test," asking the couple to mark as true or false a list of statements, such as "Getting angry is better than being critical" or "Loneliness will be cured by marriage."

Amazing things happen. Couples laugh. They disagree openly. They get nervous. They show frustration. They reveal expectations.

Getting Practical

The bulk of the sessions should cover such practical issues as:

• *Affection and sexuality.* We can ask: Where do you find information on sexuality? What is sexual love? What will you do if one of you is more highly sexed than the other?

Potential areas of tension include a partner's right to know about the other's sexual past, traumatic experiences such as rape or incest, and role expectations, including feelings about headship and submissiveness. We must be pointedly practical on these issues.

• *Values.* Issues here include occupations, whether and when to have children, and family life. A helpful exercise is to have them write their values on colored cards, using the red cards for nonnegotiable values, yellow for important but modifiable ones, and green for flexible ones.

• *Religious faith.* Couples should share their faith experiences while being made aware of how different religious journeys develop and sometimes clash. We must press for concreteness: How often do you expect to go to church? What happened the last time your fiancée asked you for forgiveness?

• *Communication.* To encourage this, we can suggest the couple promise to meet weekly to compare calenders and ask about the other's emotional well-being. Some couples commit to two mini-honeymoons yearly after their marriage, even if only overnights.

• *Nurture.* We tend to nurture a spouse in the way *we* want to be nurtured. If the wife is nurtured by exercise, she may buy a jogging suit for her spouse, who hates athletics but loves a night at home reading. The aim is for couples to respect each other's nurture needs, even if they don't understand them.

• *Christian marriage.* Psychologists say every marriage has a *contract,* perhaps implied if not written or discussed, and usually the parties perceive the contract differently. More fundamental, however, is the sacred bond of *covenant* that transcends the legal ties, and so we discuss at length what God means to their union.

• *Ceremony procedures.* We can present copies of different vows—from high church to contemporary—for the couple to consider, and then review the meaning behind the Scripture readings, prayers, and questions of intent. Then we can sit back and watch them pore over the details of the service, observing how they make decisions.

—*Bruce Rowlison*

Marriage Counseling

When marital difficulties reach the crisis stage, often that is when the pastor is called. Sometimes it is awfully late in the process, sometimes after the marriage has shattered into tiny pieces. Many times, however, the couple can return to wholeness with a little help.

Once the couple has expressed their emotions and described the basic issues during initial counseling sessions, a counselor can work on some basic objectives. Ed Smelser, counselor at Fairhaven Ministries in Roan Mountain, Tennessee, suggests five objectives for the next few sessions. These provide a marriage-counseling routine in outline.

• *Controlled release of tension.* Our initial goal as counselors is to gather data in a safe setting. We want to help the couple get things off their chests, but disallow verbal abuse and hateful statements that later will be regretted. A couple has built pressure in their relationship for a number of months or years. When they finally reach a crisis, that pressure is ready to burst out in destructive ways. Merely allowing them the dignity of being heard releases steam.

• *Increased understanding of issues.* Emotions cloud reasoning, and both parties likely come with a limited or distorted view of their marriage. Whether overly pessimistic, unnecessarily blameful, or excessively naive, their understanding often needs massive doses of unbiased observation.

"Have you considered ———?" questions help couples view their problems from a new perspective. For instance, a husband, in his hurt, may not have had the clarity even to consider how much his wife continues to be influenced by her family of origin. In counseling we might muse, "I'd probably have a hard time including new ways into old habits, too."

• *Communication with, rather than at, each other.* Since communication problems rest at the heart of so many marital crises, simply getting the two parties talking together can be a major step toward health. But the quality of that talk is important. Many of the things one person says make the other erect defenses.

For example, the wife says, "You never think about all the things I do for you."

The husband's natural response might be, "I do too! Just yesterday I thanked you for packing my lunch."

To the wife, we might say, "The way you talk seems to be triggering defensiveness in your husband. If he feels you're attacking, he's going to want to defend himself. How about saying something like, 'I sure like it when you notice the things I do to keep this family going'?"

• *Refocusing on one's own responsibilities.* By the time marital problems get out of hand, both parties likely have done a lot of brooding on what the other's failures are. The wife is full of "He doesn'ts," and the husband is loaded down with "She won'ts."

The focus must be taken from "faults I think my partner ought to work on." The issue is for each person to ask, "What am I doing to contribute to our problems? What can I work on to make things better?" It is in the present doing that the marriage is going to be saved.

• *Genuine appreciation for the other's feelings.* People don't have to agree if only they understand the other person's position. We will want to work with a couple until each develops a genuine appreciation for the other person's position, regardless of agreement with it. One woman said about her husband, "We still don't agree, but I feel so much better just knowing he fully understands my opinion and is taking it into consideration."

—James D. Berkley

Family Counseling

The Bible teaches that God has designed us to live in relationships. Therefore, no one has an individual problem that doesn't in some way affect the family and isn't in some way affected by the family. So when it becomes clear that the issue under discussion seriously affects family dynamics, we must try to involve members of the family in the counseling process. Here are some guidelines for this.

• *Prepare the counselee.* First, we need to prepare the person we're counseling. If I'm counseling a woman, and I conclude I need to see her husband, I might say, "I think I'm ready now to talk with your husband. But are you ready to discover that you may be contributing to the problem? Are you ready to find out a larger truth?" Some people are afraid of being discovered, so first we have to get the permission of the counselee before involving others.

• *Create an alliance.* When approaching another family member, we can try to create a constructive alliance. Say a distraught mother comes to see me about her 16-year-old daughter. The girl has repeatedly crashed her car, and the mother is upset. I might call the daughter and say, "Your mom has been seeing me for a couple of weeks now, but I need some other help to understand what's going on with her. Could you come in and give me your perspective?" In this way, I form a relationship with the daughter, and together we have a common cause: to understand the mother.

• *Use fear appropriately.* When the counselee's problem is serious and the family member resists coming in, we may need to build on legitimate fear to underscore the seriousness of the situation. For example, if I'm counseling a seriously depressed woman, I may tell her husband, who's reluctant to come in, "I am really concerned about your wife. She is quite depressed, and I need to give someone clear directions about what to do in case she decides to do the worst. I also need to know if she takes sleeping pills or if there's a gun around the house. I'd like you to come in and help me."

Three Cautions

As we begin working with families, we'll need to stay aware of three dangers.

• *Sabotage.* Because families develop set patterns of responding to their problems, they are reluctant to change their system of interacting, even if it is causing one person great stress. If we push families too hard for change, they are likely to sabotage the healing process: "Ever since this counselor started working with us, we've had nothing but arguments. I say we've had enough." We can prevent this problem by pacing our probing. Asking threatening questions too early or suggesting changes too quickly will likely undermine the counseling objectives.

• *Collusion.* We mustn't assume a family's "diagnosis" is correct just because they all happen to agree about the problem. Sometimes families can be gullible and believe anything a current or former counselor has said about the main counselee. Beware the family that puts up a solid front in this regard.

• *Triangling.* Avoid getting "triangled"—when the counselor and the counselee try together to solve the problem of a third party. For example, a desperate woman with an alcoholic husband pleads: "Can't you help me get my husband to stop drinking?" If an empathetic counselor does that, the third party reacts violently. The husband feels like he is being ganged up on, and he is. That usually produces more conflict than ever.

—*Archibald D. Hart*

Counseling Children

Children may be brought to our counseling offices for a variety of reasons, all of which fall into three main categories. First, they come for *emotional adjustment.* Here we assist a child to handle anger, depression, fear, or grief. Our most important task in such cases is to provide the child with the means to express his or her feelings in a safe and reassuring setting. We help the child sort through questions and provide practice in dealing with emotions. A child trying to cope with anger, for example, might be helped by learning to manage the energy that arises by hitting a pillow or bending a metal hanger when he or she feels rage.

Second, children enter counseling for the purpose of *learning to adjust to new situations.* Entering a new school, living in a new house, adjusting to the birth or adoption of a sibling—all such major environmental changes can generate significant stress in children. We can help the child express his or her fears, disappointments, and worries while encouraging the child to focus on any familiar aspects of the new situation.

One young girl went to a new school where she had to open a locker with a combination lock. She was terrified that she would not be able to open the lock and would be humiliated. The counselor asked her parents to buy her a combination lock so she could practice, and she became able to go to school with greater self-confidence.

Third, children may be brought to counseling because they need *help coping with trauma.* Children experience a broad range of traumas, including the deaths of loved ones, their parents' divorce, loss of a friend, physical injury, or sexual abuse. Children in trauma need to know they are not the source of the problem, they are safe, and they are loved. Even for adults suffering from childhood sexual abuse, their greatest emotional struggles relate to the *lack* of this kind of support as children.

Suggested Practices

Children who receive counseling can experience emotional healing. As we begin counseling a child, we will want to keep in mind a few important guidelines:

• *Seek supervision from a specialist.* Counselors who lack specific training for work with children may want to consider making a referral. The counseling of very small children (preschool age) is so specialized, few professionals will even attempt it. In general, counseling of this age should be referred to specialists.

• *Utilize the existing relational network.* The child's sessions should be followed by a consultation with the parents, explaining methods and progress. We should also be aware of other significant people in the child's life, communicating with his or her teachers, pediatrician, child-care providers, coaches, friends, and close relatives, as is appropriate.

• *Explain the limits of confidentiality.* We should make it clear to the child exactly what we will tell the parents and what we will *not* tell them.

• *Report any evidence of abuse.* Reporting abuse is required by law in every state. We must understand our responsibilities in this area.

• *Don't take an authoritarian approach.* We need to respect the personhood of each child. Counseling was probably not the child's idea, and he or she is not just a problem to be solved on the parents' behalf.

• *Consider developmental age characteristics.* Children differ socially, cognitively, emotionally, physically, and spiritually, depending on their ages. For example, 7-year-olds can't think abstractly, so we need to use concrete language with them. We can review the general developmental characteristics appropriate to the counselee's age and then compare our findings with the specifics known about the particular case.

—*Randy Christian*

Adolescent Counseling

Around 1950, the largest influence on a teenager's life was the home. Next came school, church, peers, and television. A 1990 survey found that peers now have the largest influence on teenagers, followed by rap music, television, the home, and school. Church doesn't even make the list!

In spite of this news, the large majority (92%) of youth want to learn more about values. It seems young people intuitively understand that tough problems like violence, sexual promiscuity, parental absence, drug abuse, and teen pregnancy have a better chance of being solved when moral values are taught and believed.

Yet the pastor who counsels adolescents must understand that the new teen generation is pessimistic. Many young people see their legacy as a polluted earth and a racially fractured society severely stressed with overwhelming social problems. They feel cheated and betrayed by the possibility that America's best years are over. The new generation of young people questions authority and conveys a visible disdain for hierarchy. In many ways these youth are restless, eager to grow up but afraid of the consequences.

Talking with Teens

In spite of this rather bleak picture, all is not lost. Here are some suggestions that can help us minister effectively among today's hurting teens:

- *Avoid acting like a teenager in order to relate to one.* It's a common mistake that goes nowhere fast. A counselor does not need to wear the latest styles, listen to pop music, or use slang (inevitably awkwardly) to relate to a young person.
- *Become an expert listener.* Listen to teens with what Theodore Reik calls "the third ear." Without hearing the heart-felt pain—the anxiety, the sadness, the embarrassment, the loneliness, the shame—behind a young person's seemingly mundane pronouncements, true counseling dies. "Be quick to listen, slow to speak" (James 1:19).
- *Pinpoint the severity of a teen's presenting problem.* Use assessment devices, such as *Helping the Struggling Adolescent: A Counseling Guide* (Zondervan). Such resources contain forms and guidelines for rapid assessment of such problems as depression, guilt, anxiety, grief, drug abuse, eating disorders, and dozens of other issues.
- *Challenge gross generalizations in conversation.* Many adolescents define their life situations in global terms, such as: "*Everything* is terrible," "*Nothing* is going right," "Dad is a *total* jerk." As long as they continue to see the world this way, they remain stuck. Work diligently to chip away at their irrational declarations.
- *Become comfortable with delicate subjects.* Today's teens need counselors who do not shy away from issues such as masturbation, drug use, divorce of parents, death of a friend, date rape, or other sexu-

al issues. With or without help, teens *will* deal with these issues.

• *Look to agencies and support groups for help.* Those not experienced in working with a young person's particular problem can refer the youth to someone with the required expertise. Adolescents who struggle with parental abuse, severe depression, suicide, eating disorders, phobias, sleep disturbance, or drug addiction should be treated by a trained specialist. Pastors won't be able to help every struggling adolescent.

Buddy Scott, author of *Relief for Hurting Parents,* founded and directs an agency for helping families with teenagers. His "Parenting Within Reason" support groups are an excellent resource for parents and other caregivers. (For information, call 800/28U-NEED.)

Unfortunately, there are no universal or simple formulas for resolving the complex problems of today's youth. If we are to make a difference in their lives, we'll need to practice proven principles of contemporary psychology, rely on sound biblical theology, and seek the guidance of the Holy Spirit in all our efforts.

—Les Parrott III

Counseling the Elderly

"Even when I am old and gray, do not forsake me, O God . . ." (Ps. 71:18a). In counseling the elderly, we need to hear this cry. Men and women who have lived into their old age have been forsaken by persons who were special to them. Spouses have died; children have moved away; friends no longer drop by. Yet elderly persons can draw strength and comfort from their memories as they define the kinds of control they will hold in the future.

Invite Storytelling

Consider the case of Jane. She came to her pastor and said: "I want to die now; then I could be with my husband. I have no reason to be here anymore. I was saving up some of my pills, but now I can't remember where I put them."

In her brief statement, Jane gives voice to two areas of counseling need that often confront the elderly: loss of a special person and loss of cognitive powers. Not only has Jane lost her husband, but she has lost enough of her mental acuity that she cannot remember where she put the pills that would have ended her life.

Sensitive counseling at this point would include inviting storytelling about her husband and giving an empathic response to her dilemma over not remembering where her pills are. Talking about the deceased special person brings that person back, even if only for the duration of the pastoral visit. Counseling takes place any time we invite storytelling with the elderly. Telling and retelling their stories gives meaning to their lives.

Responding with "It must be

hard to make a plan and then forget an essential part of it!" acknowledges Jane's frustration, which is real. In a situation like this, a little healthy identification is both appropriate and effective as a pastoral response.

Intervention regarding a potential suicide at this juncture would miss Jane's immediate need. That response can come later if necessary. By listening to the story and acknowledging the frustration, pastoral counseling takes place.

Name Areas of Control

John was diagnosed with depression. When the pastor visited him at the hospital, John said: "Life just doesn't make sense! I worked hard all my life. I saved and scrimped so we could have a good retirement. Now look at me! I've had a heart attack. I lost a leg to diabetes. And now I get confused. Sometimes I feel like I'm watching my own mind deteriorate and there's nothing I can do to stop it!"

John laments his loss of physical strength and his sense of losing control over his life in general. Here he needs to have that loss of control acknowledged—an empathic response—but John also needs to be challenged to name what he *does* control. If as counselors to the elderly we can help them find something to be in control of in a positive way, we will help diminish their sense of helplessness.

The elderly parishioner, patient, or client needs counseling that attends both to basic human needs and the unique needs of aging. Being human beings, the elderly need purpose, understanding, and community, as we all do. As specifically older persons, they need their personal losses named, so effective grief work can be done; their mental and physical losses attended to in a way that leaves them as much control as possible; and their life experience valued for the wisdom it holds for those who follow.

—Ann A. Letson

Medical Ethics

Most pastoral interventions in matters that involve medical ethics group around birth and death issues. Some birth issues, such as the use of anencephalic newborns as organ donors, what to do with frozen pre-embryos that are no longer needed, or whether it is right to use fetal tissue in the treatment of Parkinson's disease, present wrenching dilemmas for the families involved, but most pastors will rarely encounter such crises. Much more commonly a pastor joins parents in discussions over whether a pregnancy should be saved or terminated, or how aggressively neonatologists should labor to save an extremely premature or defective newborn.

Most death issues relate to the withholding or withdrawal of treatment. Should a "do not resuscitate" order be written? Should we remove a ventilator? Should we discontinue nutrition and hydration?

Should we attempt surgery, chemotherapy, or radiation? Or is it time to switch from cure strategies to a care plan centered on the patient's comfort until death?

Principles for Decisions

As we face such medical dilemmas, we can bring to bear at least five Christian value–driven principles to guide us through the decision-making process.

• *Face the facts.* The pastor may need to prod the family to ask direct, hard questions and insist on honest, full communication with the physicians involved. Responsible decision making begins with a thorough and rigorous exploration of the diagnosis, prognosis, medical options, and alternative therapies available.

• *Reverence life.* We must not absolutize the preservation of biological human life, since God alone is absolute. But because God's creation is good and life is precious, we will be advocates of reverence for life. Reverence should not be equated with the prolongation of physical life, but must equally concern itself with the emotional, spiritual, and relational well-being of the person involved.

• *Respect personal choice.* Paternalism, intimidation, manipulation, deceit, and coercion militate against the principle of respect for the individual. Yet we must always ask: What does the patient prefer? What would she want if she were conscious? What decisions would be most in keeping with his character and values? Pastors can encourage adults to draft care instructions, documents that declare treatment preferences if and when one becomes incompetent.

• *Improve life's quality.* Medicine's only legitimate role is to enhance the quality of life. The pastor will encourage a patient or family to weigh the burdens of a particular course of treatment against its benefits. When this is not done, the medical-industrial complex's "technological imperative"—whatever *can* be done *must* be done—may take control by default.

• *Practice good citizenship.* The Christian faith declares that we exist not as solitary, isolated cells, but as interrelated, interdependent members "one of another." Our faith challenges us to see ourselves first not as private individuals with rights, but as citizens of a colony, with duties to each other and to all humankind. Because every medical decision about a particular patient affects other individuals and institutions, we must fold societal questions into our deliberations. Will this decision adversely affect the patient's family? Are we practicing good stewardship of society's limited resources?

Conflicts may arise when one of these duties appears to collide with another. Our task is to prevent the decision from occurring in a vacuum. We must pull into the conversation people of good will, faith, and wisdom, who can add insight and balance to the decision-making process. Here, a hospital ethics committee may be helpful. The goal of all the communication is to discern, in consideration of the various parties involved and the primary values at stake, the most responsible course to take.

—*Wayne Willis*

Infertility and Pregnancy Counseling

Half of all American couples who try to get pregnant have trouble doing so. One in six couples worshiping in your congregation on Sunday morning faces the crisis of infertility. Most of these couples will negotiate an extremely expensive medical evaluation, intrusive medical procedures, or forms of drug therapy—all with no guarantees about the outcome.

Additionally, many couples will experience profound loss through miscarriage. About 50 percent of those couples eventually will conceive and bear a child, while the remaining couples will go on to grapple with adoption procedures.

Bringing Help

Infertile couples face extraordinary pressures. Here are some suggestions for helping them:

• *Affirm the infertile couple's self-esteem.* For a woman, bearing a child is often considered a confirmation of her femininity and a rite of passage into legitimate adulthood. The husband may feel threatened and frustrated as he listens to the freely shared grief of his wife. The man may suffer doubts about his masculinity, as well. In counseling, work at affirming the infertile couple as gifted and whole persons, even if they are unable to have children. Focus on their strengths and value their contributions.

• *Look for signs of marital stress.* Infertility can have devastating impact on a marriage relationship. Couples experiencing the crisis of infertility must work at redefining the purpose of their shared future. Every area of the couple's life is affected, from career decisions to sexual function to relationships with extended family members.

Childless couples typically go through three phases. First, the couple questions why this is happening to them. What have they done wrong? Why are they so defective? Why are they denied something the rest of the world takes for granted? Next, the couple mourns the loss of ability to bear children. They search their souls for many months to determine what, exactly, this will mean for them and their future identity within the extended family and society. Finally, the couple enters a decision-making phase. They will either pursue adoption or begin adjusting to childlessness, seeking fulfillment in other ways.

• *Link couples with a caring support group.* Infertile couples must know their feelings of grief, anger, helplessness, and spiritual doubt are understood and validated by others who have already walked in their shoes. A nonprofit organization called RESOLVE provides education and support for infertile couples and is located in most cities. *Stepping Stones* (2900 North Rock Road, Wichita, KS 67226) is a newsletter published bimonthly for the encouragement and support of infertile Christian couples.

• *Recognize the impact of pregnancy loss.* Expectant parents may form a deep attachment to what is called a "fantasy image" of the future child, and the death of this child may become the death of their hopes and dreams for the future. Couples who experience the loss of pregnancy usually undergo a full grieving process, often intensified for the woman due to hormone imbalance and physical exhaustion. Validating the depth of pain for the couple will allow the normal grieving process to unfold.

The couple will no doubt move through shock, anger, and self-blame before coming to full acceptance. It may take up to a year or more for this type of grieving to come to completion. It is good to connect with the hurting couple regularly over the course of the first year, being especially sensitive to the originally scheduled due date in the case of a miscarriage.

Some infertility-counseling situations require more than pastoral intervention. If you encounter extreme levels of shame, guilt, and depression, or if you discover serious sexual dysfunction, refer the couple to a trusted medical specialist, psychologist, or sex therapist.

—Leslie Parrott

Counseling People Who Are Dying

People face death asking many questions about God and the meaning of life. The truth of eternal life is only *one* question people ask as they approach their act of dying, and it is often not their most important issue. We need to be prepared mentally as well as spiritually as we approach the dying. Here are four important attitudes to take with us when we visit the terminally ill.

• *I can demonstrate appreciation, but not full understanding.* People deny that anyone else can possibly appreciate what they are experiencing. Only after they have permitted themselves to trust that we are trying to understand them—that we do not want to force our feelings on them — can we share effectively the truth of Scripture about the humanity of Jesus. Without denying the pain and specific reality of their grief, we can communicate that Jesus went through pain and grief in his own death.

People do not need trite explanations, especially at this time. A statement like "It's all for the best in God's plan for creation" most likely confirms people's worst fear: God is playing around with their lives without taking their feelings into account.

• *I can give permission to express anger.* Dying people often are thinking: *If God really loves me, why doesn't he do something?* Anger is a natural way for people to express self-concern, and it provides the energy and desire for people to take care of themselves. That energy will be needed in the stages to come. They need permission to express all their feelings, so each one can be addressed in the open. After all, life does not seem fair; we don't always like what is going on either.

People do not need our defensiveness about God. A simple listening ear and gentle probing into the depth of their anger is better than all our theological explanations about the wisdom and will of God.

• *I should extend relief of guilt.* Typically people ask, "What did I do to deserve this?" They may want to make up for some inner deficiency they assume caused their vulnerability to death. These people need to know God relates to them out of grace and not retaliation and vengeance. Sometimes they carry around leftover guilt from the past that frightens or shames them when they think about meeting God. Communion, prayer, Scripture readings, and the assurance of God's forgiveness are most appropriate at this point.

Since dying people are burdened with almost intolerable circumstances, they need hope and encouragement. What they do not need is more guilt by our suggesting they should have more faith in facing their ailment. A statement like "If you'd just put your faith in God, you would be able to accept this in peace" causes more stress than it eliminates.

• *I will offer theological assurances only at the appropriate time.* Eventually, after many side trips and much exploring, people reach the point in their journey through grief where they can accept what is happening. They have been allowed to acknowledge that death is not fair, to rule out trying to scheme their way out of it, to learn that the love of God remains even for sinners, and to accept that the family will be taken care of in their absence. Finally they ask, "What's next?"

Now we talk about Easter, the images of heaven prophesied in the Bible, and the promises of Jesus for life everlasting. Theologically, they have reached the stage of receptivity to the beauty of eternal life.

—*Linwood H. Chamberlain, Jr.*

Grief Counseling

The pain of grief is not supposed to be "cured" by counseling. Actually, the healing process of grief counseling is intended to be a journey directly into and through the pain of loss. The counselor's task, therefore, is to insure that the counselee is progressing through that process and appropriately experiencing the legitimate pain (rather than symptoms or defenses that mask or bury it).

Research has indicated that a two-year grief-recovery period is typical when healing is progressing appropriately. Since it is important for counselees to experience pain in their own unique ways, we must avoid any approaches that attempt to dictate exactly how the bereaved should heal.

Three Stages

The effective grief counselor understands that the grief process is natural. It is only when that process is interrupted that counseling—rather than basic pastoral care — is needed. In such cases, our task is to facilitate movement through the three major steps in the grieving-healing process:

• *Accepting the reality of the loss.*

Many grieving people have suffered a loss deep enough that, if possible, they would deny its reality. In extreme cases, this can mean refusing to accept the death of a loved one, pretending this person is still alive. Gentle challenges, in a supportive and caring context, can help the counselee gradually admit the painful truth.

Sometimes denial is quite subtle. A parent who has lost a son in a car accident might acknowledge the death yet refuse to allow any of the son's belongings to be disturbed. Changing the son's room would be admitting the loss at a deeper level.

We must not rush those who grieve or attempt to set up a specific schedule for their healing. Instead, we gently but candidly confirm the stark reality and pain of the loss.

- *Adjusting to the new reality.* After the grieving person has begun to accept the new reality, he or she must begin adjusting to it with practical changes in daily living. Acceptance will continue to grow even as the grieving one adjusts. A widower whose wife paid the bills will now have to assume that task for himself. A woman who relied on her father for advice will have to seek other resources.

As with experiencing the pain, adjustment can be a natural process. It is necessary to provide counseling only when the process isn't happening at all or when the circumstances demand that it occur at a faster rate. When offering help, we should avoid becoming an "answer man" by helping the client learn and utilize a personal decision-making strategy.

- *Reinvesting in the future.* This is perhaps the most difficult stage of grief recovery. When the client begins to adjust to the new reality, the full awareness of what is now missing — with all its practical ramifications — begins to hit home with profound impact. The temptation is to fill this vacuum immediately or to avoid filling it at all. We can guide the counselee between these two extremes, helping reinvestment to be gradual rather than rushed. The counselee should avoid making major commitments or decisions during the early stages of this final step in healing.

During all three of these movements, people in grief must feel free to experience personal pain in any way that "feels right." Since this pain can find expression in any and all emotions, we can allow plenty of space for crying, yelling, pleading, and questioning. By helping grieving persons feel and express their true pain, we gently bring them through to the other side of loss, where a meaningful and satisfying life can blossom once again.

—Randy Christian

Crisis Counseling

Clients should "own" as much of the healing process as possible, contends Gerard Egan in *The Skilled Helper* (Monterey, Cal.: Brooks/Cole Publishing Company, 1986). He divides counseling into three stages, each of which he further divides into three steps.

Stage I: Problem Definition

The job at this stage is to uncover the nature and dimensions of the crisis. The nature of the problem may be sketchy as we pull on a coat and hurry out the door, but at least we want to know if the person we're rushing to help is more apt to commit suicide or adultery.

1. Helping clients tell their stories. Here we facilitate the telling of what has happened and is happening, to get information on the table. We may need to draw out one person, separate another from a distracting situation, or calm another. If someone starts crying, we might say gently, "Go ahead and cry as long as you want. I'll be silently praying for you. We can talk again whenever you feel ready."

2. Focusing. This step involves screening, focusing, and clarifying. Many clues present themselves to us: bits of stray conversation, things we see, information given by others, conversations with the counselee. We perform a kind of information triage to decide what really is being said, and the person in crisis needs to determine what to talk about. We also work at uncovering parts of the crisis that may not be known or recognized even by the one in the crisis.

3. Offering new perspectives. New perspectives can provide the first glimmer of hope. We may help the alcoholic consider the effect his alcoholism has on every other part of life. The homosexual may be led to believe for the first time that there's hope for his greater healing. We need to challenge counselees to look at things a different way, to own their problems, to look for a way to change their situation.

Stage II: Goal Development

In Stage I the problem is identified and clarified, but most people don't want a clear problem; they want a solved problem. That's why Stage II focuses on goals.

1. Constructing a new scenario. Counselees need to think about which direction is up. For instance, getting arrested for indecent exposure forces a man to realize that he needs help. In talking with his pastor, he may construct a scenario with a profound new element: the ability to live without succumbing to hurtful urges.

2. Critiquing the new scenario. This step makes the counselee look closely at the newly envisioned scenarios. Will they work? Which one is most realistic? If I could have only one, which would it be? Counselees then need to consider the consequences of the choices they will make.

3. Asking for choice and commitment. This step is truly demanding. An alcoholic often balks at this point. A suicidal person may feel unable to choose life. But we can make the choice easier. For instance, clear and detailed scenarios give greater incentive than fuzzy ones; several options offer greater incentive than just one; harder, more substantial goals are actually more motivating than small plans.

Stage III: Action

It's a long way from wanting to do something to actually accomplishing it. That makes the three steps in this stage so important: (1) brainstorming strategies for action, (2) choosing strategies, and (3) devising a specific plan of action.

With the various strategies on the table, we collaborate with the counselee to decide which course of action best meets the counselee's needs, fits his or her values, and seems likely to succeed.

—James D. Berkley

Counseling Suicidal People

The distraught person has called; the suicide attempt is transpiring or at least imminent. You've gathered the basic facts of the situation. That means it's time to act. What can you do?

A Drastic Strategy

When a suicide is in progress or when a lethal and workable plan is likely to be implemented, we must act immediately. We need to determine where the person is and get help to him or her immediately and in whatever form necessary, including getting the police involved.

Most of the social rules go out the window at a time like this. The helper may worry about breaking confidences or losing the person's trust by initiating precipitous measures the caller has told the helper not to try. But even if one has promised not to call the police, strict honesty will mean little at the person's funeral.

It's a good preemptive strategy to work out a distress signal to bring a secretary or your spouse into the room where you take such calls. Then a hastily jotted note can send them to another phone to have the call traced or to dispatch an emergency team.

More Strategies

An simple strategy is to keep the person talking. As long as the caller stays on the line and talks, chances are the suicide won't take place (unless the attempt has been made and is now taking effect). Talk is an antidote, healing in itself. Just the fact of another human dropping everything to listen — really *listen* — can dissipate noxious emotions. So talk away. It's a good first strategy.

A better strategy is to obtain some kind of commitment from the caller. After a long, wrenching conversation, it's not uncommon for the caller to feel somewhat indebted to the helper. Or maybe there's a prior attachment that made the person call in the first place. Either of these debts can be used by the helper.

Make a pact with the person and hold him or her to it. Say, "You know, after all we've been through together, don't you think you owe it to me to at least give me a call before you do anything drastic? Promise me you'll do that one little thing for me." The very fact that someone feels obligated to call before pulling the trigger can keep him or her from following through with suicide plans.

An even better strategy is to work out a plan together. The suicidal person has been working on a death plan; now's the time to advance a life plan. It can begin with eliminating tools that would make a distinct suicide plan feasible. That may mean getting someone else to keep the firing mechanism for a gun or purging the house of lethal medications.

A life plan helps the caller begin to walk toward life and health. The first steps may be tiny, such as trusting the helper enough to divulge one's name, or scheduling an appointment together in person and promising to keep it. It may encompass a contract to call each other daily. It may start with a promise to make an appointment with a physician. Sometimes it will involve a step toward Christian faith.

The life plan eventually ought to get more complex, branching into a complete therapeutic program involving medical, psychological, and Christian professionals.

An Overriding Strategy

Most people can pray while listening, and bringing the power of God into the situation is absolutely necessary. It's not right to think, *All I can do is pray*. In reality, it's a case of *the best I can do is pray, and that's a lot!*

—*James D. Berkley*

Counseling the Depressed

Almost everyone knows what it means to be depressed, but it takes a special kind of understanding to be helpful to others in depression. Pastoral counselors need the ability to take control of their emotions in order to embrace the pain of depression in a truly helpful way. They must not be put off by the distressed countenance or preoccupation of the counselee. As the surgeon must be willing to encounter blood, so the counselor must be willing to offer healing in the midst of deep emotional woundedness.

Caring Technique

As we begin to counsel a depressed person, showing him or her that we understand how hurt, sad, or dejected he or she feels, there are several important factors to keep in mind:

- *Be alert to life-threatening symptoms.* Suicidal tendencies surface in most depressions. Even the most devout believer may long to be taken from this life when he or she is in a deep depression. Family members or friends can be enlisted to let us know the moment they suspect the suicidal impulses are getting out of control.
- *Uncover the causes.* After the depressed person has had ample opportunity to explore and explain his or her feelings, we can begin to focus on discovering the loss that is causing the depression. For every person, a given loss has a special meaning. We must work to discover the meaning that lies behind the loss. Often these meanings are quite

subtle and abstract and not so easy for the depressed person to recognize without help.

• *Analyze interpretations.* We should emphasize to depressed persons that the feelings they are having spring from their grief and do not alter objective reality. Depression always distorts reality and makes things look bleaker than they really are. We should keep reassuring the depressed that the feelings are genuine but their interpretation of the feelings is being distorted.

• *Move toward acceptance.* We ought to focus our attention on helping the depressed person accept the loss and release it. If someone who has been fired continues to cling to his or her old job, the depression will linger. At the point this person lets go, the depression likely will begin to lift.

• *Listen more than talk.* Our comments and interjections should focus on drawing out feelings, not on giving advice. We must place a high priority on listening and use primarily open-ended questions.

• *Don't try to short-circuit the depression.* It is callous and unfeeling to say to somebody who is depressed, "Snap out of it," or "You know, you really don't have a reason to be depressed; everything else in your life is so good." Depression *always* has a cause. If it is biological, something is wrong with the body. If it is psychological, a significant loss of some kind is at the root of the depression.

• *Don't be surprised by initial worsening.* Psychological depression is a grief response, and the more one understands the meaning of his or her loss, the more one will grieve. Usually the loss must become more apparent before it can be fully grieved. Honestly facing and feeling the pain is the key to the healing process.

• *Don't hesitate to refer.* Most pastors can help with mild forms of depression, but it's appropriate to refer people to a professional counselor or psychiatrist if two or three weeks of counseling don't yield any improvement. In clinical depression, underlying biological mechanisms are likely at work and require compensating medication from a physician.

—*Archibald D. Hart*

Counseling Homosexual People

What brings homosexuals to pastors is often one of two events: a person finally concedes preference for the same sex or the person bumps into some disturbing consequence of homosexual behavior, such as arrest, disease, or discovery. In either event, an ordered world has been disordered, and the person needs help reconstructing it.

An Understanding Presence

Initially the pastor's role is presence. The homosexual in crisis needs someone, and the genuine, unshockable presence of a caring Christian provides much-needed support.

The temptation is to try to fix the immediate crisis, but the ultimate cure comes in working on the causes of the homosexuality. Does the counselee know and understand the roots of his or her behavior? What specific activities have been involved, how often, and for how long? Does he or she want to turn away from homosexual practice?

As a counselee relates a recent experience, such as a visit to a gay bathhouse at a low moment, we may be able to tie it cautiously to earlier behaviors and make associations: "Do you realize that whenever you feel put down, you react by seeking sexual encounters? Are you looking for sex or for something else?" It is important that the counselee see the connection, what it is that triggers the behavior.

One theory advanced by Leanne Payne, author of *The Broken Image* and *The Crisis in Masculinity*, suggests an analogy with cannibalism. Cannibals didn't eat people for nourishment. They chose people with characteristics they admired — strength or bravery — and ate them, expecting to take on those characteristics. Payne believes a similar symbolic confusion is at work subconsciously in the homosexual male: he thinks he lacks masculinity, so he seeks ever more contact with the male organ to compensate. But he can never get enough.

Other theories posit a lack of male bonding with one's father, or various genetic and physiological predisposing factors. Unfortunately, there's little agreement about causation.

Meeting the Crisis

Crisis counseling with homosexuals can be frustrating. Here are some basic guidelines to keep in mind:

- Homosexual orientation and behavior is a complex, painful problem. Success rates are not good. Counseling likely will be a wrenching, difficult, and long process.
- Few homosexuals consider their preference chosen. Whatever the inception of homosexuality, they experience it as something they *are* rather than something they *choose*.
- Unless the homosexual wants to change, little we do will help. We must let them take the initiative for contacting us and making appointments, and keep them retaining responsibility for their behavior, as much as possible.
- To help bring a change in orientation, we need to bring to bear all the resources we can muster. Referral to experts is highly advised.

Difficult Choices

We can provide hope for change in Jesus Christ. God does not want anyone to be deceived or trapped in an unbiblical and self-destructive lifestyle. He can make people whole and free. We begin by valuing homosexuals as people and building up their good points, even when we cannot endorse their behavior.

We ought not condemn them or heap scorn on them. They already dislike themselves and are trying to cope with low self-image. Yet we cannot waver about the problem of homosexual practices. We do them no favor by encouraging them to continue in sin, even when the alternatives appear full of difficulty and heartache.

We shouldn't try to rescue them from all the consequences of their behaviors. They may need to feel the drastic sting of crisis to be pushed to a point of change.

Nor should we promise confidentiality that we cannot keep. Others may need to know about the homosexuality or be protected from its path, although we ought not reveal someone's homosexuality without compelling reasons, and then only to those who must know, such as a spouse.

—James D. Berkley

Counseling the Sexually Addicted

Sexual addiction is usually the result of perceived trauma, neglect, or rejection at an early age. Such trauma often results in symbolic confusion between sexuality and sexual identity. Although the sexuality (biological gender) of a child is known at birth, sexual identity (masculinity or femininity) is learned from parents—especially the father. This is one of the father's principal roles, because when he doesn't affirm his children's sexual identity, great spiritual, emotional, and sexual damage can result.

Connections and Corrections

Here are the major steps to take in work with the sexually addicted in counseling.

• *Take a sexual history.* A sexual history is taken to try to discover how the counselee found out about sex and what the childhood experiences with it were. How did he or she learn about male and female anatomy? What was known about the parents' marital relationship? What have been his or her experiences with sex? How satisfying have they been? How many partners? Questions such as these are hard to ask for most people — and difficult to answer for the counselee — but they supply vital information.

Many times the person has never talked about sex with anyone else and finds such conversations embarrassing. For instance, one counselee, Jan, was married and had also been active homosexually for years, yet his knowledge of sex was limited. Jan was shocked that Christians would actually speak openly about such things as masturbation and oral sex.

• *Connect history with present activities.* In order to heal a sexual addict, we must try to hold in tension two paradoxical beliefs: addictive behavior is both a disease and a choice, bondage and rebellion. Therefore, we want to get to the root of the disease—any trauma, pain, rejection, or poor parenting the person received as a child. In this, the child had no choice; he or she is in bondage to the sins of others. But we must face concurrently the choices the addict has made along the road — choices toward sin. If both sides of the problem aren't confronted, change is impossible.

The Book of Hebrews says, "See to it that no one misses the grace of God and that no bitter root grows up to cause trouble and defile many" (Heb. 12:15). Jan had failed to apply God's grace to himself, his siblings, and his parents. As a result, he had developed numerous roots of bitterness and didn't want to accept responsibility for his sexual behavior. Yet his only hope for healing lay in forgiving his family and in seeking forgiveness himself.

• *Break patterns of behavior.* Once a counselee begins to see patterns of avoiding emotional pain through sexual experience, progress usually follows. However, he or she will occasionally fail to deal with stress and revert back to the old patterns of using sex as a drug. When those falls occur, we may find it is the old, unrenewed belief system causing the failure. A sexual addict's belief system is filled with negative, self-rejecting thoughts.

• *Correct false beliefs.* The sexually addicted often hold a negative view of God the Father. For instance, Jan couldn't trust God to meet his needs, because he projected the failures of his earthly father onto the Heavenly Father. Over and over we washed Jan's mind with the truth of Scripture in order to overcome the lies of his irrational belief system. We showed him the ABCDs of his emotions: that Activating Events (A) are interpreted by his Belief System (B), causing Consequential Feelings (C) in him, which result in Decisive Behavior (D). We have no control over Activating Events and Consequential Feelings; the place to work is the Belief System.

—Hal B. Schell and Gary Sweeten

Alcohol Abuse

Even with all the publicity, we still understate the problem of alcohol abuse. It accounts for over 100,000 deaths every year in America alone, and this does not include the inevitable injuries, poverty, and fractured relationships. Considering the scope of the problem and the inadequacy of federal initiatives, many churches have determined to reach the alcohol abuser and offer biblical approaches to this difficult problem.

Diagnosing for Hope

If there is any hesitation from the church, it is, in part, a result of the popular literature that has proclaimed alcohol abuse a disease. If this were true, the church would be severely limited in its ability to offer hope. A more biblical understanding of alcohol abuse, however, is that it is sin that both feels and acts like a disease. Like all habitual sin, it leaves one powerless and enslaved.

Certainly, there may be people who have a physical propensity to finding pleasure in alcohol, but a possible physical predisposition does not lead people irresistibly into drunkenness. Rather, it can lead to temptation, which requires spiritual strength to resist. This description of alcoholism can be the basis for great hope for those caught in its web.

Nevertheless, in light of sin's ability to produce feelings of powerlessness, compelling solutions are essential. This means that rather than offering sophisticated new techniques, we must offer a meaningful and true model of biblical change.

Counseling for Change

The process of change begins with detection. Usually friends or family will detect physical signs of drunkenness or the more obvious sinful behaviors that result. Our intervention as pastor-counselors will likely begin after the counsel of friends and family is ignored and drinkers persist in their habits.

When counseling begins, our ultimate goal is to point ex-drinkers to Jesus. It has been said that guilt is alcohol-soluble. It may be so, but forgiveness of sins is a cornerstone for biblical change (2 Pet. 1:8–9), and a growing love of Jesus is the motive.

Here are methods to use in counseling:

- *Develop a truth-telling environment.* As with the abuse of illegal drugs, alcohol abuse is typically accompanied by secrecy and lies. We need to show counselees the biblical importance of speaking the truth, and create an atmosphere that invites honesty in counseling sessions.
- *Nurture a hatred of abuse.* A problem with alcohol abuse, as with other sin, is that it is attractive; it does satisfy certain desires. Counselees need to see their alcohol abuse more accurately, using new eyes. In order to nurture a hatred of abuse (Prov. 8:13), some people have benefited from writing a journal about the bad consequences of their alcohol use.
- *Prepare counselees for temptation.* A biblical approach does not guarantee the cessation of desire for alcohol (see James 1:14–15). In fact, the Bible indicates an ongoing battle should be expected. So, temptation should not mean hopelessness. It simply means a phone call to a friend may be necessary. If a recovering person slips back into abuse, we need to help him or her learn from the incident, know forgiveness, and continue with the process.
- *Repair damaged relationships.* Counselees must seek peace with those they have sinned against because of the abuse. This requires asking forgiveness and perhaps making restitution in practical ways. Counselees also need to learn godly skills in living, especially in areas such as resolving conflict and handling anger or depression.
- *Develop a group of partners for recoverers.* Since recovering alcoholics need strict accountability and consistent encouragement, once-a-week counseling sessions aren't enough. We can first look within Christian support groups; otherwise, Alcoholics Anonymous is a good source of support.

—Edward T. Welch

Chemical Abuse Counseling

Chemical abusers need the church because it can provide compassion, encouragement, wise and true counsel, and accountability. Frequently, however, those who struggle with addictions find the church less than welcoming. Though chemical abuse is a complex problem, the church should be ready and willing to offer its tremendous healing resources. Pastoral counselors must see themselves as agents of profound change, even in situations where the hope for change has been buried by addictive chemicals.

Detection First

Detection, the first step in counseling, may be quite difficult because most chemical abusers have a long history of secretive use. There are warning signs: weight loss, poor health, nasal problems, and unexplained changes in work and relationships. Yet our job is not merely to "catch" drug abusers. People have determined to use illegal drugs no matter what the cost, and they inevitably find a way to escape detection. Instead, the fundamental task of the pastor-counselor is to speak the truth in love and to provide an environment in which abusers can feel safe enough to speak honestly of their inner pain.

When chemical abuse is confessed or exposed, some counselors immediately ask abusers to admit themselves to a drug-rehabilitation facility. The advantage of such a decision is that the abuser will be accountable and sober during this time. Also, if there are concerns about the trauma of withdrawal, the abuser will benefit by being in a medical facility.

The disadvantages of such an immediate, live-in solution include the financial expense and the lack of evidence that in-patient programs actually do contribute to long-term abstinence. Thus, hospitalization may be helpful, but we shouldn't consider it mandatory.

When we proceed without hospitalizing the counselee, we need to find a way to verify ongoing abstinence. For example, some families volunteer to administer weekly urine screens.

A Worship Disorder

Consider this basic working biblical diagnosis: Chemical abuse, at its most foundational level, is a disorder of worship. Those committed to their chemicals often love their drugs—and their own desires—above all else. Sadly, although chemical idols promise freedom, pleasure, and power, they deliver only slavery. To break the bondage, chemical abusers, both believers and nonbelievers, need the most powerful counsel available: the gospel of Christ's kingdom. Christian counselors can introduce abusers to Jesus and his beautiful offer of love, complete forgiveness, and power over enslaving desires.

True worship requires hearing the gospel message with faith, and such worship is largely enacted in daily, small steps of obedience. To guide people in this obedience, proceed in four basic steps.

• *Confront the lies.* For many chemical abusers, lying is a lifestyle. Therefore, learning honesty is as important as staying sober. To this end, we can reveal the disadvantages of lies and offer the advantages of telling the truth (Eph. 4:25). Lying may provide a temporary reprieve from conflict, but the cost is further self-deception.

• *Break the network of old associations.* Naturally, we'll want to help counselees avoid associations with drugs and other drug users (Prov. 23:19–20).

• *Encourage alertness to the old cravings.* Being a worshiper of God doesn't mean our battle with sin is over (James 1:14–15). We can encourage recovering abusers to fight temptation even when it is only a faint voice in their imaginations.

• *Enlist helpers from the church.* The spiritual-growth needs of recovering abusers are the same as those of everyone in the church. We all need daily encouragement with the truth (Heb. 3:12–13). The best encouragers will be reliable friends in the church who see themselves primarily as fellow strugglers rather than experts.

—*Edward T. Welch*

Counseling Codependents

The subject of codependency, with a host of best-sellers to its credit, tends to have two overlapping fields of meaning. First, codependency describes the experience of having been hurt in relationships, being controlled by or dependent upon the opinions or behaviors of others.

At times, however, the codependency movement functions more like a religion that offers a new understanding of God and people. In its brand of theology, for example, codependent persons may be viewed as morally innocent, needing to love themselves more rather than love God more. Therefore, we need to be alert to how the term is used: either as a description of a client's relational experience or as an all-encompassing life philosophy. Here we use the narrower definition.

Hurts from the Past

Codependents have been sinned against in the past. Often these violations have been characterized by mixed messages, capricious and unpredictable abusive behaviors, and constant rejection—all actions that an alcoholic parent or spouse might use to control another. Counseling must bring God's perspective to this pain. The process begins with making it safe for the counselee to speak honestly of past and present hurts for as long as the wounds remain open and tender.

Alongside this experience-sharing process, we can bring the Word of God to bear. The Bible, especially in the Psalms, provides words for this kind of suffering. People can hear of a loving God who responds to their expressions of pain, speaking tenderly (Isa. 42:3) and mourning when his children are sinned against. The codependent can also find comfort in knowing that God has always been active on behalf of the unjustly victimized. To those who have been hurt, God promises his presence (Heb. 13:5–6), ultimate justice (Isa. 16:4), and the power to overcome evil with good (Rom. 12:17–21). Moreover, God promises to overturn tragedy and use it for our good, as he conforms us into the image of Jesus (Rom. 8:28–29).

What about the shame associated with past hurts? Codependents often feel as if they are constantly erecting impenetrable walls to cover their shame before other people. To this, God proclaims that he completely "covers" an even deeper problem, our sin problem. We can help counselees recognize that Jesus, the One who gives us new covering garments, has experienced an even more profound shame on the cross, on our behalf.

Relationships in the Present

Hurts from the past are one part of the experience of codependency; relational problems in the present are the other. Codependents struggle with being controlled by the perceived or real opinions and actions of others (and, in turn, seeking to control others). Again, alongside therapeutic counseling methods, we can use the Scriptures to help bring spiritual healing into the counseling room.

First, the Bible sets out clear guidelines for our duties in relationships. If codependents love in order to get love, this ruling motive must be replaced by the duty to love unconditionally as an ambassador of Christ. As counselees understand this duty, pastors and counselors can then work together with them to specify exactly what love would look like in this unique situation.

The second prong of biblical healing is for counselees to begin knowing, deep inside, that "we love because he first loved us" (1 John 4:19). The transformation from *needing* others to *loving* others is impossible without looking to Jesus as both the model and the One who empowers us to love. Codependents can begin to define themselves as *responders* to God's loving initiative. With an ever-growing understanding of God's grace, all of us can become God-dependent lovers of others.

—*Edward T. Welch*

Helping the Sexually Abused

It is easy to feel uncomfortable around young abuse victims. If we as counselors are too warm and understanding, perhaps the victim will perceive it as a come-on; if too distant, the victim won't develop sufficient trust. So how do we help the victim while remaining distant enough from the situation to be objective?

Guidelines

Here are three general guidelines that can help balance empathy and objectivity:

• *Listen ready to believe.* Child sexual-abuse victims disclose their painful story to an average of nine people before anyone believes them. They're usually told by the abuser that no one will believe their story. Unfortunately, it is often true that the victim's only escape from one adult's transgression is the righteous indignation of another adult.

Most children assume pastors are interested in truth, so many victims open up to them, even after refusing to give details to others.

Statistics tell us that only one in a thousand disclosures proves false, and most of these are misunderstood statements made to parents who turn frantic. The rest are usually from adolescent girls afraid they may have become pregnant by a boyfriend. False claims typically prove easy to check; the story changes as it is retold.

• *Blow the whistle wisely.* In nearly every state, pastors suspecting child abuse are *required* to notify authorities. But family members need to be told as well. Eighty percent of all sexual abuse occurs within the family. Fathers and step-fathers are the largest offender group. Then come other male relatives, then mothers, then baby-sitters. Only 9 percent of abusers are unknown to their victims.

Therefore, we frequently have the responsibility of informing a nonoffending parent about the details of the spouse's abuse. The best way is the direct way: "Your child found it too difficult to talk with you about this subject, so I'm compelled to tell you myself. Susie is being sexually abused by your husband."

This head-on approach has two advantages. First, the shock value definitely gets the parent's attention. Second, if we begin to waffle and say, "Well, we're not really sure if it's true, but we think maybe there could be something possibly wrong . . ." the parent will rarely act on what we report. Coming across as unsure, we give the parent license to act as if nothing is happening, and that's counterproductive. Directness imparts a sense of certainty and urgency.

• *Keep the proper distance.* We should steer away from making long-term promises to the victim of sexual abuse. The victim needs to understand our role as counselors and that we cannot be on twenty-four-hour call.

This rule is as much for the victim's good as it is for our own sanity. Sexual-abuse victims often feel the need to cling to those who show love and affection. To compensate for the lack in the past, they often will demand too much from the counselor.

For example, one young victim of abuse phoned me an average of three to four times a day. At least once a day, she would ask me to come over to counsel her. She frequently hinted at suicide, as if my refusal would set off a regrettable but inevitable chain of events. I finally had to tell her, "You just can't keep calling me like this. Let me tell you the reasons for your calls as I see them." I went on to tell her my understanding of *why* she was calling: her strong need for affirmation, her dependency, her fear of being rejected.

Support groups for victims and families, when guided by a sympathetic pastor or lay leader, can become a unique forum for significant sharing and prayer. They both help the victims and remove some of the need for excessive clinging to the counselor.

—Michael E. Phillips

Counseling Abusers

It's hard to counsel people who we may consider unlikable or who deeply repel us because of their shocking actions. Christian counselors frequently struggle with this problem when working with sexual and physical abusers, even though they know that *every* form of sin is offensive to God. Counselors who feel unable to put their feelings of disgust or contempt aside should be honest about this fact and be prepared to make a referral.

When we do take on abuse cases, we need to remind ourselves that abusers are not all alike. There is a significant difference, for example, between "normal" and "abnormal" abuse. Normal abuse is the kind most people *could* be tempted to commit, such as striking a spouse in the heat of an argument. This type of abuse is by far the most common, and the abuser is often able to change the behavior with adequate counseling.

Abnormal abuse, on the other hand, is the kind that most people would *not* be tempted to commit under any circumstance, such as sexually molesting a child. While it gets much publicity, abnormal abuse is much less common than the other type, and the prognosis for the abuser is not encouraging.

The process of counseling the abuser should focus on two pursuits: to monitor the client to reduce the risk of further offense, and to address the root problems—the deeper psychological, relational, or systemic reasons the abuse occurs.

Monitoring the Client

Regardless of people's stated intention to change, they should not be placed in a position to abuse again until they are making significant progress on the root problems. The question "Can he be trusted?" is best answered by "He can be trusted to be exactly who he is." Even though he or she may have legitimately sought and received forgiveness, the psychological sources of the abuse no doubt remain. In other words, forgiveness does not insure that sinful behavior will not repeat itself. While some Christians may feel this is unduly judgmental, the counselor has a duty to help abusers by assisting them in avoiding the temptation to sin.

We can monitor clients at two levels. At the first level, we provide accountability partners who maintain contact with the abuser whenever he or she might have access to a potential victim. This type of monitoring also provides schedules and structures to help the client avoid tempting situations altogether. The second level is involuntary monitoring or legal constraint, such as putting into effect court restraining orders, electronic monitoring, or institutionalization.

Addressing the Root Problems

Physical and sexual abuse often flow from the abuser's own history of being an abused child. In such situations, the abuser will not change without fully exploring the deep woundedness of the past. When the counselor is not able to work with these foundational issues on a long-term basis, the abuse is likely to happen again and again.

While a pastor may continue to work with an abuser in a specific role, abusers should be referred to trained counselors who specialize in working with such cases when: (1) the abuse fits the "abnormal" description, (2) the abuser has a history of previous abuse, (3) the abuser is unrepentant or justifies the behavior, (4) the abuser is not making progress dealing with root problems.

In counseling abusers, we must not forget that our first responsibility is to those who cannot protect themselves—the victims. Even if the abuser does not respond to counseling, he or she can be monitored to prevent an opportunity to abuse again.

—*Randy Christian*

Job and Vocational Counseling

Pastors often serve on the front lines of job and vocational counseling. Young people come to us searching for ways to invest their lives in the world of work. Adults come, seeking guidance for potential career changes. Retired people find their way to our doors, looking for new challenges. Pink-slip victims seek us out, too — confused, angry, and disheartened — needing support and direction.

Counseling Guidelines

Here are some general guidelines for conducting counseling sessions with all kinds of job seekers.

• *Concentrate on passion more than perks.* God created people with a variety of interests. One person's passion is another's prison, and no matter how many perks come with a job, if a person doesn't enjoy it, he or she will find it hard to continue for long. While every job has its tedious or disappointing aspects, when we're in the right vocation, our passion usually outweighs the pain. As counselors, we can help people explore and identify the kinds of activities that genuinely interest and motivate them — a productive first step.

• *Look for intrinsic value in the vocation.* Our level of commitment to a career is directly related to our perception of how much we are needed. Pastors can help by encouraging job seekers to identify the intrinsic value of a potential vocation. If people know that others really do need them and what they provide through their work, they will enjoy their work more, even if it is difficult. If, however, people feel that they and what they do are unimportant to others, then no matter how well they are paid, they will find little joy in their work.

• *Have people count the cost of becoming competent.* Just being interested in a vocation isn't enough. Louis Pasteur once said, "In the field of observation, chance favors only the prepared minds." The same principle holds true in vocational searches: opportunity favors the prepared. Competence is essential in our competitive age, and the prerequisite to competence is the discipline to prepare.

The dictionary defines *vocation* not only as a "divine call to . . . a career or occupation" but also as a "sense of fitness for a career or occupation." We can help people test the reality of their desires by asking them to consider: *Am I really prepared to become a disciple of this vocation?* And we will want to be ready with suggestions about where to get good training if the client answers in the affirmative.

• *Minister to emotional needs after a job loss.* When people lose their jobs, they experience *grief* over the loss of meaningful activities, colleagues, self-esteem, confidence, and self-reliance; *anger* at being terminated; *fear* about financial needs; and *depression* (anger turned inward), accompanied by a sense of helplessness and hopelessness. The counselor must work at two levels in such cases, providing both a listening ear during a time of great stress and offering practical resources for finding training and new employment opportunities.

• *Confirm the call through the church.* The church ought to confirm a Christian's vocational calling. When we find our calling, we sense our lives are fitting into a field of work consistent with who God has made us to be. Our inner awareness, however, can be confirmed, expanded, or corrected by others because God's call has both personal and corporate dimensions. Since vocation grows from the awareness that God uses people to meet the needs of others, the church can help awaken people to their true callings.

—*Michael Jinkins*

Counseling Cult Members

"My daughter has joined a religious cult. What can I do?" Sometime in ministry it's likely a parent will say this to us. It is a moment of enormous emotional and spiritual importance. Our response will depend on the answers we give to five key questions.

Short-term Questions

• *Is the cult dangerous?* The first thing to determine is whether or not the young person is in any physical or psychological danger. Determine the degree of danger by finding out as much as possible about the living arrangements and whether drugs are involved. Cult-watching groups, such as the Cult Awareness Network, can provide information about whether sleep and food deprivation or techniques of isolation are being used.

• *Is illegal activity involved?* Contact the police as a good source of information about different cults' illegal activities in particular locales. Don't hesitate to get law-enforcement officials involved, should either danger or illegality be present.

A positive answer to either of these short-term questions calls for immediate action.

Long-term Questions

Negative answers to those first two questions means we can focus on three long-term questions:

• *Why is this cult attractive to this person?* Sooner or later we may get a chance to counsel not only the parents but also the son or daughter involved. We need to probe to find out why the person thinks this cult is so important. Common answers include the chance to choose one's own religion, the warm community and friends the cult offers, the esoteric nature of the cult, or a fascination with the "spiritual technology" being offered. Cults typically have a sure-fire path to holiness that can be very attractive.

Once we have determined the attraction, we can begin—gently—to point out that Christianity can offer the same values. It's good to be prepared with readings the person can study. Often cult members, so motivated to discover new truths, will be impressed with the radical demands that true Christian holiness requires.

• *What is best in the long run for this person?* Patience is extremely important. Often the person is *not* ready to listen to the radical claims of Christianity and will not hear our incisive analysis of the cult in question. Then we must be patient. Maintaining the relationship is extremely important.

The average tenure in cult membership is less than two years. If no danger or illegality is involved, we can prepare for the time in the not-too-distant future when the person grows disillusioned with the cult.

• *What are my resources?* Resources will differ somewhat, depending on the person. We may work with unusually understanding parents who can rise above their natural anxiety and patiently wait and love along with us. Perhaps friends in the church will actively support the person. But three things in particular are required of the counselor:

First is knowledge of the cult in question. We must learn all we can about the experience the counselee is going through. This means studying the history, beliefs, and practices of the particular group.

Second, a listening ear. The new cult member desperately needs a sympathetic sounding board for ideas he or she is exploring. We need to be honest in our responses but also unconditional in our love.

Third, an active faith. Young people in particular often run to cults out of disillusionment with the faith of their family. More than anything, these persons need to see in us a faith that is alive and positive. We don't need to denigrate the cult in question; that is usually counterproductive. However, we do need to be an unquestioned champion and model of true, winsome Christian faith.

—*Terry C. Muck*

Part VI:

Christian Education

A major undertaking in any church is the perfection of the saints. Upon genuine profession of faith, Christians are as saved as they ever will be. But growth into Christlikeness is another matter, a process we dare curtail only when people "reach unity in the faith and in the knowledge of the Son of God and become mature, attaining to the whole measure of the fullness of Christ" (Eph. 4:13).

That may be a while. Until then, churches have a lot of Christian-education work to do.

But it's a good kind of work. It involves teaching and caring, planning and programming, sleeping on lumpy camp mattresses and participating in silly skits, budgeting for purchases and making do with less than we'd like. There's a lot of person-to-person interchange, plenty of opportunity for creativity, and definitely the need for volunteers—lots of volunteers who require training and managing and motivating.

It's also a difficult kind of work. Burnout remains an ever-present danger. Often the 80-20 rule applies: 80 percent of the work gets accomplished by 20 percent of the workers. Mix in the range of students' ages and life situations, the growing demand for variety in church programs, the never-complete nature of the education task, and the feeling that "every time I turn around, it's Sunday again," and it's no wonder Christian educators are a weary—though dedicated—lot.

A ministry so vital yet so complex ought to come with a complete set of instructions. Such a guide would fill several CD-ROM discs on the church computer, but the next-best solution probably would be a compendium of counsel from knowledgeable practitioners. That is exactly what follows.

22

The Purpose of Christian Education

Christian education is ideally a comprehensive approach to teaching and learning. It should affect every aspect of life and touch every human domain as it promotes an ongoing maturing process. This can be illustrated by exploring some basic questions about the nature of Christian instruction, looking at its theological foundations, historical background, and future directions.

Theological Foundations

Any group that values its heritage is interested in educating its future generations. Accordingly, the church must work from a clear definition of Christian instruction. By asking a series of questions about Christian education, we can give it a comprehensive description that is related to its theological roots.

• *What is Christian education?* Robert Pazmiño (1988, 81) offers six key characteristics. First, Christian education is *intentional.* It is planned, systematic, and extended over time. Second, and conversely, Christian education may also be *unintentional,* when, for instance, a teacher unintentionally displays a critical attitude toward certain students (in other words, Pazmiño's definition embraces not only intended results but any other outcomes of a teaching situation). Third, Christian education involves *shared responsibility,* since both divine and human efforts must work together. Fourth, Christian education deals with *multiple areas of learning,* including the "knowledge, values, attitudes, skills, sensitivities, and behaviors" of the participants. The fifth component of Christian education highlights the *need for change,* emphasizing personal growth while promoting strong interpersonal relationships within the church. Finally, the best Christian education advocates *a prescriptive end point,* teaching believers to "conform to the revealed will of God as expressed in the Old and New Testaments and preeminently in the person of Jesus Christ."

• *Who does Christian education include?* In a word, Christian education stands for community, which might be represented by three concentric relationship rings. The innermost ring would represent the *family,* the core of all Christian nurture. Parents receive God's call to instruct their children (Prov. 1:8; Eph. 6:4) and find many practical domestic strategies in his Word (Deut. 6:1–9; Col. 3:21). The Bible prizes family-centered education (2 Tim. 1:5).

The second relational ring represents the *church,* the extended family. From the beginning of the church, the apostles educated believers about their Savior and his teachings and about their obligation to care for one another's physical needs (Acts 6:1–7).

The third relational ring incorporates the entire *world,* the community-at-large. James condenses the Christian's life task into two assignments: to keep "oneself from being polluted by the world" (1:27b) and the parallel need "to look after orphans and widows in their distress" (1:27a). In the latter command, why are these two types of people singled out? Because God cares deeply about any loss of community, epitomized by the plight of many orphans and widows throughout the world. The "Who?" of Christian instruction, then, attends to the lifelong human need for belonging.

• *Why is Christian education done?* Discussions about the ultimate purpose of Christian teaching and learning are surprisingly rare. When it is discussed, slogans such as "to glorify God" surface immediately. Although such phrases are theologically correct, they are just vague enough to cause confusion.

Ronald Habermas and Klaus Issler (1992, 33–57) suggest the ultimate purpose of Christian education is *reconciliation,* drawing from 2 Corinthians 5:17–6:1 and Colossians 1:19–23. This ultimate purpose would then consist of four subtasks: (1) communion with God (through worship and prayer); (2) community within the body of Christ (through encouragement and admonition); (3) character formation (through godly thinking (Phil. 4:8) and godly living (Micah 6:8)); and (4) commission (applying one's spiritual gifts and responding to God's calling).

• *When does Christian education occur?* Effective Christian education purposefully connects the past, the present, and the future. This avoids the twin pitfalls of irreverence (forgetting the past) and irrelevance (ignoring the present and the future). Biblical Christian education makes use of a kind of "time travel" strategy, as illustrated in Deut. 6:20–24. Consider the nouns and verbs that identify aspects of time in this passage: "In the *future,* when your son asks you, 'What is the meaning of the stipulations, decrees, and laws the Lord our God has *commanded* you?' *tell* him: 'We *were* slaves of Pharaoh in Egypt, but the Lord *brought* us out of Egypt with a mighty hand. . . . The Lord *commanded* us to obey all these decrees and to fear the Lord our God, so that we *might always prosper* and *be kept alive,* as is the case *today.*' "

Parents pass their faith on to their children using this connect-the-dots perspective of time when they recall God's historical acts of leadership and goodness. Through persistent obedience, God's people display the relationship between past faith and future hope.

- *Where does Christian education happen?* Christian instruction occurs in three types of places, illustrated by Paul's farewell to the Ephesian elders. *Formal* and *nonformal* settings are respectively illustrated when the Apostle testified that he proclaimed God's Word "publicly and from house to house" (Acts 20:20). The first phrase pertains to a structured design; the second centers on less structured environments. The third setting reflects the least structured, the *informal.* Paul testified: "You know how I lived the whole time I was with you . . . with great humility and with tears" (Acts 20:18, 19).

In addition to types of places, we can include references to people when asking about the location of Christian education. *Domains* of human growth and *dimensions* of learning especially demand attention. Habermas and Issler (1992, 77–79) state that Elijah's conflict with Queen Jezebel (1 Kings 19) highlights interrelated human domains. Elijah's spiritual condition was negatively affected by his fear of Jezebel (the emotional domain); his paranoia, which led to separation from his servant (the social domain); his subsequent exhaustion (the physical domain); his request to die (the intellectual and psychological domains); and his later distress over injustice (the moral domain). Each domain shaped Elijah's spiritual state, and God purposefully supplied sufficient resources to meet each domain's need (for example, food and sleep were provided to meet his physical exhaustion).

Along with domains of growth, we can discern three dimensions of learning in the Scriptures. The results of Peter's sermon at Pentecost indicate that "when the people *heard* this, they were cut to the *heart* and said to Peter and the other apostles, 'Brothers, what shall we *do?*" (Acts 2:37). Here comprehensive Christian education encompasses the cognitive, affective, and behavioral dimensions of learning, respectively.

- *How is Christian education accomplished?* What means should we use to proclaim God's truth? An insightful, concise passage that addresses this matter is Matthew 17:24–27. Following an encounter between Peter and the tax collectors, Jesus initiates a discussion with this disciple about taxes. Subsequently, the Lord directs Peter to locate the necessary money inside a fish and to pay the taxes for both of them. In just four verses, the Master Teacher models seven guidelines for accomplishing Christian education.

First, instruction must be *relational.* Jesus personalizes his teaching in this passage when he calls Peter by his familiar name, Simon. Christian education should also be *meaningful* (dealing with a relevant topic, like taxes) and *dialogical* (illustrated by the Master's intentional conversation, being the "first to speak").

The fourth and fifth guidelines reveal that Christian instruction must be *honorable* (Christ did not want to cause offense (27a)) as well

The Pastor as Teacher, Catechist, Discipler

Someone has observed that average church members know their way around the local restaurant guide better than they know their way around the life of Jesus in the Gospels, and that they are more comfortable with the working of their home computer than they are with the dynamics of life in the Spirit. This state of affairs calls for teaching pastors, those who have diligently given themselves to the teaching side of the pastor-teacher role (Eph. 4:12).

Resident Theologians

Leaders like Elton Trueblood and John Stott have argued that the local church needs to think of itself as a seminary (a center for in-depth theological reflection on everyday life) and for pastors to think of themselves as resident theologians. In this view, a Christian pastor embraces and exercises the high calling of rabbi: one who serves God's people as teacher, catechist, and disciple-maker.

• *Teacher.* We pastors must find ways to teach "the whole counsel of God" (Acts 20:27), creatively taking God's people through the whole Scriptures. Obviously, this cannot be done on Sundays alone; for one thing, there is no opportunity during the sermon for questions and answers, something so necessary for real learning. So we need to offer classes and seminars at other times during the week. We can either develop our own materials (which can be tremendously rewarding) or work with the excellent resources now available in book and audio-video form.

The best teachers are, of course, those who are themselves still students. This means we'll need to give ourselves to regular, in-depth study of Scripture. Pastors who are discovering new insights in the Word

as *practical* (Peter's "assignment" to pay the tax carried specific instructions and was based on his skills and interests (vs. 27b)). Also, Christ's education was *responsible.* He instilled in Peter a sense of duty, prompting him to pay the debt for Jesus and himself. Finally, the Master Teacher modeled *memorable* instruction, for his disciple no doubt recalled the lessons each time taxes were due.

What strategies, then, should parents and educators actually follow? In general, similar to depositing money in a savings account, they must make rich deposits into the memory banks of their children. Such deposits then yield priceless living and coping resources for the future.

The Bible furnishes three specific strategies, all portrayed in the Passover Feast (Exod. 12:11–14). First, educators must establish *significant memorials* (recall other memorials, such as the twelve stones

---

are eager to teach, and the flock senses it and will eagerly want to be taught.

- *Catechist.* Along with teaching the Scriptures, we resident theologians can help God's people grapple with the foundational affirmations of the Christian faith, leading church members into an appreciation of the what and why of Christian doctrine. For example, we can teach people what they are really saying when they recite the Apostles' Creed or their church's statement of faith. In years past the catechism served this purpose, a mini systematic theology covering the essential ingredients of the Christian world-view. In some places people could not join the church until they had worked their way through the catechism. Again, we can develop our own materials or work with other resources in this area. We can carry out this responsibility through new-member seminars, small groups, or one-on-one meetings.
- *Discipler.* "Jesus is Lord" is a statement affecting every arena of human existence. We pastors are called to help people see how that is so, showing them how the great facts of the gospel speak to what is happening in the world. This will involve demonstrating how they can live out the "in the world, but not of it" tension in their finances, family life, marriage, sexuality, recreation choices, and work situations. Our calling is to give God's people a new set of glasses for a new vision of reality shaped by the gospel.

This, of course, will be a constant challenge for us personally, as we continually ask questions like: Do I do what I do because of cultural pressures or because of my allegiance to Jesus Christ and his kingdom? Am I living in my own power or in the power of the Holy Spirit?

Can you think of any greater calling or challenge—to teach God's Word, to unpack the church's creeds, to guide folks along the way of discipleship?

—Darrell Johnson

in the Jordan River (Josh. 4:1–20) and the Lord's Supper (Luke 22:19)). Second, educators must revere *healthy relationships* among teachers and learners, prizing qualities such as sincere conversation. In Exodus 12, for instance, children actually introduce questions about faith for their parents to answer. Third, educators must highlight *experiential faith.* When children inquire of parents: "What does this ceremony mean *to you?*" (Exod. 12:25), parents must be ready to respond with personal examples of faith in action.

Christian Education's History

Retaining the spirit of time travel, Pazmiño (1988, 150) states: "Viewing the past provides a rootedness from which to address the challenge of the present and future world." What are the roots of our Christian education task?

No nation ever focused more attention on educating children than the Jewish nation. This culture's approach to education was exclusively religious, since Scriptures represented the sole curriculum. The parents' primary objective was to pass on their faith to the next generation (see Deut. 4:9–10; 32:7; Prov. 10:1; 23:24; Ps. 78:4). The means of Jewish education varied. On the one hand, oral instruction and memorization of the Torah were standard; on the other hand, the celebration of the Jewish feasts (especially Passover, Pentecost and the Festival of Tabernacles) provided more interactive and experiential learning.

During the era marked by the fall of Jerusalem in 586 B.C., God often educated through the prophetic voices of Jeremiah, Ezekiel, Daniel, and others. The "schools of the prophets," described in the ministries of Elijah and Elisha (2 Kings 2:3–5; 4:38; 6:1) also contributed. In response to the conditions of the Exile, the synagogue system of education emerged. Given its instructional objectives, some have compared the synagogue to a popular religious university. Scribes took on prominent roles as public teachers. Yet schools, as they are known today, were not mentioned until Paul's ministry at the Tyrannus "lecture hall" (Acts 19:9).

Whereas Greek education did stress certain aspects of moral living, the Greek world view, in general, opposed that of the Jews. The Greek city of Sparta, for example, emphasized an education system ultimately designed to prepare young men for war: to teach them to obey commands, to endure hardships, and to be victorious. Barclay (1974) concludes that the Athenian ideal was to achieve unlimited leisure in order to pursue unlimited culture. To attain this goal, male citizens prized slavery and neglected their women. Followers of Socrates sought a moral order based on rationalism. Plato's disciples promoted an idealistic dualism, viewing the "real" as qualities established in the mind or in the heavens, with material qualities of the body being merely a dim shadow of reality. Aristotle's students espoused realism, classifying biological and botanical data and practicing the earliest forms of scientific experimentation. Finally, the Sophists advocated skepticism about any possibility of a reality beyond mere material existence, a point of view that characterizes contemporary philosophies of relativism even today.

Pazmiño (1988) believes the early church (in the second to fourth centuries) weathered the religious pluralism of its Hellenistic-Roman world by adhering to three educational anchors: (1) the *canon,* the documents accepted as Scripture, the final authority; (2) the *rule of faith,* theological resources that accompanied Scripture, such as the Apostles' Creed; and (3) the *church order,* guidelines for community organization and discipline. In these early years, *catechumenal* schools were created to preserve doctrinal fidelity, with curriculum comparable to today's forms of instruction for new believers and for baptismal candidates. *Catechetical* schools provided more advanced training, somewhat similar to our seminaries today. Two primary interpretative approaches to Scripture arose in these schools: an allegorical method of biblical education began at Alexandria; the historical-literal method prevailed at Antioch.

Various convictions about truth, education, and mission distinguished the church fathers. Tertullian (c. 160–220), finding nothing of value for the Christian within the Hellenistic culture, refused to let believers teach at secular schools. Origen (c. 185–254), the greatest scholar of that time, offered a broad curriculum with virtually no subject forbidden to his students as they studied the best of secular culture. Later, Augustine (354–430) held a similar position, valuing a form of sensory learning that would lead to absolute knowledge. For him, all truth was God's truth.

The quality of church education in the medieval era (from the fifth to the mid-fourteenth centuries) plummeted downward. Constantine's legalization of Christianity in the early fourth century initially brought vitality, or so it appeared. But catechumenal school instruction became corrupted by the middle of the fifth century, and by the seventh century, it had vanished. Not only did parents and extended family members have extremely limited knowledge of basic Christian doctrines, many clergy also suffered from the same ignorance.

B. L. Marthaler (1990) notes a shift from verbal to visual, from formal to nonformal instruction. That is, since the majority of church members were illiterate during this period, drama, architecture, and other forms of symbolic imagery offered the new means of education, primarily through worship and daily mass. Church leaders emphasized sacred times (Lent and Advent), sacred places (wayside shrines), and sacred people (the clergy, marked by their distinctive clothing).

Formal education in the church, besides listening to preaching, was reduced to learning the Apostles' Creed, the Lord's Prayer, and the Ten Commandments.

Gradually, a handful of universities sprang up about A.D. 1200. They were influenced by the monastic schools and cathedral schools (formerly a part of the catechetical education). Scholasticism (a result of Aquinas's work in 1224–1274) reigned as the predominant philosophy, attempting to combine faith and reason.

The Renaissance (from the mid-fourteenth to the sixteenth centuries) brought renewal to learning through a revived interest in classical studies. However, since this revival focused on a return to insights from the ancient Greeks, the Renaissance was, for the most part, based in humanism. In contrast, the Reformation (from the sixteenth to seventeenth centuries) promoted a theistic focus. Catechetical reform was particularly significant during this period.

Reformers stressed the sole authority of Scripture, justification by faith alone, and the priesthood of all believers. Luther (1483–1546) promoted universal compulsory education, partially for the purposes of biblical literacy. Calvin (1509–1564) devised a comprehensive educational and political system in Geneva, attempting to create a Christian society. Both men conducted extensive Bible-translation projects and developed influential catechisms.

Roman Catholic responses to the Reformers included development of the Douay-Reims version of Scripture in the common language; the organization of the Council of Trent (1545–1563) which redirected clergy education; and Ignatius of Loyola's founding of the Jesuit order, which furthered the cause of Christian schools.

Robert Pazmiño (1988) summarizes educator–church historian Lawrence Cremin's assessment of the modern Christian education era (from the mid-seventeenth century to the present) this way: *The colonial period* (1607–1783) highlighted the family and church as key institutions. During this time, three distinctive educational structures were fashioned: in New England, a common school plan, which led to current public school models; in the middle colonies, a parochial plan; and in the South, a private school plan using tutors. Complementary functions of the family and church helped shape the values and training of this time.

The national period (1783–1876) gave rise to the eventual separation of church and state. The church and in some measure the public schools were now entrusted to provide the country's moral education.

The metropolitan period (1876–1986) promoted a thorough secularization of life. The church has played a marginal role during this last period, even with the rise of multiple parachurch organizations. Society now looks to the public schools and child-rearing or rehabilitative agencies to educate children and to improve society.

Future Directions

How can we guide Christian education into a fruitful future? The key is to keep asking the kinds of questions that will help us evaluate where we've been and where we want to go. At least three broad categories of inquiry emerge.

First, we must constantly inquire about the nature of *truth:* the sources of truth (What part does natural theology play?), the interpretation of truth (When do we use literal or allegorical exegetical methods appropriately?), the structuring of truth into doctrinal positions (How should our doctrinal positions compare and contrast with those of the Puritans, for instance?), and the integration of truth (How can "all truth is God's truth" be applied to teaching and learning in Christian colleges?).

The second category that requires a careful exploration for the future is *people:* investigating the meaning of human nature (What does the image of God mean?), analyzing how people learn and grow (What can we learn from Piaget's model of cognitive development?), and understanding human similarities and differences (How can Frobel's age-appropriate sensitivity theories—which generated in the first kindergarten—be emulated in methods of Christian education?).

Finally—and most important—the inquiry into *purpose* deserves attention if we are to guide future Christian instruction effectively. Many Christian educators seem divided over their objectives in ways that did not characterize past approaches to instruction. For example, the first monastery in the West, founded by Benedict of Nursia (480–547), took on a position of separation from society–clearly assuming a posture of isolation from the community-at-large–fostering strict discipleship. In contrast, the monastery of Cluny, founded in central France in 910, integrated monasticism with the surrounding culture, hoping to infiltrate society with Christian values. Each had a different purposes, but both clearly articulated their objectives.

Believers today may opt for such divergent purposes or for other purposes, resulting in vastly different approaches and outcomes. Yet the future direction and health of Christian education will, as always, be governed by the quality of the answers we give to this overarching question (Matt. 5:13, 14): "What does it mean to be 'the salt of the earth' and 'the light of the world'?"

—*Ronald T. Habermas*

Resources

Barclay, W. 1974. Educational ideals in the ancient world. Grand Rapids: Baker.

Gangel, K., and W. Benson. 1983. Christian education. Chicago: Moody.

Habermas, R., and K. Issler. 1992. Teaching for reconciliation. Grand Rapids: Baker.

Marthaler, B. 1990. The medieval period. In Harper's encyclopedia of religious education. San Francisco: Harper & Row.

Pazmiño, R. 1988. Foundational issues in Christian education. Grand Rapids: Baker.

23

Planning Christian Education

Christian education has changed significantly in the last one hundred years. In the early 1900s, it was almost exclusively considered a Sunday school program for young children. In the 1950s its role expanded to include programs for youth and young families. Recent years have seen a virtual explosion of new areas of educational involvement in the church and community.

The Christian education program at one church will probably look different from that in the church down the road. No one model works for all churches. The size of the church, the denomination it represents, the demographics of the surrounding community, the available facilities and leadership, the funding resources, and a host of other variables will shape the kind of program a church develops.

A church's Christian education program is one of the most exciting areas of church involvement for the believer. Bringing people to personal faith in Christ and nurturing their spiritual growth is at the heart of Christian education. It ignites a passion for shared ministry on the part of the laity and helps them catch a vision for what their church can do. Consequently, volunteer leaders become disciples as they help fulfill the Great Commission.

Programming Christian Education

Understanding and applying a few basic insights will help a pastor effectively program the church's Christian education ministries.

Though simple to explain, they are challenging to implement. Yet the hard work on behalf of growing Christians will be worth it.

• *Insight #1: Christian education programs must be based on current needs.* Churches sometimes attempt to develop a new program that looks great on paper back at the home offices of the denomination, only to find that three weeks into the program it fails for lack of congregational support. Though the new program may have sizzled in the promotional materials, it simply cannot take into consideration the unique needs of each specific congregation. In addition, because these needs change with time, it is a constant challenge to stay in touch with them.

Demographic changes occur subtly in the church and community. The closing of a military installation or large-scale layoffs at a major corporation may have obvious affects on a church. However, the slow progress of ethnic variance, minor economic shifts, aging within the membership, and other social trends can also have a profound impact on the demographics of a given church and community. As each family moves in or out of a church, those moves alter the needs of the congregation.

The early church developed programs on the basis of their current needs. Whether it was creating the first board of deacons (Acts 6:1–6), establishing a pattern of home fellowships for Bible study and prayer (Acts 2:42–47), or forming a missionary-sending enterprise (Acts 13), the church developed programs on the basis of its immediate needs. Their clearly established rationale for beginning new ministries in the church should be ours as well.

Each year or two, a church's leadership team should conduct an informal assessment of congregational needs, asking themselves about changes that have occurred within the congregation. Have there been any major demographic shifts recently? Has anything occurred in the life of the church or community that would require a new program expansion? Does the church have any programs that aren't meeting people's needs as they once were? Could certain programs be combined to conserve resources? Questions such as these can help identify the current needs of a congregation and community.

• *Insight #2: Christian education programs should specifically relate to each particular church.* In the New Testament, we find ministry programs developed in one church were not always replicated in others. People in the Jerusalem church had different needs from those in the church at Antioch or Corinth. These social, cultural, religious, and geographical differences required a different approach to ministry programming.

In our day, I once served as an associate pastor in a church that was trying to decide whether to begin a ministry to single adults. I suggested holding off on developing such a program in order to further strengthen our ministry to children in the community. Already several churches within a few miles had thriving singles ministries. Only one other church had a midweek children's program, however, and although ours was one of the best in the city, it still needed improvement. In this case, the church leaders needed assurance that it was all right *not* to be all things to all people. What works for one church may not work—or even be needed—at another church just a few miles away.

• *Insight #3: Successful Christian education programs require the involvement of the entire congregation.* The theological doctrine of the priesthood of all believers indicates that God desires all of his people to be involved in ministry. There should be no ministry spectators in the church, since all members are called into action. Effective performance, however, presupposes a basic understanding of spiritual gifts and their relationship to church ministry.

Ephesians 4:11–16 states that all members of the body of Christ have been given at least one spiritual gift for the purpose of contributing to the work of the congregation and the mutual edification of believers. Gifts such as apostle, prophet, evangelist, and teacher are provided by God to form the foundation of ministry involvement.

Without a knowledge of their giftedness, people cannot be expected to engage in ministry. These gifts are to be employed in the equipping and building up of the local church to the point that it is stable and spiritually mature. As this growth occurs, the church will be unified (v. 15) and should experience numerical development (v. 16). Christian education ministry is based on helping people learn their areas of giftedness, seeking to involve these individuals in service at the points of greatest need within the body.

Organizing for Effective Ministry

The goal of any Christian education program is to meet as many needs in the congregation and community as is reasonable. This requires some forethought about how the overall program should be structured. How one goes about organizing the Christian education program of a local church depends to a large extent on the size of the church, itself. Small churches (under 200), medium churches (200–750), and large churches (over 750) require different organizational structures:

• *In the small church,* the traditional approach to organizing the Christian education program was to create a committee composed of coordinators from each church educational group, for example: Sunday school, youth group, vacation Bible school, children's church, and so on. However, although the formation of an oversight committee proved helpful, the division along agency lines did not. This approach required a great number of people with administrative skills and led to a good deal of overlap in program administration. It also contributed to competition for limited facilities, leaders, and material resources.

A better way to organize a small church's Christian education program is to create an oversight committee and divide the responsibilities according to age levels: children, youth, adults, and so on. This approach allows one person to oversee the various programs within each age level. For example, the childhood-level coordinator would oversee children's church, Sunday school, VBS, and any midweek program offered. Such an approach eliminates administrative overlap and requires fewer trained administrative coordinators.

Audio-Visual Equipment and Resources

The latest gizmos for fantastic media presentations will amaze you. In the audio-visual publications, you discover a dazzling array of equipment and materials, all "mandatory" for effectiveness. But it's wise to resist the attitude that you can't use AV effectively without the very latest products.

The Well-equipped A-V Closet

The race to stay current will frustrate any teacher. We'll no doubt have to settle for "recent" rather than "the latest." As one seminary professor advised his students, "Be not the first by whom the new is tried, nor the last to lay the old aside."

Churches and Christian institutions would do well to supply their A-V arsenal with the following:

- *Overhead projectors.* You may have heard years ago that the lowly overhead was dead or dying. Not true. It still enjoys popularity in classrooms. While easy to use, it projects a big, bright picture, and now it interfaces with computers and other newer technologies.
- *Slide projectors.* Slides are cheaper than overhead transparencies. Some of the new projectors interface with computers for random access to any slide in the tray.
- *Video players and monitors.* Everybody knows how to operate a television, and most people are used to watching videos at home. Churches should be prepared to use this excellent teaching tool.
- *LCD panels or projectors.* Plug your multimedia computer and your VCR into one of these units to project big images for large groups.
- *An enlarging/reducing photocopier* for transparency production. Also, an inexpensive computer color printer will make visuals directly from your computer.

Audio-Visual Guidelines

Consider recruiting an "owner" of the A-V closet. A media program

In addition to the various age-level coordinators, the Christian education committee also has a chairperson who is a member of the church board. This person would serve as the designated overseer of Christian education.

• *In the medium-sized church,* normally a full-time staff member provides oversight and leadership. Generally referred to as a minister (or director) of Christian education, this person sometimes assumes the position of chairperson of the Christian education committee. He or she should have professional preparation in a Christian college or seminary and should be an excellent teacher and administrator.

As the church expands into the medium range, the age-level approach to organizing the Christian education programs can expand

flourishes when it becomes evident that somebody really cares. Here are a few other keys to keeping A-V alive and well:

• *Build a resource library.* Send a postcard to all equipment and materials vendors. Their frequent mailings will keep the church current.

• *Get by with more for less.* With some basic audio-visual resources and a can-do attitude, a church doesn't need all the latest gadgets to be effective. For example, instead of using expensive dry-erase marker boards, install white bathroom panels on classroom walls (they'll get stained, but they're cheap to replace). Or use write-on slides. With these, you project 35mm instructional slides directly on a white marker board and then write on the projected images with colored markers.

• *Establish good lighting control.* Dim the lights and cover the windows so your audience can see the pictures on the screen. (On the other hand, don't show small-screen videos in a totally darkened room, or you will cause severe eye strain.)

• *Schedule regular maintenance.* As someone has said, "With A-V, it's foresight or no sight." Keep spare lamps and backup equipment handy. Simply cleaning an overhead projector can give it new life.

• *Train operators.* Even the latest technology gathers dust when nobody knows how to use it, so regularly train teachers to use everything in the A-V closet.

• *Don't misuse small screens.* The number of video viewers should not exceed the diagonal measure of the screen. In other words, use a 14-inch screen for no more than 14 people. Use a video projector for large groups. To determine the proper screen size for overheads and slides, divide the screen-to-furthest-viewer distance by six—a thirty-foot distance requires a five-foot wide screen.

• *Don't encourage bad viewing angles.* Eastman Kodak recommends that no viewer should sit outside of an area 30 degrees on either side of the projector-screen axis.

—Donald P. Regier

with it. Each category can be further subdivided. The childhood coordinator's position might be divided into both early-childhood coordinator and elementary coordinator. The youth coordinator's position can be expanded into junior high coordinator and senior high coordinator, and so on.

In addition to introducing these age-level coordinators, a medium-sized church can expand the Christian education committee to include a Christian service director and also an outreach coordinator. The Christian service director coordinates the selection of leaders and oversees the various programs' training needs. Having one person who oversees the recruitment and basic training of church volunteers helps prevent any one member of the church from being inundated by requests for involvement. It also makes sure each new worker gets a proper orientation and training experience.

- *In the large church,* a comprehensive program is required to meet

Nursery and Child Care

"What do we do about child care?" This is one of the most nagging questions faced by a pastoral staff as it plans its programs. Yet if the staff plans to enable parents to study, worship, and serve without worrisome concern over their youngsters, an effective child-care ministry is a must.

Advice for Effectiveness

A practical way to tackle the child-care problem is to recruit a ministry team. The group begins by developing a mission statement for the nursery and child-care ministry. This statement should address both the care of children and the outreach ministry to those whose babies are served. Loving care in clean, caring surroundings is essential, but we also must plan for the follow-up of visitors by someone from the child-care team. The team will want to discuss the use of music, stories, poetry, pictures, and other resources to create a teaching environment and perhaps even a structured teaching time for toddlers.

Here are other words of advice for effective child care:

- *Plan a budget.* Once the facility is in operation, needs may not be large. But some money will be needed to buy and replace equipment and supplies.
- *Develop a clear policy for hours and staffing.* Consider providing child care for each worship service as well as for other church occasions when the target audience is those with young children. Married couples frequently cannot or will not attend if child care is not provided. Special events may need to be staffed by the group planning the event, following stated policies.
- *Appoint a facilities supervisor.* This person then recruits, trains,

the numerous and diverse needs within both the congregation and the community. A Christian education program in a large church nearly always demands paid professional leaders at each age level—people who can provide the kind of experience church members will expect from a church of this size. Examples of the additional kinds of programs larger churches might offer include recovery groups, family-life programs, inner-city outreach projects, special-education ministries, latchkey ministries, and multi-ethnic programs.

In addition to having paid professionals who oversee the age-level programs, a large church will also want to develop an internship program. This program will help train one or two part-time leaders for each age level. In some cases, these interns will be Bible college or seminary students who are in training for a career in ministry. Adults considering a midlife career change into ministry also make excellent candidates for the internship positions.

---

and manages those who work in child care. Plan on one worker for every four children, and request reference checks on all volunteers. Require that *any* event have at least two child-care workers in each room. This policy can save much grief later on, should someone with a past record of child abuse volunteer to work in the program.

• *Don't skimp on space or equipment.* Churches need about 40 square feet of space per child. When there are more than 10 to 12 children for whom care will be given, more than one room is advisable, with care offered for only a narrow age range in each room. Rooms should be bright, cheerful, and colorful. Equip them with small cribs that take minimal space, play pens, a changing table properly supplied, storage areas for diaper bags and supplies, running water, and washable toys. *Sunday School Standards* by L. Brown (Gospel Light) gives a complete list of needed equipment and materials.

• *Set up a regular cleaning schedule.* The schedule should detail when sheets will be changed, toys and books washed, and floors vacuumed and mopped. A clean, sterilized room is impressive to fussy new parents. The supervisor for this program can implement the policy on a weekly basis.

• *Post a sign-in/sign-out sheet.* The sign-in system should include basic information, such as name, address, telephone number, special instructions for feeding and changing, and where the parents can be found at church. A sheet for parents can outline information on the services and rules of the nursery. Be sure parents understand that only a designated person may pick up the child—as a protection for the child.

The idea is to plan for excellence overall. This ministry may be unheralded, but it is extremely important and can become an excellent ministry of outreach and service.

—*Eleanor Daniel*

Leading for Success

An unfortunate reality of church life is that new programs require change, and change seldom comes easily for any congregation. Yet we can anticipate some of the problems that leading a Christian education program—with all its demands for change—will inevitably bring us. Here are some basic leadership strategies for confronting those problems head-on:

• *Expect some opposition.* A successful Christian education program will not blossom without challenges to those in leadership. Any new program forces the leaders to make decisions that affect the entire congregation. For example, when a church directs its outreach ministry toward the needs of street youth, a pastor should expect some opposition when these young people begin coming into the worship service.

Conducting "damage assessment" isn't taught in many seminary classrooms, but it is a helpful practice for a pastor to develop. Though not specifically biblical, the old adage that "an ounce of prevention is worth a pound of cure" contains plenty of truth.

• *Approach ministry as a team effort.* Both lay leaders and professional ministers usually develop some level of personal ownership in their areas of ministry. However, if carried to the extreme, this can undermine the church's overall effectiveness. No one program, no matter how successful, should be allowed to dominate the rest of the church.

Directing Christian education ministries will at times make us feel like the secretary-general to the United Nations. Such ministry requires diplomacy as we oversee people who have a zealous passion for their particular areas of ministry. However, distributing resources to one program while denying it to another will create some degree of tension and misunderstanding. Leadership requires wise decision making, and decisions must be made on the basis of what is best for the whole church, not just a special-interest group.

• *Don't strangle frontier ministries.* From time to time, people ask their pastors about starting a new ministry. Though these requests may come from well-meaning members, those making the request sometimes do not understand that most pastors are already overworked. When this occurs, the tired pastor may look for ways to gracefully deny the new program the church's support.

One of the best responses to such a request, however, is to turn the tables around and ask the person making the request to take ownership of the program. For example, I might tell the person the new ministry does not fit into the goals established by the governing board for that year. But if the requester would like to see such a program developed, he or she will need to assume the responsibility for the details of the ministry. In such a case, no church resources would be allocated to the new ministry until it has been in operation for a period of at least eighteen months.

Such an approach allows frontier ministries to be developed by those who have the passion to direct them, without sidetracking the church staff from their responsibilities. If the new ministry program begins and then dies in a couple of months for lack of involvement, it is not the church staff's responsibility to try and save it. But the fact remains that not all church programs have to be designed and developed by the professional pastor. Many of the most successful programs may have little or no pastor involvement at all.

We can take the counsel of Gamaliel to heart in these situations: If their plan of action is not of God, it will not last; but if it is of God, we won't want to end up fighting against him (see Acts 5:38–39).

• *Accept input from volunteers.* It is sometimes difficult for a minister to accept input from volunteers who have little or no ministry training. Accepting criticism about how a ministry is going is especially hard on the ego. It takes a great deal of self-control to receive the input without being defensive. However, the spiritual gifts of wisdom and knowledge also reside in lay leaders, and their input and recommendations can prove effective and beneficial.

When lay input is helpful or has prevented waste in the way a program operates, we should give the volunteers public recognition for their contributions. This encourages others to speak up when they have a suggestion, and it helps others in the congregation realize that their pastor is approachable. It also lets them know we are human and can make mistakes, too.

• *Don't view people as interruptions.* Successful Christian education programs involve detailed planning, staff recruitment and training, leadership development, conflict management, and constant assessment. The time constraints on the director of Christian education can be demanding. If we are not careful, we can become so fixed on accomplishing a goal that we forget the reason for doing the job in the first place. Christian education has the evangelism and discipleship of *people* as its primary purpose. We must never get so wrapped up in the development and maintenance of programs that we forget about people. Ultimately, only the people count!

• *Protect your own family.* Crises in the lives of our parishioners come at the most inconvenient times. Families don't always fall apart between 9:00 A.M. and 5:00 P.M. The minister who seeks to nurture people will need to be accessible beyond normal working hours. Naturally, this produces considerable stress on our personal and family life. Therefore, we must seek a balance between being accessible and protecting our family commitment.

In particular, a pastor who oversees Christian education programs will need to guard against overinvolvement in the details of the job. At some point, the pastor must learn to let go and let others assume responsibilities for the programs as well. If this important lesson is not learned early in ministry, the minister's own health, spiritual vitality, and family life will suffer.

Successful Christian education programs are exciting and contagious. When done right they can propel a congregation into shared ministry involvement. Healthy families are the building blocks of the local church, and programs that nurture family growth deserve the church's full attention and significant resources. Christian education programs should be viewed as the church's investment in the lives of the congregation, an investment that will reap rewards both in the current life of the church as well as in the eternal body of Christ.

—Michael Anthony

Resources

Anthony, M. ed., 1992. Foundations of ministry: An introduction to Christian education for a new generation. Wheaton, Ill.: Bridgepoint.

Gangel, K. 1985. The church education handbook. Wheaton, Ill.: Victor.

Gangel, K. 1989. Feeding and leading. Wheaton, Ill.: Victor .

Pazmiño, R. 1988. Foundational issues in Christian education. Grand Rapids: Baker.

Vacation Bible School

Vacation Bible school remains a great opportunity for teaching and outreach—if we plan carefully. Though the planning team must not overlook publicity, special events, preregistration, and arrangements for transportation, the major pre-VBS activities will center on recruiting the staff and selecting the curriculum.

Staff Work

The VBS team's basic decisions include dates of the program, time of day offered, goals and objectives, curriculum, and special emphases. This group sets policies and prepares an organizational guide to direct recruitment and preparation efforts. For help with planning, see *The ABC's of VBS* by Eleanor Daniel (Standard). It's wise to begin planning and recruiting early—no less than six months before the event to do the job well. Teams may, in fact, begin preliminary planning when VBS is over the year before.

Smart teams recruit plenty of workers so they can plan for small classes. This allows for outreach without any one class becoming unmanageable (the fastest route to worker burnout). The usual rule of thumb is to provide one worker for every four babies and toddlers, every five preschoolers, every six first and second graders, every seven third and fourth graders, every eight fifth and sixth graders, every ten junior highs, and every dozen teens.

The team should divide tasks so that no one person is overwhelmed. For example, recruit teachers' aides to assist with memory work, attendance taking, and other routine tasks, and recruit craft leaders and aides to handle that part. Plenty of support workers are needed—secretaries, kitchen workers, recreation leaders, supply clerks, and worship leaders. The more people involved in VBS, the greater the enthusiasm for it. The more people involved, the less the likelihood of worker burnout.

It takes plenty of work to recruit a staff. Likely recruits include Sunday school teachers, youth coaches, public school teachers who may not teach Sunday school regularly, newcomers to the congregation who may not yet have found a place of ministry, college students home for the summer, and high school students to assist an experienced teacher. And these workers need the necessary know-how and materials to do the job.

One idea that works well is to have a VBS director-in-training working alongside the current director, with the understanding that the person in training will lead the effort the following year. This arrangement assures continuity and creativity—and saves considerable supervisory time.

Curriculum and Followup

The choice of curriculum is critical. Most leadership teams prefer to select a published resource, while a few teams choose to develop their own materials. The wide array of colorful visuals, teacher's and pupil's books, songbooks, and environmental helps is the strong lure of commercial curriculum. The opportunity to meet specific needs is the appeal of developing curriculum locally. Whatever curriculum is chosen should be Bible-based, need-related, educationally sound, attractive, and easy to use, even by relatively untrained teachers.

Followup assures success. The planning team should have a strategy for contacting newcomers. They should decide how to express appreciation to workers and how to integrate them into other places of ministry within the church program. They may want to plan follow-up activities (day camps, Bible clubs, youth groups, etc.) to maintain contact with new participants as well to provide further ministry to children within the congregation.

—Eleanor Daniel

Children's Ministries

Children's ministry is a relative newcomer to the church vocabulary. Though churches have carried out ministry to children for years through programs such as Vacation Bible Schools, it is still in many ways an emerging field that calls for creative planning and programming.

A Total Church Effort

What do we mean by children's ministry? It is a total church effort to meet the needs of children, from birth through elementary school. Naturally, it includes Sunday school, children's church, vacation Bible school, Bible clubs—all covered elsewhere in this book. But it may also include camps, tutoring, after-school activities, choirs, support groups for children with special needs or problems, special summer activities, latchkey day-care programs, and services for parents.

The objectives of children's ministry should be consistent with the objectives of the church. It should seek to meet the identified needs of children within the congregation and in the community. It should also reach out to find children—and their families—and attract them to the church. A third objective would be to minister to the children's families.

Planning children's ministry can be the function of a ministry team charged with the responsibility. The team may be a subgroup of the Christian education ministry team or it may be organized by the pastor or the general church leadership. The children's ministry team can evaluate existing programs (the scope defined by their supervisors), identify areas of need, prioritize the needs, and launch the programs chosen.

The team needs to exercise two cautions: Not to try to do more than the money and people resources will allow, and not to program so much that the ministry infringes on family time. It is far better to confine efforts to two or three special programs, doing them with excellence.

Many Avenues of Approach

Churches have found diverse ways to carry out good children's ministry. Some churches have developed outstanding latchkey programs that meet the needs of elementary children after school. These programs often provide tutoring, supervised study times, recreation opportunities, and spiritual teaching. Other churches offer a day-care program for the community and then follow it up with ongoing ministry to parents in order to integrate them into the total ministry of the church.

Summer is a special time to plan children's activities. Some churches make sure that children from both inside and outside the church go to camp, even if that means providing camp scholarships. Some churches have planned day-camp programs. Many have a special activity day per week in which children are involved in fun and educational activities.

Providing support groups for children is a growing area of ministry opportunity. Children who have experienced divorce often need special help. Children dealing with grief (the loss of a parent or grandparents, especially) can benefit from a support group. The same is true for children with special physical, intellectual, emotional, or social problems. The parents of these children have similar needs and would profit from ministry that parallels the support they themselves may be receiving. Many congregations already have a cadre of professionals who can use their skills in support-group settings.

Effective children's ministry requires spiritually mature, compassionate, stable adults to lead it. Many adults with these basic qualities can be taught the leadership, teaching, and listening skills necessary for the specific ministry. College interns may well make a valuable contribution, but they rarely carry out good children's ministry without the continuing involvement of more mature adults.

The future of children's ministry is limited only by our imaginations. Plenty of needs permeate our communities and churches, and we can find the needs and meet them.

—Eleanor Daniel

Christian Clubs

Club programs for children and youth have served North American churches for more than a century. Many continue to function as parachurch agencies, though denominations and local congregations have often absorbed them or created their own club programs. Historically, the club phenomenon can be traced to the Sunday school and nineteenth-century youth organizations such as the Society of Christian Endeavor and the YMCA, begun by Christians eager to evangelize and disciple young people whom they believed churches were neglecting. Today, most clubs are sponsored by churches.

Club Characteristics

Christian clubs perform various functions, including: evangelizing youth, teaching and applying biblical principles to life, supplementing Sunday school while providing physical activity and social development for the church's youth, providing a Christ-centered alternative to secular youth organizations, and fostering healthy adult-child relationships, often to compensate for family failures. Churches investigating sponsorship of a club should examine their own goals and determine which club programs are a suitable fit.

Almost all Christian clubs offer a similar set of program elements, with the curriculum emphasizing Scripture memorization, Bible stories, and discussion. Most clubs include games and craft projects in their meetings, while many add personal-achievement activities (outlined in handbooks) with appropriate awards and recognition. Invariably, club meetings conclude with devotions or personal testimonies. Camping, service projects, and competitive sports lend the extracurricular dimension to regular club meetings.

Churches typically consider clubs a part of the Christian education program, to be supervised by a Christian education director or committee. Since the clubs are often more successful than the Sunday school in attracting unchurched youth, a club should be treated as an outreach arm of the church, as well. These clubs effectively utilize volunteer leadership that may not be available to other educational programs (for example, men with limited Bible knowledge, college students, or retired adults).

Clubs that operate independent of local churches (Young Life or Good News, for instance) may be perceived as competitors by church leaders, though a cooperative relationship can benefit both the congregation and the organization.

Choosing a Program

Three main guidelines help a church choose a Christian club program:

• *Assess the available volunteer base.* A large percentage of Christian clubs flounder, often within two or three years of their beginning, because volunteers are not trained properly and find leadership too demanding. Churches should try to maintain a ratio of one adult leader to no more than eight children. Effective leaders have either been mentored by veterans or formally trained by the club program's professional staff. Club meetings and activities demand that leaders have solid administration skills, a strong commitment to reaching youth for Christ, and the ability to provide group discipline.

• *Count the costs.* Clubs require a financial investment by the church, otherwise all the expenses are borne by the participants. Costs for curriculum materials, awards, uniforms, dues, and craft resources can add up quickly. Most churches attempt to cover leadership expenses and charge club members only for individual costs. A club of 20 to 25 members and several adult volunteers can expect to spend at least $500 annually.

• *Evaluate various club curricula.* Observe how the Bible is used, and don't be misled by the total number of memory verses, a favorite marketing factor. Ask: Are meeting plans outlined for easy use by busy volunteers? Are club activities attractive and meaningful to children? Does the curriculum give adults the opportunity to develop friendships with youth? How complicated is the program for volunteers to operate? How much emphasis is placed on external rewards compared to personal development and relationships?

Selected Christian Clubs

Awana Clubs
International
1 E. Bode Road
Streamwood, IL 60107

Calvinist Cadet
Corps/Calvinettes
Box 7259
Grand Rapids, MI 49510

Christian Service Brigade
P.O. Box 150
Wheaton, IL 60189

Girls in Action (SBC)
P.O. Box 830010
Birmingham, AL 35283

Good News Club
Child Evangelism Fellowship
Warrenton, MO 63387

Pioneer Clubs
P.O. Box 788
Wheaton, IL 60189

Royal Ambassadors
1445 Boonville Ave.
Springfield, MO 65802

Word of Life Fellowship
P.O. Box 600
Schroon Lake, NY 12870

Youth for Christ/
Campus Life
P.O. Box 228822
Denver, CO 80222

Young Life
P.O. Box 520
Colorado Springs, CO 80901

—*Paul Heidebrecht*

Young-Adult Activities

Young adults are not all alike. In this group, ranging in age from 18 to 28, a church might have college students living on campus or commuting, college-age people working and living at home or away from home, unemployed people anxious to find a job, military personnel, blue-collar workers, executive types, yuppies on the rise, and yuppies on the decline. We might have singles who have never been married and singles who once were, along with young marrieds with children and young marrieds without children, and the unmarried with children. We can have the disabled and those on the comeback trail from drugs, alcohol, illness, or bankruptcy.

Target Your Audience

What we *can't* have very effectively is just one group for everyone of young-adult age! If we are going to minister to young adults, we will need to target our audience by either looking at what kinds of young adults are already in our church or what kinds we'd like to reach. For instance, if a church is near a college campus and has a few students in the congregation, it might want to begin a ministry geared specifically to undergraduate students.

Suppose we survey our community and discover that no one is doing anything in the area of divorce recovery (a big young-adult need). We could do more research, gather resources, recruit a leadership team, and begin a six-week course that helps people pick up the pieces after a divorce. As people finish that experience, we might decide to begin a continuing group for them and others in a particular age range. We would now have three separate ministries: a college ministry, a divorce-recovery program, and a group we might call Genesis, for those, say, in their middle to late 20s.

Perhaps a church is near a military base and not near a college. That church could begin a ministry to military folk. At the same time, the church might be near some apartment complexes primarily occupied by young families. If so, it could begin a couples ministry and also set up a support program for young mothers.

One church is near a downtown office park, so instead of doing a college or military ministry, it emphasizes midweek Bible studies and support groups for business people. The point: We can't just throw open the church doors and expect to meet all the needs through one group called Young Adults.

Constant Change

Young-adult ministry requires enormous flexibility to meet the needs of groups in constant transition. Young-adult leaders must be ready to cope with this continuous flux, because young adults are at a transitional point in their lives, and they are on the move (24 is the median age for those who move five times or more in three years). They may choose to change careers and move to another part of the country, or their employment situations may suddenly change, forcing them to make such moves. So as we encourage long-term commitment to a group, we need to be realistic about the turnover bound to happen. Leadership changes constantly, too, so an ongoing leadership-training program is crucial.

Another dynamic of young-adult ministry is that few people want to leave a group once they have been in it for a while. If the cut-off age is 28 for a group, are we going to ask people to leave on their 29th birthdays? Hardly! Thus it's important to keep developing new young-adult ministries that will offer attractive options for this diverse and energetic group of Christ's disciples.

—Denny Rydberg

Singles Ministries

Approximately 60 million adults in the United States are not married (about 40 percent of our adult population over the age of 18). The rate of increase in adult singles between 1970 and 1990 in our country was 85 percent (source: "Married and Singles," *American Demographics*, 4/92). Few churches come close to this percentage in the makeup of their memberships. Therefore, we may assume that a large unreached mission field of adult singles exists in every community.

How can the local church respond?

Singles as Adults

First, the church needs to recognize that the key word in single adults is not *single;* the key word is *adults*. Adult single people are adult first, and single is an adjective that describes a secondary aspect of their lives and lifestyles. Churches too easily fall into the error of treating single adults like teenagers, giving them an autonomous status and a youth group–like program accompanied by sponsors. Single adults are capable of designing and developing a ministry for their affinity group. They simply need to be given permission. When single adults feel they are integrated into the total life of the church, they will have the support to reach out in ministry to others.

The ABCs of Intimacy

Another key word in this ministry is *intimacy*—the opportunity to share with others one's needs, concerns, struggles, dreams, hopes, defeats, and achievements. Single adults need at least one close friend with whom they can share their lives without the pressure to live together or experience a sexual relationship.

The church can be the best place for *A*ccepting, *B*uilding up, and *C*aring for single adults. This ABC approach will attract single adults from many corners of the community; a church won't need to advertise. It doesn't take long for singles to know which church loves, forgives, and gives grace to the wounded.

Strong Leaders

Churches can begin their ministries by identifying single adults who have the capacity and interest to lead. They should look for people within the church, but can go outside if necessary.

The next step requires training and building personal accountability. The method is to bring a core group of potential single adult leaders together, spend time building them up in the faith, train them for ministry, and learn about single adults in the community that the church can target for outreach.

It is important to identify a target group at the beginning, such as single parents, single adults in their twenties, or those going through a divorce. Informed, aware leaders will know who is the most reachable target group in the community. This group can be a beginning place for outreach efforts, but ministry to other categories of single adults can soon follow.

As a church envisions the possibilities for a singles ministry and as they talk with potential leaders, here are some key questions to keep in mind:

- Do we really know the needs of the single adults in our church, regardless of their age or status?
- Do we need to wrestle with any theological questions, status stereotypes, or media issues that might keep us from understanding and loving single adults?
- Are we forsaking the pain of some single adults in order to protect the prestige of our church or established programs?
- Will the new single-adult ministry confine singles to a specialty group, or will they be encouraged to become an integral part of the church?
- Are we willing to give ministry ownership to single adults and embrace them as peers in leadership, or will they carry a secondary status?

—*Doug Fagerstrom*

Adult Activities

Why are some adult programs boring, lifeless, and unattractive to outsiders, while others are lively, invigorating, and seemingly magnetic? Church-growth research points to several common denominators found in flourishing adult ministries.

Here are five of the those important characteristics:

- *A mission beyond the church.* Effective adult programs have a sense of purpose that clearly includes reaching out to those not yet part of the Christian community.

Leaders of growing adult groups clearly communicate to their members the centrality of Christ's command to make disciples.

That does not mean every activity is explicitly evangelistic; these groups have wonderful social events, special outings, study groups, and more. But the activities of effective adult ministries are considered means to an end, not ends in themselves. The end, or goal, is to model and share Christian love, not only among those in the group but also with those who have yet to experience it.

• *A focus on relational webs.* The method of outreach by which the church has grown since the first century is also practiced by effective adult groups today. It is the process of household evangelism—reaching out to one's friends, relatives, and associates.

Growing adult groups regularly invite and involve people from these existing webs of relationships. They plan special events specifically designed to aid members in inviting friends and family, and the church intentionally sets up programs to encourage this natural and most effective means of bringing others to faith.

• *Intentional assimilation of newcomers.* Every adult group has a tendency to become closed off to visitors and outsiders. Once a group has been together for over two years, the history and traditions of that group make it difficult for a newcomer to break in.

The adult groups that see a high percentage of visitors become active participants intentionally open their arms to newcomers by involving visitors in conversations and activities. People also do personal follow-up on their guests, perhaps inviting a newcomer to join them for lunch during the week or dinner at home. The group's overarching sense of mission makes extending a warm welcome to newcomers an important priority.

• *Regular new-group start-ups.* Growing adult groups have discovered a simple but powerful formula for success: New groups = new growth. One lone group simply can't minister to the variety of adults in a particular church and community, with their different ages, marital statuses, interests, lifestyles, needs, and time constraints.

Churches with effective adult programs continually start new groups based on common interests, common needs, and common goals as they arise. New groups form as soon as people agree on when they can meet, what they want to do, and where they want to go. Regularly starting new groups is a key to keeping an adult ministry in touch with people's practical needs.

• *Opportunities for friends and fun.* Numerous studies have shown that the friendship factor is a key ingredient in the glue that keeps church members coming back. Adults like to be with others who enjoy common interests, who are compatible, and who help them enjoy the experience of living.

Therefore, effective adult ministries plan social events for members and potential members that are just plain fun. Leaders realize that such functions significantly contribute to the overall mix of opportunities in an effective adult ministry.

—Charles Arn

Seniors Ministries

It is no secret that the church is aging. Demographers tell us that a huge age wave is rolling toward our shores, a phenomenon that has been called the most important trend of our times by futurist John Naisbitt. Will the church catch and ride this wave? Or will it miss this great opportunity?

Prepare for the Age Wave

For the churches that can see this wave coming and prepare for it, this radical demographic change brings hundreds of opportunities. Here are five beginning steps for those churches desiring to adapt themselves in order to reach the age-wave generation for Christ:

• *Recognize your introversion.* A traditional senior-adult group is probably unable to reach the secular, unchurched senior adults in our communities, because most senior-adult groups in today's churches are inward focused and self-centered. This is not an indictment of these groups; it is simply what happens to groups that have been together for many years. This realization leads to the next step.

• *Create new groups.* Newly retired or soon-to-be-retired persons have little interest in joining a group with members ten to fifteen years older and with dissimilar interests. (We'd never ask a junior high teen to join the college group!) Medium-sized churches should have three to six groups for persons 55 years old and above, each appealing to a different piece of the age/interest mosaic. Larger churches should have ten to twelve such groups.

• *Train lay leadership.* Leaders of senior-adult programs face a challenge in recruiting and equipping lay persons for leadership. On the one hand, older adults are often the most spiritually mature persons in the church family and therefore the most qualified for such leadership. On the other hand, these older adults tend to shy away from long-term commitments in pursuit of other interests they may have postponed. Consequently, older adults usually respond more readily to short-term tasks rather than long-term responsibilities.

A second recruiting and training obstacle is the scarcity of effective training resources in this specialized area. To respond to this need, L.I.F.E. International has developed the *New Senior Study Center,* which offers extension courses for pastors, staff members, and lay volunteers. These guided learning experiences include important readings in the field, interviews with senior adults, and ways to senior-adult activities.

• *Change your paradigms.* A paradigm is a grid of values and principles through which we interpret our lives. Paradigms provide structures for solving our problems, telling us why we do things and how we believe things should be done. Here are some old and new paradigms concerning senior adults:

Old paradigms: Senior adults *require* volunteers; they *need* caretakers; churches have *apathetic* outreach to seniors; *one* senior-adult group is adequate; the retirement motive is *play*.

New paradigms: Senior adults are a *source* of volunteers; they *are* caregivers; churches have *intentional* outreach to seniors; *multiple* programs are required; the retirement motive is *work, learn, serve, play*.

• *Appoint a director of adult ministries.* To catch the age wave, a church needs a leader. This person may be a part-time volunteer or a full-time staff member, but he or she must have a genuine love and concern for older adults. With love, one cannot fail; without such love, one will not succeed.

The church of tomorrow will be composed mainly of adults. Those who effectively reach out to them will have anticipated the age wave and the exciting ministry opportunities it brings to the shores of the local church.

—*Win Arn*

Ministries for Those with Disabilities

"I am a person, and though some of the machinery doesn't work quite as well as it ought to work, I am *still* a person." The wheelchair, the cane, the physical or mental limitations—all of these deflect our attention from the real person. Yet, behind all of these distractions is someone who desperately wants to be treated as a valuable person, as someone with something to offer, as someone who needs fellowship.

Most people with disabilities feel alienated from society as a whole. Prejudice—or at least discomfort—still abounds. It's the reason most people with disabilities (estimated to be as high as 95 percent of them) do not attend church. Frankly, they just do not feel welcomed.

Disabilities, unfortunately, are not only restricted to a single individual. Family members often feel as alienated and imprisoned as the person with the disability for whom they care. The families, too, need to be a part of the church fellowship.

The care of a family member with a disability can add four hours or more per day to the regular routine within a home. Church members enlisted to assist with the care of the disabled person can free family members to participate in various activities within the church. An alternative approach would be to recruit help for the ordinary tasks, such as grocery shopping or housecleaning. A mother with a severely disabled child would welcome an offer from a retired nurse to come in and watch a child so she could attend the neighborhood Bible study.

Creative Inclusion

Working to include people with disabilities in the regular fellowship activities of the church will take some creative energy, but the church will be incomplete without the rich experiences of those with disabilities (see Luke 14:21–23). We need to consider the ministry of involving disabled people a responsibility, not an option.

Here are some recommendations for planning inclusive activities:

• *Work to raise awareness.* An investment in helping church members become aware of and sensitive to disabilities will generate huge dividends throughout the church body. Often people unintentionally exclude others because they don't know what to say or how to act around someone who is not "normal." We can ask the person with the disability to assist in the process of educating others.

• *Practice inclusion whenever possible.* With few adjustments-,most people can be included in normal fellowship activities, such as Bible studies, home fellowship groups, women's and men's groups, and youth groups. That option would be the choice of most disabled people, if asked. Mental retardation or severe mental illness may warrant the formation of a distinct group.

• *Be flexible and creative.* Often a bit of creative thinking can make what seems an impossible situation work. For instance, suppose the regular meeting place for a home fellowship group is in a split-level house with numerous steps—a seemingly hopeless situation for the woman with multiple sclerosis in a wheelchair. However, after a discussion with her and her husband, the group could decide to move the meeting to the woman's own home.

• *Expect contributions from the physically and mentally challenged.* While a disability may affect mobility, speech, or some other function, it does not mean a person cannot be actively involved in the church. Leading a Bible study, sharing in discussion, bringing the brownies to the next meeting—all are realistic expectations. If assistance is needed, the disabled person will ask.

When we seek out the gifts and talents of those with disabilities, we'll be richly rewarded.

—Conrad Mandsager

24

Teaching Methods

The Greek word *methodos* contains in its last five letters the term for "road" or "way." There are many effective avenues we can take in order to get to where we want to go in our teaching. Yet all effective methods have certain general characteristics:

• *Reality related.* The methods we choose will work best if they approximate real life. For example, suppose I arrange to have a person (unknown to the group I'm teaching) drop in on a home study on cults and pretend to be a Jehovah's Witness? This method might generate a much more realistic interaction about cults than the mere dispensing of information on that subject.

• *Audience adapted.* A group of 5-year-olds would probably be fascinated by a collection of brightly colored rocks that could serve as a springboard to discuss the issue of inheritance (from Luke 12:13). By contrast, a group of 60-year-olds probably would not get too fired up by this method. Factors such as age, culture, region, and background can make a decided difference in what method we choose.

• *Need oriented.* Felt needs provide the electricity for what appear to be the rather innocuous wall sockets of some subjects. For example, having my best friend, a first-rate intellectual, jettison Christianity in college would make the subject of apostasy in Hebrews 6 come alive for me. Thinking backward from our material to its matching need is to hunt for an effective port of entry for our subject.

• *Regularly evaluated.* Our teaching goals give us "the before" and help us craft the methods we choose. Evaluation is "the after," which forces us to revise, clarify, or modify the teaching techniques we've been using.

Evaluation can assume various forms. Handing out a printed questionnaire after a six-week class can help us size up weaknesses and strengths if we sense the class coming to a consensus on particular items. We can also invite into class a trusted friend to take notes on our class and provide possible pointers. For still greater objectivity of evaluation, we could ask a professional to critique our class. That may seem scary but might provide the best results.

Guidelines for Working with Groups

Maximum active participation by as many class members as possible generates maximum learning possibilities. This arrangement can be subdivided into a number of formats, such as total group interaction, small groups within a larger group, pair-offs of people who report results to the larger group, and so on. In such situations the leader will function as facilitator, moderator, or catalyst.

Here are ten valuable suggestions for effective facilitation of groups:

• *Be prepared, organized, thorough.* Do your own groundwork by in-depth study of your subject beforehand. You may wish to bring an index card with a series of ten to twenty questions for the class to deal with, highlighting in colored pencil a key word in each question to prompt your mind. If necessary, list corresponding times (for example, five minutes for question #4) beside the numbered questions.

• *Be courteous, nondogmatic, nonthreatening.* Group leaders need to learn to disagree agreeably at times ("I wouldn't agree with your opinion on that issue, Teresa, but there are a lot of people who would." Or: "I'd take issue with that on a biblical basis, Jerry, but I appreciate you sharing your opinion."). To say something blunt like "That's not what Scripture teaches!" is to put a damper on the participant—perhaps permanently. This principle is vital if there are non-Christians in the group who won't offer the expected, time-honored answers.

If we sense a respondent has become extra quiet, we may need to talk personally after class with that individual. Our goal in class is to create a comfortable, informal environment where all feel free to share their deepest selves.

• *Be affirming.* "I never would have thought of that, Greg" is a compliment. "Now, that's an interesting observation, Terri"—if it is—is a compliment, too. We shouldn't just use schmaltz to get on people's good side, however. People will open up like morning glories if they sense our acceptance. Conversely, they will skitter for shelter like repulsed fawns if they feel invaded.

• *Be firm (as well as affirming) if necessary.* Almost always there is one problem person in a group who will seek to domineer or in other ways create problems. It's usually best to begin any group-study series by saying, "Let's operate with the ground rule of a maximum of three out-loud participations per person so that everyone may contribute to our discussion." If someone is rude to another member, it may prove necessary to say, "Now, wait a minute, Joe. Think about how Mary might be offended by that."

• *Be directive.* We must keep discussions from getting bogged down on one question, unless we sense it's an important issue to be addressed. Living people are more important than lesson plans.

• *Be specific.* We can keep asking questions that press for more specific, close-to-home, real-life answers ("But can you think of a particular time when this very thing happened to you? Would you mind sharing it in some detail?"). General answers tend to be hiding places.

• *Be open-ended with questions,* not asking questions that elicit merely a yes or no.

• *Be relational.* We must plan to ask questions that relate the Bible to modern, everyday situations ("Would you share a specific case of how someone you know modeled compassion when you needed it?"). Our goal is to build group rapport. As people dig deeply into their experiences and become more vulnerable, this happens quite naturally.

• *Be inclusive.* To involve as many people as possible, it's entirely appropriate to call on individuals (gently) by name if they haven't said anything ("Ted, what do you think you'd do in that circumstance?"), asking questions we know they can answer. Temporarily pairing up with partners on a question can also help generate participation.

• *Prepare an opening and closing.* An ice breaker (such as a fun question for pairs to share) helps loosen people up. Also, we need to leave a minute or two at the end in order to give a sense of closure to each lesson.

Many Ways to Study

Our group methods of study will vary according to our purposes and goals. Here are a few samples of possible study methods:

• *Inductive Bible study.* Induction is the process of examining in particular what is there. Some proponents of this method move from (a) observation (What does it say?) to (b) interpretation (What does it mean?) and on to (c) application (What does it mean for me? What do I do now?).

• *Finding principles and illustrating.* In an hour, a class can study a chapter from the Bible, alternating between principles and examples.

First, the class filters from the text a principle (or timeless truth), such as "Temptation often strikes hardest when we are under duress" (from Matthew 4:2). Next, members of the class come up with real-life illustrations of that same principle ("I remember when I had been away from my wife on a two-week business trip when this good-looking woman started coming on strong. . ."). By constantly alternating between principles and their real-life illustrations, classes members begin to see that the Bible really does deal with reality.

- *Elective topics.* Relevant issues tend to attract extra participants who might not otherwise participate. In these sessions, techniques such as brainstorming, buzz groups, round-the-circle answers, and analyzing case studies have proved effective for group involvement.
- *Focused participation.* Occasionally classes may enjoy having outside guests take the primary leadership. Such classes may take the

Preparing to Teach

Sometimes on Sunday morning we stand behind a lectern and, for any host of reasons, haltingly lead a Bible study that just goes nowhere. The symptoms of such classes vary: use of cliches, due to a shallow grasp of the text; fogginess, due to heavy biblical spade work but light cultivation for human consumption; or apathy, due to sparse focus on the implications of the text.

These defects can be corrected. We can avoid Sunday meanderings by cultivating three fluencies during the week: textual fluency, people fluency, and schedule fluency.

Textual Fluency

Textual fluency means knowing the content of a Scripture passage thoroughly enough that it leaves its mark on us. It requires a journey from biblical text understood to discipleship implication addressed. In my journey, I take five steps, posing five sets of questions to every lesson passage.

- *Technical questions.* This generally means vocabulary study. C. S. Lewis said, "Tell me what the hard words mean" (in their own setting, when they were first said).
- *Historical questions.* We must view the text in its own setting, both the historical setting within the material itself and that which lies behind the material. "Who is John the Baptist?" "What issue caused Paul to write what he did to Timothy?"
- *Theological questions.* "If that's what it *says,* what does it *mean?*" This requires some interpretation, which is the dynamic part of the great journey.
- *Contemporary questions.* "How would Christ's point collide with his own world, with his contemporaries?" Now we're getting inside the skin of a first-century person — what some critics call audience criticism — to understand how and why the collision would occur.
- *Discipleship questions.* I must ask, "What is this text saying to

form of debates, forums, panels, committee reports, lectures by well-known specialists, a husband-and-wife dialogue, or unusual testimonies. We can demonstrate that we value in-class members by inviting them to share their expertise, give reports, or otherwise lead the group.

When One Leader Predominates

Probably the lecture method has predominated in most traditional church settings. The lecture format does not need to be a boring, changeless monologue. We live in an era heavily conditioned by the televiewing format (that is, ten-minute segments of programming interrupted by several commercials). Here are some important items to remember when lecturing:

me? How does it intersect with my life? Where am I challenged to change?"

People Fluency

Some pastors love working the early stages of the journey but never get around to asking what it all means. They can stun us with Greek word studies but never arrive at discipleship implications. That's where people fluency — understanding myself and my people — comes in. By sustained listening, we come to understand what is happening in people's lives and what questions are on their minds. We can be prophetic speakers only when we've been prophetic listeners.

A prophetic listener is quick to hear and slow to speak. When we have a great text to communicate and we're trying to find a window for our listeners, it's essential to know the questions they are asking and how they're asking them. There are hardly any new questions, just ancient questions asked in new ways. We must listen for how the questions are being asked, so we can pose questions to the text on behalf of our people.

Schedule Fluency

Pastors have the gift of time more than most professionals. Except for Sunday morning, we wield the whip hand over most events in the church week. We largely control when people will schedule appointments with us, when special classes will be offered, when we'll talk with outsiders. Granted, this scarcely means we abound in free time, but we can, if the resolve is there, establish a rhythm to our week.

I have found that in order to be a good teacher, I must finish my sermon and lesson preparation for the coming Sunday on Thursday morning. Advancing the deadlines for essentials, like the sermon, has helped me escape the garbled tyranny of the urgent. When we wait until Saturday to pound out our lessons, the undone presentations have overshadowed every day of that week. This kills thorough research.

—*Earl Palmer*

• *Be prepared.* Bluffing it and playing it by ear won't work here. Inspiration is almost in proportion to perspiration. One teacher said, "You have to dig a hundred pounds of dirt to get a pound of gold." Topflight resource books can supplement our firsthand spadework. Bible commentaries such as William Hendriksen's *New Testament Commentary,* William Barclay's *Daily Study Guide, The Expositor's Bible Commentary,* the *Word Biblical Commentary,* the *New International Greek Testament Commentary,* and the *Tyndale Old Testament Commentaries* are excellent resources.

• *Be interesting.* If something is old hat to us, it probably will be old hat to a class. We must introduce ideas and information we have gleaned from our reading and experience. When using a published curriculum, it is pointless to rehash material students have already read.

• *Be picturesque.* Use lots of word pictures. Vivid examples can be found in Micah 1:8–16 in the NIV Study Bible footnotes and James

Finding Study Time

Pastors shouldn't need to ask for time to study. Does a doctor ask a patient, "Would you mind if I consult books?" Rather, in preparing to preach or teach, study is a *sine qua non.* Gordon Fee, the New Testament scholar, once said to a group at a pastor's conference, "We've got the best story to tell; we must believe this in our bones and know, therefore, that it deserves thoroughgoing study."

Nevertheless, pastors need cooperation from the congregation in this area. I've found that people will grant freedom for whatever we hold to be the linchpins in our ministry, especially if we are careful to "pay the rent." A pastor pays at least four rents for the freedom to pursue adequate preparatory research before teaching.

• *People must perceive that we know and are under the text.* A physician won't be allowed to treat a patient's ills unless the patient is confident the physician knows the medicines being prescribed. Otherwise, the patient will be jumpy, watching the doctor's every move, worrying about the accuracy of everything he says.

Pastors must master the Scriptures and proclaim them clearly. In addition, our lives are to be under the Word, congruent with it. In his letters to the Ephesians and Philippians, Paul says, "I want your life to be worthy of the gospel." The Greek word for *worthy* also means "congruent." We don't have to be perfect, but people must feel that our lives affirm the message.

• *People must sense growth in us.* If not, they worry about us and, ironically, give us less time to study. They begin to hover around us, discipling us because they think

Moffatt's Version, as well as Matthew 7:3–6.

• *Use variation.* Following the TV format, we need to break up class time into segments, using such variables as maps, time lines, stories, guest mini-reports, charts, handout sheets, overhead projector transparencies, skits, video snippets, slides, visual aids, object lessons, or a planned interrupter.

• *Use questions.* The four Gospels record over one hundred questions Jesus used.

• *Be specific.* Generalities help no one. People can relate better to "a garage full of hand tools" than they will to that greatly overused word *materialism.*

• *Give take-home assignments.* Have class members see if next week they can spot one example of sexism. Ask them to cut out a magazine picture or a newspaper article illustrating oppression. Then we must make sure we use the assignments in the next class at the appropriate time.

we're going stale, going downhill.

People expect a payoff for the study time they allow. When they see growth, they want us to do even more of whatever caused it. They'll say, "Hey, listen; whatever you're doing, keep doing it."

• *People must know we're working hard.* We don't have to publish a work schedule, because most of the time people can catch it when we're working hard. By our actions and demeanor, people sense our vigor. They sense an honest day's work for an honest day's wage. It's not the pastor waving a flag and saying, "I work so hard." They just sense the pastor is pulling his or her oar.

• *People must know we love them.* When we show that we like our people and treasure them, the people go to bat for us. If they are convinced we are for them, they'll let us take the time to become textually fluent.

There is no substitute for learning the names of people and giving them our full attention when we are with them. We can't be everywhere at every time we are needed. But when we are with people, we must really *be there.* Preteens and teenagers especially appreciate that nonexploitive adult who is simply friendly. It isn't necessary to have a profound word to say, but it is important to use their names and work at knowing them individually.

I once read an article in *The New York Times* by Norman Mailer on the subject of writing. He observed that some of his best writing had been done at times when, ironically, he was the driest. That's because when dry, he did more research, which resulted in some of his best breakthroughs.

At any given moment, effective teaching can seem like an unreachable goal. Yet that's just the time to give ourselves wholeheartedly to becoming fluent with the text. We may be closer to eloquence and effectiveness than we think.

—*Earl Palmer*

• *Be relevant.* No one is grabbed by meat offered to idols in 1 Corinthians, but they may be interested in exploring their choices in videos. We must also weed our vocabulary of Christianese (bow in prayer, blessings, fellowship, here I raise my Ebenezer, and so on) if we expect to hold the unchurched.

Forms of Teaching

We do not merely manufacture methods for methods' sake, but, ideally, should select methods that are congruent with our goals. When we know where we're going, we can employ some of these forms:

• *Visuals.* Jesus picked up a tot as a visual (Matt. 18:2). Ezekiel is a veritable cornucopia of visuals (see 3:1, 4:1–4; 5:1–4). Many Christian publishers provide visual aids for purchase with their curricula. The frugal ones among us will develop a filing system for their reuse.

Homemade and close-to-home objects can also serve as teaching tools. A real plumb line brings home Amos 7:7–9. The crack of a bullwhip wakes people up to a lesson on Jesus' temple cleansing. A borrowed exotic sword swung over children's heads makes Ephesians 6:17 come alive.

Word pictures embed truth into memory. One of Howard Hendricks's colorful statements is that Elijah (in James 5:17) was "no fugitive from a wax museum."

• *Eatables.* Perhaps a most frequently neglected teaching tool is food. Even teachers who are not cooks know someone whose services they can borrow. After a lesson for children on the Red Sea, why not have a rectangular glass dish full of red Jello, complete with a path cut through the middle and store-bought gummy figures sprawled around? A golden calf can be made out of cheddar cheese with raisins for eyes and carrot sticks for legs and horns. Why not do some research on ziggurats and get a baker to make a multilayered cake like the archaeological specimen to use with a lesson on the Tower of Babel?

• *Dramatics.* Imagine how blind Bartimaeus felt after being healed, use your imagination to create a dramatic monologue, and then don your bathrobe and tackle the task from that perspective. Or, employ four class participants (based on Genesis 27) for Jacob's dysfunctional family to imagine out loud what each of them would have thought.

Come up with an imaginary character from the sidelines of some biblical scene in order to shed new light on an old story. For instance, we all remember lovable Lemuel, the Used Camel-Lot salesman who sold Joseph and Mary their donkey for the trip to Bethlehem, right? Or how about Reuel, the roof-repair estimator, who talks about what happened to that roof in Mark 2:1–12? We can use church children, teens, or adults to do short skits with our main point.

- *Projects and games.* Children could build a wall of Jericho out of marshmallows. Adults could cut or fold paper into shapes that say something significant about their identity.
- *Technological tools.* Computers, VCRS, overhead projectors, tape recorders, music cassettes—all are strategic for our commuter and computer, instamatic and microwaving generation. We can use our hi-tech buffs as resource people.

Flexibility is the key to effective teaching, regardless of the methods we choose. It's no use trudging through Ezekiel with a droning lecture Sunday after Sunday when we can take a clue from God (in Hebrews 1:1) who used multiple methods ("various ways") to communicate content. God values variation (see Job 33:14 and Hosea 12:10). If God isn't stuck on saying the same old thing in the same old way, why should we be? We can try mime, arts and crafts, sketches, clay sculptures, montages, cartoons, interviews, cell groups, question boxes, charades, handbooks, memorization, show-and-tell, or hobbies. "The field is the world," so to speak.

Part of the "image of God" (Gen. 1:26) is probably our ability to use our imaginations. Simply thinking about a single subject from varying viewpoints usually results in fresh fodder for lessons. God is creative; we must be imitative of God's creativity.

Jesus pulled a shocker when he invented a "good" Samaritan (What Jew ever imagined such a foreign notion?). God did the unpredictable when the God-Man was born somewhere other than a Versailles. God unpredictably used people whose testimony was outlawed in a law court (namely, shepherds) as his public-relations people for the birth of births on this planet.

Nothing retains and sustains attention like being unpredictable. A basic law of learning is: It is very difficult to learn while sleeping. The Holy Spirit, who is the Holy Wind, will teach us his techniques of unpredictability if we are open to learning how he operates.

—Jim Townsend

Resources

Gangel, K., and H. Hendricks, eds. 1988. Christian educators' handbook on teaching. Wheaton, Ill.: Victor Books.

LeFever, M. 1985. Creative teaching methods. Elgin, Ill.: David C. Cook.

Mabry, S., and B. McNabb. 1990. Teaching the Bible creatively. Grand Rapids: Zondervan.

Pressau, J. 1983. Teachniques: Creative designs for teaching. Louisville: Westminster/John Knox.

Rice, W., and M. Yaconelli. 1991. Creative activities for small groups. Winona, Minn.: Saint Mary's.

Learning Styles

We don't all think—or learn—alike. Just as people finally "hear" the gospel when it is translated into their mother tongue, they best learn it when it is taught in their native style. Educators have found at least four separate learning styles, each with its own optimum teaching methods. Though individual educational theorists label their quadrants differently, the schema Bernice McCarthy outlines in *The 4MAT System* distinguishes these four kinds of students:

Innovative Learners

Innovative learners seek meaning, learning as they listen and share ideas. For them, being personally involved in the learning process is crucial. They like to participate in small-group discussions because they're idea people (they typically hate art projects) whose favorite questions are "Why?" and "Why not?" We often find innovative learners in careers in the humanities, in counseling, or in organizational development.

Debates, skits, role plays, and other interactive methods work the best with these learners. Put them into a small group at some point in the learning experience and let them discuss with others the application of biblical truths.

Analytic Learners

Analytic learners say, "Just give me the facts." For them, learning occurs as they think through ideas to form reality. They tend to have less interest in people than in ideas and concepts, enjoying the process of critiquing information and collecting good data. They'll excel at creating concepts and models, often clustering in careers that involve them in math, research, or the basic sciences.

Because they want to know the mind of the experts, these learners usually love the traditional classroom. Straight lecture suits them well, as long as the lecturer truly is qualified. To best teach analytic learners, give them details, lists, technical information, and quotes from authoritative scholars.

Common-Sense Learners

These people don't want to talk about something; they want to *do* it, getting involved in practical, hands-on approaches to learning. Common-sense learners filter learning through the screen of usability. Because they typically desire to take things apart to see how they work, these learners may actually resent being given answers, preferring to solve problems themselves.

Set common-sense learners free to work (with their hands) on a project that has some tie to "real life." For example, if a Bible lesson is on stewardship, common-sense learners might enjoy working on a system for paying the church bills. Give them a copy of the church budget and expenditures, and then set them loose to plan, experiment, and solve the problem.

Dynamic Learners

Hidden possibilities excite dynamic learners. Their favorite question: "What can this become?" The world comes to people like these in rather concrete principles, but they process it actively and with flair. They don't so much absorb reality as enrich it. People like this often seek careers in sales, action-oriented managerial positions, and marketing.

This group functions best by acting and then testing their experience. To best reach them, we need to make things happen in the classroom, to inject action into mere concepts. For a lesson on evangelism, we might charge the dynamic learners with designing a strategy to reach a local apartment complex with the gospel. However, the task would involve not only designing the plan but also finding ways to bring it to reality. Dynamic learners wouldn't necessarily want the hands-on experience of printing the brochures (as the common-sense learners would), but they would certainly like to brainstorm the program design. This is a *real* task, one they would consider worthy of their enthusiasm and creativity.

—*Penny Zettler*

25

Sunday School Programs

More than 200 years ago Robert Raikes, credited as founder of the first Sunday school, wanted to minister to the needs of street children in late eighteenth-century England by providing them with a basic education. His curriculum consisted of reading, writing, and simple arithmetic, the Bible being used as the textbook. As a result of Raikes's efforts, children learned the Word of God, and it changed their lives.

By 1785 Sunday schools were formed in the United States, where there was not as much need for literacy education. The Sunday schools here promptly focused on teaching Christian doctrine, encouraging Bible memory, and accomplishing the evangelism of local neighborhoods.

In the nineteenth century, the Sunday school movement experienced significant growth, especially in the frontier areas of the United States. During this time national Sunday school conventions attracted the attention of significant national leaders, involving people like the Rockefellers and Carnegies. Political leaders, including presidential candidates, often would appear on the convention platforms. One of the key reasons for the Sunday school's success at this time was the significant involvement of lay leaders. Thousands of churches were started as a result of mission Sunday schools.

In the early 1900s, however, something happened that continues to affect the Sunday school movement today. Leadership was taken out of the hands of lay leaders and given to professionals. Many of these professionals were heavily influenced by liberal theology, resulting in a curriculum that at times included little Bible and focused primarily on a secular, character-development education. Interest and attendance declined for a while.

From the 1930s, however, evangelical involvement in the Sunday school movement increased. Today, with over 200 Sunday school conventions a year, the influence of biblical curriculum, and the development of the field of Christian education both in colleges and seminaries (along with church staff positions in education), Sunday school attendance in the United States averages around 36,000,000 each week.

Defining a Purpose

Leaders who want to revitalize their Sunday schools must articulate a distinctive purpose and communicate it to all involved. Over the years the Sunday school has focused on different purposes, including social action, evangelism, doctrinal catechism, Bible memorization, character education, fellowship, and mutual edification through spiritual gifts.

"Teaching the Word of God" can be considered the overall purpose, but what should happen to the learner as a result of this teaching must be clearly stated. Result-statement possibilities might include: bringing people to faith in Christ (outreach and evangelism), growing in the Christian life (application of biblical truth, resulting in Christian discipleship), fellowshipping with other believers (nurture and edification), and helping people in need (ministry and service). Historically, a major purpose was outreach and evangelism, but in the sixties, many churches moved to an emphasis on Bible knowledge. Consequently Sunday school attendance declined, even in evangelical churches.

A good purpose statement must include all that is implied in "teaching" the Word of God. Bible knowledge alone will not suffice. Though knowing the Scriptures and applying biblical truths in the lives of the learners is an appropriate purpose statement for today's Sunday school, we must be certain to include, in a specific way, everything that well-rounded, relevant biblical application can really mean.

Leadership and Structure

One big reason for the success of Sunday schools in the nineteenth century was the strong lay leadership. We need to remember this valuable lesson today. In fact, Sunday schools still could not exist without lay people serving as workers, teachers, and administrators.

This is not to suggest the pastor should turn over all of the Sunday school ministry to others and remain isolated from the program. Pastors can work with the lay leadership by serving as resource persons and by encouraging and providing the necessary training. Pastors should constantly demonstrate support for the Sunday school ministry through verbal announcements during worship services and through articles in bulletins and newsletters. Pastors can also offer personal encouragement to workers by visiting in their departments, leading training sessions, and helping in the recruitment of teachers. Pastors must be enthusiastic about Sunday school if it is to be effective.

The Sunday school leadership team includes a superintendent or director (departmental directors in larger schools), teachers, and other workers, such as secretaries, teacher's helpers, and class officers. Often there is a Sunday school council or Christian education board or committee to oversee the program.

Sunday school can offer ministry for all ages. In fact, the church is one of the few truly intergenerational organizations in society. Though educators recognize that learning can take place both in carefully age-graded structures as well as in intergenerational settings, most Sunday schools today are organized around age groupings. These four divisions are common, though they are not set in stone:

- *Early childhood,* with cradle nursery; toddlers; nursery (2s and 3s); and beginner, kindergarten, or preprimary (4s and 5s).
- *Children,* with primary (grades one and two), middler (grades three and four), and junior (grades five and six). Some smaller Sunday schools will form this division into two departments: primary (grades one through three) and junior (grades four through six).
- *Youth,* with junior high or middle school (grades seven through nine, or six through eight) and high school (grades nine through twelve, or ten through twelve).
- *Adult,* with a young-adult department (ages 18 through 35); middle-adult department (ages 36 through 60s), and senior-adult department (ages 60s and older).

In these divisions, middle schools may include sixth grade, while college and career groups may still fall under the youth division. In determining divisions and classes for school-age pupils, it is best to follow the divisions of local public schools. This way students will be in the same groupings in church and in school. Depending upon the size of the Sunday school, each division would be subdivided into classes or departments.

Though these divisions, departments, and classes are quite common for early childhood, children, and youth, the adult divisions can provide several different options. Some possibilities include offering classes for singles, single parents, men, women, couples, college, career, and professionals. Classes may be organized around specialized topics or Bible book studies, with adults selecting the elective course they desire. These classes may gather adults from age 18 through the oldest senior. Specific age grading for adults in Sunday school is not as popular as it once was, but educators do see the importance of life-stage grouping, bringing together learners facing similar developmental issues.

A Means of Education

The Sunday school cannot be found in the Scriptures. It was begun in England in 1780 as one means of Christian education. Does this

Choosing Curriculum

To look at curriculum clearly, three factors must be in focus: Why, what, and who.

Why Evaluate Curriculum?

Churches normally find three good reasons to evaluate Sunday-school curriculum:

• *Discomfort among teachers.* This problem — indicated by such factors as poor morale, resignations, and alternative curriculums being used — is the most common reason.

• *New education goals.* With new goals, churches often rethink teaching materials. For example, they may want more seeker-focused programs to appeal to non-Christians, or they may want a more conservative view of Scripture.

• *Desire for better materials.* This may be the most neglected reason, since it doesn't spring from the assumption of necessary change. Yet, churches want to ensure that teachers have the best resources available, so it is a good idea to evaluate materials for quality every three to five years.

What's Our Bias?

The second factor essential to clear curriculum evaluation is an understanding of the teaching staff's educational bias. Otherwise a church may find the newly chosen materials do not fit the teaching staff.

Churches tend to have one of three biases:

• *Application to life.* This is the strongest concern among teachers today. The "So what?" question appears constantly. Materials must help students live their faith.

• *Educational methodology.* Many teachers with this bias feel it is a sin to bore a student, so lessons focus on learner participation, and predictability is anathema. The classroom may expand into the community, sometimes at the expense of Bible content and direct application to life.

• *The mastery of Bible content.* These Christian educators decry the absence of biblical knowledge today. They believe that children should know the truth, and the

mean that the Sunday school is not biblical? Of course not; we have the clear teaching of the Scriptures on the importance of educating the members of Christ's body from their earliest years. Jesus, of course, was the greatest teacher who ever lived, and the Bible identifies the various approaches that were used to fulfill his injunction to teach all of his future disciples (Matt. 28:20).

All of the apostle Paul's letters were teaching documents for the churches, and his ministry was primarily educational. The early church used schools to teach the new converts about Christianity. Both Calvin and Luther devoted much of their time to teaching. Lu-

truth will set them free to apply scriptural teachings.

Obviously, curricular materials should do justice to all three biases. But if the teaching staff's pet area appears to be slighted, the materials are not likely to gain wholehearted staff support.

Who Gets Involved?

The third focus in a curriculum evaluation is *ownership* of both the process and the decision. This brings up further questions:

• *Who evaluates?* It is important to create a broad base of ownership in a curriculum study, and the key concept is balance.

For example, in a children's department, three groups should participate: teachers, parents, and Christian-education specialists. Each group should have an equal voice in the process, including the selection of evaluation tools and the curricular products to be reviewed, and the hands-on evaluation. Older students may join the process for the upper grades.

• *Who decides?* Once the evaluation leads to recommendations, someone needs to make a decision. Key to success is that whoever decides must previously hold the respect of the congregation.

Usually a church board or committee makes this decision, but in some cases, a staff member can decide. In either case, it should be someone knowledgeable in Christian education but other than those who did the evaluation. This provides a check against evaluators becoming too close to the decision, and it lends authority to the decision.

• *What if it fails?* Because teachers may find the curriculum choice to be ineffective, leaders need to define publicly how the changes will be evaluated — before changes are implemented. A means of redress should be built into the process. It's wise to allow the new curriculum a full year's cycle for adequate in-use evaluation, but people need to know how and when the effects of the change will be critiqued.

When we keep these points of focus in mind, a visit from a curriculum representative will provide information and stimulation that can shape our ministries while not forcing a premature or inappropriate curriculum choice.

—*Mark H. Senter III*

ther even wrote a catechism for children and held classes much like today's Sunday school. So we can see that much teaching and learning took place in the church prior to the Sunday school movement.

Sunday school is one *means* of assisting the church in fulfilling its mission of teaching and learning. Yet in its 200-plus years of existence, the accomplishments are remarkable.

The church's mission of teaching and learning will continue, while the means to accomplish that mission may change. As a means, Sunday school may change, or a new means may take its place. If a better strategy is developed, churches must be willing to embrace it in order to better accomplish the unchanging mission of Christian education.

In a recent meeting that brought together over twenty educational professionals from some of the largest churches in the United States and Canada, several different strategies surfaced to assist the church

Teaching Adults

A common attitude in our culture is that education is for children: The sooner you're through with it, the better. In the church, too, theological schooling may seem like a relic from childhood, because many Christians have never brought their adult minds to bear on an understanding of the Bible.

Fortunately, this situation can be turned around. First we need to know the special characteristics and needs of adult learners, and then we can launch into teaching that really connects with them.

How Adults Learn

Adults learn differently than do children. For example:

- *Adult learners are self-directed.* Adults like to see themselves in charge of their own lives, making their own decisions and directing their own learning experiences.
- *Adult learners have large reservoirs of experience.* As adults grow, they learn to trust their own judgment and test what they hear from others against their own sampling of reality. They will not take a teacher's message seriously if it contradicts their own experience.
- *Adult learners are oriented to their tasks, roles, and identities.* The learner's identity—as parent, spouse, worker, professional, or recreational hobbyist — profoundly affects what he or she is willing to learn about.
- *Adult learners want practical knowledge.* Unlike many children and youth, most adults are unwilling to store up theoretical knowledge that may or may not someday be of use to them. The "someday" has arrived, and adults want information they can use *now.*

Teaching that Connects

Keeping in mind the characteristics of adult learners, we can structure teaching so that it connects

in its educational responsibility. After sharing their personal experiences, the group members unanimously agreed, however, that the Sunday school was still the best strategy for accomplishing the educational goals of the church for all age groups. Other strategies were fine for specialized groups and ages, but the Sunday school continues to be the viable program for the entire church. Since this is the case, churches and leaders need to get behind the ministry of the Sunday school and work to make it as effective as possible.

Keeping Sunday School Effective

Revitalizing the Sunday school is a major concern for today's church leaders. Prophets of doom declare the organization dead. Others continue its existence—or at least tolerate it—but do not give it a

with adults. There are at least four keys:

• *Provide learning space with an adult feel.* The room itself must respect their sensibilities. As we look at our churches, we should ask ourselves: Is this a place where adults would enjoy gathering and spending time together? Does it look clean? Are the chairs comfortable? Can people hear? Are the aesthetics pleasing to adults?

• *Diagnose individual needs.* One way to do this is through personal interviews, asking questions such as: In the last two years, have you undergone a transition or crisis? How might the church have helped you to cope during that time? What stage are you at in your spiritual pilgrimage? How can the church help you grow as a Christian?

When the answers are gathered, they shed light on how best to teach a particular class.

• *Involve learners in planning their own learning.* The most effective courses begin this way. For example, in preparing to teach a course on women in transition, begin by discussing questions such as: What would you like to learn in this area? What transitions do you think women are experiencing? What are some of the hardest issues faced by women in transition?

Planning with people helps them stay in control of their own education.

• *Make adults responsible for their learning.* Avoid coaxing adults into learning. Instead, make them responsible for the learning they want to do. I might begin a class in the Book of John by asking group members to make a learning contract: "There are three levels at which you can take this class. Level one: You can come and receive whatever is presented; just be willing to enter into the discussion. Level two: As you take this class, you will read William Barclay's commentary on John. Level three: Bring a notebook and plan to do your daily devotions and meditations in John." At that point, I can hand out a simple questionnaire and ask people to make a personal commitment.

—*Roberta Hestenes*

high priority in the church's ministry. Sunday school workers sometimes receive little support or encouragement from the church leadership, and in some areas the training of workers is almost nonexistent.

Sunday school continues week after week in many churches because there has always been Sunday school. Little thought is give to its purpose or to what should actually be accomplished. Sunday school evaluation appears to be a word from another language that cannot be translated, or at the least is seldom done.

Revitalize may not be a strong enough word. Perhaps we should use *resuscitate!* Here is a simple, beginning strategy to use in revitalizing a Sunday school ministry, based on having the leaders ask themselves six critical questions.

• *Why have Sunday school?* A clear understanding of the Sunday school's purpose is essential to its success. Sunday school is not a church but a part of the church ministry and a means of assisting the church in fulfilling its mission.

Call a meeting to discuss and adopt a Sunday school purpose statement. Include as many of the teachers and workers as possible and encourage full discussion, bringing the group to a consensus on the purpose statement. Lead them to study the important Scripture passages, and from these develop a purpose statement. Working with the group in this way will demonstrate the crucial administrative principle of ownership—involving in the planning all those who are going to do the work. This is wise, since it is the mission or purpose that motivates people to serve.

A sample purpose statement might read: "To teach and apply the Word of God. Elements involved in the application of biblical truth might include outreach and evangelism, spiritual growth and discipleship, ministry and service, and fellowship."

Rather than copying a statement already developed, it is better to lead the group in writing its own, as long as it contains the important elements. With a clearly defined purpose, it will be possible to determine how well the ministry is going, since the statement provides a standard for meaningful evaluation.

• *What are the leadership needs?* Certainly a director or superintendent must be enlisted. This person would have the responsibility for the overall ministry of Sunday school. If the right person cannot be found, it will be necessary for the pastor or a staff member to assume this role until someone can be trained to assume the duties. Look for someone with administrative gifts who has a burden for educational ministry.

Other leadership needs include teachers and department directors. How many workers are needed? A handy ratio for the typical Sunday school is one worker for every ten people enrolled. In the early-childhood department the ratio is much smaller, while in the adult area it is larger. The average, though, is 1:10, and a church with fewer workers may be understaffed.

• *How will we organize and train?* Details of structure will depend on enrollment, but a good place to start is with the four basic divisions of early childhood, children, youth, and adults. Within each division, then, leaders can create the classrooms necessary to provide the best environments for learning.

Each class and department will require trained teachers and workers as well as space. Each worker will need training in how to perform the assigned task. Training can be as simple as a brief meeting for secretaries on how to take the records. For teachers, training likely will require a continuing series of workshops lasting several months. A personal commitment to ongoing training must be a standard qualification for all prospective workers.

• *Are the facilities adequate?* Not every church has ideal facilities, so Sunday school leaders often must take a creative, improvisational approach to setting up the best possible learning environments. Generally speaking, classes should be clean and comfortable, providing a positive environment for learning. If space is limited, consider multiple Sunday schools or off-site facilities. The key is to provide quality learning regardless of the location.

• *What curriculum resources will we use?* Churches should develop a comprehensive curriculum plan that not only provides for quality learning for each age group but also considers the progression of learning from year to year. Does the junior curriculum take into account what was learned in the primary department? How will the youth material incorporate the content offered in the children's department? A total curriculum plan for the church will coordinate the scope and sequence of learning through the age groups.

Several publishers provide quality materials for Sunday schools. A church that stays with a single publisher can tie into the publisher's curriculum plan. Churches that decide to use materials from different publishers for different age groups will need to study the plans carefully to avoid unnecessary duplication or the omission of significant biblical teachings.

An important part of training for teachers will be showing them how to use the curriculum materials. When teachers complain about their curriculum materials, often leaders will discover the teachers are not using the materials as they were designed. Consider inviting local publishing house representatives to train teachers in effective curriculum use.

• *What regular meetings will we schedule?* Most people are not interested in going to more meetings, but in order for the Sunday school to be effective, the team of workers must meet on a regular basis for prayer, training, preparation, and planning. Sometimes a meeting will bring together only those who work in a department. At other times the entire staff of workers must meet together. Many Sunday schools have opted for the smaller departmental meetings on a regular basis and for combined-staff meetings once or twice a year.

Departmental agendas should devote significant time to prayer, both for the needs of the workers and for the Sunday school ministry in general. Each meeting should provide some kind of training. No one should leave a meeting without learning at least one way in which to become a better worker or teacher. Beginning topics might include teaching a particular age group, understanding developmental characteristics, leading a person to Christ, and ministering to people in need.

If all classes in the department are studying the same lesson, teachers can spend valuable time preparing together for future lessons. Planning for upcoming events such as promotions, special days, ministry opportunities, and socials completes the agenda of the departmental meeting.

Some schools combine the full-staff meeting with departmental meetings. When this is done, it's good to give careful attention to the assigned time for each activity. When the entire staff meets together, workers should experience encouragement and renewed motivation for the task. Leaders can make announcements of general interest to the entire Sunday school, with special attention focused on departments and classes that have achieved their goals or accomplished a significant task. Visiting speakers and appreciation dinners should be used regularly.

In addition to the staff and departmental meetings, meetings between the Sunday school director and the pastor or another staff member need to be scheduled regularly. This underscores the importance of the director's position and keeps communication lines open. Such meetings can be used to evaluate the Sunday school program, discuss personnel needs, plan for special events, and contribute to the ongoing training of the director.

In any organization as old as the Sunday school, problems will arise. Most of the problems result not from the concept of Sunday school but from the faulty ways its ministry may be attempted. When there is no clear purpose, when unqualified people are recruited, when the church leadership does not adequately support the ministry, when the workers and teachers are given assignments without adequate training, or when ineffective teachers continue to serve, we can be assured of a Sunday school fraught with continuous problems. Following the steps listed above will help leaders overcome problems.

Some researchers report that Sunday school attendance continues to decline, while some curriculum publishers report their sales are the highest ever. We could say the decline is confined to particular denominations, but that would be inaccurate. In any denomination, some schools are declining while others are growing. Those that continue to grow are serious about their ministry and are giving it their best efforts.

It is important to remember that Sunday school is about teaching people. The administrative structure is important. We need good curriculum materials. And dedicated teachers and workers must be on hand. Working together with the Holy Spirit as the Master Teacher, we can have effective, vibrant Sunday schools today.

—*Dennis E. Williams*

Resources

Brown, L. 1986. Sunday school standards. Ventura, Cal.: Regal.

Clark, R., L. John, and A. Sloat. 1991. Christian education: Foundations for the future. Chicago: Moody.

Dean, K. 1992. Sunday school handbook. Nashville: Convention Press.

Westing, H. 1980. The super superintendent. Denver: Accent.

Williams, D. 1993. Volunteers for today's church. Grand Rapids: Baker.

Teacher Recruitment

People get excited about ministry; they get scared off by jobs. Here are five recruiting practices that can help potential teachers see teaching as a ministry, while making recruiting itself less of a chore and more of a ministry.

• *Recruit through relationship.* Recruiting basically is matching people with needs. In order to find a good match, however, we need to know the people in the church: what gets them enthused, how they enjoy spending their time, and what their passions and motivations are.

For example, let's say we've noticed a young mother who has been attending church for some time. We may be tempted to ask her to babysit in the nursery. But when we get to know her, we discover she is gifted in relationship skills and has a desire to evangelize. So, instead we might ask her to design a meaningful outreach program for young mothers. We cannot help people find a ministry if we don't know their gifts, abilities, and interests.

• *Tap by team.* A recruiting team represents a variety of interests, backgrounds, gifts, and passions. The best recruiter for a ministry is the person on the team who is closest to that ministry, the person who is the most excited about it. So the person who is enthusiastic about working with second graders is a better recruiter for second-grade teachers than even the pastor. With a team approach, individuals can be delegated to contact prospective teachers for the areas in which they have the most interest.

• *Set the setting.* The recruiting conversation ideally involves sitting down in quiet, comfortable surroundings and sharing the vision, explaining the objectives, spelling out the expectations, and detailing the support we are willing to give. We can ask people what they think they will need to do the job, think through the outline of the course with them, and ask what books, tapes, or other resources would help them prepare for teaching the class.

The recruiting experience should not be a contract negotiation done hurriedly on a Sunday morning, but rather the creation of a partnership between friends, an informal time of thinking and praying together and reaching a decision. We shouldn't say, "Please respond to the terms written on this paper before you leave today." Rather, we want to arrange an informal meeting that conveys "Let's seek the will of God together."

• *Interpret excuses.* Dealing with excuses is one of the most delicate aspects of recruiting. For one thing, "excuses" are sometimes valid reasons. Learning to tell a reason from an excuse is part of the discernment that goes with recruiting.

Confronted with an obvious excuse, we will need to discern whether to take the excuse as a no or change the job description. Sometimes an excuse simply means "I can't make that big of a commitment. If the commitment were smaller, I would consider it." In this case, we may want to break the job into two or three parts, offering the prospective teacher a portion.

No one feels adequate. The apostle Paul didn't feel adequate, Moses didn't feel adequate, and I sure don't feel adequate. But often we can answer an inadequacy excuse by offering the prospective teacher help, training, prayer support, and resources.

• *Delay for discernment.* We should discourage immediate response during the initial conversation. Our job is not to rope people into our program but to help them discern the will of God. We can close with words to the effect, "Let's pray and think about this possibility for the next few days. Then let's get together a week from now and talk again."

—*Roberta Hestenes*

Teacher Training and Support

Virtually all ministers would agree that a key pastoral task is "the equipping of the saints for the work of service" (Eph. 4:12). Since we can't do everything ourselves, we must give significant attention and encouragement to ongoing teacher training. Fortunately, none of us in North America can say we lack training opportunities and materials. Here are some of the many options available:

• *Curriculum.* If teachers want to improve their skills, the place to start is to study thoroughly the teaching material. A church I know has a particularly good early-childhood department. The coordinator believes it's because the teachers meet together, study the curriculum, and work out ways to apply it to their students.

Most publishing houses employ professional educators who understand learners and design methods to reach them. Volunteer teachers who ignore the curriculum only deprive themselves and their students.

• *Department meetings.* Regular meetings are essential for planning and coordination, but we also can use them to build skills. When workers join together for prayer and program concerns each month, they enhance accountability and encourage fellowship among the team members.

For example, the boys in a church I served wanted a club program, so several men met for training. The club began with much enthusiasm, but after four or five months, something seemed to be missing. As I checked with the program director, I found the men were no longer meeting for training and prayer once the program got going. Each man was simply doing his thing, resulting in a loss of overall direction, teaching skills, and team spirit.

• *Individual training.* In the average college dorm, though some students enjoy studying as a group for exams, others prefer to isolate themselves in the library. In the same way, some teachers benefit greatly from using a correspondence course, a book, or a tape in the privacy of their homes.

Many churches have assembled a library of training books and cassettes for individual use. When teachers are willing to work individually, we can provide the materials, encourage them, and try to follow up later with "I'm so happy to see you investing personal time in the ministry of teaching."

• *Guest speakers and workshop leaders.* An outside "expert" can inspire and motivate our teachers. By providing opportunities for teachers to hear stimulating educators, we not only give them bits of information to use in their teaching but also renew their enthusiasm for the Lord's work.

We can strengthen an educational program by bringing in a consultant to conduct a Sunday school evaluation, scheduling an evening for teachers to listen to a local expert speak on building self-esteem in children, inviting a Christian education professor from a Bible college to conduct a Saturday morning seminar, scheduling a Walk Through the Bible seminar, or using a publishing-house consultant to help the teachers learn how to use their curriculum.

• *Conventions and seminars.* The cost of outside training opportunities can be significant but is usually well worth it. For instance, when I was a freshman in college, our youth leader took five of us a hundred miles to attend the InterVarsity conference on missions at Urbana. The sessions were meaningful to me, but equally special was the time I spent with my spiritual mentor and the other committed collegians. The same thing can happen with pastors and Sunday school teachers as they drive to weekend seminars with better teaching on their minds.

—John Cionca

26

Youth Ministries

Though the youth group has flourished during the last half of the twentieth century, youth ministry is a rather new phenomenon in the great developments of church history. Christian youth movements were a product of the Industrial Revolution, which took place first in Europe during the late eighteenth century and later in America. The structures of society fundamentally changed when the means of making a living moved from the home to the factory, from the village to the metropolis, from the controls of church and community to the freedom of boarding houses and bars. Parents feared their young people would forget the values of their heritage. Into this spiritual vacuum stepped a variety of youth ministries that attempted to pass Christian convictions from one generation to the next.

Many strategies were formulated at the grassroots level for the purpose of nurturing the children of the church and evangelizing children from lower socioeconomic levels of the community. Friendly societies, mutual-improvement societies, Sunday school teachers' meetings, singing schools (the forerunners of today's church choirs), temperance and missionary societies, literary and devotional societies—all provided safe places where boys and girls could meet Christian peers.

The birth of the Society for Christian Endeavor in 1881 was the genesis of the modern youth group. Its structure still provides the skeleton upon which the meat and muscle of modern young people's fellowships are supported today.

The denominational youth organizations, which emerged during the last two decades of the nineteenth century, and the parachurch youth ministries, which reached young people for Christ a half century later, flourished and then settled into comfortable patterns of ministry.

Yet one question needs to be asked: Has there been any continuity in youth ministry since its beginnings? In other words, is there anything in youth ministry over the past two centuries that appears to contribute consistently to success? The answer is a resounding Yes! Here are a few basic principles that have insured effective youth ministry across generational, socioeconomic, and cultural barriers.

Enter the Student's World

The most basic principle of youth work—making contact—has been described in many ways. "Contact work," "earning the right to be heard," "building relationships," and "incarnation ministry" are some of the most common descriptions. The cornerstone principle is that youth ministry begins when a spiritually mature adult finds a comfortable way to enter a student's world. Francis Clark made contact with young people through the structured meetings of Christian Endeavor. Jim Rayburn showed up at athletic events, talked with young athletes on their own turf, won their confidence, and eventually invited them to Young Life clubs. David Wilkerson showed up at a police station in the Bronx on behalf of members of a street gang, and from this contact was born Teen Challenge.

Consider these four distinctives of the contact principle:

- *An emphasis on Christian ministry.* Many worthwhile activities benefit young people, and many sponsoring organizations share a Judeo-Christian value system. The goal of Christian youth ministry, however, is fulfilling the Great Commission, which includes both evangelizing and discipling. Without this dual emphasis, youth ministry degenerates into mere youth work.
- *Leadership by spiritually mature adults.* Though some youth movements have been student led initially (for example, the Student Volunteer Movement and the Student Foreign Missions Fellowship), the continuity of vision and leadership over the long haul has always been in the hands of people older than the young people the movements have served. Where youth ministry has been effective, it has had adult leaders who were secure in their relationship with God and with other people. For such people, youth ministry is not a method of prolonging one's adolescence but a mission of helping youth in their spiritual journeys.

To provide this type of attention to the discipleship process, the ratio between leaders and students needs to be at least one adult for every ten young people. Student leadership is not negated by the adults who are involved in youth ministry; it is enhanced. The adult serves as a coach, while the young person calls the signals and leads the team on the field of play.

• *Activities that are mutually comfortable to student and adult.* Mutual interests most frequently provide a point of contact between students and adults. Music, drama, sports, service activities, camping opportunities, Bible quiz teams, ski trips, and weekly youth group meetings all provide environments in which youth and adults can get acquainted and grow to like each other. Only after the comfort level has been established can evangelism or discipleship take place.

• *Ministry that takes place in the student's world.* Just as the Son of God left the splendor of eternity to become incarnate in the hostile world of fallen humanity, so Christian adults must be willing to take the risk of leaving their comfort zones to become pilgrims in a new world. The people in this world are usually more familiar with current musical groups, professional athletes, and TV celebrities than they are with Moses, David, or the apostle Paul. For many adults this initial plunge into the land of youth is akin to a jarring cross-cultural experience.

Lovingly Confront with the Gospel

To enter a student's world, as difficult as it is for many adults, is only the beginning of youth ministry. The most significant part of the ministry equation emerges when young people are lovingly confronted with biblical truth and its implications in their lives. Adolescents are attempting to become their own people. They are sorting out what convictions they hold and what standards they reject. To become mature, youth will take frequent opportunities to reject the convictions of the adults who surround them—parents, teachers, pastors, doctors, and even police.

Youth-ministry people stand between the generations, imploring the old to understand the young and the young to appreciate their elders. Such ministers stand in the gap, holding out the Word of Life. To enter a student's world without teaching him or her to view the world through the lens of Christian conviction hints at personal or spiritual immaturity on the part of the adult leader. It takes skill and conviction to induce students to confront themselves in the light of biblical truth.

Confrontation in youth ministry seldom means preaching at passive learners. Though preaching is appropriate in many settings, most of the time students need to discover biblical values through both a social and biblical process of induction. They need to discover, experiment with, and eventually internalize biblical truth. Youth groups, from their beginning, have been places where students could come to grips with the Christian values of their parents' generation.

With what should the young person be confronted? The Christian gospel is the core message, with all of its implications for salvation, personal lifestyle, interpersonal relationships, and stewardship of God's creation.

There is a danger, however, for youth ministers as they confront students with the gospel. Some expect youth to respond as adults might respond, failing to account for the maturing process that has happened in their own lives during the ensuing years since adolescence. In frustration at the lack of adequate response, Christian youth leaders may resort to manipulative tactics to produce "results." Seldom are these strategies effective in bringing the freedom of the gospel to young people.

Junior High Ministries

Junior high kids are special. Caught in a whirlpool of change, they are growing and developing in every area of life as they transform from children into young adults. *Physically,* limbs and bodies seem to gain inches and pounds overnight, and adult hormones kick in, bringing new sexual awareness. *Socially,* junior highers aggressively seek out friendships, with the phone becoming a social ally and a constant companion.

Mentally, early adolescents navigate the uneasy path from the concrete to the conceptual, viewing life mostly in black-and-white tones; things are "excellent" or "stupid." *Emotionally,* junior highers experience great highs, followed by rapid descent into deep lows. Their psycho-emotional focus is on competence—learning new skills in order to answer the questions "What can I do?" and "What am I good at?"

Spiritually, these kids begin to question what they've been taught in Sunday school. Church isn't considered "cool" in junior high, and many young teens stop attending church as soon as they can manage it with their parents.

Reaching Junior Highers

Unfortunately, during these difficult years, just when they most need mature guidance, faithful relationships, and overt expressions of love, junior highers are sometimes deserted or ignored. They tend to fall into a ministry gap—stuck between the children (with their colorful and creative programs and Christmas pageants) and the senior highers (with their full-time, professional youth worker).

Junior highers do need lots of love and attention. Here's how to reach and help them.

- *Provide positive adult role models.* Junior high students still look up to adults. They will respect those who respect them and follow those

Develop a Delivery System

Youth for Christ rallies and, later, Campus Life clubs, Fellowship of Christian Athletes' huddle groups and conferences, Young Life clubs and camps, denominational youth programs (such as Free Church Youth Fellowship, Lutheran Youth fellowship, Royal Ambassadors, and Young Calvinist Federation) are examples of youth ministry delivery systems. A delivery system is an organized means of getting students from the point of contact to the moments of confrontation with the Christian gospel.

Competition, humor, skits, testimonies of Christian personalities, discussions, concerts, and a host of other program elements can move students from a casual commitment to an adult or peers to a serious consideration of the gospel message. While dozens of models of youth

---

who spend time with them. Parents can make excellent volunteers, because most junior highers still enjoy having Mom and Dad around.

• *Give them a safe place.* Every event and program should provide a safe haven where kids feel affirmed, where they can experience success instead of failure. Leaders should allow no name calling or belittling, and games should give everyone an equal chance to win.

• *Relate the Bible to life.* Kids reared in church know the Bible stories; now they need to sense the Bible's relevance to life, *real* life. Otherwise they will discard the faith with their childhood toys. Teach junior highers how to read, understand, and apply the Bible. Make Christianity practical to their growing and changing world.

• *Exercise discipline.* Early adolescents seem squirrelly and out of control—because they usually are! Often when they act up, they can hardly help it. They need well-defined rules and limits administered by adults who will firmly and kindly enforce those rules. A stern look, a hand on the shoulder, or a quiet but direct "That is not acceptable" communicates concern for the individual as well as the group.

• *Teach life skills.* Because junior highers want and need to learn "how to," this is the ideal time to teach them how to succeed in life. Design or find lessons that teach "How to Make Friends," "How to Get Along with the Opposite Sex," "How to Get What You Need," "How to Resolve Conflicts," and other clearly relevant topics. Also include spiritual-life skills such as "How to Pray," "How to Worship," and "How to Explain What You Believe." Teach these skills by following three simple steps: explanation, demonstration, and supervision (active practicing).

• *Have fun.* Filled with boundless energy, junior highers are fun, and they like to have fun. In fact, two sixth-grade boys can spend hours chasing each other around the yard or family room. Laugh with them, play with them, and enjoy life with them.

—*Dave Veerman*

ministry exist, there are four broad families of delivery-system strategies:

- *Leadership-development strategies.* The oldest family of youth-ministry strategies grows from the model pioneered by the Society for Christian Endeavor, in which the youth group was divided into committees (sometimes called commissions) led by officers elected from within the group. The committees were responsible to provide weekly meetings along with periodic social activities and service activities. The purpose of these activities was to pass the values of one generation to the next and to produce a new generation of leadership for the church. In these arrangements, the energy of the group is focused on students whose parents attend the host church. When youth join the church as a result of conversion, the student has typically come to faith away from the weekly youth group meetings.

Senior High Ministries

Senior-high teens have a unique and complex relationship with adults and adulthood. On the one hand, adulthood, with its autonomy and freedom, is the pearl of great price, the goal toward which every teen is straining. On the other hand, teens often view adults with suspicion, seeing them as the old people who want to "hold me back" from the freedoms of full membership in society.

Those of us who wish to minister to senior highers must launch ourselves into the middle of this love-hate relationship. As we attempt to navigate these turbulent waters, we'll want to keep in view two key traits of the senior-high teen.

Craving for Autonomy

Because the autonomy of adulthood is so compelling, older teens crave experiences in which this autonomy can be tried on for size. Such experiences stand in contrast to the "student activities" that senior highers may view as being concocted by adults to shield them from the realities of life. Such a contrived experience presents no real risk and offers little opportunity to make important choices with real-world consequences.

The difference between "adult" and "student" experiences can be highlighted by contrasting a church overnighter — including a video on ministry to the poor — with an actual trip to the inner city. The inner-city trip brings the teens into contact with the dangers they read about in the paper.

Though it must be carefully managed, this risk factor makes the event attractive. It thrusts the students into the real world of real gains and real casualties. They can hold a baby or pass out food, rather than watch a video of someone else doing it.

This *youth fellowship model* is most commonly found in smaller churches or in congregations that lack the financial resources associated with the middle class. Seldom are there paid youth ministers to help develop this type of ministry. Most of the responsibility for leadership rests on young adults (who are often not viewed as being old enough to be leaders in the larger church) and student officers. Young people are forced to rely upon their own ingenuity to make the gospel come alive to peers who might otherwise be bored by another meeting in church.

A variation on this approach is the *community model.* Here church members view the youth group as a vital part of the larger community of believers. Qualified students may even serve on the board that governs the church, since student opinions are important to the community of believers. Youth group meetings tend to be for the purpose

As the students begin to realize their actions have real-world consequences, they display new levels of responsible behavior. In fact, the teens may begin manifesting a maturity that adult leaders thought impossible from those who, for example, recently poured salt into the junior highers' punch bowl.

Craving for Relationships

Junior highers, when presented with a church program, will ask, "What are we going to do?"

Senior highers will ask, "Who is going to be there?"

This attraction to relational intimacy includes a desire to have a significant and genuine relationship with an adult. However, the senior higher often raises temporary defenses that may convince adults the student wants nothing to do with them. Adults must understand that this is not the case. The adults are simply being kept at a distance (almost unconsciously by the student) until they can be evaluated. If a favorable evaluation occurs, an open and trusting relationship can develop.

During that evaluation period, students are looking for some specific things. They want to know that the adult in question is being open and honest about himself or herself. Though senior highers are curious about adulthood, they want the truth, not an "edited for television" version. If they perceive the adult is for real, they probably will want to pursue the relationship further. This requires our commitment to personal vulnerability. It feels risky, but it will pay off in huge relational dividends.

Senior highers tend to gravitate toward people who are saying, "This is who I am. I am not someone or something else. I like what I have become and who God has made me to be." Such persons can give students hopeful insights into what adulthood is really like. This positive information will help allay students' fears about being trapped in an adulthood they can neither enjoy nor change.

—John Hambrick

of discussing issues that should be of concern to the church. The church's progressive leaders may look to the idealism of youth to stimulate the consciences of the more conservative church elders. Young leaders emerge before the eyes of the believing community.

The *facility model* rounds out the leadership-development strategies of youth ministry. Buildings provide a place of safety in which leaders can develop. Found most frequently in urban and rural settings, the mind-set seems to be: "If we can keep the kids off the street, they will grow up to share our value system." As a result, many churches have gymnasiums, student lounges, or activity rooms for their youth. When staffed by people who know how to turn conversations about school and sports into an examination of Christian values, these facilities may well become places where new leadership indeed begins to develop.

• *Consumer strategies.* There was no pre-established constituency for parachurch youth ministries. Every week the club rose or fell on its own merits. If a student stopped attending, there was no parent on the phone with the youth sponsor expressing concern. If anything, parents from secular homes likely expressed relief that their son or daughter had gotten over this religious phase of life!

Parachurch means "alongside the church." The Sunday school and YMCA/YWCA movements were the earliest parachurch agencies doing youth ministry. Believing that there were tens of thousands of youth the church had no way of reaching with the gospel, these movements replaced the church with the high school as the most popular gathering place for adolescents. The Youth for Christ movement (with Saturday night rallies described as "the hottest place in town") and Young Life clubs (built around personable adult leaders who won the loyalty of student leaders) soon found hundreds of young people showing up for meetings.

Though the youth culture has changed in the past fifty years, the consumer strategy remains in effect for both parachurch agencies and a widening circle of seeker-oriented churches. The formula is simple: Make the gatherings fun, even exciting; address subjects that relate to students' felt needs; employ the authority of Scripture while speaking to students with dignity and respect; be sure each student will be missed when not present; and don't be afraid to ask for appropriate spiritual decisions.

As the twentieth century draws to a close, one of the largest youth ministries in the United States is Student Impact at Willow Creek Community Church near Chicago. Despite the fact that this is a ministry of a single church, the consumer strategy drives the ministry. Students are attracted to a Tuesday-evening gathering (of over 1,200 kids) by the games, music, media shows, relationships, and pure fun. They are then willing to stay to hear student need–related talks based on the enduring principles found in the Bible.

• *Service strategies.* Tired of singing songs in retirement homes, taping bindings on aging hymnals, and handing out gospel tracts in front of rescue missions, a new breed of youth ministers in the mid 1960s began looking for service projects that challenged the imaginations of youth-group members. Operation Mobilization had set an example on Christian college campuses by calling students in their late teens and early twenties to carry the Christian message around the world in short-term missionary efforts. Local churches from middle-class communities began exploring the possibilities for high school students.

Soon parachurch agencies began to catch the vision and assist churches in sending young people into short-term, cross-cultural ministries. Youth for Christ promoted Project Serve; Youth with a Mission advertised "Get Dirty for God" and brought young people from all over the United States to form ministry teams and send them around the world for a summer of ministry. Youth with a Mission expanded the idea into a ministry of youth to youth, eventually reaching into every nation in the world. Denominational youth programs once again followed the lead of the parachurch agencies, primarily focusing on native Americans, ethnic minorities, and the urban and rural poor.

The primary problem with these service strategies was that they were often merely offering experiences, much like that of a weekend retreat or summer camp. Seldom, however, did the entire youth group go on the trip. It was a great time of training for student leaders. Yet even with ten weeks of orientation before the missionary trip and a debriefing time afterward, the experience seldom lasted more than three months. The problem became, What does the youth group do during the rest of the year?

While the service strategy has been incorporated into other strategies, some youth groups have made service a year-round proposition. They design trips to accommodate all youth-group members. Thanksgiving projects and spring break expeditions complement the summer excursion. Weekly ministry in the community provides the opportunity for adult coaches to work with students on a week-to-week basis as they assist latch-key children, the homeless, or other troubled youth.

• *Cell-group strategies.* Small groups became a normal part of youth groups in the late 1960s. The idea of using clusters of six to twelve people gathering to study the Bible or pray was not a new idea for adults in Christian movements. Now the antiauthoritarian mind-set of the Vietnam era and the influence of the "Jesus Movement" made small groups attractive for youth, too, who wanted to get to know their peers better while holding each other accountable for spiritual growth. While a professional youth ministry was emerging in churches, unpaid young adults usually took over the leadership in cell groups.

The goals for high school cell groups varied widely. For many, the group was a place to get to know other Christian students and talk honestly about the problems they faced. Bible study and prayer were usually a stated priority, but unless the youth minister was actively involved in training small-group leaders and then supervising their efforts, cell groups frequently lost their discipling focus. Yet the cell-group strategy allowed an adult a comfortable way to enter the students' world. Even if the Bible study faltered, young persons still had a role model to confide in during times of stress.

In most youth groups, the cell group is a subset of a larger group gathering. For some, weekly or monthly evangelistic meetings establish the tone and character of the youth group. For other churches, the Sunday school or midweek program provides the youth minister an opportunity to instruct and challenge those who attend. Small groups can make sure each member of the larger youth group is enfolded and nurtured.

Finally, the *Meta-Church strategy* views the cell as *the* church and the larger group meetings as a support and expansion of the small group. Youth groups that adopt the Meta-Church strategy eliminate large-group activities, which consume the energies and time of both students and leaders. The cell group is the focus of evangelism, and volunteer leaders are trained to keep an empty chair for spiritual seekers who are brought to the group by their friends. Bible study, prayer, and worship are similarly the responsibility of cell groups. When groups grow beyond about a dozen in attendance, they are divided and expected to reach out to nonbelievers—and in the process continue to grow and multiply.

—*Mark H. Senter III*

Resources

Benson, W., and M. Senter. 1987. The complete book of youth ministry. Chicago: Moody.

Ratcliff, D. and J. Davies. 1991. Handbook of youth ministry. Birmingham: R.E.P. Books.

Richards, L. 1985. Youth ministry: Its renewal in the local church. Grand Rapids: Zondervan.

Senter, M. 1992. The coming revolution in youth ministry. Wheaton, Ill.: Victor.

Veerman, D. 1992. Small groups ministry with youth. Wheaton, Ill.: Victor.

Yaconelli, M., and J. Burns. 1986. High school ministry. Grand Rapids: Zondervan.

College Ministries

College ministry can be tremendously exciting and fulfilling. College students are an energetic group of bright, talented, articulate folks who are making key decisions in their lives. They have the ability to make an impact on other students and, later, their communities and the world. What a privilege to spend time with them and have an influence on their lives!

What Are They Like?

The most important thing for a college minister to know about college students is that they are not just older high school students. Neither are they like young adults in their late 20s. College students have their own unique set of priorities, needs, and experiences.

In one sense, today's college students haven't changed much from those of the past. They still struggle with leaving home and saying goodbye to the familiarity of high school life. They still face crucial life decisions—determining college majors, making career plans, and establishing relationships that might lead to marriage. They are still coming to grips with who they are and who they will be beyond their parents' direct influence.

In other ways, students are different from those of twenty, or even ten, years ago. More are from dysfunctional homes and need reparenting to some degree. More are nonchurched and biblically illiterate. In addition, today's student faces stiffer competition in the classroom than ever before.

How Can We Minister?

What is a college minister's best approach? Naturally, we need to love the students, developing a ministry that meets their needs and calls them into a deeper relationship with Jesus Christ. We can go where they are, hang out on the campus, have lunch with students, meet them where they live. Since we won't be able to give this kind of time to everyone, we need to recruit a team to help out.

Then we can achieve a ministry of balance by building in four key elements. First, in "the gathering" all the students involved in the ministry can get together regularly, at least monthly. Since college students are typically people of the night, having this meeting late, say 9:30 to 10:45, minimizes scheduling conflicts. This larger meeting should include worship, teaching, and fun.

Second, we can set up cell groups of five to eight people that get together weekly for sharing, Bible study, and prayer.

Third, we need to develop some form of outreach ministry that moves students into the community (tutoring disadvantaged kids, teaching English to immigrants, building homes for Habitat for Humanity, etc.). Community outreach lets students test their faith and discover that Christ crosses every cultural boundary.

Fourth, we can work with the students to start investigative Bible studies in dormitories or other popular gathering places.

Common Mistakes

What typical blunders should we avoid as college ministers? Consider these three:

- Don't assume an interest in the institutional church. Students might drop by for worship one week and not be around for the next three weeks. One thing is sure, however: they won't show up at all if we try to lay a guilt trip on them.
- Don't underestimate students' talents and abilities. They can do so much! Challenge them to become leaders; give them every opportunity to display their gifts and to succeed in ministry to their peers.
- Don't forget the amount of pressure on students. Along with studying for tests and meeting term-paper deadlines, they face the challenge of coming to grips with who they are, developing a social life, and living out their values in a place where morality is typically minimized. Students need to know that we appreciate their pressure-cooker existence.

—Denny Rydberg

27

Camps and Conferences

We all share a deep need periodically to get away from it all, to leave our routines and familiar surroundings for places of relaxation, recreation, and renewal. In large part, that is what Christian camping is all about. While providing physical retreat, camping can also help the church meet many of its spiritual-growth and nurturing objectives. Those who have yet to involve their church family in camping experiences will no doubt ask at least three big questions about how that can happen.

What's Our Reason?

Why go camping? For starters, there are some things that the church can do better at camp than it can do anywhere else. Consider these five benefits:

• *Effective evangelism.* Tony Campolo, while speaking to a thousand Christian camp leaders at a banquet, was on a roll with his opening remarks, and everyone else was on the floor—with laughter. Then he asked a quick series of staccato questions: "How many of you became Christians watching television?" One hand went up. "How many accepted the Lord listening to a fine sermon during a church service?" A half-dozen hands were raised. "How many accepted Christ in a Sunday-school class? A youth-group meeting? At home?"

Two or three hands went up each time. Then he paused for a moment, grinned impishly, and asked, "How many of you became Christians at a camp?" The hotel dining room was filled with hands lifted high!

He assured us that his survey has never failed to produce the same results in any group. Camp is a most fruitful setting for reaping a harvest of new believers, whether among children, youth, or adults, though significant amounts of planting and watering back home help produce it.

- *Rest and relaxation.* Another activity the church can do better at camp than at home is exactly what Jesus invited his disciples to do: "Come with me by yourselves to a quiet place and get some rest" (Mark 6:31). Jesus practiced what he preached, starting off with a forty-day camping trip that he shared with angels and wild creatures. Consider the spectrum of activities a church family can share during a weekend at camp and the potential for Christian fellowship those activities hold: sharing meals with leisurely time for table conversations during and after the meal, setting tables, washing dishes, cooking, playing table tennis, dressing up for skits and performing them, taking one-on-one walks in the woods, building a snowman, singing around a campfire, floating down a river in an inner tube, studying the Bible in a mountain meadow, doing a puzzle with friends, climbing a craggy peak at sunrise, conversing under a tree, paddling a canoe, sharing in small groups, worshiping out of doors . . . and the list goes on.
- *Continuous quality time.* Someone may say that many of the activities named above could be done back home. That's true, but it's here that camping offers perhaps its greatest advantage: continuous quality time together for church members. Getting away together for a weekend or longer provides a church family with not just little windows of quality time snatched from a hectic week, but continuous, uninterrupted hours of meaningful fellowship.

For instance, let's say a Sunday school teacher has about 45 minutes with her class every Sunday. In a year, she'll have had her students for a total of 39 hours—if her students are there every Sunday. With 75 percent attendance, that's about 30 hours scattered over a year's time. Contrast that with a weekend—at least 30 waking hours —or a week, with at least 96 waking hours. No wonder so much is accomplished when we can get those kids to camp!

Of course, it is not only the youth who can benefit from continuous quality time. The entire church family, whether they come all together during a family camp or attend in specialized groups (retreats for men, women, singles, seniors, etc.), will experience significant spiritual growth.

- *Modeling opportunities.* Not only are camping activities deeply beneficial for the relaxation and recreation they provide, but as they are shared by a church family, ministry leaders have premium opportunities to model the winsome love of Christ. Scripture teaches that modeling the truth is critical to the effectiveness of teaching. Paul said, "Follow my example, as I follow the example of Christ" (1 Cor. 11:1), and "Whatever you have learned or received or heard from me, or seen in me—put it into practice" (Phil. 4:9). The writer of Hebrews admonishes the church to "remember your leaders, who spoke the word of God to you. Consider the outcome of their way of life and imitate their faith" (Heb. 13:7).

It's not uncommon for church members to see their pastors only during a sermon, or to meet with an esteemed Christian friend only for a brief hello in the church parking lot. Effective modeling calls for significant time together for the model and the student. Camp provides wonderful opportunities for the "out of the pulpit and onto the softball diamond" phenomenon.

What specific traits might be modeled? Within the camping experience, leaders can convey the value of family togetherness, sincere interest in others, good sportsmanship, the ability to laugh at oneself, loving discipline, time for fun, openness to interruptions, eagerness to learn, and serving unselfishly. Living together for days at a time provides a much more realistic classroom for modeling lessons like these. The church body at camp offers a great place for positive friendships to blossom and deepen.

It's also a great place to build esprit de corps among church members. This can happen back home, to be sure, but living together at camp for a little while nurtures a church's family identity. "We really are family; we even live together every now and then!"

There's an old camping axiom: If you can go camping with someone and come home friends, you're *really* friends.

• *Outdoor worship.* Worship together out of doors leads Christians to a deeper appreciation of the Creator through various close encounters with the creation. It enables people to involve all the senses —hearing, touching, tasting, and smelling, as well as seeing, God's wonders. It encourages worshipers to move around, carrying their services to different locations and perhaps singing as they go. This kind of worship teaches a strong and positive lesson to those young in the faith, that true worship is not confined to one building or to one place of any kind. True worship takes place in the heart.

Many pastors cherish every chance they get to involve people in worshiping out of doors. It provides a fitting opportunity to encourage good stewardship of the beautiful world God has given us. As Christians, we are commanded to subdue, replenish, and have dominion over the earth. We're called to be responsible environmentalists. Camp is an ideal place to look at the creation firsthand and foster deeper respect and appreciation for it.

What's Our Plan?

As we weigh the pros and cons of a church going to camp, we should keep in mind that good planning makes a lot of difference. Four areas of planning need consideration as we gather our resources and set to work toward a camping experience:

- *Purpose.* What do we see as our primary objective? This is a planning committee's initial question. Is the main purpose to evangelize, to build relationships, to train disciples, to plan a program for the year, or to combine any of these purposes? Do we expect to take teenagers, children, the church board, men, women, young couples, the church choir, or the whole church family? Perhaps we see the need for a retreat devoted to prayer, or an adventurous outing for fathers and

Camp Operation

In our day, local, state, and federal regulations affecting camps are multiplying exponentially. Camping leaders must stay attuned to the times in order to stay in operation. A carefully formulated purpose statement, excellent neighbor relations, full compliance with mandates and ordinances, and adequate insurance coverages—especially liability—are all more important than ever. Christian camping will continue to be a powerful arm of the local church as long as members understand that camps are businesses that require professional management.

A Dedicated Board

A camp is a multifaceted concern. It's a hotel, restaurant, bank, retail store, park, recreation complex, daycare center, senior-adult center, counseling center . . . and the list goes on. To make a camp profitable and keep staff and constituents content, the primary entity behind the camp—namely, the supporting church or churches—must fully understand the complexity of ownership and operation.

Governing with a dedicated camp board—rather than having a church board include camping on its list of responsibilities—is a preferred arrangement. As a rule, a separate board has more time to get closer to the operation and enact policies that enable growth.

A Competent Staff

A competent staff is the foundation for building a successful operation. Staff members must be team players who are comfortable with the stated philosophy of the camp and who assume the vision as their own.

Depending on the size of the operation, a resident caretaker may be able to handle the job, provided program or "platform" responsibilities are assigned elsewhere. Key volunteers must also be on hand to

sons to strengthen their relationships. Once we choose our primary objective, that objective will exercise a lot of influence on our next planning decision.

• *Place.* No matter where one's church is located, no doubt great camping locations are nearby. The camping purpose, however, narrows the list of potential destinations to those that meet the camping purposes.

For instance, backpacking and car camping are fun-filled and inexpensive, and they work well for multiple objectives. Relatively few adults, however, really get into such primitive outings, so they work best for young people and special-interest groups, rather than for a church-board planning retreat.

Christian campgrounds and retreat centers abound and vary widely in

---

fill critical operational positions, such as food service and housekeeping.

If a camp has five or more buildings and 75 or more beds, or operates year-round, additional staff, perhaps part-time, should be a serious consideration. Staff burnout is common at camps in which the governing body does not understand the demands of full-time ministry (sometimes 24 hours a day!). Keeping a camp presentable, profitable, and safe is hard work.

Provisions for staff members should include adequate housing along with a salary and benefit package that camp board members are not embarrassed to disclose. Depending on dining hall left-overs to round out the fare for the director and his or her family may be economical, but it's not respectable.

A Thorough Cost Analysis

If staffing is the foundation of a successful operation, financial management is the mortar. It's important to start with a thorough understanding of fixed and variable costs. For example, one camp, after completing a cost analysis, found that over $135 a day was needed to cover fixed utilities, liability insurance, operating permits, long-term maintenance, and indirect salaries. Costs directly traceable to camper usage, such as program supplies, food, and honorariums, then had to be added to the fixed expenses.

Unless the primary supporting entity is committed to subsidizing camp operation, the fee charged to every camper should cover: (1) variable, direct costs and (2) a prorated portion of the fixed, indirect costs (the total fixed costs divided by the number of campers projected for the entire operating season). This pricing method allows other contributions to go toward sponsorships and capital improvements.

In the formula above, the number of campers in the operating season may be so low that the camper fee is unacceptably high. In that case, the camp must either increase its operating season (adding midweek programs during the cooler months, for instance) or increase its fund-raising efforts.

—John Ashmen

cost, luxury (or lack of it), and the nature of recreational features they offer. An extensive catalog of these facilities is available from Christian Camping International, in Colorado Springs, Colorado.

When choosing a location for a church-camp experience, the following suggestions will improve the likelihood of success:

Visit the site or camp and take a tour before you commit yourself. Check out the beds, rest rooms, athletic equipment, and meeting spaces. Arrange your visit to include a meal so you can sample the food yourself. In other words, minimize the surprises.

Read the standard contract and the "guest group responsibility list" thoroughly before signing, noting particularly the guaranteed minimum and maximum for which you'll be responsible to pay.

Counselors

"Kevin, can you be a counselor at church camp next week? All you have to do is keep the kids from hurting each other and pray with them at night; our speaker will do the rest. We start on Sunday at three o'clock. Bring a sleeping bag, ball glove, and Bible . . . and try to get there before the kids do."

This recruitment pitch typifies the way some groups view the role of the counselor. In reality, few tasks related to camp are as important as counselor selection and training.

Where to Find Them?

Traditionally, senior high and college-age young people are sought first for counselor positions. If the program activities are not extraordinarily strenuous, older adults should not be ruled out as counselor candidates. Most states set a minimum age for counselors and have mandates for camper-counselor ratios based on camper age. Some states even require fingerprinting and background searches. It's important to check with the appropriate state agency to learn the requirements.

If camp leaders need to go beyond the church membership to find staff, a Christian college or a campus ministry at a secular university is a good place to look. Leaders should start the search early, since many young people put their summer schedules together right after Christmas. Regardless of a candidate's appearance or reputation, it's wise to get three references before signing an agreement.

Even if campers are sopped with rain from dawn until dusk, carefully selected counselors can save the day and can make camping an enjoyable, life-changing experience. Camping enthusiast Lloyd Mattson pointed out years ago that counselors of distinction have three traits in common:

- *They enjoy kids.* They don't just adore kids when they're combed and cute, or when the kids become momentary heroes on the

Get an easy-to-read map to include in your camp brochure.

Ask about menu choices. Consider whether you want to cook for yourselves or have the meals provided. Most camps offer one option or the other.

Choose a camp location far enough away from home, especially for adult retreats, that still guarantees full participation. Men are the worst offenders at wanting to slip in for only part of the event. This practice, regardless of the age group involved, tends to disrupt the continuity of what you intend to accomplish. It also tends to diminish the commitment of those who are attending for the entire event. Many leaders adopt a "no drop-in or part-time attendance" philosophy if they must choose a nearby conference center.

---

ball field or talent-show stage. The best counselors relate, communicate, and affirm no matter what the situation.

• *They surrender self-interests.* Subduing the desire to lounge by the pool or catch the lake's legendary trout, these counselors submit to a juvenile agenda so the kids in their care can be coddled, coached, and counseled in the things of the Lord. Harder yet, they do not permit an infatuation with a counselor of the opposite sex to steal valuable time from the campers.

• *They accept accountability.* With an unusual maturity, they are committed to seeing the camp's objectives fulfilled in campers' lives. Meanwhile, they are equally concerned about safety and the protection of camp property. Outstanding counselors pray regularly, realizing their ultimate accountability is to God.

How to Train Them?

An ideal staff-training program takes about a week. This allows sufficient time for program orientation and bonding. Campers can readily tell if counselors are excited, personally prepared, and united as a ministry team. If a one-week program is not possible, orientation can be trimmed by one or two days if counselors are already familiar with the camp schedule and training materials are mailed in advance.

Staff training should cover such topics as camping dynamics, age-group characteristics, various counseling techniques, and camper follow-up. Equally important are sessions on handling emergencies, administering discipline, and recognizing and reporting child abuse. If recreation or outdoor skills are to be taught by counselors, include practice sessions. Training materials on these and other related subjects can be provided by Christian Camping International, P.O. Box 62189, Colorado Springs, CO 80962; phone (719) 260-9400.

In larger programs, an effective way to assist and supervise counselors is through senior counselors or unit leaders. Experienced people positioned between the program director and counselors can provide guidance and ongoing encouragement. They also can step in to handle emergency situations.

—John Ashmen

• *Personnel.* The best family camps typically are planned and executed by lay leaders in the local church. On the other hand, professional youth workers often lead the best youth retreats. Churches that don't have a youth minister can take advantage of camps that offer youth retreats blending small groups from various churches.

Whoever leads any conference should have great enthusiasm for the project. All camp personnel—leaders, counselors, cooks, baby-sitters, and speakers—should have adequate training and be given a written job description detailing their responsibilities.

Those who plan children's or youth retreats are wise to recruit and train counselors from their churches to counsel their campers. Sharing the camp experience brings the campers and counselors close as they play, pray, sleep, eat, study the Bible, talk, and laugh together. The experience lays a foundation for continuing nurture and discipleship. Much is lost if the last time campers see their counselor is on the final day of camp.

• *Promotion.* Church families are bombarded with a propaganda blitz from every direction. To capture people's attention for camping opportunities, consider these guidelines:

First, assign one person to be in charge of promotion and nothing else, someone who is creative, outgoing, and energetic. Then start the promotion early and keep it going full steam ahead.

A variety of approaches works best, including brochures, posters, announcements with humorous skits, sincere testimonials, phone calls, and personal invitations. When a church publishes its schedule early in the year, it displays good organization and increases anticipation.

It's important to emphasize a registration deadline and encourage early sign-ups by tacking on a late fee for registrations received after the deadline. In reality, early sign-ups are the best promotion. People who have already signed up are walking, living ads for the camping program.

What's Our Program?

Good programs begin at the point of departure, where transportation and luggage handling should be well-planned. Assigned leaders can be on hand to assist with details, including welcoming campers and making everyone feel a part of things. At least one leader should arrive at the camp a few hours ahead of everyone else to verify room assignments and perhaps post campers' names on their rooms. These room assignments should be made before the departure day.

The camp schedule is important enough to be posted in every room. Those who want a surprise element at camp are better off to let the surprises stem from how excellent each activity is, not from a moment-by-moment curiosity about what will happen next.

Good camp programming depends, of course, on our goals and our style of reaching them, but I recommend the following guidelines:

- *Structure the entire day* with time slots, but be sure to include generous portions of free time. We can encourage and model genuine leisure for work-weary adults. Youth groups generally call for a little tighter schedule.
- *Play!* With kids on computers and adults on the run, experts are calling for a return to pure, unadulterated play. Recreation equals re-creation.
- *Plan enough time for sleep* and gently but firmly insist on sticking with it. For example, if you have some junior-high boys who just won't quiet down at midnight, try this: "Okay, guys, we've had a good time talking and laughing. Now it's time to get some sleep. I've asked you a couple of times, and this is the third and final time. If anyone makes any more noise after I'm through with this warning, you'll spend your entire free time tomorrow on your bunk. Have a good rest; we have a big day ahead!" Lack of sleep will diminish every other aspect of a camping program.
- *Balance social input.* People need active times of fellowship and quiet times of solitude. The discipline of spending perhaps thirty to sixty minutes without talking to anyone but God can be an enriching exercise for youth and adults.
- *Be flexible.* There are times when we must take that structured day of ours with a grain of salt. We shouldn't let any plan gone awry rob us of our joy. Certainly a back-up plan is wise. Rainy days, broken-down buses, or power failures should find us with an alternate activity or program in our back pocket.
- *Make meal times special.* Use themes (for example, Christmas in July, Valentine's Day, or movie titles) and decorate the place. Provide background music. Do skits. Suggest table-discussion questions.
- *Emphasize fellowship.* The dinner table at mealtime used to be a premium place for sharing, but its importance appears all but lost in the hectic pace of today's family. But we can nurture dinner-table fellowship at camp. The best argument for structuring such fellowship is a statement by Jesus in Revelation 3:20, where we read that his entrance into our lives will be like we're having supper together. What a high view of mealtime fellowship!

How do we get campers to stay for fellowship after they've eaten their food? We can save important announcements for the meal's end and ask everyone to stay until we've made those announcements. If we have many people who aren't used to talking around the table, we may want to provide a card at each table that lists several fun or interesting discussion questions. Or we can offer a prize to everyone at the table who uses a secret "Prize Word" in their after-meal table conversations.

What's Our Cost?

There *is* considerable effort and expense to consider. When we sit down to budget a retreat, we may want to start by pricing several nearby camps. The national average in the early 90s is around $24 a day per person for lodging and three meals. If a conference center that provides meals costs too much, a church can consider sites that allow groups to bring food and do their own cooking.

Many churches set up a camp scholarship program, considering it a solid investment in the Christian education of the church family. Who would ever refuse a college scholarship? We can help our church families see scholarships enabling camp attendance in the same light.

Is Christian camping worth the cost? At the national average, camp costs about a dollar an hour. Compare that to a movie in a theater ($2.50 an hour), baby-sitting ($4 an hour), bungee jumping ($50 for five minutes), or a visit to the dentist! Certainly camping is a bargain by anyone's standards—for the child who finds a friend, for the family who finds a deeper bond, for the teenager who finds Jesus. Camp can be a priceless treasure that any church can help its people discover.

—*Sonny Salsbury*

Resources

Dausey, G. 1983. The youth leader's sourcebook. Grand Rapids: Zondervan.

Cagle, B. 1989. Youth ministry camping. Loveland, Colo.: Group.

Cockrell, D. 1991. The wilderness educator. Merrillville, Ind.: ICS.

Focus series pamphlets. Colorado Springs: Christian Camping International.

Raus, B. 1990. Ministry through camping. Martinsville, Ind.: American Camping Association.

Wright, N. 1986. Help, I'm a camp counselor. Ventura: Regal.

Travel Camps

A travel camp is a mobile classroom for growing Christians. It provides a number of impressive benefits, such as the adventure and educational opportunities of travel, a variety of recreational options, built-in small-group times, and exposure to a wide array of mission endeavors. Lodging is virtually free, and so are many meals. In fact, it's a low-budget dream.

Travel camps offer wonderful settings for Christian education, providing all the variations normally associated with mission treks, choir tours, or recreational outings. Why settle for one or two dimensions when we can expose campers to the whole rainbow? The witness of a gospel concert or of physical labor on a needed project is meaningful, but they represent just two elements of a much broader spectrum of Christian-growth opportunities. A travel camp is a means of training Christians in personal disciplines, life in the body, and service in the world.

From years of experience, here are some guidelines for leading an effective travel camp.

Broad Experiences

We need to aim for balance and variety. Luke 2:52 presents a great model of balance: "Jesus grew in wisdom and stature, and in favor with God and men." This verse describes the four basic areas of our lives: mental, physical, spiritual, and social. The best possible travel camp will stretch travel campers in all of these areas. Some ideas:

• *Mental.* Assign each camper a Christian book to read during the trip and perhaps a second book of their choice if the trip takes three weeks or more. Hold an awards banquet near the trip's end for all those who complete their reading.

• *Physical.* Arrange to do some hard, meaningful manual labor for a church or mission. Go backpacking for a few days. Involve your campers in some physical challenge that is new to them, such as kayaking, surfing, or rock climbing.

• *Spiritual.* Have daily Bible studies together, with various students taking leadership. Arrange for your group to visit great teachers and speakers along the way. Give each camper a cloth-bound diary book in order to keep a spiritual journal during the trip.

• *Social.* Have your group members pair up in twos every day for a half-hour session of "the two of us." Instruct campers to pair up with the person they know the least, get better acquainted by discussing your suggested questions for the day, and close by praying for each other.

Logistical Suggestions

• *Transportation.* If possible, use twelve-passenger vans. They create automatic small groups, and they are inexpensive, compared to buses. A group also can visit different sites simultaneously.

• *Lodging.* Mix the options. Sleeping bags on church floors are great for building community, emphasizing the servant nature of our calling. Random pairs staying in host homes build one-on-one relationships and provide opportunities to witness as gracious guests. An overnight campout can be an exciting variation.

In planning stops along the way, it's best to utilize contacts you know personally and to visit each site before you commit your travel group.

• *Food.* Some meals will be provided free where you are doing work projects or a concert. Typically, you'll have breakfast and a sack lunch provided by host homes and dinner together at the church.

Provide a variety for other meals: feast for a meal; fast for a meal. A cook kit allows you to make lunches by the road. Each person should take a turn serving as a cook for at least one meal.

The time that Jesus spent with his disciples was, in effect, a travel camp. We can use it as our model for optimum discipling.

—*Sonny Salsbury*

Wilderness Camping

The wilderness is an excellent learning context and practical change agent. We may teach in a number of classroom settings, but nothing can produce change like the wilderness.

The wilderness offers unique opportunities for new starts, discovery of the incredible things Christ can do in and through us, and indelible transformation and growth. Take Rick, for example—a high school dropout who considered himself an extremely poor learner. Over the years he became a fine wilderness instructor, and later he received a master's degree in English—with a 4.0 average.

The Real Thing

Wilderness experiences are a time of training for a purpose—a critical ingredient in people's faith journeys—never an end in themselves. The Bible is full of wilderness experiences, and it's a book about transformation, not just information. Abraham, Moses, Paul, and even Jesus remind us that the wilderness is a place of radical dependence on God. Wilderness and change go together; participants learn because they have to.

The wilderness is a nonneutral learning environment because it forces change; the learning curve is at its steepest. A subtle tragedy of our culture is that people can go through life without getting really cold or hungry or thirsty or tired. And because so much of our educational process is vicarious—indirectly learned through books, the media, teachers, and other people's experiences—learning often fades under the test of life's many great pressures. Not so in the wilderness!

I remember Janet, who had tried to rappel at lest six times but each time was driven back by fear. Later, she insisted that she be given one more try. When she got to the edge, just as she was about to back over the cliff, she looked at us and said boldly, "This is to *prove* that Jesus Christ is real in my life!" And off she went, learning more about herself and life than she ever could in a classroom.

God created everything except a substitute for experience.

Making It Safe

The Boy Scout motto, "Be prepared," is never more important than in wilderness camping. Any leadership post requires a level of expertise, but leading a group in the wilderness demands a wide range of skills, experience (both technical as well as relational), training, and judgment.

Groups need at least one trained leader for every five students. These leaders need to know such things as advanced first aid, CPR, evacuation procedures, survival techniques, how to safely manage a group in the wilderness, map and compass skills, how to stay warm and dry in inclement weather, how to protect the fragile environment, and what kind of clothes and equipment each participant will need. But of all the mountaineering skills, good judgment remains the most important.

If a church group is unable to provide experienced leadership, Christian wilderness programs can offer assistance. Most will supply not only trained guides but also appropriate equipment and supplies. Many church leaders consider such camping programs the best way to experience the wilderness. By utilizing experienced Christian guides, group leaders not only insure safety and fun, but also give themselves the freedom to cultivate relationships and provide spiritual leadership.

Group leaders will want to check the church's insurance policy for coverage of wilderness excursions. Both medical coverage and adequate liability insurance are highly recommended for adventure activities.

Two Christian wilderness ministries that can set you up for adventure or direct you to other resources are:

• Summit Adventure, P.O. Box 498, Bass Lake, CA 93604; (800) 827-1282.

• Second Wind, c/o JH Ranch, 8525 Homestead Lane, Etna, CA 96027; (205) 822-2929 or (916) 467-3468.

Helen Keller once said, "Life is either a daring adventure or nothing at all!" Wilderness camping is about life.

—*Tim Hansel*

Specialized Retreats

Someone has said, "We must come apart for a while to prevent us from coming apart permanently." We need to remove ourselves periodically from the normal ministry routine and make time to restore our vision and renew our passion. Jesus said to the first disciples, "Come with me by yourselves to a quiet place, and get some rest" (Mark 6:31).

Note the words carefully. Yes, there is restoration in the quiet places, a measure of renewal in getting away by ourselves. But the key lies in the phrase "with me." It is his presence in the quiet place that makes for the miracle. Church historians tell us that nearly every period of revival in the church's vitality has involved retreat ministries — believers intentionally going away to meet with their Lord for particular purposes.

We need to plan for specialized retreats, getting away with people in similar life circumstances for the purpose of addressing, in the Lord's presence, particular common needs. We should also design retreats for teaching on and actually doing prayer, for covering specific portions of Scripture, for grappling with sensitive issues believers are facing.

Ideas for Effectiveness

Those who regularly plan and lead such retreats advise:

• *Worship, worship, worship!* Through worship, tension is released, perspective is regained, hearts are softened, and God becomes more real and present. We can begin and end with worship — and worship, even if for only a moment, along the way.

• *Work with a team.* It's good to recruit and train a team of people, giving each person particular responsibilities. One or two of the members might do the teaching, and one or two the music. Others may handle supplies (from providing notebooks and Bibles to securing extra toothbrushes and aspirin). Other team members may focus on simply making themselves available for conversation and counseling.

• *Plan carefully — and then let things evolve.* Those who repeat the same retreat often tell us that each one takes on a life of its own. Though the schedule of events may be the same as the one before, the mix of people and the freedom of the Holy Spirit make for something unrepeatable. We can be open to the Lord, who wants to create something no one in the planning process could have anticipated.

• *Go with the flow of energy.* Certain kinds of activities work best in certain time frames. Week-long retreats, for example, tend to bog down during the third day. So, plan for a change of pace: a recreation day, or a field trip away from the retreat center. Weekend retreats tend to work best with the following rhythm:

Friday evening: worship songs are strong and lively; content of messages requires lots of vivid imagery.

Saturday morning: worship can begin lively and become more meditative; content of messages can be more didactic and informational.

Saturday evening: worship will be meditative; content should stress the personal and devotional.

Sunday morning: worship needs to be bright, more concrete; content should focus on "Where do we go from here?"

• *Plan for follow-up.* It's a good idea to give participants specific suggestions about what they can do when they return to their routines (including how they might change any routines that hinder spiritual vitality). We may want to plan a follow-up event, such as a Friday-evening potluck, a Saturday picnic, or several small-group meetings.

As leaders we need to relax and enjoy the benefits of retreating with our flocks. We can find a level of healing and transformation taking place that simply cannot happen in a one-hour time span on Sunday mornings.

—Darrell W. Johnson

28

Christian Schools

Although some Christian schools are more than a century old, the great majority have begun since 1950, shortly after the end of the Second World War. The early postwar wave of these new educational institutions consisted mostly of parent-society schools. Church-controlled schools became prevalent as legal problems intensified for the schools and as more Christians came to believe that operating a school was a valid church ministry.

Why Start a Christian School?

Since the early sixties, major legal decisions have prohibited the Bible and prayer from having a role in the nation's tax-supported schools. As a result, the differences between the secular school and the Christian school have become clearer, year by year. No secular school, private or public, is based on the unique and distinctive world-view of the biblical Christian. Thus churches and parents begin and operate Christian schools in order to have their children educated in the light of God's truth.

It is the broad purpose of the Christian school to teach children and young people that the Lord Jesus Christ is preeminent in all of life. That truth is the unifying principle of Christian education and underlies every aspect of academic learning and school life. "For by him all things were created: things in heaven and on earth. . . . He is before all things, and in him all things hold together. . . . that in everything he might have the supremacy" (Col. 1:16–18). With this underlying foundation, those who enter into Christian schooling can tackle the three foundational tasks involved in the initial planning stages for the school: developing a sound biblical and educational philosophy, setting clearly defined objectives, and defining the ongoing relationship between the school and its sponsoring congregation.

Developing the Educational Philosophy

A growing number of national and international organizations exist to serve congregations desiring to create a Christian school. Their help and advice is backed by years of experience and is a great advantage to those developing an educational philosophy. These organizations can be identified and located by asking existing schools for information or by contacting the largest Christian school organization—the Association of Christian Schools International.

In spite of this excellent available help, each sponsoring church will be responsible for sitting down with church members, interested parents, and the school-planning committee to hammer out a clear set of philosophical statements detailing mission and educational objectives. Churches approaching this crucial task must keep in mind at least three philosophical and theological principles about which most Christian school planners have sought consensus before moving any further in the process:

• *Parents are ultimately responsible for the education of their children.* Parents, not the state—or even the Christian school—are the ultimate educators of their children. During the school day, Christian school teachers act in place of the parents, and the biblical injunction to raise children in the nurture and admonition of the Lord transfers to them. Parents, teachers, and the church are thus partners, teaching children at home, at church, and at school with the understanding that the parents are the primary educators.

Children's concepts about education and its importance begin with the parents, and the home is the center of educational and spiritual development, a bastion of learning that cannot and should not be replaced by the school. The school simply supplements the home and the church, and parents are to be living examples of what they want their children to imitate. Parents who exhibit in their lives a commitment to continuous learning help their children realize that excellence in Christian education cannot be achieved without prayer, intellectual discipline, and moral integrity, coupled with hard work and commitment to God's will.

• *All truth is God's truth.* A primary concept in a Christian school philosophy of education should be the recognition that reality—truth—is knowable through God's general revelation in creation and through his specific revelation, both the living and written Word of

God. There is no truth apart from the person or actions of God. All truth is God's truth, without division into so-called "sacred truth" and "secular truth." Such a division indicates faulty thinking about the nature of God as Creator of all that exists, including history and mathematics, science and language, music and the arts. Jesus Christ is to be the center of all learning and living, because in him "are hidden all the treasures of wisdom and knowledge" (Col. 2:3).

Yet there is a basic, critical difference between the Christian and the secular *approaches* to education. The facts of knowledge are identical for both to explore. The difference is in the interpretation of those facts. The Christian school purposes to integrate facts with the Word of God, believing that no subject can be understood in totality when the Creator-Savior is ignored or denied. The secular approach to education teaches facts but omits God. The integration of a God-centered world-view with a sound academic curriculum need not be strained or forced in the Christian school but can be natural, "for in him we live and move and have our being" (Acts 17:28).

• *Life has a divine purpose and a moral design.* Everyone involved in launching a Christian school must be convinced that human beings are to live their lives as a response to their Creator-Savior, enjoying him and endeavoring to please him through doing justly, loving mercy, and walking humbly with him. The eternal state of each human being is determined by that person's response to the call of God in Christ Jesus.

It follows that the absolute determination of what is morally right or wrong is the prerogative of God alone, revealed to us in his Word, both written (the Bible) and living (Jesus). Since the Holy Spirit indwells every Christian and he convicts us of sin, guides us into all truth, and magnifies Christ, we can agree to accept the values for life that are derived from the Word of God.

Setting the Student Objectives

The goals of Christian school education rest on the philosophical underpinnings stated above. Building on these broad statements, school planners can begin working on specific teaching and learning objectives for the students. These will no doubt include, at the least, foundational statements such as these:

• *The Bible will be presented as the basis for the most fulfilling life.* Students not only should be taught what the Bible says but should learn how to study it for themselves. Bible content is best taught in a devotional manner, so students learn to be open-hearted and affected by the revelation of God's will for their daily lives. This approach fosters the best kind of character development, in which students are growing into the likeness of Christ.

With the Bible as the foundation, the teaching of related truths naturally follows. Students are encouraged to receive Jesus Christ as Savior and Lord, the master of their lives. Through an ever-deepening commitment, they are encouraged to become disciples who submit themselves to his direction throughout their lives. In addition, biblical standards of morality and ethics are set forth as absolute truth, not relative. They are presented as God's standards for our good in this life. The lifelong objectives of doing justly, loving mercy, and walking humbly with God are presented as reachable goals, not as mere idealistic visions.

• *Care for the human welfare of others will be cultivated.* Students are shown how to relate to non-Christians and to Christians who hold differing points of views. Involvement in practical ways with world missions—and with local missions projects for the hungry and homeless—is set forth as urgent. Students are taught to pray for their neighbors and their world, seeking practical ways to get involved with the needs of those around them.

The Pastor-Administrator Relationship

A church school is best administered when the personal relationship between pastor and administrator is strong and amicable. The pastor should be confident that the administrator is well-qualified for the job and is to give the administrator the freedom to do it.

Keeping Strong Relationships

Unless the administrator can independently lead the school in a way that reflects the church's beliefs and complements its ministry, both institutions will suffer. Here are some essential requirements for an effective pastor-administrator relationship. They'll need:

• *Theological compatibility.* Compatibility on theological beliefs and on the principles of daily living is essential, since both the administrator and pastor offer spiritual leadership. Since the pastor is the administrator's pastor, however, the administrator should experience him or her as understanding and open to different points of view.

• *A respect for separate ministries.* The pastor needs a strong, genuine commitment to the ministry of the school, seeing that the school gets proper visibility in the church and that the administrator is recognized for leadership. At the same time, the administrator is responsible to provide adequate data, so the pastor can feel comfortable discussing the school with any audience.

• *Public solidarity.* It's best for the administrator to have a specific, visible ministry in church on Sundays. The pastor should speak in chapel periodically and to the

• *The knowledge and skills required for higher education, occupational competence, and lifelong learning will be taught.* The school should work at developing young minds that can be discriminating and wise throughout the whole of life. Students are encouraged to perform to the limits of individual ability in ways that test and push back personal intellectual boundaries. In other words, students would be encouraged to stretch their minds to full capacity from early childhood through adulthood, becoming lifelong learners who continue learning as the world itself changes.

Students are taught to think courageously and to stand up for their spiritual beliefs under pressure, as they learn to study and to work independently and cooperatively. Communication skills, creative skills, and proficiency in music, art, and drama would be developed, along with physical education that stresses wholesome, lifelong recreational participation.

• *The importance of personal, civic responsibility will be enhanced by the school's activities.* Christian schools should be in the business of

faculty as well, while the administrator should participate in the meetings of the church staff.

Both need to build up the other in public contacts. They should be open with each other and friendly, scheduling time to pray and talk together at least once a week. Problems arising between them need to be resolved directly and immediately, without defensiveness, because each desires the Lord's will.

• *A commitment to loyalty.* When approached about a problem concerning the other person or that person's domain of responsibility, they should support and defend the other's integrity by getting the reporting party to go directly to their colleague to solve the matter.

If the pastor is also a parent in the school, he or she must never pull rank on behalf of the children. Pastors need to observe the same rules and work through the same channels as any other parent.

• *A plan for decision making.* The administrator should be allowed to make independent decisions, keeping the pastor informed and asking for counsel so that such decisions will not be contrary to the overall ministry goals. However, the pastor dare not become overinvolved with the school to the detriment of pastoral work or the work of the administrator. There should be a balance, a symmetry. This requires a deepening of the relationship, so the trust level remains high.

There is wisdom in having the church board supervise the administrator, yet the pastor must have direct access to the administrator without going through the board. This would be pastoral access rather than administrative, however. The pastor is not to go above the board or around it for administrative purposes.

—*Roy W. Lowrie, Jr.*

developing good citizens, in light of the apostle Paul's teachings in Romans 13. Civic participation should be taught, encouraged, and modeled by the school staff, who demonstrate how Christians can live faithfully in their culture, being in the world but not of the world.

Teachers would emphasize cultural heritage and the need to find solutions to the serious issues facing the country and the world. This is done in light of the centrality of the healthy family as established by God. Biblical precepts would be conveyed for the present and for the future when students marry and establish their own homes, all based on the biblical call to view life as sacred.

Financial Support for Christian Schools

It is better to build children than to repair adults. Perhaps that is why private Christian schools are springing up all across America. How to fund these schools, though, is the big question school founders and administrators are continually asking.

Spiritual Foundations

Building on a firm spiritual foundation is crucial, because it takes a miracle in our present economy to find sufficient money to pay for private education! Only God can perform miracles, but we human beings can participate in those miracles. The key is to find out what God is doing, translate God's will into a clear vision we can interpret to others, and then identify with God in the work he is doing. We can then expect the winds of heaven to drive us on to success.

Naturally, along with a spiritual foundation of prayer and seeking God's will for funding our schools, we must offer a product that parents desire for their children. They invariably want a wholesome Christian environment and quality education with high academic standards. So the curriculum itself must have a spiritual foundation. It is important to teach basic Christian truths and ethics along with all the cultural subjects that will enhance the capacity of children to enjoy full lives. Regular chapels also build a worshiping community.

Sources of Funding

Once we have laid the spiritual foundations and made plans to offer a well-rounded, quality education, we must gain the enrollment numbers to fund the program through tuitions.

In the early 1990s, the average tuition for independent Christian schools was $3–4,000 a year. Tuitions for independent schools are usually higher than those for church-sponsored schools because the independents must buy land and build buildings. Church-related schools using facilities provided by the church can often reduce fees

Defining the School-Church Relationship

Schools that are thoroughly integrated into the ministry of the church have the fewest problems. But problems that can occur without a close, highly communicative relationship might include tension between Christian-school students and secular-school students together in Sunday school and the youth group, an elder board that is not unified in its endorsement and support of the school, and public-school teachers in the congregation who may begin to feel the Christian-school supporters are subtly indicting their work. In addition, a

by approximately one-third, making the tuition about $2,000 per year on the average.

A rule of thumb in budgeting is a third of income for salaries, a third for operational costs, and a third for land and buildings. Adequate enrollment numbers are necessary to provide sufficient funding. I have found good results in designing facilities for 900 students.

Approximately 80 percent of the funds to run a private school will come from tuitions and fees. The remaining 20 percent can come from various sources. Here are some revenue sources to tap:

- *Matching funds.* Hundreds of corporations are willing to give matching funds through their employees (the parents of the students). These companies typically promise to give—dollar for dollar—the same amount an employee gives to the school. Matching funds can speed classroom construction and equipment purchases during the beginning of a new school.
- *Grandparents.* Consider holding a Grandparents' Day, inviting these folks to the school to visit their grandchildren's classrooms. Discuss the program and needs of the school in a large-group meeting and appeal for grandparents' financial support.
- *Capital drives.* Make a practice of running a capital-fund drive once every two years. Call upon donation-capable parents to help meet the capital needs of the school.
- *Foundations.* In California alone, there are about forty foundations that might be interested in supporting special programs, such as building a computer lab or a vocational workshop. We simply need to find out how to apply for funds—and then ask.
- *Memorials.* Make a list of needs, such as classroom furnishings, science and computer equipment, and playground structures. Certain parents will appreciate the opportunity to give a memorial in the name of a deceased loved one. Attach tastefully designed nameplates to the equipment.
- *Philanthropic gifts.* Invite qualified people who are capable of giving large gifts to become members of your school board. Acquaint them with the benefits of private Christian education and with the larger capital needs of the school. Many will be happy to offer their financial support.

—*Ernest D. Sillers*

significant problem can arise if people begin to believe Christian-school education is the primary church priority or that it is the only way for children to grow in Christ and develop spiritually. Then the broad ministry of the body of Christ for mutual edification is downgraded.

To avoid dissension in the church, the pastor has to deal continuously with the ebb and flow of church members' attitudes toward the school. Some will always strongly oppose it, and others will always faithfully support it.

The following insights regarding issues in the school-church relationship were contributed by pastors who are strong proponents of the Christian school and have a demonstrated commitment to its welfare. But each also acknowledges that there have been problems for his ministry caused by the school. Understanding and wisdom permeate their observations.

- *The school and pastoral involvement.* Without good, open communication between members of the church and school staffs, problems will arise for the pastor. There also will be a significant problem if the school begins taking the minister's time and energy away from pastoral tasks and priorities. Unfortunately, the pastor may have chosen—to the detriment of the church—to be more involved in the school administration than is prudent, thereby neglecting the church. It's no secret that the school can be demanding; the pastor, however, must have the utmost confidence in the school administrator and governing board.

Pastors must be on guard about subtle dangers to their church ministry: The school can drain leadership away from the church, especially if the church is small; the school increases the pastor's counseling load because school parents who go to other churches come to the school pastor for counseling; and interpersonal problems between parents, teachers, and administrators can quickly sap the pastor's emotional energy.

- *Enrollment from church members.* Here's a grievous problem for the church leadership: Encouraging high numbers of students from the church to enroll in the Christian school can actually keep families whose children attend other schools from coming to the church! This fact makes necessary a different kind of program for youth—all the youth in the community, whether they are involved with the Christian school or not.

Another problem in this area relates to who is qualified for school leadership. One rule of thumb is that church members not enrolling their children in the school should not be given positions of authority in the school. This is similar to rules requiring an elder or deacon to be a church member.

- *Financial responsibility and accountability.* Developing financial stability for the school is critical and requires great care. The handling of money is a spiritual matter, demanding that salaries, fringe benefits, raises, and vacation time be made equitable among the school and church staff. Yet, the most potentially divisive question will be: How large should the school become in terms of constructing new buildings and investing additional church monies?

The student-teacher ratio is the biggest single factor in financing the school. The cost of tuition needs balance, so that it is not so low that the church acquires a monumental bailout burden each year and not so high that all but the financially elite are priced out of the market. Tuition should cover faculty and staff salaries and fringe benefits, usually about 80 percent of the budget.

Preparing for the Future

As we approach the new century, more students are enrolled in Christian schools than at any time in the nation's history. As the secularization of public schools continues, Christian schools based upon the Bible are increasing in number and in size. This relationship is a striking phenomenon: Cultural decadence appears to stimulate Christian growth! At the same time, there is an ebb and flow of enrollment in individual Christian schools, depending on local and national issues. Also, the regions of the country vary in their rate of growth.

As we look to the future, we see that the Christian-school movement confronts challenges similar to those of churches, mission boards, and other Christian endeavors, such as: (1) keeping the vision bright, (2) finding good leadership, (3) obtaining adequate financing, (4) maintaining quality facilities, and (5) creating effective internal and external public relations.

Christian schools will continue to have problems, as will churches. Small Christian secondary schools experience the most difficult challenges of all, often making their very survival problematic. Yet the results of this educational ministry in the lives of students and families are worth the sacrifices involved in resolving the problems. A typical testimony written by a parent said, "The school strengthens the Christian foundation of our home. Our entire family has grown and matured from this experience."

Churches interested in starting a Christian school need to consider these brief but basic guidelines:

- *Seek legal counsel.* Do this right at the outset of the planning process. Get ongoing advice from an educational lawyer whose work has been with Christian schools.
- *Take the time to hire the right staff.* It's crucial, for example, to hire a proficient administrator, since the head of the school is the linchpin of the entire enterprise. The school exists for the students,

and they deserve qualified teachers who are assigned to their major fields of study.

- *Seek staff input on construction plans.* Have the administrator and teachers work with a school architect in designing or adapting facilities. Work to design church educational facilities to *school* specifications. A congregation never knows when it might need to use supposedly church-only spaces for dayschool purposes.
- *Start a school only if you believe in it with all your heart.* And, incidently, a pastor's level of commitment to the school will no doubt be judged by whether or not his or her children are enrolled.

—Roy W. Lowrie, Jr.

Resources

Enderlin, A., and R. White, eds. 1986. The manual of administration for new and young Christian schools. Whittier, Cal.: Association of Christian Schools International.

Gaebelein, F. 1985. The pattern of God's truth. Winona Lake, Ind.: BMH Books.

Kienel, P., ed. 1978. Philosophy of Christian school education. Whittier, Cal.: Association of Christian Schools International.

Knight, G. 1989. Issues and alternatives in educational philosophies, 2d ed. Berrien Springs, Mich.: Andrews University Press.

Teachers and Staff

The effectiveness of any Christian school rises and falls with two vital factors: philosophy and staff. The school that is founded on strong biblical principles and hires the right people to carry out that biblical philosophy will certainly be the dynamic school God desires.

Any school striving for spiritual academic excellence must set high standards when seeking school employees. If a school board becomes nervous and quickly hires someone to fill a position for fear they may not find another candidate, they often will regret such haste later. On the other hand, the school that is willing to be patient in searching for the best candidate will usually be blessed with God's choice.

Staffing Guidelines

Here are specific suggestions to keep in mind when seeking to hire and retain the right teachers and staff:

- *Bathe hiring decisions in prayer.* Luke 6:12 gives us an excellent personnel principle. Here Jesus spends the entire night in prayer, and the next day, from among all his disciples, he chooses twelve to be his close apostles. We must exercise great caution against hiring in a hurry, especially if chance circumstances happen to bring potential employees to the school.
- *Interview thoroughly.* During the interview all major concerns should be covered, namely: philoso-

phy of the school, standards and expectations for students and staff, and evaluation procedures for workers. Salary and related fringe benefits should naturally be covered in proper detail.

Employers make a major mistake by presenting only the most positive image and skipping sensitive or negative issues. It is best to present a perfectly honest, clear picture of the job situation.

• *Streamline the hiring process.* Once candidates are located, implement a simple procedure from interview to hiring. All of the regular hiring steps, such as the detailed interview, careful assessment of past performance, and proper reference checks must be followed for each candidate. We must realize, however, that often good people are lost because the process is too long and cumbersome. For example, if a strong prospect is asked to change an interview date several times because the committee can't get together, this person easily could change her mind about accepting the position.

• *Don't overlook the most obvious sources of candidates.* Sources for staff prospects may be right next door. We should include in our search the church body where the school is housed, local churches that are in harmony doctrinally, and colleges and seminaries that may be located nearby.

• *Don't dictate exactly how the job is to be done.* A common error is to carefully and prayerfully hire the right person and then turn around and handcuff that person, almost making it appear as if the new employee is under suspicion. This type of job environment causes the new person to be tentative, lacking creativity.

There is nothing wrong with providing training sessions for new workers. Many assignments, however, can stand some new approaches, and employees should be encouraged to find them.

• *Don't neglect regular reviews.* A mutually developed evaluation system is one of the best motivators. When workers feel they are appreciated by their supervisors, they will be happy. Therefore, we need to offer evaluation conferences once or twice a year. (In the difficult times when a staff member may have to be dismissed, these conferences also can be a source of documentation of the problem.)

In harmony with the Bible's sowing and reaping principle, if a school treats each employee fairly and kindly, regardless of position, God in turn usually blesses that ministry with good workers.

—*Art Nazigian*

School Facilities

One of the most deeply challenging ministries a church can undertake is starting a Christian school. The need for Christian schools grows by the day with humanism increasing around us. As a church earnestly prays and seeks God's will about starting a school, it must, at the same time, assess its facilities to see if they are adequate.

Questions Needing Answers

What does a church need to know before determining what facilities to provide? Or how will it assess whether present facilities can adequately house the Monday school? Answers to the following questions should have a major impact on faculty decisions.

• *What grade levels will the school provide?* Most churches that have or are starting a Christian school begin with the first three or four grades. They add one or two grades each year thereafter until the grade that completes the school is reached. It is not difficult to launch a school that will eventually cover grades K–8. The greatest amount of effort is involved when the church wants to have a quality high school.

The cost of a high school program is about three times greater than that of an elementary program. Having 20 to 24 students in a class will cover the expenses of an elementary classroom, including the teacher's salary. In high school, however, the classes are much smaller, and there are many more classes to choose from, thus driving per-pupil costs much higher.

• *What will be the class size limits?* Ideally, for elementary school (grades K–6), classrooms that provide for 30 square feet per child are standard. This space allows for the basic educational needs, such as areas for doing small-committee work, a reading corner, a science center, a closet, and storage areas. For example, a class of 20 students should have a classroom at least 20 feet by 30 feet in size.

The floor space needed for junior and senior high is only 20 square feet per student, since less physical activity will take place in the room. Churches that may not have this recommended floor space can still meet minimal requirements, provided classrooms are well lighted and ventilated, with at least ten square feet per student.

• *What is the political climate for permits?* Securing a permit or approval to operate a Christian school in a church is generally not difficult, since, presumably, the church already is conducting a safe and proper Sunday school. However, it is always wise to check with the proper officials to be sure you aren't overlooking any major building codes or other requirements for running a weekly school program.

• *Will we have a library?* The "facility heart" of the school is its library. One of the largest, most attractive, centrally located rooms should serve as the library and the multimedia center. All films, audio and video cassettes, computers, and other like equipment can also be housed in this room.

• *Will we offer special courses?* Does the school plan to provide art, music, or physical education classes? For high school programs, science and computer centers are essential, and churches will need to single out the larger rooms to accommodate these two subject areas. The type and quantity of science equipment and materials will determine the size of the room needed. Students and teachers must take extreme safety precautions when doing chemical experiments, so running water, excellent ventilation, and easy-access fire exits are absolute necessities when setting up the science room.

—Art Nazigian

Preschools

Naturally, the first step in organizing a preschool is to canvass the church, neighborhood, and community to assess the need for such a program. This assessment will also provide information about the specific type of child the school might serve, particularly whether the program will be limited to church children or include other children in the community. A congregation also begins to see potential students' needs through this assessment activity.

Six Steps to a School

If the assessment effort shows the need for a preschool program, at least six subsequent steps are in order:

• *Hire a professional consultant.* It's wise to engage the services of a competent preschool consultant, at least during the initial creation and organization of the school. Each state has strict regulations, and the consultant will contact the proper state and local departments to learn those regulations and see that they are implemented. A consultant will also evaluate the potential facilities to determine whether they comply with government regulations and support school goals. The consultant can also lead the church through each of the subsequent steps, saving valuable time and expenses.

• *Set up a board.* The school board will provide essential support for the director and staff. Describe, in minute detail, the roles and responsibilities of the school board members. The board could be composed of parents, members of the church, people elected by the church membership, or people appointed by a church board. They must be individuals of high moral standing in the community and thoroughly dedicated to childhood education. They need not be professional educators but must be open to learning everything they can about the schooling task.

• *State your educational philosophy.* This philosophical statement will determine the school's overall mission. Include descriptive statements about the nature of the preschool child, the reason for learning at this age level, and the course of the maturation process. Identify the mission, goals, and specific objectives of the school. Define the roles of both the learner and the teacher. Address the relevant biblical issues related to spiritual growth as well as academic learning. A statement of philosophy provides the rationale upon which all future decisions will be made.

• *Develop the budget.* This initial financial statement should include startup expenditures, employee costs, rent, health insurance, taxes, scholarships, the cost of equipment and instructional materials, and other items peculiar to the specific school. Identify income sources with the estimated amounts to be received. Possible sources of income include tuition, grants, fundraising projects, gifts, and church subsidies. Obviously, there should be adequate income to meet projected expenses.

• *Design the curriculum.* The educational objectives and curriculum design flow from the philosophical statement. Educational objectives should speak to the three basic areas of learning: cognitive, affective, and psychomotor. The curriculum should also consider the social and personal needs of the child. The 3- or 4-year-old child learns primarily through doing, and all learning activities should be based on this fact.

Preschool leaders can contact established Christian school organizations to obtain information about instructional materials that integrate faith and learning. Two national associations are Christian Schools International (Grand Rapids, Michigan) and the Association of Christian Schools International (Whittier, California).

• *Staff the program.* Identify the staff to fill, such as director, head teacher, teachers, cook, nurse, janitor, and bus driver. For each position, determine the credentials needed and write a detailed job description before interviewing and hiring the candidates who best fit the school's needs and philosophy.

—*John A. Burgess*

Part VII:

Chaplaincies

It's tough to be a pastor on someone else's turf. But every day, thousands of clergy provide pastoral care in decidedly unchurchly situations—dusty military compounds, frantic hospital emergency rooms, down-and-dirty cell blocks, and speeding patrol cars. Some pastors live out their faith and their calling in the oddest of places—much like the kinds of places in which Jesus placed himself during his earthly ministry.

While the functions of ministry remain similar in these places, the rules are often different. There are questions of command and authority. Role conflicts arise more easily. Church-state policies thrust themselves to the fore. Loneliness and professional isolation eat at chaplains. People don't know what category to place them in, and so they're the oddity, the unusual agents in most situations.

But amid such struggles, ministry continues. The Word gets preached on the poop deck, in pediatrics, and at the police officer's funeral. Counsel is given on death row, at a crime scene, and in the ICU. Teaching is communicated under a camouflage canopy, in a hospital conference room, and at a work-farm Bible study. Captive audiences and begrudging respect are part of the mix for chaplains.

To keep chaplains from being the Lone Rangers on the frontiers of Christian ministry, congregations have a supportive role to play. And parish pastors can stand beside chaplains of all kinds, even serving as volunteer chaplains in many situations. The main idea is that all people need ministry, even those in unusual circumstances. For their benefit, the following advice is offered.

29

Military Chaplains

The military chaplaincy predates both the U.S. Constitution and the Declaration of Independence. The origin of the U.S. military chaplaincy is generally traced to an action by the Continental Congress on July 29, 1775, which authorized a pay scale for army chaplains. While chaplains had served in British units and on board ship, this congressional action was the earliest official legislative recognition of chaplains as a part of the U.S. military establishment. Appointments of chaplains to the Continental Navy soon followed, and by 1777 chaplains were serving in large numbers in both services.

Interestingly, many chaplains who served in the Revolutionary War were also active combatants. Some even led troops into battle. Not until later in military history were chaplains considered noncombatants. In the early days, few chaplains saw any conflict between the roles of clergyperson and combat soldier. Over the years chaplains came to enjoy a reputation in the services as courageous guardians of moral, ethical, and spiritual truth.

The Nature of the Chaplaincy

The unique status of the military chaplain as a staff officer serving on the personal staff of the commander presents both a challenge and an opportunity. According to Army regulations, chaplains are "expected to speak with a prophetic voice" and to "confront the command when the religious rights of soldiers are affected." It is this requirement to be an integral part of the command that sets chaplains apart from other clergy or lay persons that carry on ministry with the military community. Access is the key. Being a part of the unit, living with and working with service members, the chaplain has the opportunity to be salt and light to an entire community.

• *Becoming a chaplain.* The educational and physical requirements for appointment as a military chaplain have changed little during the past 40 years. Since chaplains are commissioned as officers in the armed services, they must be physically and morally fit. They must meet the educational standards for other officers (a bachelor's degree) and must also have completed three years of resident theological education at an approved seminary. A Master of Divinity degree or equivalent is required prior to appointment.

Furthermore, chaplains must be endorsed by their respective denominations and then serve at the pleasure of their denominational bodies. Should a chaplain be at odds with his or her church body or unresponsive to its discipline, that church body may withdraw its endorsement and recall the chaplain to civilian life. When this occurs, the service terminates the chaplain's commission, and he or she is released from military service.

The services do not evaluate chaplains on theological or ecclesiological grounds, nor do they train them in those areas. Chaplains are brought into the services based on formulas designed to ensure an equitable distribution by denominational affiliation. While the services do not use a quota system, they do try to maintain a "faith balance" within each service. Once chaplains enter the armed services, they are treated as other officers in terms of promotions and assignments, except that they are separately managed by the respective Chiefs of Chaplains.

• *Serving as a chaplain.* The rank structure of the three service chaplaincies parallels that of the regular armed services. Chaplains begin their ministries as First Lieutenants (Army and Air Force) or Lieutenants, Junior Grade (Navy) but are usually promoted in a year or less to Captain (Army and Air Force) or Lieutenant (Navy). After three years of service, they are selected for continuation for an initial indefinite term.

At about the six-year mark, they are eligible for selection to the next higher grade. If promoted to Major (Army and Air Force) or Lieutenant Commander (Navy), they are then integrated into the regular force and, barring a disciplinary or behavioral problem, can continue to serve for at least 20 years. If promoted to Lieutenant Colonel (Army and Air Force) or Commander (Navy), they can serve for 28 years. If selected for Colonel (Army and Air Force) or Captain (Navy), they can serve a full 30 years or longer. Two senior chaplain officers are selected from each service for promotion to the rank of Brigadier and Major

General (Army and Air Force) or Rear Admiral (Navy) to serve as Chiefs and Deputy Chiefs of Chaplains in their respective services.

Service as a chaplain requires keeping two seemingly conflicting responsibilities in healthy tension. On the one hand, chaplains are public servants, paid by the government to minister to all personnel. On the other hand, as ordained clergy they must remain true to their ordination vows and particular theological distinctives. Fortunately, the services make allowances for this, and chaplains are not required to participate in activities or perform duties contrary to the tenets of their faith traditions. This important understanding is essential to the chaplain's performance in the military environment. The key words are "cooperation without compromise."

• *Maintaining professional status.* As commissioned officers, chaplains are expected to meet and maintain the standards of a highly trained, elite group. At the same time they must be able to relate to the most junior and sometimes immature service members. However, in so doing, they cannot compromise their professional status. Commanders at all levels expect their chaplains not only to set a high moral, ethical, and spiritual tone, but also to exhibit competence and professionalism in their work. Often, chaplains are judged not by how well they do as pastors but by how well they perform as professional staff officers.

Although wearing two hats (or serving two masters) presents a challenge to the chaplain, the professional status conferred upon him or her can also be of great value when it comes to communicating the gospel and penetrating the military system. The chaplain speaks with the authority of both church and state as an insider. If the chaplain has cultivated and maintains good relations with the command leadership, he or she can exert a profound influence for good. On the other hand, some chaplains are co-opted by the system and end up muting their message and compromising their values in order to get ahead.

Duties and Responsibilities

Chaplains have a unique opportunity to exercise influence not only through their ministry to individuals but also as they speak to the institution. As staff officers, chaplains often participate in the decision-making process, bringing a moral-ethical-spiritual perspective to the internal debate on strategy, tactics, or operations. Thus, chaplains serve as prophetic voices, bringing a "word from the Lord" to the most secular of discussions. In this sense, when obedient to their calling, they are indeed salt and light.

• *Religious duties.* While military chaplains are essentially pastors, priests, or rabbis carrying on religious ministry, the diversity and extent of their religious duties set them apart from civilian clergy. First, they are required by law to conduct public worship services and burial services for members of the command to which they are assigned. While they may normally conduct denominationally distinctive worship services, when ministering to the community at large, chaplains must provide opportunity for all service members to worship. They need not *conduct* services inconsistent with the tenets of their faith, but they must *provide* such services for their people.

Further, chaplains are expected to administer sacraments, ordinances, and ministrations upon request. They are expected to participate in military and patriotic ceremonies, provide pastoral care (including visitation and in-depth counseling), and supervise or conduct religious education for service members and their families.

While there are areas of specialization within the overall chaplaincy

Authority and Conscience

The year was 1967. The place was Vietnam. Members of a Special Forces unit were on a search-and-destroy mission deep in Vietcong-controlled jungle territory. Continually harassed by sniper fire from an elusive enemy, these soldiers were on edge, their nerves raw. The commander's jeep driver, a young soldier of good reputation, well liked by both his compatriots and his commander, had gone down to the nearby stream to get water. Rising out of the water behind him, a Vietcong soldier had seized him and, without mercy, had slit his throat, killing him instantly.

When the chaplain arrived on the scene, he found the Vietcong soldier seated cross-legged on the ground, his arms pinioned behind him, his head pulled back by one of his captors. A distraught company commander, sobbing with grief and rage, held a pistol to his enemy's head. As the chaplain pieced together the story, fellow soldiers urged their commander to take revenge and "waste this miserable animal."

The chaplain knew what he had to do. But, as he described it, he seemed frozen to the spot. For a moment, he couldn't move, couldn't speak. He wanted to turn away and let it happen — just so he didn't have to *see* it happen! After all, this enemy deserved to die, didn't he?

Then, praying silently, he approached the commander. "Sir, you can't do this," he heard himself saying. The officer turned on him, sobbing and screaming in his grief and anger. Then, again, the chaplain spoke in a quiet voice, "Sir, you can't do this."

The commander turned from his prisoner, threw his pistol to the ground, and walked away, sobbing. The prisoner was taken away for interrogation. The crisis was over.

An Important Role

This true story illustrates the chaplain's role as the *conscience* of

ministry, when chaplains are assigned to military or naval units or to ships of the line, they are expected to minister to and meet the needs of *all* members of that command. This is why there is great emphasis on continuing education in various pastoral skills within the chaplaincies.

• *Combat duties.* Regardless of the effectiveness of ministry in peacetime, it is in combat that the true value of the chaplain is revealed. Combat tests the limits of human endurance and quickly brings soldiers, sailors, airmen, and marines back to the basic, essential questions of life. In a life-threatening environment of maximum stress, opportunities for life-changing ministry are limited only by the chaplain's physical endurance and spiritual stamina. It is for this reason that chaplains undergo the same rigorous training and must

---

the unit, speaking with the *authority* of a prophet of the Lord. The chaplain had to settle the questions of conscience with himself before the event. After the fact would have been too late.

Military regulations not only permit but actually require chaplains to be the conscience of the command. While chaplains are under authority in the military services and are expected to obey lawful orders, they also represent and must communicate what God says about the actions of human beings prone to sinful actions. Therefore, soldiers look to chaplains for guidance on matters of conscience. Chaplains exercise spiritual authority while serving under secular authority.

Military chaplains are protected by regulation from performing any act at variance with the tenets of their faith. Since they are noncombatants with special recognition under the Geneva Conventions, they do not bear arms. They can assist the wounded, but they are not expected to participate in offensive operations, except to the extent that they are a part of the military unit engaged in the offensive.

A Continual Duty

Decisions about when to speak out are not confined only to wartime or combat situations. The chaplain will be confronted with this challenge sooner or later in peacetime. The chaplain must raise the moral banner — through lifestyle, speech, sermons, counseling — *before* a crisis, however. This is absolutely essential. Seeking redress *after* the fact (unless the actions were taken without the chaplain's knowledge) is invariably treated as griping, and the chaplain loses credibility.

The conflict between authority and conscience will always be with us. When military chaplains take the courageous route and raise issues of conscience before the fact, and when they speak with the authority of Almighty God, they usually have little difficulty with the authority of men.

—*James A. Edgren*

---

maintain the same level of physical fitness as the service members to whom they minister. They must also concentrate on maintaining themselves in a high state of spiritual readiness, so that they are prepared to carry on a dynamic ministry in a combat environment.

Chaplains must have worked through the issues of conscience and the whole spectrum of arguments on the question of bearing arms. They should be well versed in just-war theory and be able to provide assistance to service members who struggle with these issues.

While chaplains need not endorse uncritically the actions of commanders or troops in a combat situation, they are a part of the military establishment being paid with public funds and have taken an oath of office, just as line officers have. They must, therefore, be pre-

Morale and Family Concerns

Chaplain ministry in the armed services takes place in the environment of the total institution. In the civilian world, there is a certain "apartness" of the church from the community it serves. This is not so in the military. The chaplain eats, sleeps, and trains with his or her congregation.

The chaplain also is one person in a larger leadership team, and this leadership team is ultimately concerned with the fulfillment of the unit's mission. Anything that detracts from training and completion of the mission is of interest to the command. If a member of the military community worries about family or experiences family problems, the motivation for fulfilling the unit's mission will be hampered. Since the person in tune with the difficulties and morale of the troops is the chaplain, commanding officers expect chaplains either to assist in the resolution of family problems or to refer matters to the proper agency.

A Proactive Approach

Although the command expects the chaplain to be involved with families, a basic motivation for such action is the chaplain's personal understanding of ministry. Stresses from separations, long periods of training, and living with the threat of war—all make the family a logical place of entry for the chaplain. Rather than being reactive, chaplains need to be proactive in this work. The following suggestions will assist the chaplain in ministry to families.

• *Become active in the command's family-support program.* Deployed units appoint representatives in the community to assist during the service member's absence. Given various names—ombudsman, key volunteers—these are people with whom the chaplain needs to develop a positive, supportive relationship. Contact with these unit representatives is vital not only when stateside but also

pared to be a part of a military action that may bring death and destruction upon an enemy of their nation. Chaplains who are uncertain about their feelings on this issue can exercise the option of resigning their commissions and separating themselves from the armed forces *before* entry into combat. Even in combat, chaplains are expected to challenge and confront immoral or unethical actions, and they have a history of having done so.

• *Leadership duties.* Chaplains must exercise moral and spiritual leadership in a military society increasingly hostile to the gospel. How do they do this? The key to the whole process is the word *service.* Chaplains are expected to take the lead when it comes to making the hard choices on moral, ethical, and spiritual issues. In fact, the chap-

while deployed. This link is crucial to building chaplain rapport and opening avenues for ministry.

• *Address the stresses of the military lifestyle.* As an institution, the military says both "We care for you" and "The mission comes first." The service member is subject to frequent short-term separations from spouse and family as well as multiple home relocations. While each branch of service has developed a Family Support Program, the chaplain within the individual unit must be particularly sensitive to such issues, developing unit activities that will assist personnel in transitions, in marital communication, and in independent living. Priority goes to predeployment and return programs that address the dynamics of military lifestyle. Parenting programs that teach the skills of communication and discipline are essential for ministry to the whole family.

• *Take special interest in the single-parent family.* Units now include people who are attempting to rear children alone. For these individuals, field training and deployments are potential crisis experiences. Chaplains can assist by keeping up-to-date listings of competent weekly daycare providers and helping to make arrangements for child care during deployment. The pure fatigue of a single parent is the touch point for significant ministry.

• *Acknowledge your vital role within the institution.* Chaplains often leave the programs suggested here to the Family Services Center of the command. Such an approach fails to acknowledge who the chaplain is. The chaplain represents both the command and a particular faith group. Is the faith community's message relevant to any of the above concerns? Can strength from a person's faith assist in meeting the stresses of military life?

While a chaplain can bring many resources to bear in meeting the problems of military lifestyle, his or her role within the system points beyond the mundane to an eternal faith relationship with God. Abdicating our responsibility to meet family needs means limiting our witness to the power of God to feed hungry souls.

—Gerald T. Richards

lain can and will provide a true service when he or she assists the commander in making the right choices.

The chaplain's effectiveness in communicating God's Word to this unique segment of society is directly related to how creative he or she is in ministry. Although the military community has accepted the chaplaincy as a fact of life, for many within that community, the chaplain is irrelevant. The challenge is to rise above that image and conduct a ministry that provides real answers to real problems, demonstrating that the gospel meets needs and that the Christian life is exciting.

In a world in which clergy from many backgrounds are falling into moral impurity, chaplains must set and maintain high moral standards. Even if they never voice it, superiors, colleagues, and subordinates have the highest expectations for chaplains in terms of conduct. They watch the chaplain's lifestyle closely and expect a godly presence that reflects light in a dark world. At the same time there will be pressure to conform, to laugh at dirty jokes, to join in debasement of the opposite sex. Resisting that temptation is absolutely essential to effective ministry.

Chaplains have insider status in a way that most civilian clergy do not. They are a part of the organization by regulation and by law. They have both the right and duty to participate in the policy-making and decision-making processes. Though some commanders may attempt to deny chaplains their seat at the table, relegating their program and input to the periphery, wise commanders will ensure that chaplains are really heard. Chaplains themselves must aggressively work at maintaining their leadership status.

The expectation that chaplains will speak prophetically to the institution is foreign to bureaucratic thinking: Let the chaplain sermonize and give guidance, counsel, and comfort to the religious, but God forbid that he or she should influence policy or have any impact on the decision-making process! This prevalent point of view reveals a misunderstanding of the chaplain's role.

Nathan the prophet could say to King David "Thou art the man!" because he had access to the king. He had won the right to be heard because, as a prophet of God, he regularly spoke to the institution with a prophetic voice.

Governmental and Popular Support

The military chaplaincy is deeply rooted in the constitutional and statutory foundations of our country and has, from the earliest days, enjoyed popular support by our people. Congress appropriates public funds year by year to support the service chaplaincies and their programs. These funds pay salaries, build chapels and religious-education facilities, provide equipment and transportation, and buy Bibles, hymnbooks and religious-education materials. In addition, public funds pay for conferences, training programs, retreats, and professional development for chaplains and assistants. The three chaplain schools are also publicly funded.

Chaplains Funds (offerings given in chapels) are used to supplement public funding and "to meet [the] social needs of the religious community." Receiving of offerings is also viewed as an integral part of worship. As a result, it is not unusual for military chapels to give 15 to 25 percent of their income to charitable, humanitarian, and missionary enterprises outside the military establishment.

The chaplaincies of the three armed services are established and defined in public law (Title 10, United States Code). This statutory authority confers an official status upon military chaplains within the federal government that is unique in American public life. In no other sector are chaplains as firmly established. Although this official status of the chaplaincy has been challenged in court (most recently and notably in the case of Katcoff v. Marsh [1979–1986]), the courts have consistently upheld the constitutionality of the military chaplaincies. The first amendment of the Constitution prohibits enactment of any law "respecting the establishment of religion or prohibiting the free exercise thereof." In striking a balance between the "establishment" and the "free exercise" clauses, Congress has recognized the necessity of the chaplaincy to protect and enhance the "free exercise" rights of service members. At the same time, chaplains are trained to avoid even the appearance of any "establishment" of religion. Yet, Congress has, in essence, allowed for limited establishment in order to protect individual religious rights.

In recent years there has been increasing pressure from various segments of society to eliminate the chaplaincies or to at least cut back their public funding severely. So far the military chaplaincies have survived these attacks. However, as this nation becomes more secular in character, it will become increasingly necessary to justify the chaplaincy. That can be done, though, as long as chaplains continue to provide quality ministry in the toughest of environments. As they do, the chaplaincies will no doubt survive and thrive.

—James A. Edgren

30

Hospital Chaplains

Throughout its history the church has held in high esteem those who compassionately minister to the sick. Of course, Scripture clearly encourages such ministry. In Matthew 25 we hear Jesus saying, "I was sick, and you looked after me. . . . I tell you the truth, whatever you did for one of the least of these brothers of mine, you did for me." Though reaching out to the sick is a supreme act of love worthy of every pastor's time and energy, this special form of ministry presents difficult challenges, demands a solid sense of personal identity, and requires a specific set of purposes.

Challenges

The hospital has been and will continue to be a fertile field for Christian ministry. However, the very nature of the hospital has changed, making effective ministry somewhat more difficult. Consider:

• *The rapid change of the hospital.* After World War II, government subsidy programs helped fund hospital construction, and many new hospitals were built. Federal expenditures for research also expanded — from $73 million in 1950 to over $2 billion in 1972. As a result, technology advanced dramatically. As Medicare and Medicaid were incorporated into social security, the best medical care became more available to everyone, regardless of socioeconomic status.

Recently, DRGS (diagnosis related groups) and their reported rates have become a large determining factor in treatment plans. If a hospital can find a way to treat a patient for less money than the specific rate of reimbursement designated by a DRG, it can keep the difference as profit. If the hospital's treatment occasionally costs more than the designated reimbursement, it absorbs the loss.

The trend appears, therefore, to have been a move away from the more personal care that was available years ago. Most observers see a movement toward larger, perhaps more impersonal facilities, where patients may suffer greater feelings of anonymity. Many hospitals have become serious about making a profit and being cost driven. Today's chaplain enters an environment in which hospital managers may be more financially motivated than service motivated.

• *The inner tension of the chaplain.* What is the chaplain's role and responsibility in the midst of all of this change? Lawrence Holst describes the tension a chaplain faces when he or she attempts to minister within two worlds, the worlds of religion and medicine. We can readily identify the source of the tension. The chaplain, often being an ordained minister, usually has specialized training as a pastor in the context of a local church. This pastor then becomes a chaplain and is thrust into a foreign, highly specialized medical field that uses a distinct vocabulary and delivers a unique set of problems.

The chaplain identifies with both worlds, yet does not feel entirely at home in either. Chaplains are an enigma to both worlds: Medicine does not consider them "medical enough" and questions their relevance; the church often does not consider them "pastoral enough," questioning their essential identity and calling. But despite the tensions and enigmas, the hospital chaplain can be very much committed to both worlds and can serve as a vital link between them (Holst 1985, 12–27).

• *The complex environment of the ministry.* In visiting the sick, then, the minister encounters a unique and challenging environment for ministry. People involved with illness, both patients and patients' families, need so many things on so many levels. Almost everyone at this time desires spiritual counsel and encouragement.

Patients and their loved ones are often more open to considering spiritual truths during a physical crisis. Granted, sometimes this openness is motivated by pure fear over the current situation or extenuating circumstances, yet the opportunity to draw near in ministry is still present and valid. For patients and patients' families alike, a time of sickness encourages evaluation of life's past choices and future plans. Priorities and schedules are challenged and will often be reevaluated. People make significant decisions, charting new courses of action for the future.

As a patient evaluates decisions and contemplates choices, the chaplain often has a unique opportunity to help guide the process. The chaplain also has an unparalleled opportunity to demonstrate God's love and concern.

Identity

What kind of person ministers effectively in the hospital? In today's technological society, the pastor and chaplain must have a sure sense of personal identity. Apart from some specific techniques, strong Christian character is the crucial requirement for developing and maintaining that identity. Three Bible passages give insight into these traits: 2 Corinthians 5:20, Luke 10:30–37, and 2 Corinthians 1:3–4. According to these passages, a chaplain must be:

• *One who can represent Christ in a secular environment.* In 2 Corinthians 5:20, Paul writes that we are "ambassadors for Christ." An ambassador speaks on behalf of the sovereign who sent him or her, and it is the duty of the ambassador to proclaim faithfully and accurately the sovereign's message. In a real sense, therefore, it can be said that the message of the ambassador *is* the message of the sovereign.

All believers should serve as Christ's ambassadors, whether in the marketplace, a recreational area, or the hospital. By the nature of our relationship with Christ, we are automatically identified with him, and our actions and words are a direct reflection upon him.

As a minister for Jesus Christ enters the hospital environment, his or her responsibility as ambassador does not automatically go on hold or into remission because of entering a secular institution. Ambassadors for Jesus Christ are ambassadors no matter where they happen to be at the moment. Often the sufferer is looking for a word from God and is trying to make some sense out of his or her pain, waiting for God's ambassador to help. Christ's ambassador, through words and actions, can function as the hands and mouth of Jesus in a powerful, incarnational form of ministry.

• *One who can show mercy to all.* In response to the question "Who is my neighbor?" Jesus told the story of the Good Samaritan in Luke 10:30–37. On the surface, we might understand Jesus as teaching that a person should always help others in need. However, in light of the context of Jesus' rejection, we could view this parable as a reflection of his own ministry. Jesus, like the Samaritan, was the outcast one who was nevertheless willing to seek and save people who were perishing. Whether one looks at the surface interpretation or views the passage as a reflection of Jesus' ministry, the message remains that we are to "go and do the same." A chaplain should be able to demonstrate compassion and mercy freely.

What does it mean to behave like a compassionate and merciful neighbor? What are we do to? The Good Samaritan felt compassion for the man along the road and therefore he responded. Compassion calls for sympathy, understanding, patience, and sensitivity to those who are underprivileged, sick, or suffering. To show mercy means to give of ourselves willingly and cheerfully.

• *One who can offer comfort based on a close relationship with the Comforter.* The chaplain should also be a comforter of those who suffer. Paul writes in 2 Corinthians 1:3–4, "Praise be to the God and Father of our Lord Jesus Christ, the Father of compassion and the God of all comfort, who comforts us in all our troubles, so that we can comfort those in any trouble with the comfort we ourselves have received from God." All Christians experience affliction. Probably no one experienced more afflictions as a Christian than Paul, who was beaten, stoned, shipwrecked, robbed, and starved (see 2 Cor. 11:23–30). Through all of this, Paul encouraged his readers to shift their perspec-

Chaplains and the Health Care Team

Effective hospital ministry requires the ability to function as a member of an interdisciplinary team, working on a daily basis with nurses, physicians, technicians, social workers, and other health care professionals. Chaplains must both demonstrate the need for their place on this team and then function as true professionals among their care-giving peers.

A Needed Ministry

Even though the hospital as a modern institution has blossomed from its Christian roots in monastic hospices, we can no longer assume clergy will be working in health care environments. Pastoral care departments typically fall first to the fiscal axe when budgets tighten. Therefore, hospital chaplains must learn to defend their roles to hospital administrators and medical practitioners, especially if they minister in medical centers unaffiliated with a religious body.

To maintain adequate administrative support, chaplains can regularly document the services they provide and the ways the quality of care has improved through chaplaincy ministry. In a sense, chaplains can "market" pastoral care creatively by identifying new areas in which the needs of patients, families, and hospital staff can benefit from pastoral resources. Such marketing involves research, education (of hospital staff and administration), and promotion. For example, research could help establish pastoral ministry as a valued part of hospital services in such areas as pain management, ethics education for medical staff, outpatient care, and the development of various support groups.

A Dual Focus

Chaplains assess and respond to the spiritual needs of patients and their families. Nurses and nursing aids can be most helpful in this ministry, since they interact the most with patients and their families and can provide crucial insights about family dynamics and

tive from the temporal to the eternal (see 2 Cor. 4:17–18). Christians are to keep their eyes focused on Jesus Christ, not upon the temporal things that might steal their attention away from the Lord.

The source of all comfort in the midst of our afflictions is God himself. He is the God of all comfort. Receiving comfort from God during their trials enables the comforted believers to comfort others.

What does it really mean to comfort? The word *comfort* means to impart strength and hope. The original Greek root used in this passage is *paraclete,* which is also used to describe the ministry of the Holy Spirit. The word describes one who stands beside another per-

patients' needs. Ideally, all team members consult in weekly interdisciplinary team meetings to develop a care plan related to the physical, emotional, and spiritual aspects of each patient's situation.

Chaplains, however, have a second focus. They not only care for patients and their families but also minister to the medical staff, who typically experience high levels of stress in their work. Research has shown that clergy offer significant support to other members on the health care team, helping to counter burnout. Thus, time spent at the nurses' station listening to and supporting fellow team members is as much a part of hospital ministry as bedside visits with families in crisis. Chaplains may establish support groups for medical staff in critical-care areas, they may conduct grief workshops, or they may offer worship services for hospital staff.

The Necessary Competence

As each profession represented on the health care team performs a different function, members expect each other to be competent in their various fields. A chaplain can enhance professional competence in the eyes of colleagues in at least three ways:

- *Learn to communicate special expertise.* Pastors are the experts in spiritual life, ethics, and methods of pastoral care. They must communicate this knowledge and its practical applications to the other team members.
- *Develop objective assessment methods.* Colleagues can be shown that the chaplain is not just dealing in subjective generalities. A chaplain can demonstrate empirical assessment by using detailed evaluation forms or inventories. See, for instance, George Fitchett's *Spiritual Assessment in Pastoral Care: A Guide to Selected Resources* (Decatur, Ga.: JPC Publications, 1993).
- *Become familiar with the technical side of health care.* To work effectively with other caregivers, a chaplain must become thoroughly conversant with the terminology of medical diagnosis and treatment. The challenge is to work professionally within the relationship that exists among theology, medicine, and the behavioral sciences, without losing one's identity and profile as a minister of the gospel.

—*Frank Milstead Woggon*

son to encourage him or her when that person is undergoing severe testing. The Holy Spirit as Paraclete strengthens and guides us, comforts and consoles us (see John 14:16, 26; 15:26). Likewise, when we minister to others who are suffering, we go to them in order to stand beside them, comforting and encouraging them during their time of need.

Purpose

The ministry of the hospital chaplain is broad and can be wonderfully rewarding. To the chaplain, the patients become a mission field, and the hospital staff becomes a congregation. Ministry takes place when divine resources touch human needs through loving channels, to the glory of God. This is possible when the chaplain is clear about his or her specific purposes and roles:

Dealing with Death

Chaplains are considered the death, bereavement, and grief experts on the health care team. Yet death in the modern hospital is a medical pronouncement and ideally should be announced to the family by the physician. The chaplain can coach the physician on how to break the news and can pick up the pieces and shepherd the family after the physician is gone.

Good Grief

To minister effectively with grieving people, we must be convinced grief is essentially therapeutic rather than pathologic, and "the best way out is through." It's important to get the bereaved into a private space where wailing and screaming will not be upsetting to other families. Any strong expression of grief—short of doing violence to oneself or others, or tearing up the premises—is permissible.

All the tasks surrounding death in the hospital, such as contacting relatives, choosing a funeral home, and discussing organ donation, potentially contribute to good grieving. In cases of infant death, for example, naming and holding the dead baby can help bereaved parents move through denial to the acceptance of reality and the experience of its pain.

Chaplains help to bring closure to the immediate bereavement experience by gathering the family around the deceased, inviting all to join hands, and reciting a psalm or leading a prayer of thanksgiving for the life of the deceased and for passage to God's safekeeping.

First Facing Death

Chaplains can spend years in training, learning techniques and methods for dealing with the dying and counseling the bereaved. No

• *To provide pastoral care for patients.* The primary thrill of the chaplaincy comes from working directly with patients. The staff chaplain makes daily rounds and is available 24 hours a day to offer spiritual counseling and emotional support to the sick, recovering, and dying patient. A normal day includes not only daily rounds, but also visitation of patients who are scheduled for surgery the next day.

Making rounds involves visiting patients who have recently been admitted into the hospital. The chaplain is clinically trained in making effective calls in these situations. The techniques used to enter into conversation with a patient vary, but the goal is always to be an ambassador for Jesus Christ, offering personal availability for ministry in ways the patient might request.

The chaplain will find patients dealing with grief, joy, fear, anxiety, or any other emotion. Specific problems range from the evident physical ones to financial and marital concerns. Any problem that a

---

amount of training, however, can take the place of the one foundational prerequisite that will determine the true effectiveness of those who wish to minister compassionately to the bereaved: thoroughly confronting one's own mortality.

Here are some key steps involved in that process:

• *Make a will.* Contemplating your death and what will become of your possessions powerfully confronts you with your own mortality.

• *Compose care directives.* Think through how much treatment you would want should you be dying, and document this in a living will. Stipulate the person you would want to serve as surrogate decision-maker for you in the event you become unable to speak for yourself.

• *Draft a list of the ten persons or things you value most* and prioritize them. Imagine losing them one at a time, from the least to the greatest. Write your feelings and thoughts upon contemplating each loss.

• *Fill out a hospital Report of Death on yourself.* This would include information such as the hour, day, month, and year you imagine you will die; the cause of death; the identity of the next of kin; and the funeral home or crematory to which you expect to be released.

• *Observe an autopsy.*

• *Identify the three greatest losses you have experienced in life.* Recall your feelings and thoughts in great detail. Let your emotions open up to the pain of loss in your own life.

• *Write "To be opened only on the event of my death" letters* to your most significant others and place the letters in your safe-deposit box.

• *Write instructions about your funeral* or memorial service that you want your survivors to follow.

• *Say your "I love you's" today to those who need to hear them.* Christopher Morley once said that if we all suddenly learned we had only five minutes left to live, every phone booth in the country would be filled with people blurting out, "I love you!" Why wait until the last five minutes?

—*Wayne Willis*

pastor would face in a pastor's study, the chaplain will face in the hospital room; however, in the hospital the problem is accented by the patient's physical trauma.

If a patient has no minister from home, the chaplain serves as friend and pastoral figure, providing neutral ground for discussion of spiritual matters. The chaplain may not be the patient's continuing pastor but can still provide God's perspective during a needy time.

The primary tools available for the chaplain's use are good listening techniques, Scripture, and prayer. Listening, sharing a verse of Scripture, and praying helps bring fractured lives back into focus. A good chaplain is able to maintain a proper balance between inviting consideration of the eternal perspective and dealing practically with temporal reality.

• *To offer support to patients' families.* Sometimes the patient is in no condition to speak with a chaplain. During those visits, the chaplain focuses on the patient's family, being available for calls to the emergency room, intensive-care unit, and surgical waiting areas to help with the distressed family of a critically ill or dying patient.

In this ministry, the chaplain can provide crisis counseling and support. This is an exciting and rewarding ministry. Deep and lasting friendships often develop between the chaplain and family as the chaplain provides guidance and directs attention toward the One who is able to provide stability in the midst of instability.

• *To serve as pastor for the care-giving staff.* The chaplain is able to be, in an often stressful and demanding environment, an understanding friend and confidant with a sympathetic listening ear. Staff members who do not have a minister of their own often seek the chaplain's counsel, especially during times of personal and family need. Whereas the average stay of a patient is only four days in an acute-care hospital, the staff member may remain in the hospital for years. Chaplains should therefore seek to develop long-term ministry with the personnel working in all areas of the facility on all three shifts.

The chaplain, working in cooperation with the care-giving team, can also serve on a bioethics committee, counsel in the chemical-dependency unit, make rounds with the oncology team, and supply crisis counseling during emergency-room trauma. These contacts open ample opportunities to meet, encourage, and pastor an often stressed-out staff.

• *To function as a liaison for local clergy.* The hospital chaplain typically sees a patient before his or her own minister is aware that hospitalization has occurred. With the patient's permission, the chaplain can call the family pastor, priest, rabbi, or other spiritual leader. The chaplain then remains available and ready to provide pastoral care until the patient's minister arrives. In this ministry, the chaplain serves as an arm of the local pastor's ministry. When chaplains build a foundation of trust with the local clergy, they will be genuinely appreciated for this transitional role. It is exciting to see shepherding members of the body of Christ working together.

• *To do public-relations work for the hospital.* Chaplains often serve as the hospital's religious-community public-relations person. This ministry includes coordinating any services that might be held in the hospital, providing pulpit supply for vacationing pastors, or acting as community-resource person on topics such as hospital visitation, terminal illness, death, and the grieving process. This ministry calls the chaplain to function as a minister-at-large for the community. Funeral services and other public duties often fall to the community chaplain when a family has nowhere else to turn.

The thrill of the chaplaincy flows from being uniquely involved when a sufferer experiences fresh awareness of the greatness of God's grace. To encourage that miracle, chaplains rush into emergency rooms late at night to stand with the loved ones of those seriously injured. They minister amid all the tubes and equipment of life-support systems. And they stand at the graveside, comforting the grieving, before driving back to the hospital to smile and congratulate a proud new father. It is to these godly, humble, untrumpeted servants of the Lord that Christ will say, "Well done."

—Douglas M. Cecil

Resources

Holst, L. 1985. Hospital ministry: The role of the chaplain today. New York: Crossroad.

The hospital chaplain: A training manual for instructors and chaplains-in-training. 1987. Anaheim, Cal.: Hospital Chaplains' Ministry of America.

31

Prison Chaplains

Over 1.2 million men and women are locked up in the jails and prisons of our nation today. Constituting only 5 percent of the world's population, we Americans incarcerate over 50 percent of the world's prisoners. Our prisons are full and desperately overcrowded, and as quickly as we build new ones, we cannot keep up with the need for more beds and cells. The demand for ever-increasing prison space is fueled both by a rising crime rate and by the fact that between 60 and 70 percent of those released from prison commit new crimes within four years.

Before we become overwhelmed by statistics like these, we must step back and consider how the power of the gospel can make a difference in our prisons through the critical ministry of prison chaplains. We might begin by asking these four basic questions: What is a prison for? What does a prison chaplain actually do? What are the special challenges of chaplain ministry? And how can a congregation fit in with chaplain ministry?

Places for Repentance and Restoration

Our Savior's pointed words in Matthew 25 about involvement with people who are hurting, destitute, or locked away in jails has throughout history generated Christian concern for the prisoner. Though often thought of as places for punishment, prisons do not have to serve this primary role. In the eighteenth century, for example, Pope Pius IX organized a papal prison for juveniles, placing them in individual cells for the purpose of spiritual reflection, not for punishment.

The Quakers in 1772 built a prison in Philadelphia—the Walnut Street Jail—taking punishment off the streets and placing offenders in private cells so they could meditate and repent of their sins. Here the name "penitentiary" was used to express a philosophy of redemption and restoration, not merely retribution and strict justice. A chaplain was employed in the Walnut Street Jail to address the spiritual needs of those imprisoned. As the American prison system evolved through periods of what can only be viewed today as incredible brutality, the role of chaplain gained considerable significance.

Today there are basically three different levels in our criminal justice system, and each has its unique dynamics and ministry challenges. The upper level consists of the Federal Bureau of Prisons, a federal agency with over 70 institutions housing over 83,000 prisoners at present. This prison system has a more sophisticated clientele, in general, than the state systems'. The federal determinate-sentencing law means that federal prisoners will be serving longer sentences and more of their sentenced time. With a high level of educational qualifications required for all of its personnel, these prisons usually employ chaplains from mainline (or at least the larger) denominations.

The middle level is the state prison systems. Each state has its own body of laws and often its own correctional culture. Many of the state systems have death rows and house a larger number of violent inmates. Penal philosophies vary widely from state to state. Today, some states, implementing rugged cost-cutting measures, are exploring cutting back on chaplaincy services or at least moving them to a contract status outside of the prison structure. This is a cause for concern in the ranks of chaplains and could seriously affect the delivery of religious services to inmate populations.

At the lower level of criminal justice stands the network of county and city jails where inmates are either serving relatively short sentences or awaiting trial. The dynamics in these institutions are quite different from those of a prison. Often the men and women housed in these institutions are reeling from the first shock of losing jobs and income, trying to cope with all the attendant trauma to their families as car and house payments come to a stop. These men and women typically have their families and roots in the local community and, therefore, church members can have a powerful outreach to their own neighbors in these local jails.

Many prisoners go through these various criminal justice systems feeling discouraged, angry, bitter, and totally rejected. Prison tends to make them dependent and often leaves them unprepared for life in society when they get out. Learning to survive in a violent prison culture with its unique codes of morality, and facing a perceived rejection by society, few prisoners become more functional on the outside world as a result of supposed "rehabilitation" on the inside.

A Ministry of Uncommon Compassion

From a spiritual perspective, a prison is one of the great bastions of the Evil One, a place where men and women are shackled in the chains of hopelessness and despair, violence and hatred, and all the attendant negative emotions. Yet it can also be a place of tremendous opportunity, where men and women meet the person of Jesus Christ and his loving acceptance. This can take place in a setting where, perhaps for the first time, people have significant time to think, to study, and to act on their new spiritual insights.

Standing in the gap, holding out the possibility of this incredible inner transformation for those so long without hope, is the small band of prison chaplains. These men and women have committed their lives to that difficult ministry of bringing the Good News of God's grace into our penal institutions. Today the office of prison chaplain is well established, even while its job description and philosophy is constantly changing to meet the growing complexities of the correctional field. It is a ministry in one of the most demanding and stressful fields of service, yet it is so little understood by the average church member. What in particular do prison chaplains actually do?

The opportunities for different forms of ministry can be almost overwhelming in terms of time and numbers. At the most basic level, the chaplain schedules regular times for worship and Bible study, led by both the chaplain and outside volunteers. In addition, individual and group counseling sessions provide opportunities for the chaplain to hear prisoners' concerns and problems, while often confronting their attitudes and lifestyles.

A chaplain's work almost always includes meetings with inmates to notify them of family emergencies, severe illnesses, and deaths. He or she makes the necessary arrangements required by these crisis situations. Often these emergencies—always traumatic—are even more so for those who are locked up and feeling utterly helpless.

Another area of responsibility for the busy chaplain is the management and coordination of outside ministries and programs for prisoners. These ministries bring tremendous and welcome resources to the religious program in a jail or prison. They expand and multiply the ministry of the chapel-related community far beyond the capabilities of a full-time chaplaincy staff, and they reach into the rest of the prison population, as well. Such resources include many different kinds of programs: evangelistic crusades, marriage seminars, preaching missions, and concerts.

On the downside, however, chaplains know that each outside program demands tedious and meticulous preparation and planning, placing an added burden of security measures on the correctional staff. This management of the volunteer program is a demanding task, one that is seldom appreciated or understood by outside ministries.

Special Problems in Prison Ministry

The chaplain's work can bring deep satisfaction. Being a primary source of comfort, hope, and personal acceptance to those who so desperately need it is certainly one reward. It's also gratifying to know that one is working with the kinds of people with whom the Savior spent so much of his own time, with those who are hurting and those who do not fit easily into our church culture. Christ's habit of working with these kinds of people was what caused so much consternation and uproar in the Jewish religious community of his day.

Christian Rehabilitation

What does it mean for a prisoner to be truly rehabilitated in Christ? Only God knows the heart of an individual, but we in the church can have God's heart as we reach out to prisoners and support the work of the prison chaplain. This ministry demands an abundance of discernment, common sense, nurturing ability, and patience.

Difficult Distinctions

Prison ministry is difficult. Anyone who reaches out to prisoners with the gospel must be cautious and wise, recognizing that true rehabilitation springs from a radical change of heart. There is little behind a prison's stark concrete walls and cold bars that can accomplish lasting change other than a genuine encounter with Jesus Christ.

Here are some recommendations for pastors or church members assisting the prison chaplain.

- *Discern the truth in behaviors.* Is the conversion real, or is the prisoner just faking it? Is it true rehabilitation or simply a "jailhouse conversion"? Naturally, we must be alert to the reality of manipulation; some prisoners will mimic evangelical jargon that we call "church talk." The one true indication of conversion is Christlike behavior, and not returning to crime is the most compelling evidence of rehabilitation.
- *Use common sense in giving.* Avoid giving a prisoner material goods, such as money and stamps, and avoid having an ex-offender move in with a church family just after release. These practices often are a violation of prison policy and can lead to victimization.

Working with the prisoner or ex-offender will sometimes require making hard decisions and being confrontational in love. Simply giving in to every request for money, materials, or other assistance is not good for the prisoner or the church.

At the same time, there are also significant problems and difficulties for anyone involved in this ministry. Here are just four of the unique problems prison chaplains face:

- *Struggling with mountains of paperwork.* Because of the security problems inherent in such a climate of restraint, there is an almost endless flow of paperwork to be done. Time and energy for direct ministry with persons seems constantly drained into the writing, signing, and filing of countless reports. How frustrating!
- *Watching "successes" walk out the door.* The people who excel in spiritual growth often become a parish pastor's strongest supporters, moving into Christian service and taking up positions of leadership in the congregation. For a chaplain, the greatest people successes are the first to leave the prison and never come back. Unless they get into

---

- *Offer biblical nurture in abundance.* Make sure the prisoner's conversion is built on a solid biblical foundation and visit regularly to conduct in-prison Bible studies. A conversion that emanates from a knowledge of God through the Scriptures has a better chance of being genuine than a spontaneous decision rooted in the emotion of a prison chapel service.

Occasionally it may be appropriate to have an ex-offender give his or her testimony in the local church, but avoid the temptation of a speaking circuit that puts ex-offenders in a spotlight. They should not be given a responsible position in the church, either, until there is enduring evidence of growth.

Do create mentoring relationships, though. One of the best ways to stabilize the Christian life of an ex-offender is to get him or her into a strong discipling relationship with a mature Christian. Accountability rooted in biblical principles can lead to genuine rehabilitation.

- *Be patient in viewing slow progress.* The longer someone has been in prison, the more emotional baggage he or she carries. Prisoners often come from dysfunctional families, and their complicated problems have developed over a long period. Simply stated, when working with prisoners and ex-offenders, we will often experience "two steps forward and one step back." Though the negative effects of long-term incarceration may frequently surface, our gentleness and patience will develop a trust relationship that can help heal the wounds.

Several years ago a church pastor told me, "We tried prison ministry once, but it didn't work." He told of bringing an ex-offender into the church who had then apparently stolen a member's watch. Of course, anyone coming into that church could have been a thief. If we are looking for reasons to label people or to eject them from our communities, we will find them. May we see instead the great potential for good that God has built into every human being (Eph. 2:10).

—Don Smarto

some kind of prison ministry, they'll try to forget the painful memories associated with the prison experience and will seldom be heard from again.

• *Working under secular values.* Pastors' supervisors almost always share in their vision for ministry and espouse similar values. The supervisors of chaplains, however, too often hold a different set of values, viewing chaplains' work from a thoroughly secular perspective.

• *Feeling like a loner.* Chaplains are often misunderstood by their denominational peers, who have difficulty relating to the kinds of concerns with which prison chaplains wrestle daily. Their work is usually done behind the scenes and out of the spotlight, unrecognized by the community on the outside. Their spouses typically are minimally involved in the work of the prison or jail chapel. A chaplain's

Prisoners' Families

How can the local church bring aid and comfort to prisoners' families? We in church leadership might first identify the chaplain of a local jail or prison and then give that person visibility in the church. For example, we might bring him or her to the church to speak, or display a photograph of the chaplain along with those of our foreign missionaries. This will pave the way for a good working relationship between chaplain and church.

Supporting the Chaplaincy

The church can be supportive of the chaplain's work with prisoner families as he or she cares for the spouse and children during the prisoner's incarceration. This relationship works best when the church determines to work within the rules and policies of the institution and accepts the chaplain's limitations on involvement. Specifically, here are guidelines for those becoming involved with prisoners' families:

•*Respect the chaplain's authority.* Never go around or over the chaplain to implement any form of ministry. We may know the warden, sheriff, or an elected politician who can exert influence on the chaplain, but the chaplain is the pastor of the prison, and the Christian inmates are his or her congregation. We must work with and through the chaplains, respecting their authority.

• *Help the chaplain follow policy.* The chaplain is a part of the administrative team of the facility, and he or she is aware that the first obligation of the prison is secure custody. Therefore, we must not pressure a chaplain into making exceptions in policy.

For example, we should avoid asking for special favors, such as visitations at unreasonable hours, which would be burdensome to cor-

family often has its own involvement in a local congregation, leaving the chaplain with a vague sense of rejection, or at least a sense of detachment from the church community with which he or she was once involved.

How the Local Church Fits In

Prisoners have been intentionally separated from society at large. As Christians, however, we must never separate members of Christ's body from brothers and sisters in the church. The daunting challenge of chaplaincy is to make the connection between the two communities in every possible way, within the obvious restrictions.

So how can chaplains most effectively work with the church? Con-

rectional staff. Do not ask the chaplain to give a prisoner unauthorized books, cakes, clothes, or other materials that are usually restricted. Also, do not pressure chaplains into becoming advocates for a prisoner's case or lure them into a situation in which they must become a character witness on the prisoner's behalf at a hearing or trial. This can create a serious role conflict.

• *Work through established programs.* Two programs that help prisoners' families are the Prison Fellowship Angel Tree Program and the Salvation Army. At Christmas, the Angel Tree Program helps buy gifts for the children of inmates (the incarcerated parent signs the card to the child). Several Salvation Army programs give gifts, food, and clothes to prisoners' families.

• *Don't embarrass the spouse.* Often, because of the social stigma of incarceration, the spouse of a prisoner will stop going to church because of embarrassing questions he or she receives. Some spouses even prefer to tell people they are separated or divorced.

This is where the church needs to be especially sensitive. We can invite the prisoner's family not only to a church service but to social activities as well.

• *Offer marriage enrichment.* Over 80 percent of inmate marriages result in divorce. The chaplain and the local pastor working together can help stabilize the marriage through counseling, marriage-enrichment seminars in the facility, and eventual supportive follow-up in the church after the prisoner's release.

• *Don't neglect the children.* The most neglected members of a prisoner's family are the children. The money drain of the trial and incarceration often results in a woman going to work for the first time or even becoming dependent on welfare. If the prison is far from the home, church members could take turns giving family members a ride to the facility for visitation. The church could also consider setting up a car pool for such routine needs as shopping and doctor's visits.

—Don Smarto

sider these five suggestions that can help strengthen relationship with the local church, thereby enhancing our mutual ministry:

• *Maintain a special identity and authority.* The chaplain is the legitimate authority in the institutional community. Though they are the gateway to the Christian community in the prison, too often they may be regarded as an obstacle to be overcome or by-passed by those who would bring their ministries directly to prisoners.

Parish pastors who differ from chaplains in tradition or doctrinal convictions must yet honor chaplains for their personal commitment to a demanding ministry. Chaplains dare not let others undermine their work because of differences. If the local church is serious about this kind of outreach ministry, it is essential that the ministry leaders begin with a serious commitment to the spiritual support of the chaplain, including daily intercessory prayer for his or her ministry.

• *Be open to pastoral support and nurture for personal needs.* Chaplains work constantly with people who are trying to build a relationship solely for the purpose of manipulating them for some personal goal. This can produce great stress, and chaplains need the support and nurture of the church to cope. So chaplains need to let pastors get to know them as people.

It's good to spend unstructured time together whenever schedules allow, perhaps away from the institution. The chaplains' job is a relatively lonely one, but they can begin to share their perception of their task in all of its aspects by exploring such questions as: How do I feel about prison residents in general? What is it about my job that excites me as a pastor?

Chaplains can let pastors in on their hopes and dreams for their work. They can speak at churches or groups and share their vision for ministry among prisoners.

As chaplains get to know local pastors, they sometimes receive from them resources such as books, Bibles and New Testaments, and study materials to strengthen their work and program. Also, professional meetings might significantly enrich a chaplain—if he or she can afford to go. Many churches would be happy to supply this need if they were only made aware of it.

• *Gently confront stereotypes and prejudices.* Many church members hold uninformed attitudes toward prisoners and those released. The church community tends to reflect the basic attitudes of society in general toward prisoners and ex-offenders, rather than a scriptural perspective. That attitude of fear and mistrust has always been a problem, just as it was in Jesus' day. As redeemed children of God, we need to remember we have been forgiven of far more than any convicted person has ever been accused of by society.

We in the church should know more about forgiveness than anyone else. Our criminal justice system makes judgments on the basis of behavioral acts. We serve a holy God who has forgiven us not only of the outward actions but of a far greater body of sin, that of our desires and true motives. Our failure to obey the first two commandments—to love the Lord our God with all our heart and mind, and our neighbor as ourselves—is a shortcoming many too easily excuse. Yet, in spite of these unfortunate tendencies, many churches joyfully welcome ex-prisoners into their fellowships.

- *Work together to form support groups.* As churches express the desire to be involved in prison ministry, chaplains can work to form a small group for the support of an ex-prisoner upon release, providing training to these group members and helping them understand the difficult work of maintaining loving accountability and understanding. Particularly in the case of prisoners released without any other kind of support, such a group can identify a place to live, refer to job possibilities, and organize personal support with a clearly defined structure of loving accountability. The first 180 days after release from incarceration can be the most difficult part of the incarceration experience. For a Christian expecting to be accepted by a Christian community upon release, the reality of nonacceptance can be absolutely devastating.
- *Prepare converted prisoners for church membership.* Some prisoners begin taking an active part in the ministry within the institutional setting. The basic ministry goal here is to establish a strong personal relationship with the particular inmate who has made a profession, to disciple him, to prepare him, and to help him make a commitment to the structure of the welcoming church. This preparation on the inside is as valuable and important as the actual experience upon release.

A sad fact is that of those involved in the Christian community in an institution, 90 to 95 percent do not find a church home on the outside after release. A significant church outreach project, then, is to encourage local churches to enhance inside ministry by building a bridge of relationships that will take a prisoner from his or her institution into the fellowship of the local church after release. Such a program, thoughtfully and carefully carried out, will extend a chaplain's ministry beyond the prison walls and create an effect on the church community on the outside.

Various national revivals and awakenings have generated within the church a concern for prison reform. Christians have played a significant role in past efforts to make the institutions of justice more humane and less destructive, more geared toward bringing about true repentance and personal renewal. Any such trend should be supported by believers with diligent work and constant prayer. Men and women reborn into newness of life out of the correctional context can add a richness of experience to the life of any local church body.

—George Soltau

Resources

Colson, C., and D. Van Ness. 1989. Convicted: New hope for ending America's crime. Wheaton, Ill.: Crossway.

Costantino, F. 1981. Crimefighter. Orlando: International Prison Ministries.

Pace, D. 1976. A Christian's guide to effective jail and prison ministry. Terrytown, N.Y.: Revell.

Smarto, D. 1987. Justice and mercy. Wheaton, Ill.: Tyndale.

Van Ness, D. 1986. Crime and its victims: What we can do. Downers Grove, Ill.: InterVarsity.

32

Police Chaplains

"Are you a priest or a cop?" I must have been asked that question two dozen times an evening while I patrolled the local fair. I cannot fault people's curiosity. After all, I was outfitted like a police officer — badge, portable radio, baton, chemical Mace, handcuffs, and uniform — but I also wore a clerical collar. I typically responded, "I am the police chaplain — a pastor who works with the police department." Most people seemed to like the idea, although a few shook their heads in disbelief.

A chaplain for a police department seems to many a novel idea. However, some police chiefs, street cops, and progressive communities are beginning to recognize the need for a chaplain in today's law enforcement agency. Unfortunately, few departments have chaplains and few pastors have given serious consideration to this field of volunteer ministry. This uncharted territory needs to be mapped.

Who Needs a Police Chaplain?

Police chaplains first minister to the departments they serve. Peace officers occupy a frontline position when it comes to stress and difficulty. The seamy side of life, criticism and hostility, and sometimes even physical abuse constantly barrage police officers. Burnout presents an ever-present risk, divorce is common, and a creeping cynicism pervades their outlook. Feeling misunderstood by most people, cops tend to stick together in a quasiparanoid state of isolation.

Chaplains serve as an outlet for anger and frustrations, and as a rare source of nonpolice thinking. This role in maintaining the mental health of the officers alone justifies the position.

A chaplain serves the police department in guiding conflict resolution, lending the department his or her reputation as a community leader, providing training insights from the social sciences, and standing ready to give spiritual counsel when asked.

Chaplains also minister alongside the department to serve the community. For example, while on patrol or on call, a chaplain often contacts the victims of crime. Mere presence often adds reassurance and comfort at a stressful time. Suspects in custody will often talk to police chaplains freely, and women prisoners especially appreciate the "protective" presence of a chaplain. Family arguments have been known to calm suddenly when a "priest" appears at the door with the cops. Who wants to beat his wife with a priest watching? People will sometimes avail themselves of the chaplain's crisis counseling, while the authority of the police officers may only set them off.

What Is at Stake?

Prior to serving as a police chaplain, a pastor must resolve certain questions:

• *Why am I doing this?* Pastors seeking only thrills and excitement will have more fun at Disneyland. Police work is usually highly routine, and when it gets exciting, the officers need something more than a thrill seeker beside them. A frustrated, would-be cop will make a poor chaplain. Likewise, someone out to prove something about his bravery or masculinity has a poor motive for serving as a police chaplain. The authoritarian personality who enjoys the power of law enforcement will also make a poor cop and a poor chaplain.

Why *am* I doing this? If the answer is to gratify my own needs rather than to serve the department and the community, then I should take a second look. Chaplains must determine to function as servants — always. They certainly should enjoy the service, but service must come first.

• *How do I feel about law enforcement?* A pastor will make a poor chaplain who generally considers cops to be slow-witted, heavy-handed Neanderthals. Such prejudice would render him or her ineffective.

Likewise, potential chaplains must also come to grips with their feelings about the use of force, including deadly force. Is it necessary? Is it legitimate? Romans 13:1–5 is the standard many chaplains fall back on. A police chaplain must consider the police function to be a necessary and legitimate force within the community. Antipolice crusaders might as well stay clear of the police department.

I, personally, decided to carry chemical Mace and a baton because of the potentially dangerous situations I encountered with a solo partner. If order collapsed, I might be his only backup. The decision was made not without some doubt and even conflict, but it had to be made. Fortunately, I never needed to use either defensive weapon.

• *Can I work in this general atmosphere?* A chaplain does not work in a rarefied atmosphere. The language he or she hears, the people encountered, and the things seen may often be of the crudest variety. The chaplain needs to be able to take these factors in stride. The person who cannot abide profanity or who is easily shocked or flustered will have difficulty with police work.

• *How do I feel about myself?* Do I have the maturity to handle the situations I will encounter? Do I have something vital to offer as a Christian chaplain? Can I remain calm in stressful situations? Do I have the courage to face dilemmas and perhaps physical dangers? Can I retain my Christian perspective and my ability to relate to others amid difficult circumstances? Will I be accepting of others, and do I expect the cops to accept me? Do I plan to give the job the time and commitment it will require?

In others words, do I believe I have what it takes to be an effective chaplain? If I have grave doubts, I'll no doubt project them to those around me.

How Do I Prepare?

Once a chaplain is approved for a department, he or she needs extensive orientation. From the beginning the chaplain, to be effective, must have rapport with the chief and the officers below him, and a chaplain needs to maintain an open line of communication with the top administrators.

Riding on patrol with many different officers is indispensable for getting a feel for what it is like for the beat cop out on the streets. As the chaplain begins to feel the stresses, learn the jargon, get comfortable with the procedures, befriend the patrolmen, and catch the style of police work, effectiveness increases considerably.

Becoming known personally and breaking the barriers of suspicion and doubt are crucial. Until the patrolmen trust a chaplain, he or she will be merely someone to babysit. The patrol car proves a marvelous moving arena for conversation and bridge building. Chaplains know that they've found acceptance when patrol officers let them use the radio and start kidding them as mercilessly as their fellow officers. In my case, when the cops' language remained salty around me and I was invited to an off-duty poker party, I knew my orientation was completed.

Beginning chaplains will find reserve officer training at a police academy to be another valuable asset. In some states a minimum class of twenty hours or so may be required, but often one can continue with additional hours to qualify as a full-fledged reserve officer. Classes may be held in evenings for part-time students.

Not every chaplain will have the time or inclination to take significant police training, but the ones who do will find their effectiveness increased. In my case, this reserve-officer training gave me a new edge with the department. They considered me one of them and showed new confidence in me. Knowing their business better gave me a new confidence, too. I considered it far better to be trained for something I hoped never to use than to come up short in some dreadful emergency situation.

Attending departmental training sessions also improves police skills. Camaraderie grows when the chaplain and the officers practice on one another with a baton! It pays to be one with the troops in as many ways as possible.

Continuing education for police chaplains proves more difficult. There are few seminars for police chaplains, although at least one academy near Los Angeles offers a short course. A chaplain can also cull journal articles from such publications as *Police Chief, Journal of Police Science and Administration, Police,* and *Law Enforcement News,* since there is no journal devoted exclusively to chaplains' concerns. Chaplain Bob Turnbull's book *Calling Angel One* provides an interesting look at one chaplain's style.

The International Conference of Police Chaplains also offers information and guidelines for chaplaincy programs. Classes on crisis intervention, psychology, and criminal science also prove useful for practicing chaplains. As in any other professional field, continuing education is essential to improving skills and broadening one's expertise as a police chaplain.

What Is My Role?

Maintaining the role of police chaplain becomes a delicate balancing act. Role pitfalls abound, such as:

- *Supercop.* This is the chaplain trying to "out-cop" the cops. Chaplains must not become so involved in the police game that they forget their role. When a chaplain begins telling the officers how to do their job or becomes overinvolved in the functions a police officer should perform, he or she is forgetting the role. The role is not competitor to the cops. A chaplain is there to learn from them and help them. If the department wanted another patrolman, they would have hired a police officer. A pastor is brought aboard to be a chaplain.
- *Snitch.* Police officers call an informer a "snitch." Nobody really

likes snitches, not even the officers. A police chaplain must take pains never to become a snitch, even inadvertently. Confidences simply must remain confidential.

Every department has its personnel disputes, its power plays, its misunderstandings and disagreements, and its rumors. Chaplains become privy to many privileged communications and even more rumors and complaints. Breached confidences will ruin credibility, since the chaplain's effectiveness is pegged to the trust officers have in him or her. Chaplains must learn to remain both neutral and trustworthy in all their dealings with department members.

- *Cynic.* The cynic has also lost role identification. Healthy skepticism keeps a police officer effective — and alive — but skepticism easily slides over into cynicism. Too much dirt and pain and frustration can make a cynic of about anybody. Chaplains must beware, lest overidentification with the police officers robs them of the very thing they have to offer: themselves.

If chaplains become hardened and uncaring, if they lose their perspective, if they begin to divide the world into good guys and bad guys, they need to withdraw and reevaluate their attitudes. Cynics will be of no help as police chaplains.

- *Preacher.* While *preacher* is a marvelous title for parish pastors, it can be a derogatory label for police chaplains. Chaplains with a reputation for preaching to their partners will be ineffective at the very task they attempt to undertake.

Preachers are chaplains who consider the patrol car a pulpit, taking advantage of their captive audience. They ooze platitudes at every opportunity and lecture patrolmen incessantly. Without taking the time to earn the right to be heard, they assume they have a pat answer for every situation. A preacher will be tuned out permanently.

Chaplains do have a relevant message to proclaim — a message of God's love and reconciliation. However, wise chaplains learn to wait until the message is practically drawn out of them by an officer at the proper time. Effective chaplains are heard and do minister, simply because they understand their role and capture the right moment. They learn to separate their Christian function from their service function, and then blend them together when the moment is ripe.

- *Martyr.* Such a chaplain will burn out before he or she has accomplished the task. No chaplain will ever perfect the department and convert every cop. These are just not practical goals. Problems remain, cops hold out, and chaplains feel terribly insignificant at times. The martyr cannot live with this and will destroy himself or herself trying to be a savior.

Yet, while such chaplains incessantly chase sirens, who is with their families? Who is pastoring their churches? Chaplains must pursue realistic expectations and set sane schedules. As in any other ministry, chaplains who do not want to become martyrs must live with their own less-than-perfect efforts.

What Am I Doing out There?

The police chaplain has an interesting and often unique ministry. He may be out on the streets at midnight with a vomiting drunk or in a smoky police lounge talking to a desperate rookie about to lose his job. Sometimes she views the vilest of human motives and other times may witness true human courage. Through routine hours of patrol, to awful moments of stark tragedy, to joyous times of deep brotherhood, the police chaplain ministers. The chaplain is a servant, much as Christ served those around him.

Jesus Christ ministered among people of all kinds. He worked with the tax collectors and harlots and sinners. He took his message and himself out into the world to the places where he found need. The chaplain in the patrol car, in the precinct station, in the dark alleys and wounded homes and seedy bars, the chaplain among the pimps and thieves and wifebeaters and drunks, the chaplain encouraging and supporting the men and women who keep our lives safe — that chaplain is doing the work of Christ. He or she is bringing salt and light to the disheartened and those in the dark.

Police chaplains have two things to offer: themselves, in loving, caring service, and a message of hope and renewal found in the gospel of Jesus Christ. Either of these alone remains inadequate for the situation, but combined together, they have transforming power.

On the doors of the Los Angeles Police Department patrol cars is painted the motto: "To serve and to protect." Across the heart of every police chaplain should be stenciled: "To serve and to protect those who serve and protect."

Police chaplaincy is a high calling in an often-lowly place. While frequently routine, many times frustrating and discouraging, occasionally dangerous, at times hilarious, and only sometimes fulfilling, police chaplaincy is always worthwhile. In serving both the police and the community, the police chaplain serves Christ.

—James D. Berkley